DOMESTIC INTERIORS

DOMESTIC INTERIORS

The British Tradition 1500–1850

JAMES AYRES

Yale University Press
New Haven and London

FOR ANNABEL

Designed by Ruth Applin
Set in Bembo by SNP Best-set Typesetter Ltd., Hong Kong
Printed in Singapore

Library of Congress Cataloging-in-Publication Data

Ayres, James.
  Domestic interiors : the British tradition, 1500–1850 / James Ayres.
    p. cm.
Includes bibliographical references and index.
  ISBN 0-300-08445-5 (alk. paper)
  1. Architecture, Domestic – Great Britain – History. 2. Vernacular
architecture – Great Britain – History. 3. Interior decoration – Great
Britain – History. 4. Vernacular architecture – Great Britain – Sources.
I. Title.
  NA7328.A88 2003
  728'.37'0941 – dc21

                          2003005824

Frontispiece   Frederick Daniel Hardy, *Interior of a Sussex Farmhouse*, detail of Fig. 36

Endpapers   detail of anthemion decoration stencilled on plaster from a house in Widcombe, Bath, late eighteenth-
           early nineteenth century.

Contents

Acknowledgements

The earlier smaller version of this book, published in 1981, owed much to numerous individuals (and institutions). Relatively few books had been published on interior decoration in England. In those that had appeared the country house was the primary concern. They referred to the large and elegant houses of the rich who, until the Industrial Revolution, were necessarily landed. A possible exception to such an exclusive view was Sir Osbert Lancaster's *Homes Sweet Homes* which, in both line and word, bestowed the 'common touch' with such an imperiously sure hand. There was no such prejudice against the smaller house in the United States and I must therefore express my gratitude to a number of American scholars and institutions. Until the emergence of the barons of industry in late nineteenth-century America, no large houses were built there. By English standards Mount Vernon and Monticello are modest manor houses. As a result, organizations such as the Society for the Preservation of New England Antiquities and the Henry Francis du Pont Museum, as well as individuals like Mr and Mrs Bertram Little and John Sweeney have perforce done much to show us in Britain how to look at our vernacular interiors. It was their published research over the years as well as their personal advice that proved invaluable to me in the preparation of the first edition of this book. I am indebted to Mrs Little's *American Decorative Wall Painting*, for without it I doubt that I would have discovered examples of early nineteenth-century stencilled wall decoration in this country. Similarly, had Rodris Roth not published her research on *Early American Floor Coverings* it is unlikely that the great importance of oil cloths in the eighteenth century would have occurred to me. Such points are not only clearly but beautifully demonstrated at the American Museum in Britain. For my part I owe a considerable debt

of gratitude to the Fulbright Commission, the Ford Foundation, the Museum School, Boston, and the Institute of International Education for without the munificence of these institutions my experience of America would have remained that of the tourist.

In their turn the Americans owe much to the first open air museums in Scandinavia of which the earliest was Skansen, near Stockholm, opened in 1891. Just as American vernacular architecture shows us what became of the British tradition when transported to the west, so some of our traditions originated to the east of the North Sea. I therefore acknowledge the assistance of the Norsk Folkemuseum, Oslo, the Frilandsmuseet, Copenhagen, and my Danish mother.

All writers on any aspect of vernacular architecture in Britain must salute S. O. Addy and C. F. Innocent for their pioneer studies which contain important descriptions of details of small domestic interiors. In recent years research has been more concerned with statistical matters of the distribution of house types. Nevertheless, the work of scholars like M. W. Barley provide an indispensable matrix for the study of interiors, whilst folklorists like E. Estyn Evans, I. F. Grant and Iorweth C. Peate have written on the use of interiors.

In travelling around the British Isles it soon became evident that many of our folk life museums are recently founded, like the Museum of Scottish Country Life at East Kilbride which opened in July 2001. This museum was not open when the last book was published and has since closed and been taken over by the Museum of Scottish Country Life. One of the first and finest of these institutions was the Welsh Folk Museum (founded in 1946) at St Fagans and I am especially indebted to J. Geraint Jenkins and Derick Jenkins for their help and advice. Another inspiring establishment is the Folk and Transport Museum, Holywood, Northern Ireland and, after the most fruitful and enjoyable days spent there, I would like to thank the Director, G. B. Thompson OBE, Joan Morris and Dr Philip Robinson. My gratitude is also due to Alan Graham of Queen's University, Belfast; Wendy Osbourne of the Ulster Museum and the staff of the Department of Post Medieval Antiquities of the National Museum of Ireland, Dublin. In Scotland my research was eased with great generosity by Gavin Sprott of the National Museum of Antiquities, Edinburgh; R. Ross Noble of the Highland Folk Museum, Kingussie; J. Hugh M. Leichman, the National Trust for Scotland; Andrea Kerr, Kirkcaldy Museum and Art Gallery; Angela Weight, Aberdeen Art Gallery and Museum, and the Scottish Women's Rural Institute.

In England numerous organizations and individuals were kind enough to enter into the spirit of my enquiries and give of their time and knowledge. I would like to thank the staff of all those institutions and in particular to acknowledge the help of the staff of Bath Public Library (Reference Department), the British Library and the Historic Buildings record of English Heritage. I gratefully acknowledge the assistance, when they were at the institutions referred to in brackets, of Ashley Barker (GLC Historic Buildings Council), Martyn Brown (Somerset Museum of Rural Life, Glastonbury), Anthony Davis and Ron Clarke (Coventry City Museum and Art Gallery), John Gere (Department of Prints and Drawings, British Museum), John Hardy (Department of Woodwork, Victoria and Albert Museum), John Harris (Drawings Collection, Royal Institute of British Architects), R. W. Higginbottom (St Helier Museum, Jersey), Tiffany Hunt (Salisbury and South Wiltshire Museum), Michael Middleton (Civic Trust), John Renton (Museum of Lakeland Life), John Rhodes (Oxfordshire County Museum), Peter Robshaw (Civic Trust), Dr Sadie Ward (Museum of Rural Life, Reading), Group Captain W. R. Williams OBE DFC (Landmark Trust), and Cleo Witt and Katherine Eustace (Bristol City Museum and Art Gallery). In addition, essential help was provided by the Avoncroft Museum of Buildings, Worcestershire, the Bath Preservation Trust, Bramish Open Air Museum, the Bradford-on-Avon Preservation Trust, the Museum of East Anglian Life, Suffolk, and the Weald and Downland Museum, Sussex. I would also like to pay tribute to the National Trust who own a number of small properties because of their architectural importance (such as the Priest's House, Muchelney) or literary associations (as with Beatrix Potter's house in the Lake District).

Among the individuals whose advice was invaluable as well as those who were kind enough to show me their houses I would like to thank Ian Bristow, Jeanne Courtauld, Dr and Mrs Andrew Crowther, Anthony Dale, Mrs C. L. du Pre, Sir John Eardley-Wilmot, Commander and Mrs Colin Ellum, the Hon. Desmond Guinness, the Revd Terry Hampton, Morrison Heckscher, Anthony Herbert, Martin Holmes, Stanley Jones, Francesca Jordan, Mr and Mrs Stanley Lewis, Dr A. T. Lucas, Ian McCallum, Mrs M. Maurin, Mr and Mrs Kenneth Monkman, Dr Dallas Pratt, Mr and Mrs M. F. Pratt, Mrs Polly Rogers, Mr and Mrs Charles Smith, Gordon H. Smith, Sir Robert Spencer-Nairn, Lisa van Gruisen, David Whitcombe and Robin Wyatt. The correspondence generated by the book was capably handled by Sarah Trevatt.

To my father I owe an early upbringing in the building crafts which I hope brought to the book a physical understanding of the timeless skills that wood and stone demand.

I remain indebted to many of the aforementioned individuals for this revised and enlarged edition. Since then further research has owed much to the example and help of the following: Malcolm Airs, Mary Countess of Bessborough, Peter Brears, Freddie Charles, Charles Lenox-Conyngham, Debbie Dance, Timothy Easton, John Gall, Henry Glassie, Ian Gow, Ian Grant, Michael Gray, Richard Harris, Barbara Hutton, Pricilla Minay, Nicholas Mander, Peter McCurdy, Alison Mills, Brian Owen, Derek Parker, Jane and Mark Rees, Pamela Slocombe, Margaret Swain, Andy and David Snell, Peter Thornton, Jeremy Uniacke, Eurwyn Wiliam and David Yeomans.

Research of this kind necessitates the use of libraries and museums in London and I am therefore indebted to Dr and Mrs Crowther for providing me with a base in the capital. No less practical help was given by Gillie Cannon who, with skill and good humour translated my illegible handwriting into typescript.

Over the years I have benefited enormously from protracted, frequent and entertaining conversations with John Steane. I am also grateful to Claudia Kinmouth for introducing me to the publishers, Yale University Press, where John Nicoll and Ruth Applin have worked on the production of this book with great flair and professionalism. As always deficiencies are the responsibility of the author.

My penultimate acknowledgement is to Giles de la Mare who, at Faber and Faber, published the first incarnation of this book and who now gives this revised and enlarged edition his imprimatur.

Finally, to my wife and family I owe the greatest debt of all. They accepted, if not exactly welcomed, my physical presence, if absented mind, over a period of many months.

Foreword

Over the last twenty years there has been an extraordinary growth of popular enthusiasm for interior decoration in Britain.[1] Indeed it has now reached a position where it almost threatens gardening as a national obsession. Oddly enough, and despite the numerous television programmes and magazines that have emerged in response to this demand, little has been published on the history of the smaller domestic interior. Consequently I am grateful to Yale University Press for this opportunity to revise and expand my *Book of the Home in Britain*, which was first published in 1981 by Faber and Faber.

One of the reasons for this relative lack of published research may have something to do with the origins of connoisseurship.[2] The cognoscenti in their libraries seldom ventured beyond the green baize door. As a consequence art history is predisposed to being concerned with what is aesthetically significant rather than historically characteristic. To that extent 'art history' is more about art than it is about history. With regard to interiors this situation is compounded by the sheer richness of many patrician houses and their documentation. At the vernacular level written records are rare with the result that we are more often dependent upon physical evidence. The approach is more archaeological than historical. We know from both sources that, for many people, primitive conditions long persisted in Britain (Fig. 1). In *The History of Myddle* (Shropshire) Richard Gough (b. 1635) describes a family on Harmer Hill living in a cave and 'One Thomas Chidlow' who dwelt in 'a poore pitiful hutt, built up on to an old oak butt'.[3] Archaeological investigation has shown that temporary 'earth-fast' or 'stave-built' structures, with a life of about twenty-five years, were built by British settlers in the Southern Colonies of North America.[4] By definition

such fragile shelters are elusive, but of recent years some attempt has been made to trace them through history.[5] Stone-built dwellings, although relatively permanent, could be equally rudimentary. The so-called black houses (windowless) of the Western Isles of Scotland, with their central hearth, exemplify a type which continued in use well into the twentieth century.

The regular and inscrutable façades of the eighteenth century masked a consistency of plan but a great diversity of interior treatment. These interiors responded successively to the fashion of the day. At the provincial or Colonial level rooms may be found which are subdued interpretations of the Baroque and the Palladian, but they less often encompassed the more trivial confections of the Rococo, Chinoiserie or Gothic. An exception to this may be found in furnishing and furniture. Here a detail, such as the back-splat of a chair, may adopt one of these fashionable styles. In contrast to the eighteenth century the vernacular interior of Tudor and Stuart England bore a more direct relationship to its external elevations. A timber-frame wall is visible as such, both inside and out. Although its presence may be suppressed or emphasised with distemper, or clad with roughcast or plaster, weatherboarding or panelling, such walls may not disguise the slender nature typical of timber-frame construction (a wall thickness of 5 or 6 ins (12.7 or 15.2 cm), being common). This is a feature with inevitable consequences for the treatment of interiors. For example shutters cannot be accommodated in the embrasure of a window – a circumstance that may have encouraged the development of sash shutters (a possible ancestor of the sash window). In contrast a cob wall is disciplined by the limitations and possibilities of mud, manure and straw which combine to impose a minimum thickness of about 2 ft 6 ins (76.2 cm). Random stone walls generally possess a comparably ponderous magnificence for reasons of economy (Fig. 2). As with dry-stone walling, cut stone is minimised – hence the resulting thickness of each. Consequently elevations constructed of such substantial materials inspired a vigorous treatment of internal detailing and furnishing.

Because of the ephemeral nature of interior decoration, especially at the vernacular level, the following chapters are intended to sample various details in more permanent domestic buildings – the ones that have survived. For practical reasons this is a history of the homes of 'the middling sort'. In the earlier periods under review this means the yeoman farmers or lesser gentry although, in the south-east of England, this could extend to a rich, but nevertheless landless, peasant. In a primarily rural economy these layers of social class were relative positions, largely measured by the ownership of land.[6] As education increasingly began to signify middling social status (lawyers, doctors, etc.) in late Stuart and early Hanovarian Britain the divisions between classes became ever more graduated. In contrast the divide between town and country could be visually abrupt with a terrace in north London ending in a cornfield.[7] These urban fingers stretching out into the countryside did not, at first, signify the townsman's appreciation of the timeless beauty of the landscape; they rather reflected a lack of transport. This can be seen in the City of Bath, the growth of which, so it was argued in 1743, was conditioned by the fares charged by sedan chair men.[8] The vistas which the spa offered of rural Somerset had little to do with early Georgian developments in the City, although the surrounding hills were always appreciated for their 'healthy situation and fine prospect[s]'.[9] If one considers urban schemes like Queen Square (1728) and the King's Circus (1754) they are inward-looking spaces conceived by John Wood the elder (1704–54), whereas the younger Wood (1728–81) created the Royal Crescent (1767) as an extrovert series of thirty houses facing a rural prospect – with a ha-ha to protect the front lawn from too close a proximity to pastoral agriculture. This reflects a growing awareness of landscape, an appreciation that manifested itself in the work of Richard Wilson (1714–82), 'the father of English landscape painting'.

The square, circus and crescent provided the grand 'set pieces' in a species of town planning which was, in fact, conceived and carried out bit by bit. The associated dwellings which occupy the lesser streets were essential components of the 'support system' enabling the Georgian city to be both functional and pleasing. These lesser houses demand more serious consideration; they were a new vernacular, a revised tradition.

The notion that vernacular building coexisted with the architecture of Hanovarian Britain may need some

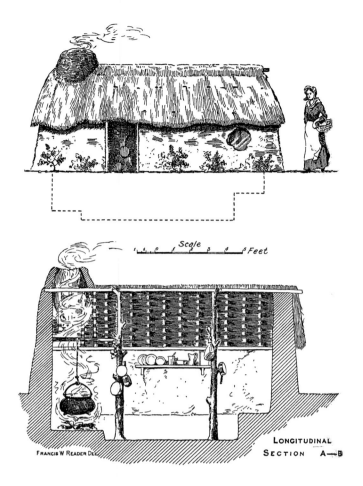

1   In 1846 Henry Laver recorded this cob-built dwelling, one of a group, near Boroughbridge, Somerset (Somerset Archaeological and Natural History Society, Vol. 55, 1909). The only concessions that this Saxon house type makes to the mid-nineteenth century are the chimney and the hole in the wall which, being glazed, serves as a window. The central trough improved the head-room and provided seating on three sides with a hearth at one end.

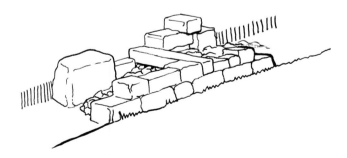

2   Rubble or random stone walls, coursed or uncoursed, were traditionally a minimum of 30 ins (76.2 cm) in thickness for reasons of economy. Such a wall enabled rough-masons to use stones of numerous dimensions on both the inner and outer faces (united by through-stones) with the space between being filled by a 'hearting' of gallets and stone dust. (Frederick Rainsford Hannay, *Dry Stone Walling*, 1957)

3   Charles L. Eastlake's *Hints on Household Taste* (1868) took as its inspiration a reasonably objective analysis of the vernacular interior, as in this illustration of a farmhouse fireplace at Chambercombe, Devon.

justification. Undoubtedly the timber-frame tradition persisted and the use of 'bonding-timbers' may be seen as a further extension of these age-old methods.[10] However, the conundrum of 'Georgian vernacular' is, I believe, best examined through a consideration of the builders, rather than the buildings – not so much a 'reception' theory, or even a 'production' thesis, as a sociological question. Take for example the convex crescent of some twenty-four early sixteenth-century, timber-frame dwellings in Church Street, Tewkesbury. As a 'product' they offered shops with living accommodation above and to the rear. They presumably met the needs of their original occupants ('reception'). As architecture they were no less 'designed' than the three curved blocks of which the King's Circus in Bath is comprised, except that the latter was conceived by a joiner, the former by a carpenter. Similarly a brick terrace in London, or a row of stone houses in Stamford, were the product of craftsmen, working on the basis of an empirical understanding of materials but who, for all that, were far from ignorant of the prevailing idioms of their time.[11]

There was also, it should be added, the potential for an extraordinary continuity of tradition in both craft methods and stylistic convention. This situation was not confined to those many families in which a particular trade was passed down through the generations. Apprentices generally began their training as children of fourteen years of age. In a time when retirement was an unheard of luxury a craftsman, health permitting, worked into his seventies and even his eighties. Such a circumstance brought about a considerable mingling of the generations in the workshops and on the building site. Thus age-old methods of working were perpetuated and aesthetic idioms maintained, over periods of a century and more, and certainly well beyond the compartments into which art history is too often neatly divided. For these reasons it is not the persistence of tradition but the presence of innovation that is remarkable.

For demographic reasons the earlier periods of furnishing and decoration sampled in the following pages are more likely to be drawn from rural districts whilst later examples are often from urban areas in which the 'row house' became dominant. These 'terraced' houses, as they were to become known, were a response to population growth and a developing consumerism.[12] This was mass-housing built on speculation 'for the chance of letting' or leasing.[13] For this reason houses were sold 'in that state denominated by builders "a shell"', so that they could be finished to meet the taste and pocket of the purchasers.[14] This finishing would have included much interior joinery and plasterwork. As is well known, the status of town houses was defined in relationship to their size, location and quality as first, second, third and fourth rate (see p. 2 and Figs 9, 10). What is less well understood is the extent to which 'customised' interiors extended down the 'pecking order' to the third and fourth-rate dwellings. It is known that the best of the first-rate houses were very radically treated once the 'shell' was complete. On the face of it, it seems likely that more modest dwellings were finished in accordance with their occupants' wishes, at least insofar as painting and decorating were concerned. For example, the less affluent were unable to afford printed wallpaper, still less silk hangings, but they might well have discussed a stencil design or applied such ornament themselves as suggested by John Claudius Loudon (see p. 161). And the importance of Loudon in the second quarter of the nineteenth century may scarcely be over estimated. George Eliot offers the following dialogue in her novel *Middlemarch* (1871–2):

'Will you show me your plan?'
'Yes certainly. I daresay it is very faulty. But I have been examining the plans for cottages in Loudon's book, and picked out what seem the best things. Oh what happiness it would be to set the pattern about here! I think, instead of Lazarus at the gate, we should put the pig-sty cottages outside the park gate.'

As an aesthetic manifesto Charles L. Eastlake's *Hints on Household Taste* (1868) began where Loudon's pattern book had not ventured (Fig. 3), and his contemporary, William Morris, would leave an even more indelible mark.[15]

Although for Sidney Oldall Addy the interior remained a central concern of his pioneering study *The Evolution of the English House* (1898) his example, in this respect, has only occasionally been maintained. The journal *Vernacular Architecture* is typical in being primarily concerned with matters like structure, planning, house type, geographical distribution and, more recently, dendrochronology. Despite this relative, if far from absolute, paucity of published research on the vernacular interior, there are two areas of enquiry which have proved to be of value to this emerging field. I refer to recent studies concerning social history and also vernacular furniture.[16] This book owes much, but probably not enough, to these two areas of research. In particular, social and economic historians,[17] backed by the statistical analysis of probate inventories, have done much to illuminate the fundamental trends in household life so that the more complex questions as to how an individual small house was handled in real life can be more satisfactorily examined.

At a practical level this book would not have been possible without the example of a number of American colleagues who, in effect, showed me what to look for in this country.[18] Finally, whatever the limitations of this publication, it remains my belief that it is at the vernacular level that our shared trans-Atlantic culture is most evident (Figs. 290–1).

Introduction

If the peasant can be satisfied with his establishment, and the gentleman could not tell how to live without his, one would be almost persuaded that they could not be of the same class of animals.

William Howitt, *The Rural Life of England*, 1837[1]

This is a book about vernacular interiors: that is to say, it is concerned with interiors which may sometimes be quite large but in their arrangement and construction draw from tradition. Today small houses have often reverted to their original middle-class status, but in the past housing has tended to descend the social scale as expectations of comfort and privacy have risen. Many so-called cottages were intended for the yeoman class just as many farmhouses were built for the lesser gentry. The last traces of the Saxon hall (Fig. 4) once suitable for kings and princes may be seen in timber-built barns; such a transition was no doubt caused by the ancient tradition for man to cohabit with his domesticated animals (Figs. 6, 7). Thus we may view the stone-built beehive pigsties of Wales (Fig. 5) as being related to the ancient and primitive houses of similar construction found in Scotland and Ireland.[2]

It is exceedingly rare for small houses in Britain to be 'listed' for preservation because of their interiors, and fairly common for them to be listed without knowledge of their internal appearance. Although existing legislation theoretically makes provision for the statutory protection of all listed buildings inside and out, in practice it is not effective. This matter demands further exploration and debate. To admire the external elevations of architecture is for most people a cerebral activity, whereas to be within an historic building, to be enveloped by history, is an important emotional and physical experience.

The fragmentary condition of the interiors and decoration of many small houses is to some extent reflected in the form of this book which gives an account of a succession of details. This approach should make reference easier, but a concluding chapter has been added to this edition in an attempt to unify these various elements into a cohesive whole. Some consideration is given to the practical details of construction in wood and stone, as well as to paint and painting, in the hope of assisting those concerned with the restoration and maintenance of similar buildings.

The vernacular interior was not designed on paper in an office; it evolved on carpenter's bench and mason's 'banker' and was mostly built *in situ*.[3] In other words, vernacular building is arrived at either by individuals constructing shelter for themselves or (more often) by trained craftsmen, both categories of builder drawing upon the traditions of the culture at large, inspired and disciplined by local materials and climate. Until the late sixteenth century those who designed buildings were trained craftsmen: masons or carpenters. In the seventeenth century and afterwards these artisans often had little understanding of the basic thinking behind the Classical Orders, whilst architects sometimes had little appreciation of materials or craftsmanship. The technical proficiency of the master craftsman, dominated by the architect with his aesthetic manifestos, reached its height in the late nineteenth century. Today the position of the architect as master is now threatened by the structural engineer or 'project manager' whilst, according to *The Times*, architecture is considered to be 'a profession and not an art'.[4]

4   The hall of Plas Uchaf, Llangar, near Corwen, Clwyd, Wales. This interior may date from 1400 or even earlier and is a rare survival of an aisled hall in a domestic building although it was to remain common in barns in Britain. Despite its relatively small size this house was of very high status in relation to its time and place.

5   Pigsty at Penddeucae Fach, Bedlinog, Gwent, Wales. The beehive construction was used in many of the early stone-built single-cell dwellings of Celtic Europe. The transition from human to animal occupation is a recurring theme.

Buildings surviving from before 1600 tend to belong to the upper levels of society. The mud shelters of the peasants have been dissolved by the action of rain and time, although at higher social levels houses of cob or clay lump have survived in considerable numbers in counties like Devon or Norfolk. There are also examples of features long since rejected by the aristocracy that continued in use in houses built for the gentry and yeomanry. An obvious example was the declining use of timber. This had been the primary material used in the construction of the halls used by Anglo-Saxon kings. *The Domesday Book* lists only seven quarries confirming that, apart from the reuse of material from Roman buildings, stone was not much used at this time.[5] On the other hand some features, like the central hearth open to the roof, persisted amongst both the aristocracy (who had a choice of rooms) and the poorest (who had no choice at all). With furnishing, the woven tapestry persisted in patrician households long after the humble stained hanging had gone out of use in more modest dwellings.

The emergence of the middle classes following the Reformation gave rise to more substantial homes for lesser men (Fig. 8). Inevitably much of this book is concerned with the middle classes as represented, in an urban context, in the engravings of 'Third and Fourth Rate Houses' illustrated in Peter Nicholson's *New Practical Builder* of 1823–5 (Figs. 9, 10). By the time of the 1851 Exhibition the vernacular traditions were dying as a result of the mass culture brought about by industrialisation and the concomitant improvement in communications. After 1851 the rich were not so easily recognised as an élite by the quality of their surroundings so much as by the quantity of objects in those surroundings.

Many of the features with which this book is concerned are more important than architecture or decoration, and even more fundamental than craftsmanship. In 1963 after a fire at Lauderdale House, Highgate, London, builders discovered bricked-up in a wall near a first-floor fireplace a basket containing two shoes, a candlestick, a goblet, two strangled chickens and two chickens that had been walled-

6, 7   Byre dwelling (two views) from Magheragallan, as re-erected at the Ulster Folk and Transport Museum. The tradition of man cohabiting with his domesticated animals is well illustrated in this nineteenth-century example. The 'house-part' is separated from the byre by an open drain.

8   Greive's Farm, Northumberland, drawn by S. H. Grimm in the late eighteenth century. It conveys the effect of such domestic interiors as they were lived in. Note the half-door, the coal-burning bar-grate and the washing line.

up alive. This miscellaneous collection had been ceremonially incarcerated as a builder's offering circa 1600,[6] a religious and mystical approach to building that declined with the emergence of the architectural profession.[7] The extinction of this type of superstition has been confirmed by such prosaic matters as planning regulations. The concept of the home as a near holy place with its lares and penates is ancient. Indeed, for the liturgy of daily life the threshold and the hearth may be seen as equivalent respectively to the church porch and altar. Such a reverential attitude to man's shelter produced an outlook that regarded comfort as a proper but subordinate consideration. Health, as defined by government edict and imposed by local officials, was yet to be invented. Before houses were 'designed' they evolved, with a sensitivity towards their environment that may be seen as truly organic. It is such values that we have lost today and thus it is that we so cherish them.

I see the barns and comely manors planned
By men who somehow moved in comely thought,
Who, with a simple shippon on their hand
As men upon some godlike business wrought.
John Drinkwater

9, 10   A 'third' and a 'fourth-rate' terraced house from Peter Nicholson's *New Practical Builder* (1823–5).

James Ayres
Bath 1979 and 2002

Chapter 1

The Vernacular Interior

House: a building wherein to shelter a man's person and goods from the inclemencies of the weather and the injuries of ill-disposed persons.

Anon, *Builder's Dictionary*, 1734[1]

Decor: the keeping of due Respect between the Inhabitant and the Habitation.

Richard Neve, *The City and Country Purchaser*, 1726[2]

The main sources of reliable information on small domestic interiors are contemporary descriptions[3] and pictures (Fig. 11). In general only the grander houses were considered valid subjects; but travellers often had to accept accommodation where they could find it and if particularly primitive it was just as worthy of record as the 'big house'. Today the growing number of open-air museums which exhibit reconstructed and furnished houses provide an interesting picture of the past but, as they necessarily involve some speculation, they should be treated with caution. In the present state of knowledge so many issues are unresolved. How widespread were wire-gauze window blinds, floor cloths or chimney boards in eighteenth-century England? In gentry or aristocratic houses these questions are less difficult to answer. The larger the house, the more easily rooms could be left unchanged for a century or more, a situation which was particularly true of state apartments used only on formal occasions. In small houses the clutter of human occupation and activity had greater effect, and as each successive innovation was introduced so it either overlaid or destroyed earlier decoration or previous ways of life. There is almost a case for including here a history of

costume; certainly agricultural and fishing implements were likely to stray indoors (Figs. 12, 13) where they inevitably played a part in the appearance of relatively small rooms.

In the reconstruction of a modest interior the degree of speculation involved very much depends upon period and geographical location. An interior of *c.* 1750 could be arrived at with reasonable accuracy if it came from the south-east of England, but in many parts of the British Isles it could not be assembled with confidence unless dating from the mid-nineteenth century or later. So long as, and wherever, the basics of the medieval tradition persisted the use of paint for colour and pattern was probably more pungent than we would now suspect. In contrast textiles, which are so often today's vehicle for colour and pattern, were exceedingly scarce until after the Industrial Revolution.

The Reformation brought with it effects that were to prove more far-reaching than a shift of power (from mason to architect) or style (from medieval tradition to classical innovation). It introduced the middle classes.[4] Later, a hundred years elapsed between the appearance of a prophet like Inigo Jones and a disciple of Palladianism like Lord Burlington, that 'Apollo of the Arts' whose 'proper Priest' was William Kent. In the intervening years the Dutch influence and the use of brick made possible the emergence of a new vernacular which contrived to unite the seemingly irreconcilable by acknowledging the influence of both the English weather and the Italian Renaissance. In Isaac Ware's inimitable phrase, 'climate induces as necessary a deviation in copying their [Italians'] works here, as the ceremonies of their religion.'[5] The simple brick town houses devised in the mid-seventeenth century were to become ubiquitous after the

11   J. Van Aken, *Grace before a Meal, c.* 1720. This painting by a Dutch artist offers a remarkable glimpse of middle-class life in England. The family, or its servants, are about to dine in the kitchen at a gate-leg table which, for compositional reasons, is unconvincingly small. Judging by the thin walls the house, in which this scene is set, is of timber-frame construction. Although the family is well dressed the absence of textile furnishing (neither curtains nor rugs) is typical of pre-industrial Britain. Ashmolean Museum, Oxford.

12 An Orkney living-room in about 1930. In pre-industrial communities the house was a place of work as much as a refuge for relaxation. Note the fishing floats visible in the top left of the picture.
Photograph: Bryce Wilson.

13 Interior of a croft on Foula, Shetland in *c.* 1900. Note the fish hanging up to dry and smoke over the fireplace.

Great Fire of London where, under the supervision of Wren and others, they were to form the basis of British domestic architecture for over two hundred years (Figs. 14, 15). Even the nineteenth-century stucco-clad houses of Nash and his Victorian followers conform, in their internal planning, to these seventeenth-century origins. This was what the late Sir Albert Richardson, rejecting that vague term 'Georgian', sensibly dubbed 'the English Style', an unspoken reference to Muthesius.[6]

The development of urban centres in the seventeenth century resulted in a division between the character of life in town and country. A situation that was confirmed by the spectacular growth in population in the nineteenth century. The medieval burgage plots gave each property a street frontage the narrowness of which was compensated for by their depth; an early manifestation of the effects of urban congestion. Up to the seventeenth century the width, or rather the narrowness, of the burgage plot was emphasised, on the street elevation, by a gable. This would give way, in the interests of Classicism, to a roof in which the ridge, or rather the ridges, ran parallel to the frontage, in turn resulting in the 'M' roof with a central gutter. The use of dormer windows made attics more useful and the provision of a roof with a double pitch created more head-room. This feature is known in England as a 'curb roof' but the old English term 'gambrel' is still used in America.[7]

Before the coming of the railways the self-sufficient economy of many villages was maintained. In some towns a degree of specialisation in the manufacture of certain products developed in the late seventeenth

14   A terrace of brick-built
houses on the north side of
Newington Green. At the time
they were built in *c.* 1650
Newington was a village to the
north of London. Although the
gables define the width of the
traditional burgage plot the
horizontal emphasis afforded by
Classical architectural details
like cornices and plat bands
make these houses the
precursors of the Georgian
terraced house.

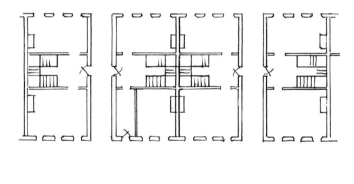

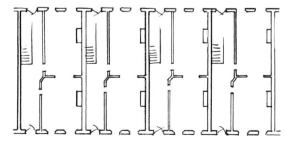

15   Sketch plan (above) of mid-seventeenth-century row houses of
the Newington Green type compared (below) with a typical terrace
of the eighteenth or early nineteenth centuries.

century on the basis of locally available materials.
Nevertheless, in much of the country conditions had
scarcely changed for three hundred years. William
Cobbett's description of a farm sale near Reigate in
October 1825 shows that even in the Home Counties a
sixteenth-century farmhouse would have just one room
that was Regency in character and thus of its time:

Every thing about this farm-house was formerly the
scene of *plain manners* and plentiful living. Oak clothes-
chests, oak bedsteads, oak chests of drawers, and oak
tables to eat on, long, strong, and well supplied with
joint stools. Some of the things were many hundreds of
years old. But all appeared to be in a state of decay and
nearly of *disuse*. There appeared to have been hardly any
family in that house, where formerly there were in all
probability, from ten to fifteen men, boys, and maids
and, which was the worst of all, there was a *parlour*! Ay,
and a *carpet* and *bell-pull* too! One end of the front of
this once plain and substantial house had been
moulded into a '*parlour*'; and there was the mahogany
table, and the fine chairs, and the fine glass, and all as
barefaced upstart as any stock-jobber in the kingdom
can boast of. And, there were the decanters, the glasses,
the 'dinner-set' of crockery ware, and all just in the true
stock-jobber style. And I dare say it has been *Squire*
Charington and the *Misses* Charingtons; and not plain
Master Charington, and his son Hodge, and his daughter Betty Charington, all of whom this accursed system

has, in all likelihood, transmuted into a species of mock gentlefolks, while it has ground the labourers down into real slaves. Why do not farmers now *feed* and *lodge* their work-people, as they did formerly?

★ ★ ★ ★ ★

When the old farm-houses are down (and down they must come in time) what a miserable thing the country will be! Those that are now erected are mere painted shells, with a Mistress within, who is stuck up in a place she calls a *parlour*, with, if she have children, the 'young ladies and gentlemen' about her: some showy chairs and a sofa (a *sofa* by all means): half a dozen prints in gilt frames hanging up: some swinging book-shelves with novels and tracts upon them: . . .[8]

This could almost be a description of George Morland's set of six paintings of *The Story of Laetitia* of 1786 and it is possible that Cobbett was familiar with the popular engravings based on these canvases. On the other hand the accuracy of Cobbett's description is of great value, emphasising little-known details like the rarity and high social status of carpets and the better-known issues of changing social organisation. Because standards varied so much, descriptions of interiors are only of value if their approximate date is known together with their geographical location. Of the urban centres London was pre-eminent in terms of the material standards of living enjoyed by its inhabitants. Indeed the capital, Cobbett's 'great wen', was the engine of change for the country as a whole.[9]

In small country towns Celia Fiennes was able to describe the occupants of the old timber houses of Goudhurst, Kent, in 1697: '. . . they are a sort of yeomanly Gentry, about 2 or 3 or 400 £ a year and eate and drink well and live comfortably and hospitably; the old proverb was a Yeoman of Kent with one year's Rent could buy out the Gentlemen of Wales and Knights of Scales and a Lord of the North Country.'[10] A situation often referred to by today's politicians as 'the north/south divide'. The rich soil of the Weald, coupled with close contact with the latest ideas from the Continent, had early established a level of household comfort unmatched elsewhere in the country, and which, although by then 'old fashioned', was still adequate for the standards if not the fashions of the late seventeenth century. In contrast the Welsh at this time lived in such primitive conditions that Miss Fiennes ventured no further into the principality than 'Holly Well' (Holywell) where 'they speake Welsh [and] the inhabitants go barefoote and bare leg'd, a nasty sort of people'. Conditions at Aitchison Bank in Scotland were not much better:

The houses lookes just like the booths at fairs . . . they have no chimneys their smoke comes out all over the house and there are great holes in the side of their houses which lets out the smoke when they have been well smoked in it; there is no room in their houses but is up to the thatch and in which are 2 or 3 beds even to the parlours and buttery; and not withstanding the cleaning of their parlour for me I was not able to beare the roome; the smell of the hay was a perfume and what I rather chose to stay and see my horses eat their provender in their stable than to stand in that roome, for I could not bring myself to sit down.[11]

If Miss Fiennes had been less 'stand-offish' she would have been below the level of the smoke. In contrast to the surroundings she was offered both salmon and trout to eat and 'some of their wine, which was exceeding good Claret which they stand conveniently for to have from France'.

Tudor writers, living in a time of great social, religious and aesthetic change, note improvements in comfort. William Harrison wrote (1577) that fine possessions extended to 'the lowest sort (in most places of our south countrie)' and that possessions had 'descended yet lower, even unto the inferiour artificers and manie farmers, who . . . have (for the most part) learned also to garnish their cupboards with plate, their (joined) beds with tapistrie and silke hangings, and their tables with (carpets and) fine naperie, whereby the wealth of our countrie (god be praised therefore and give us grace to imploie it well) dooth infinitelie appeare.'[12]

In the far south-west, twenty-five years later, the situation was very different, as Sir Richard Carew's *Survey of Cornwall* of 1602 makes clear. In the duchy, the aristocracy and gentry kept liberal

but not costly builded or furnished houses . . . Touching the Yeomanarie . . . Suiteable hereunto was their dwelling, and to their implements of household: walles of earth, low thatched roofes, few partitions, no planchings or glass windows, and scarcely any chimneys other than a hole in the wall to let out the smoke; their bed, straw and a blanket: as for sheets, so much linen cloth had not yet stepped over the narrow channel, betweene them and Brittaine. To conclude, a mazer and a panne or two comprised all their substance: but now most of these fashions are universally banished, and the *Cornish* husbandman conformeth himself with a better supplied civilitie to the Easterne patterne.[13]

Thus even in Cornwall, where Carew compares a hostile attitude to the English with 'the Welsh, their auncient countrimen', the population was gradually beginning to enjoy some of the comforts of their despised neighbours.

By the eighteenth century many of the comforts that we now take for granted such as window glass and fireplace chimneys were all but universal, although carpets, curtains and plumbing remained uncommon. The improvement in living conditions in the second quarter of the eighteenth century was, with some implicit self-praise, well summed-up by John Wood in his *A Description of Bath*:

> About the Year 1727 [when Wood returned to his native city], the Boards of the Dining Rooms and most other Floors were made of a Brown Colour with Soot and small Beer to hide the Dirt, as well as their own Imperfections; and if the Walls of any of the Rooms were covered with Wainscot, it was with such as was mean and never Painted: The Chimney Pieces, Hearths and Slabbs were all of Free Stone, and these were daily cleaned with a particular Whitewash, which, by paying Tribute to every thing that touched it, soon rendered the brown Floors like the Stary Firmament: the Doors were slight and thin, and the best Locks had only Iron Coverings Varnished: The Looking Glasses were small, mean, and few in Number; and the Chimney Furniture consisted of a slight Iron Fender, with Tongs, Poker and Shovel all of no more than three or four Shillings Value.
>
> With *Kidderminster* Stuff, or at best with Cheyne, the Woollen Furniture of the principal Rooms was made; and such as was of Linnen consisted either of Corded Dimaty, or coarse Fustian; the Matrons of the City, their Daughters and their Maids Flowering the latter with Worsted, during the Intervals between the Seasons, to give the Beds a gaudy Look.

★ ★ ★ ★ ★

> As the new Buildings advanced, Carpets were introduced to cover the Floors, though laid with the finest clean Deals, or *Dutch* Oak Boards; the Rooms were all Wainscoted and Painted in a costly and handsome Manner; Marble Slabbs, and even Chimney Pieces, became common; the Doors in general were not only made thick and substantial, but they had the best Sort of Brass Locks put on them; Walnut Tree Chairs, some with Leather, and some with Damask or Worked Bottoms supplied the Place of such as were Seated with Cane or Rushes; the Oak Tables and Chests of Drawers were exchanged, the former for such as were made of Mahoggony, the latter for such as were made either with the same Wood, or with Wallnut Tree; handsome Glasses were added to the Dressing Tables, nor did the proper Chimneys or Peers of any of the Rooms long remain without well Framed Mirrours of no inconsiderable Size; and the Furniture for every chief Chimney was composed of a Brass Fender, with Tongs, Poker and Shovel agreeable to it.
>
> Beds, Window Curtains and other Chamber Furniture, as well Woollen as Linnen, were, from time to time, renewed with such as was more fit for Gentlemens Capital Seats, than Houses appropriated for common Lodgings; and the Linnen for the Table and Bed grew better and better till it became suitable even for People of the highest Rank.[14]

Later writers, unless straying into those parts of Britain where primitive conditions could still be found, tended either to reflect a rather bourgeois smugness or to react to some extraordinary feature. J. T. Smith, for example, mentions the Italian artist Capitsoldi who 'upon his arrival, took the attic storey of a house in Warwick Street, Golden Square [London] and being short of furniture, painted chairs, pictures and window-curtains, upon the walls of his sitting room, most admirably deceptive'.[15] This account indicates that the furniture in this *trompe-l'oeil* must have been ranged round the walls in a regimented fashion, as is known to have been the eighteenth-century practice in the houses of the gentry and aristocracy. Judging by Grimm's drawing of the interior of the Saracen's Head, Southwell, Nottinghamshire (Fig. 16), such was also the custom in smaller rooms where the resulting spaciousness was the more valuable. The great variety, in terms of quality and size, of tilt-top tables and corner chairs provide still further evidence of the constant ebb and flow of furniture within a room.

Good, bland, middle-class household comfort in cottage surroundings is expressed by Goldsmith through the Reverend Dr Primrose in *The Vicar of Wakefield* (1766):

> My house consisted of but one storey, and was covered with thatch, which gave it an air of great snugness. The walls on the inside were nicely whitewashed, and my daughters undertook to adorn them with pictures of their own designing. Though the same room served us for parlour and kitchen that only made it warmer. Besides as it was kept with the utmost neatness – the dishes, plates and coppers being well scoured, and all disposed in bright rows on the shelves – the eye was agreeably relieved, and did not want richer furniture. There were three other apartments – one for my wife and me; another for our two daughters within our room; and the third with two beds for the rest of the children.

This description is a remarkably early example of the middle classes returning to the type of house in which their ancestors lived. It was probably on the basis of the need for economy as much as upon French precedent and the Romantic Movement that the *cottage ornée* took root in Britain.

As early as the 1730s estate workers had been housed in rows of cottages at Boxworth, Cambridgeshire,[16] and at the same period Ralph Allen built a terrace of houses

16   S. H. Grimm, *A Part of the Parlour at Saracen's Head at Southwell, called King Charles's Room, Nott.*, drawn *c.* 1793. The arrangement of furniture against the walls is typical.

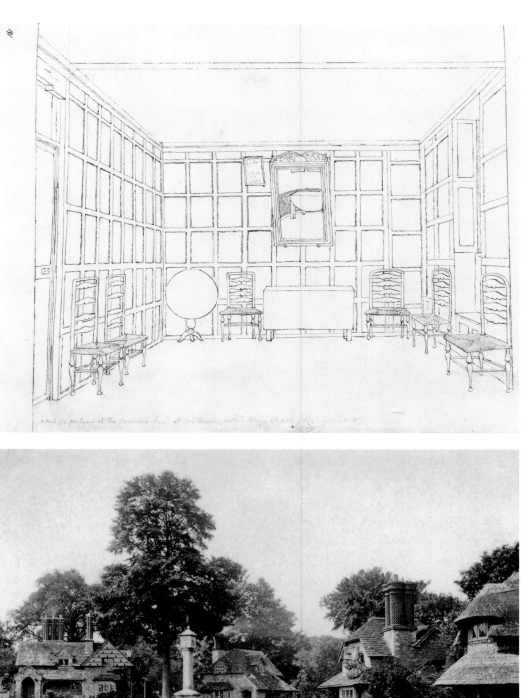

17   A self-conscious awareness of vernacular domestic buildings began with the French *cottage ornée*. Numerous architects in Britain designed schemes in this idiom, among them John Nash as here at Blaise Hamlet (1810–11, photograph *c.* 1860) just north of Bristol.

for his masons and another for his quarrymen at Bath.[17] In general, landowners removed such buildings from the view of the 'big house' but the later desire to combine an ornament to the estate with a home for its workers could also develop into a matter of social conscience. Blaise

Hamlet (1811), by Nash, may have been built to give greater amusement to the rustic scene but it also provided comfortable if improbable housing (Fig. 17). John Papworth's *Rural Residences* (1818) is mainly preoccupied with the external appearance of such buildings, in con-

18   S. H. Grimm, *Privy at the decoy, Abbotsbury, Dorsetshire 1790*, watercolour drawing. The earliest water closets date back to the sixteenth century but were rarely deployed until the nineteenth century whilst, for most people in Britain, indoor plumbing was a twentieth century innovation.

trast to Loudon's *Encyclopaedia of Cottage, Farm and Villa Architecture* (1833) which is also concerned with the practical arrangements within them. Loudon's book was avowedly designed to increase 'the comforts of the great mass of society'.[18] Such books must be seen as the precursors of the Prince Consort's attempts to improve the living conditions of the urban masses. Despite the efforts

of the establishment and the example of the radical Chartists, these activities and activists had little impact on the housing problems of the nineteenth century. The writings of Richard Jefferies and Flora Thompson show that in the country little changed except for the worse, whilst the indescribable squalor of some areas of the large towns remained to be graphically recorded by Gustave Doré.[19]

The 'Necessary House', or as William Halfpenny (and others) described it in the eighteenth century, the 'Bog House', was simply an outside shed, providing a degree of privacy which many houses lacked even in the nineteenth century (Fig. 18). The privacy of the privy was important. In 1755 Ann Shaw was presented in court in Ormskirk 'for not having a door to screen her necessary and dunghill from public view'. In this case failure to meet such a need resulted in a fine of £1 1s.[20] The water closet within the house, though invented as early as 1596 by Sir John Harrington, and installed in some houses in Hanovarian Britain, remained a luxury not widely introduced until the twentieth century.

Eventually it was not the well-meaning condescension of the rich[21] so much as industrialisation and transport that were to improve the quality of life for the mass of the population. At first this new-found means of producing objects cheaply tended to result in greater elaboration of the product at the expense of increased production. *The Report to the Juries* regarding the exhibits at the 1851 Exhibition sensibly remarked that 'It is not necessary that an object be covered with ornament; or extravagant in form, to obtain the element of beauty; articles of furniture are too often crowded with unnecessary embellishment, which besides adding to their cost, interferes with their use.'

It was neither judgements like these nor the increased profits that simplified design would bring to industrialists that ultimately exerted the restraining hand on the excesses of Victorian decoration. It was the attempts of the Arts and Crafts Movement to turn back the clock that succeeded in providing a less cluttered aesthetic though failing to create a new society.

Chapter 2

Heat and Light

THE FIRE AND THE HEARTH

The domestication of man probably began when he tamed fire. Even before houses were built fire was central to man's life and in the earliest house it was the focus (Latin for hearth) of the room. Indeed the central hearth open to the roof persisted in England well into the sixteenth century and remained in use on the fringes of the British Isles within living memory (Fig. 19). The fire was the heart of the house.

Two of the words most intimately concerned with this fundamental subject – 'fire' and 'hearth' – are Germanic in origin. The hearth was practically a synonym for the home, as in the phrase 'hearth and home'. In the north of England the room with the fireplace was once known as the 'fire house'.[1] Because fire was seen as being so crucial to man's survival it was used in England as a yardstick for taxation – 'the hearth tax'.[2] The presence of this '*fumage*' tax discouraged a proliferation of hearths, with profound effects on the planning of houses in England, and probably encouraged the retention of the more efficient if less convenient open central hearth which provided warmth, light and heat for cooking, although in summer some cooking would have been done out of doors. In Viking Denmark and Iceland separate rooms designated as kitchens within the main body of the house have been found, but in Britain they are generally a later innovation and in some areas a recent one. There was also a tradition for kitchens which were detached from the dwelling house, a feature adopted in the southern states of Colonial North America with some enthusiasm.[3] It was here that the climate encouraged the use of a winter kitchen in the body of the house whilst in the summer months the heat of the fire was removed to a separate building –

'the summer kitchen'. In most smaller pre-Reformation houses only one room, known as the 'hall', would have had a fire in it. The parlour, if one existed, would have remained unheated; such grandeur was a cold privilege in winter and for this reason these rooms were not elaborately decorated. Accordingly, the central hearth may be seen as not simply more efficient but, in winter at least, more socially cohesive at a time when a yeoman's household would be comprised of the farmer, his family, and the farm servants (the labourers, etc.). The central hearth was the natural theatre in which to gossip and recite traditional stories and songs.

The hearth itself was of earth, clay or stone and was known, before the advent of the grate, as a 'downhearth'.[4] Where wood was burnt, firedogs were necessary to provide a good circulation of oxygen to assist combustion. Being made of iron, a valuable commodity in a pre-industrial society, these must have long remained a luxury available only to a few. At first these firedogs took the form of a horizontal bar supported above the hearth by a pair of feet, from each end of which sprang vertical members, later known as staukes,[5] which prevented the logs from falling outwards. Such firedogs have been found over much of Celtic Europe from the British Isles to Czechoslovakia, as have many other examples of early domestic ironwork. Celtic firedogs of the type from Capel Garmon, now in the National Museum of Wales, and another in Colchester Museum are terminated at each end by magnificent ox heads (Fig. 20). The alternative name for a firedog, 'andiron' from the French *landier*, may preserve 'through late Latin forms a common Celtic root meaning a bull-calf or a heifer'.[6] The type, though lacking the zoomorphic detail, persisted wherever central hearths were used.

19   Interior of an Orkney croft in *c.* 1900. The central hearth, hanging chain, timber and straw chairs and the cupboard-beds are typical.

20   Early Iron Age firedog from Capel Garmon, Gwynedd. The double-ended firedog was intended for use on a central hearth. The zoomorphic detail on this example is typically Celtic. National Museum of Wales.

A good sixteenth-century example survives on the central hearth of the great hall at Penshurst. With the introduction of fireplaces a pair of firedogs placed side by side with their staukes facing outwards became necessary. This break with tradition encouraged greater variety in form and even name, 'cobiron' being an alternative which may refer to their being knobbed (Fig. 43).[7] In Britain the availability of wrought-iron firedogs and cast-iron fire-backs from the Weald of Kent and Sussex may well have been severely circumscribed until improved transport made them more widely available. Such an hypothesis would explain why ceramic firedogs and fire-backs were made by the potters of north Devon (Fig. 21).

The firedog was the perfect means of supporting a roasting spit (Fig. 22). At first these were turned by hand, sometimes by 'poor Industrious Boys . . . for small Perquisites of licking the Dripping Pans'.[8] In due course various mechanical devices were developed, the most sophisticated of which was a turbine installed in the flue. These turbines were activated by rising heat. This contrivance was known to, and possibly devised by, Leonardo da Vinci. A Regency example may be seen in the kitchen of the Royal Pavilion, Brighton. Lesser households used the clock spit (operated by clockwork and attached to the chimney bressummer), the 'jack' (Fig. 23, also operated by clockwork), and the dogwheel. An aquatint by Rowlandson showing such a wheel occurs in H.

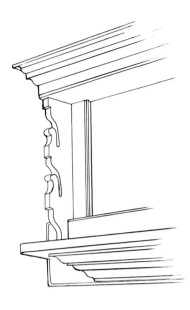

21 Reconstruction of a north Devon pottery fire-back and firedogs (the latter dated 1708). The fire-back is based on a fractured example at Docton House, Appledore and the firedogs derive from the fragmentary survivals in Barnstaple Museum (see Figs. 41, 42). By the late eighteenth century better transport systems made the cast-iron products of Ironbridge, Shropshire and Falkirk, Scotland, available throughout Britain and beyond to overseas markets.

22 Spit rack (one end) at 21 Grove Terrace (begun 1761), Highgate, north London.

Wigstead's *Remarks on a Tour of North and South Wales in the Year 1797* (1800) and a surviving example was located some years ago in the Old Manor House, Mitford, Northumberland – a house of modest size.[9] In the City of Bath a special type of dog was used for this purpose. They were characterised by their 'exceedingly long backs, but short bandy legs' and, like their masters, were well known 'for their Daily Assembly together in one part of the City or another'. The notion that these were a special kind of mongrel seems to have been first noted by Dr John Caius (1510–73) of Cambridge. He described them as 'the curs of the coarsest kind, a certain dog in kitchen service excellent. For when any meat is to be roasted, they go into a wheel, which they turning about with the weight of their bodies, so diligently look to their business, that no drudge nor scullion can do the feat more cunningly, whom the popular sort here upon term turnspits.'[10]

Any fire which is exclusively wood-burning needs encouragement. As we have seen, firedogs helped air to circulate, but there were times when the more vigorous action of bellows was necessary. The word 'bellows' is probably derived from the Anglo-Saxon *blaest balg* or blast bag, so clearly they have a long history. Most primitive of all was the iron blowing tube. In contrast the rather sophisticated looking 'centrifugal hand blower' was, in fact, confined to peat-burning districts.[11] Other items

23 Wood engraving from Thomas Bewick's *British Birds*, Vol. II, 'Water Birds' (1804), 6th edition 1826, p. 243.

24   The 'New' Church (St George's), Portland, Dorset in *c.* 1790. Watercolour drawing by S. H. Grimm. Note the 'cow clotts', on the block of stone in the left foreground, being dried as fuel.

were also necessary to adjust the logs, and references to 'fire forks' abound in sixteenth-century inventories.

In general the preferred fuel was timber, with the hardwoods being the most favoured (see Appendix VII). Wood such as oak was slow burning and produced the greatest heat. One exception was elm, which is a poor combustor and once lit produces little heat; for this reason elm was usually selected for the fireplace bressummer in houses that were otherwise framed-up of oak. In regions that were not forested, and amongst those individuals who did not possess woodland, or hold common rights that enabled them to obtain firewood, other kinds of fuel had to be gleaned. The poor in the region of Swanage were exceptionally fortunate in the availability of Kimmeridge shale. Celia Fiennes states that 'they take up stones by the shores that are so oyly as the poor burn it for fire, and it's so light a fire it serves for candle too, but it has a strong offensive smell (Fig. 67).[12]

Another source of fuel was dried dung, the removal of which impoverished the land worked by the crofters in Scotland, adding to the downward spiral of their poverty. A late eighteenth-century drawing of the New Church at Portland by S. H. Grimm[13] shows a block of stone in the left foreground with cow 'clots' (also known as 'dyths' and in Yorkshire dialect as 'cassons'[14]) left to dry on its top (Fig. 24). The indefatigable Celia Fiennes also saw, near Peterborough, 'upon the walls of the ordinary peoples houses the cow dung plaister'd up to drie in cakes which

they use for fireing – its a very offensive fewell but the country people use little else in these parts'.[15] Again her acute eye noted the lack of fuel around Penzance where they burnt 'turf and furse and ferne; they have little or noe wood and noe coale. . . . I was surprised to find my supper boyling on a fire always supply'd with a brush of furse and that to be the only fewell to dress a joynt of meat and broth, and told me they could not roast any thing, but they have a little wood for such occasions but it's scarce and dear.' In many parts of Cornwall the 'intolerable price' of wood for the domestic hearth was due to the voracious needs of the tin smelters, a situation acknowledged by Carew as early as 1602.[16] Gorse, twigs and fern were also used as fuel in parts of Wales and in some regions it is likely that fires were lit only when there was cooking to be done.[17]

In Scotland dried horse and cow dung supplemented with seaweed was burnt in houses on the Orkneys and the Hebrides, and in Fife and Angus cow dung was mixed with coal or sawdust dried in the sun to form cakes known as *dalls* or *daws*. Peat was a basic fuel not only in much of Scotland but also in Ireland, Wales and various parts of England such as Cumbria. In areas where it was scarce or where old-established communities had used up all the nearby peat, turf was sometimes used as a substitute with disastrous long-term effects on agriculture.[18]

When the tax on coal was abolished in 1793 its use became more widespread. In some parts of Scotland, as

25   Central hearth with reredos in a croft on Birsay, Orkney (photograph *c.* 1900). The cupboard-bed in the background is particularly well 'grained'.

early as 1795 coal was burnt in the 'front room' but peat continued as the fuel in the kitchen. Coal not only provided a greater heat, it also produced a better light. In the parish of Dyke and Moy in Morayshire even the poorer households burnt coal quite early as it provided enough light to continue the domestic industry of spinning after dark.[19]

In the Yorkshire Dales knitting was an activity which could be carried on in the semidarkness of firelight. William Howitt, in his *Rural Life of England* (1837), gives the following description: 'As soon as it becomes dark . . . they rake or put out the fire; take their cloaks and lanterns, and set out with their knitting to the house of the neighbour where the sitting falls in rotation, for it is a regularly circulating assembly from house to house . . . The whole troop of neighbours being collected, they sit and knit, sing knitting songs, and tell knitting-stories . . . All this time their knitting goes on with unremitting speed. They sit rocking to and fro like so many weird wizards. They burn no candle, but knit by the light of the peat fire.'[20]

The utensils of the hearth were always kept to a minimum, metal being expensive and a profusion of gadgets confusing. The 'great dripping pan'[21] was always important for cooking as was the pot-hook and chain, known in the Isle of Man as the 'slouree'. Chains of an early type if not date (their use persisted in the so-called black houses of the Outer Hebrides) are fitted with

hooks to facilitate raising and lowering the chain in a loop (Figs. 25, 26, 28, 31). Again the introduction of the fireplace brought about change and although the chain continued in use it was generally displaced by a trammel which provided the necessary adjustable height for the cooking pot. The trammel hung from a green-oak log, known as a 'lug pole', which was built into the throat of the chimney.[22] The Scottish 'swee' or 'swey', known in England as the chimney crane, was made of iron and in the south some were devised so as to adjust the height of the cooking pot (Figs. 34, 35). All had the advantage of being capable of swinging the pot away from the fire to inspect the progress of the cooking. These devices were probably first constructed of wood and the Ulster Folk Museum possesses a specimen in wood which nevertheless imitates those made of iron. Another example of wood imitating iron is the trammel hanging over the fire in the 'smoke-room' in the house from Mule, Bord, Faeroe Islands,[23] but wood trammels true to their material were made in Scotland.[24] The Irish example may also relate to the *gjoye* of late medieval (if not Viking) Norway. These were great logs which swung out from the wall to provide a point in space over the central hearth (Fig. 236) from which cooking pots were hung; it served the same function as, and was very similar to, the chimney crane.

Many utensils were of iron including the cooking pots, but posnets (three-legged vessels also known as skillets) of bronze or bell metal were preferred. According

26   John Phillip (1817–67), *The Highland Home*. This painting shows the appearance of the interior of a croft in the second quarter of the nineteenth century. The reredos to the central hearth may have inspired this typical transverse partition. Aberdeen Museum and Art Gallery.

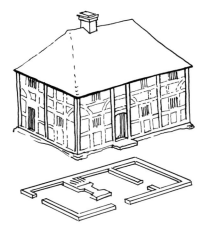

27   The position of the cross passage was to become the traditional location for a half-bay which, at first, accommodated a smoke hood and later (as here), a flue. This resulted in a lobby entrance with a ladder or stair on the other side of the flue – as in this example based on a timber-frame house in the south-east of England.

to sixteenth-century inventories they are often referred to as 'brass', and until the end of the century such objects were the most valuable possessions in many households. Food in medieval Britain was generally boiled (stews and boiled puddings) – ovens, other than 'pot-ovens', being a rarity until the introduction of chimney flues made them more possible.

The greatest single disadvantage of the central hearth was the smoke it produced. For this reason the reredos was introduced to control the direction of the draught, and these continued in use in the Orkneys until the end of the nineteenth century (Fig. 25). The hearth remained in a central position but the reredos could be enlarged to form a partition wall. In John Phillip's painting of a Highland home it can be seen that this transition has taken place (Fig. 26). The migration of the hearth to the wall has begun; the development of the chimney hood and flue is made possible. Most authorities tend to argue

28   A smoke bay in the cruck house from Stangend, Danby of 1704 as re-erected at Ryedale Folk Museum, Yorkshire. Note the witch post with its hex sign on the left (see also Fig. 38) and the built-in salt cupboards at the back of the fire to the right.

that the evolution of the flue at the vernacular level may first be seen in certain adjustments to the roof. It is perhaps more logical to see this innovation beginning at the hearth.

Although chimney flues were used in Royal Circles, at least since the Norman Conquest, their use at the popular level was possibly accelerated by the rigours of the 'Little Ice Age' which began in the mid-sixteenth century.[25] A more efficient variation on the open central hearth was the location of the fire off-centre in a bay or half-bay rising to the full height of the house (Fig. 27). This probably developed from the practice of enlarging the reredos into a transverse wall and subsequently screening over, with lath and plaster, a pair of adjacent trusses in the roof above but somewhat forward of the fire. Where this feature occurs within part of a full bay it was probably an afterthought, but when it is seen in a purpose-built half-bay it was, from the start, in line with

the most up-to-date notions of domestic comfort.[26] In cruck-built houses where the hall was a bay-and-a-half or two bays long, a smoke hood could be supported on the tie beam that united the pair of crucks, thus producing a smoke bay, a feature common in Yorkshire (Fig. 28). In Westmorland, in the dwellings of 'statesmen' or yeomen and in many smaller houses as well, this 'bay' was loftier than the room and was screened by a 'heck', a spur wall of stone or timber. The smoke was collected in a funnel of lath and plaster and discharged into a short stone flue at the top of the wall against which the fire was placed (Fig. 29).[27]

Because the smoke bay was both defined and created within the trusses of the roof the hearth was necessarily situated against a transverse partition. In some counties with a mild climate, such as Devon, the high status symbolised by the chimney led to it being placed more visibly on external flanking walls rather than against

transverse partition walls or at the gable. It is impossible to talk with any certainty about the development of the flue in terms of date as documentary evidence is scarce. Evidence for central hearths has been found throughout the British Isles,[28] whilst they continued in use in Scotland and Ireland within living memory. It will therefore be necessary to look at various surviving types of fireplace of miscellaneous date which may suggest the likely sequence of their evolution.

Following the smoke bay the earliest type of flue was simply a hood attached from within to an internal or

29   Chimney hood (photographed in 1934) in a derelict farmhouse at Boundary Bank, Underbarrow, Cumbria. The floor (ceiling) is almost certainly a later addition. A smoke funnel constructed of timber and fire-proofed internally with a parget of clay was known in the North American Colonies as a 'Catted Chimney' (A. L. Cummings, *The Framed Houses of Massachusetts Bay, 1625–1725*, 1979, p. 119).

30   Nineteenth-century smoke hood in a single-room dwelling from Meenagarragh as reconstructed at the Ulster Folk and Transport Museum. The roof lining is confined to the bed outshot.

31   Interior of a souter's cottage on Tayside, Scotland as recorded in this mid-nineteenth-century painting by Robert Roland McIan (1803–56). The timber smoke hood or 'hangin' lum' is typical. National Museums of Scotland.

external wall and constructed of lath and plaster. Such an example may be seen in the late nineteenth-century one-roomed house from Meenagarragh, Co. Tyrone, reconstructed at the Ulster Folk and Transport Museum (Fig. 30). In the north of England and Scotland a cowl of overlapping boards was usual. In the Highlands of Scotland this feature was known as the *similear crochaidh* or hanging chimney,[29] and in the lowlands as the 'hangin lum' (Fig. 31). When such fireplaces were constructed of stone or brick it became necessary to support them on either corbels or piers and most surviving examples are a combination of both (Figs. 32, 33). Once a floor is inserted obscuring the flue they assume an appearance compatible with modern ideas of a fireplace in which the lower part of the flue is visible as the chimney breast (Fig. 34).

In his *Description of England* (1577) William Harrison remarked that old men in his village (Radwinter, Essex) had seen great changes in their lifetime, among them 'the multitude of chimneys latelie erected, whereas in their yoong daies there were not above two or three, if so

manie, in most uplandish townes of the realme (the religious houses, and manour places of their lords alwaies excepted, and peradventure some great personages), but each one made his fire against a reredosse in the hall, where he dined and dressed his meat'.[30]

The 'Great Rebuilding'[31] of the fifteenth, sixteenth and seventeenth centuries is characterised by three main features: (a) the insertion of chimneys, helped in many regions by (b) the reintroduction of bricks, and (c) the insertion of upper floors resulting from the introduction of chimneys.[32] The latest dated and recorded 'built-in' chimney in the south of England is at Chodd's Farm, Handcross, Sussex, and it bears the inscription 'Bilt 1693'.[33] One of the earliest datable floored-in halls is at Great Worge, Brightling, East Sussex which had been modernised in this way by 1567.[34] In the north modernisations of this kind tended to take place somewhat later. In Ulster all types of fireplace from the most primitive to the more sophisticated were in use in the nineteenth century. It is therefore all the more remarkable that the

32   Carved fireplace lintel at Handois, Jersey, dated 1659. The keyed lintel is typical and is related to certain types of flat arch, the individual *voussoirs* are known in French as *crossettes*.

33   (*right*) Late eighteenth-century fireplace in a house in the Market Place, Kendal, Cumbria. The corbelled lintel derives from the smoke hood but persisted in the Lake District thus producing a curious combination of vernacular forms with 'polite' details.

34   Fireplace in a house from Cruckacady as re-erected at the Ulster Folk and Transport Museum. A fireplace with a chimney made possible the insertion of upper floors, an innovation that did not generally occur in some regions and provinces until the nineteenth century – as in this example. The location of the bed outshot adjacent to the fireplace is typical.

double flue should have been in use there — a truly belt and braces method of extracting smoke (Fig. 35).[35]

In districts where brick was used the introduction of the chimney flue in the sixteenth century was most often celebrated externally on stacks with horizontal corbelled courses and vertical ribs whilst the finest were, in addition, elaborately carved. Internally these large brick chimney pieces were masked by elaborate stonework, often used in conjunction with a plaster or timber over-mantel. Where the brickwork was left visible it was often treated quite simply, although the sophistication of 'tuck pointing' was sometimes counterfeited with rodel (red lead) and white lime distemper emphasised with 'pencilling'.[36] The remains of such a treatment were found in 1986 on the hall fireplace of Northeycote Farmhouse (*c.* 1600) on the outskirts of Wolverhampton.[37]

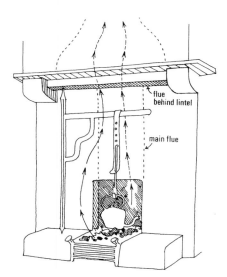

35   Nineteenth-century Ulster double flue.

36   Frederick Daniel Hardy (1826–1911), *Interior of a Sussex Farmhouse*, dated 185?. A valance was often hung on the chimney bressummer where flues failed to contain the smoke from the fire. The three-legged 'cricket' table and the buffet chair to the left (see Fig. 250) were once typical examples of English country furniture. Leicester Museum and Art Gallery.

All early fireplaces with flues have openings which are large in size; they are high and wide. In early Stuart England Sir John Coke advised that 'The rule for height of Chimneys [i.e. chimney pieces] and under manteltrees [bressummers] is this. Divide the wideness into 4 parts . . . three of them is the height but they use now to make them higher'.[38] The height and bulk of the bressummer or mantel-tree probably has something to do with its origin as a tie beam in a smoke bay or in its function in supporting a chimney hood. Their width was desirable to save labour in sawing wood for fuel. Nevertheless they were and are inclined to smoke, a fact which was of little

concern at first as they represented such an improvement on previous methods of extracting smoke. However, it was probably soon discovered that a chimney cloth or fire cloth alleviated this problem. Such a feature may be seen in Hardy's *Interior of a Sussex Farmhouse* dated '185?' (Fig. 36). These chimney cloths were sometimes made of leather and were occasionally stretched on a frame.[39] In lowland Scotland a strip of sheet metal known as a 'smoke board' was used in the nineteenth century.

Once windows were shuttered or glazed and external doors closed the presence of a chimney introduced the one orifice through which, it was believed, evil spirits

37   Apotropaic marks on the chimney bressummer in the hall of the Swan, Worlingworth, Suffolk. Doors (see Fig. 99) and windows were believed to provide access to evil spirits but the ever-open chimney flue was much the weakest point of entry – hence these marks. The letters 'A' and 'M' are thought to stand for Ave Maria – even in post-Reformation England. The 'P' may be some form of Chi-Rho – ☧. Drawing after Timothy Easton (1999).

38   Witch posts from North Yorkshire with their apotropaic hex signs – from left to right: Postgate Farm, Glaisdale; Church View, Gillamoor; and Scarborough (after Peter Brears, *North Country Folk Art* 1989). For greater efficacy in warding off evil spirits these posts were usually made of rowan wood. A 'witch post' *in situ* is illustrated in Fig. 28.

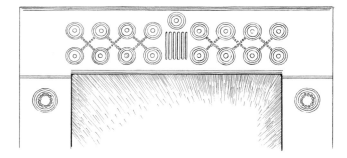

39   A carved slate fireplace surround, second quarter of the nineteenth century, from Dyffryn Ogwen, North Wales. The extent to which apotropaic devices become 'traditional designs' is not easily gauged. Drawing after Gwenno Caffell, 'The carved slates of Dyffryn Ogwen'.

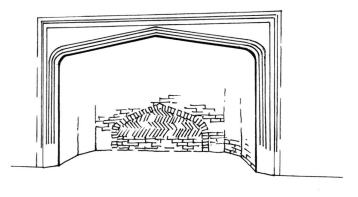

40   Sixteenth-century tiled nogging used as a 'fire-back' in Norwich.

could enter. Recent research in East Anglia by Timothy Easton and further work in Sussex has shown that, for this reason, fireplace bressummers were often incised with apotropaic marks to turn away such spirits.[40] These marks become most visible in a raking light (Fig. 37). They generally take the form of a rather geometric, not to say runic, version of Christian symbolism such as ✻ (Chi-Rho) or AMR (Ave Maria Regina). Although these marks will sometimes be found on other important structural members such as tie beams,[41] they are not to be confused with carpenters' assembly marks. In some ways the hex signs carved in the 'witch posts' of Yorkshire smoke bays (Figs. 28, 38) relate to these scribed emblems in the south-east of England, and later if comparable work in North Wales (Fig. 39) (see also Appendix VI).

Wood-burning down hearths of the type described above are capable of generating sufficient heat to cause the bricks at the back of the fire to become friable and collapse. In Norwich it was usual for a panel, headed by a four-centred arch and set in the back of the fireplace, to be fitted with a herring-bone arrangement of tiles and in Essex with a panel of brick nogging. This use of tile or brick is non-structural, and could be easily replaced (Fig. 40).[42] In Devon the potters of Barnstaple made fire-backs (and firedogs) in gravel-tempered salt-glazed ware (Figs. 21, 41, 42). The Weald of Kent and Sussex, known since Roman times for its iron industry, once again had active blast furnaces by about 1540,[43] and iron fire-backs became usual, fulfilling the dual role of protecting the brickwork of the flue and producing radiant heat. As we have seen, the marketing and distribution of these iron products was, at first, both socially and geographically limited. Even in Sussex the presence of cast-iron fire-backs may not always be presumed. In the late sixteenth-century Leabridge Cottage, West Burton, a simple panel of projecting brickwork[44] was found in the back of the fireplace, analogous to the use of tiles in Norwich and brick nogging in Essex. Early Sussex fire-backs are wide and low and carry simple designs impressed into the sand mould – sections of rope being particularly popular

41 Fragment of a ceramic firedog dated 1708 from north Devon (see Fig. 21). The overall height of these fragments is from 9 to 10 ins. Barnstaple Museum.

42 Fragment of a ceramic firedog from north Devon. The heat of the wood-burning fire accounts for the fragmentary condition of surviving examples. Barnstaple Museum.

43   Cast-iron Sussex fire-back dated 1598 and a pair of wrought-iron firedogs of a type sometimes known as cob-irons. The vertical 'staukes' are ratcheted at the back to enable the pair of hooked rings to be raised and lowered for the precise positioning of a spit.

44   Cast-iron fire-back (Sussex?), late seventeenth century, showing Dutch influence. The tall proportions are typical of its period; a century before fire-backs were typically long and low – see Fig. 43. Victoria and Albert Museum, London.

(Fig. 43). Eventually wood patterns were used to press into the sand and late seventeenth-century examples betray considerable sophistication and some Dutch stylistic influence (Fig. 44). They are taller than they are wide so as to be in proportion with the fireplace surrounds of their day.

Because of the tendency of smoke to permeate even the best-built brickwork or masonry, flues were generally lined with 'Pargetting Mortar' comprised of four parts lime and one part fresh horse dung[45] to which mixture goat hair was added. This mortar was applied either by bricklayers or rough masons and sometimes by plasterers.[46] The flues of No. 36 Craven Street, Westminster (built *c.* 1730) were lined, both inside and out, in this way – as became apparent when the panelling and the fireplaces were temporarily removed for conservation work. It is remarkable that this sort of care was taken in a speculatively built third-rate terrace – in a house in which Benjamin Franklin lodged for many years.

In mid-seventeenth-century Devon, Somerset and Wiltshire the pargeted lining of the flue extended down to line the back and cheeks of the fireplace (Figs. 46–50, 212). This was also done some fifty years later in Aberdeen, Scotland,[47] and in Boston, Massachusetts (Fig. 45).[48] At first the extension of the pargeting down behind the fire was generally whitewashed; certainly Sir Roger Pratt (1620–85) gave instructions for this to be done.[49] Inevitably this surface was to be given a decorative treatment. This took a geometric character which derived from the use of a sgraffito technique in which black plaster was scraped back to reveal the white plaster beneath it,[50] a craft that extended to other details of interior decoration at this time (such as the reveals of windows) and is also found on external elevations.[51] The earliest surviving examples in fireplaces appear to date from the mid-seventeenth century and their designs tend to echo the character of the ironwork which would have inhabited these spaces (Figs. 45, 46). By the third quarter

45   A room in the Moses Pierce-Hitchborn House, North Square, Boston, Massachusetts. Although dating from the early eighteenth century this painted plaster fireplace lining and skirting 'board' is similar in character to the sgraffito work of half a century before found in Britain in Devon, Somerset, Wiltshire and Aberdeen.

46   Sgraffito plaster, worked in two coats, one black, one white, from 21 High Street, Plymouth (now demolished – drawing after S. R. Jones). This probably dates from the mid-seventeenth century and would have been close in character to the ironwork that once furnished this hearth.

47   Seventeenth-century plaster decorations on the back and jambs lining a fireplace in the first-floor room at 21 High Street, Plymouth (now demolished – drawing after S. R. Jones). Such work was evidently regarded as ephemeral, this being the second scheme to occupy this space – the first is shown in Fig. 46. The geometric character of early work of this kind owes much to the sgraffito technique.

48, 49, 50   Three painted fireplace linings ranging in date from the mid-seventeenth century to the early eighteenth century – a span of perhaps fifty years. Clockwise from top left: Alhampton, Somerset; Totnes, Devon; and the acanthus leaf from a house in Milverton, Somerset – see also Fig. 210.

of the century the inspiration appears to be an informal and vernacular response to the use of ceramic tiles of the type used in Holland, Portugal and Spain. In the 1660s Pepys had a number of his fireplaces 'done with Dutch tiles' and others survive *in situ* from a decade later in Ham House, Surrey.[52] The later examples of these plaster fireplace linings employ a faux sgraffito technique (Fig. 49) whilst in their final phase they were simply decorated with free-flowing designs in distemper (Fig. 50). In many instances this sequence of design and technique is found layered one on top of another. In such a location it is clear that the decoration demanded regular reworking due to smoke-blackening. In its original form the sgraffito technique was fully within the province of the plasterers. However these craftsmen were, by tradition, permitted to apply distemper (but not oil paint) in all-over washes. The final phase in this type of decoration, with its free brush-work, impinged on the frontier that marked the demarcation between the roles of the plasterer and those of the painter-stainers (see pp. 125–7). An extension of this type of work, and one often found in association with it, is the use of a painted skirting – often worked in black or dark-brown distemper at the base of plastered walls (Fig. 45).

The large open fireplaces of the past were used for cooking as well as for general heat and it was common practice for a bread oven, and sometimes an auxiliary smoking flue for curing bacon, to be built into them. The bread oven was usually constructed of brick but in the potteries of north Devon around Barnstaple, and in Truro, Cornwall, they were prefabricated in earthenware. These 'cloam' ovens were made until the early twentieth century, the last being 'built' at Lake's Chapel Hill Pottery in 1935 (Fig. 51).[53] They had a wide distribution, being found in much of the West Country as well as South Wales;[54] they were exported to America in the seventeenth century and have been found at Jamestown, Virginia.[55] In 1716 the 'Barnstaple Ovens of Devonshire' were described as not only 'cleaner and cheaper' than the alternative brick or stone ovens built *in situ*, but they baked 'with more Evenness and Certainty, and consumed not a Fourth of the Fuel, which is wasted in those of the ordinary Fashion in London and elsewhere'.[56]

In houses of the North Yorkshire moors salt-boxes hewn out of two great blocks of sandstone were built flush into the back wall and fitted with a small wooden door. The largest recorded example has external measurements of 31 by 21 by 23 ins (78.7 by 53.3 by 58.4 cm). The access to these boxes was usually about 6 ins (15.2 cm) square, surrounded by an oak frame in which was hung an oak door suspended on leather hinges (which the salt would not corrode). In North Yorkshire the 'Great Rebuilding' did not begin until the second half of the seventeenth century and so most of these salt-

boxes date from this time and later.[57] Roughly equivalent to these Yorkshire salt-boxes were the 'keeping holes' found in Ulster, one on each side of the fire.[58]

As fireplace openings became smaller, the presence of the chimney piece was emphasised by the chimney breast, the visible part of the flue (Fig. 66). The great size of early fireplaces (Fig. 52) had stressed the importance

51 Cloam oven of north Devon type. These earthenware bread ovens were exported to South Wales and North America. They were made from the seventeenth century to the 1930s. Castle Museum, Taunton.

52 Fireplace in Hassage Farmhouse, Wellow, near Bath. The wider opening of the early seventeenth century was reduced a century later.

53 Stone fireplace dated 1707 in the cruck and cob-built Burgh Head Farmhouse (now destroyed), Burgh-by Sands, Cumbria. The bolection moulding surrounding this fireplace is typical of its period.

54 Overmantel from Wayne's, Queen Street, Coggeshall, Essex, early eighteenth century. The sections of the mouldings are considerably more sophisticated than the carving.

accorded to them, both visually and as a source of heat, and made them appropriate centres for embellishment. It was here that the four-centred arch of late medieval fashion was used (Fig. 103), and it was the chimney breast that bore on its generous proportions the first essays in the Renaissance. The first flush of Italian influence did not appear in smaller houses, but *The Designs of Mr Inigo Jones* were later processed for popular consumption, together with those of *Mr William Kent*, by John Vardy (1744). Before the second coming of Palladianism in England the bolection moulding was used around almost everything: windows, pictures and fireplaces (Fig. 53). It might be added that this moulding was not much used externally except in the Bath area where the soft free-stone made this a cheaply produced sign of opulence. Internally the mantelshelf may well be a late innovation; certainly it seldom occurs in conjunction with the use of bolection mouldings.

Some types of fireplace popular in the grandest circles did not descend the social order, among them the corner fireplace with its surmounting stepped pyramid on which could be displayed collections of rich and rare porcelain from Cathay, or delft pottery. In general the grand designs of the Renaissance were scaled down to a size that was large enough to accommodate wood fires but could also house coal-burning grates.

At the vernacular level the fielded panel was popular throughout the eighteenth century and the chimney breast became the main wall surface for its orchestrated use (Fig. 54). In most compositions this work naturally falls into two main areas, the fireplace itself and, above the horizontal line of the mantel, the overmantel. Batty Langley's *The Builder's*

and Workman's Treasury of Designs (1750) contains no less than twenty designs for fireplaces with 'Tabernacle Frames'. In the early seventeenth century mirrors were generally too small to occupy such a position worthily and until the nineteenth they were too expensive to be found in smaller houses. It therefore became usual for this space to be furnished with a panel painting, most often a landscape. The proportions of these panels, as with the similar 'over door' panels, were conditioned by the height of the room and by the size of the opening. Linda Hall[59] has demonstrated that ceiling height is very much associated with social status. For example, in South Gloucestershire almost all gentry houses have ground floor ceiling heights of 8 ft or more. Consequently overdoor paintings will, in general, only be found in the houses of the aristocracy, gentry and rich merchants where ceiling heights were sufficient to accommodate such embellishment (Figs. 55, 56). Where possible, square over-mantel panels were favoured, and among Langley's designs only two were for panels that were considerably wider than they were high. Overmantel pictures of a surprisingly primitive sort, although not found in the houses of the nobility, may be seen in the homes of the gentry. Urchfont Manor in Wiltshire contains an almost complete series of six such panels painted with representations of the house and gardens; naive renderings of a splendid Continental formal garden – see p. 152 and Fig. 217.

Early fireplace surrounds in the south-east of England were often of brick, this being the material out of which the flues were constructed. As Isaac Ware pointed out in *The Complete Body of Architecture* (1756), such brickwork was inclined to crumble and break off and the problem was solved or masked by 'a frame of wood [which was

55, 56 Examples of some of the seven overdoor paintings recently discovered in Melrose House, Whittox Lane, Frome, Somerset. The house dates from the mid-seventeenth century but was radically modernised about forty years later when these paintings were installed as part of the panelling.

57 A chimney board of the second quarter of the eighteenth century. Victoria and Albert Museum, London.

then] carried round it'.[60] This became something of a fire hazard and was soon replaced by stone. These fire surrounds were inevitably given decorative treatment of various kinds. In nineteenth-century Scotland, Ulster and the north of England the jambs and lintel of the fireplace were sometimes painted with flecks of different colours to give a suggestion of granite or, possibly, marble. Between 1830 and 1845 the valley of the river Ogwen in North Wales saw a brief flowering of elaborately engraved slate fireplace lintols and jambs (Fig. 39).[61]

In summer the fireplace presented a rather forbidding black hole, relieved in winter by the fire itself. In many households it was a traditional point of honour to maintain the near-sacred fire year in, year out. I remember visiting a farmhouse near Chagford in Devon in the late 1940s and being told that the fire had not been allowed to go out for three hundred years. The truth of the statement is far less important than the sentiment expressed. Undoubtedly, the tradition of the never-to-be-extinguished fire is ancient.[62] Before the days of matches the creation of a flame with a steel and tinderbox was not easy.[63] In the town of Ormskirk, Lancashire, a regulation of 1746 dictated that 'no inhabitant of this town shall fetch or give any fire to any Neighbour, to be carried into the Street uncovered, upon pain, both to the fetcher and giver thereof, to forfeit for every time so doing each of them [6d]'.[64]

Eighteenth-century genre pictures suggest that in less traditional houses it was usual in summer, then as now, to place a vase of flowers or leaves in this otherwise empty space.[65] Wedgwood wrote to his partner Thomas Bentley on 29 July 1772, 'Vases are furniture for a chimney piece, bough pots for a hearth. . . . I think they can never be used one instead of the other.'[66] Judging by the large size of the bough pot in the fireplace which is illustrated in Joseph Highmore's (1692–1780) portrait of Samuel Richardson (1689–1761) this is quite understandable.[67] In 1767, Jones's of 71 Holborn Hill (William and Thomas Jones – the latter moved in 1774 to 57 Shoe Lane and in 1778 William Jones is recorded at Ray Street, Clerkenwell) supplied a 'Great Variety of Flower Pots and Vases for Chimneys'.[68]

Another method of obscuring the hearth when it was not in use was the chimney board, also known as the fire board (Fig. 57). These should not be confused with fire screens which were not designed to cover the fireplace but were intended to protect a fashionably pale complexion from the effects of the fire when it was in use, as shown in Hogarth's *The Lady's Last Stake* (1758–9). The fire board on the other hand was designed to fit the fireplace opening exactly and was therefore tailor-made. In the eighteenth century it was possible to purchase panels of wallpaper to decorate such boards or to have them painted especially by a decorative painter such as 'Matts Darly Painter, Engraver, and Paper Stainer at the Acorn facing Hungerford, Strand', whose trade-label is dated 1791 and who provided 'Ceilings, Pannels, Staircases, Chimney Boards etc. Neatly fitted up with Painting, or Stainings in the modern, Gothic or Chinese Tastes for Town or Country'. They could also be commissioned through a retailer such as the 'Upholder', John Potts, who provided (*c.* 1760) 'Ornaments for Halls, Ceilings, Stair-cases and Chimney Boards'.[69]

Fire boards were probably most necessary in large houses, where a fireplace could remain unused for months on end, as well as in garden pavilions which would receive only occasional visits. Elegant examples survive at Osterley and at Audley End. When the Earl of Orford's house in Chelsea was sold on his death in 1747 the 'Summer House' contained a lot which consisted of 'Eight Green painted chairs, a walnut table and a chimney board: £0-10-6'. An amusing reference to these boards is to be found in the description of the exhibition that was organised in 1762 by the fictitious Society of Sign Painters but was in fact put together by William Hogarth and Bonnell Thornton: 'On entering the Grand Room . . . you find yourself in a large and commodious Apartment, hung round with green Bays, on which this curious collection of Wooden Originals is fixt flat . . . and from whence hang Keys, Bells, Swords, Poles, Sugar-Loaves, Tobacco-Rolls, Candles and other ornamental Furniture, carved in Wood, that commonly dangle from the Penthouses of the different Shops in our Streets. On the Chimney-Board (to imitate the Style of the Catalogue) is a large, blazing Fire, painted in Water-colours.'[70] Chimney boards must have once been very well known items of furnishing. In David Garrick's farce *Bon Ton: Or High Life Above Stairs* (produced 1775) Colonel Tivy hides behind such a board to escape a confrontation between Lord and Lady Minikin and Miss Tittup (Fig. 58).[71]

In America a great many fire boards dating from the late eighteenth to the mid-nineteenth century survive. A number exist *in situ* and in museums on the Continent. The Stedelijk Museum, Amsterdam, possesses a fine example painted by an unknown artist showing an orange tree growing in a large blue and white pot.[72] In England they are exceedingly rare – why? No doubt the reliable North American summers meant that the fire board could be used confident in the knowledge that it would remain *in situ* for six months. In one remarkable and surviving case in Pennsylvania a large fireplace in the Marshall House is enclosed in summer by folding doors with six leaves united by strap hinges.[73] In Britain, on the other hand, our climate is less predictable. Furthermore, the introduction of coal-burning grates with narrow-throated chimneys in the late eighteenth century made the draught-proofing properties of the fire board less essential. In fact most surviving American examples date from the very time when their use in England, which was probably always less widespread,[74] was declining. Their mobile nature has resulted in their destruction or, with the more sophisticated examples, their reuse as easel paintings for the decoration of the walls of a room. One of the earliest surviving English fire boards is in the Victoria and Albert Museum. It has a distinctly late seventeenth-century Dutch appearance. It is painted on a sheet of pine ¾ in (1.9 cm) thick and shows no sign of originally having had battens on the back, though these

have been added (Fig. 59). As with many of the American examples,[75] it depicts a vase of flowers of the type that was placed in the fireplace as an alternative mode of decoration and, again like a number of the American ones, it is surrounded on three sides by a painted rendering of the decorative delft tiles customarily used in fire surrounds. It probably dates from the first decade or so of the eighteenth century and its proportions would suggest that it once stood in front of a coal-burning grate.

Coal began to be used in London at the end of the thirteenth century but at first only for manufacturing purposes as it was considered a health hazard. In the early years of the seventeenth century the Port of London handled 11,000 tons, but by the end of the century 500,000 tons arrived annually from Newcastle. No wonder that it was possible for Wren's St Paul's Cathedral to be built on the tax levied on this mineral and that coal represented one third of all cargoes carried by British shipping at this time.[76] Mendip coal from Somerset and 'Cannel' coal from Newcastle-under-Lyme was also important. In commenting on the abundant use of coal in Newcastle-upon-Tyne itself Celia Fiennes describes not only the pollution of the air but also the cinder paths used in gardens and parks.[77] In the course of the eighteenth century the use of coal became general in urban homes, but it was not used in America in significant quantities until the nineteenth century.

The introduction of coal-burning grates had far-reaching effects upon the design of 'chimney pieces' (as they were called, in preference to 'fireplaces' – a place of fire could be anywhere and did not necessarily demand a flue). The proportions of the rooms in which they were located underwent no less radical changes. The earliest literary reference to a coal grate in *The Oxford Dictionary* is of 1605. By 1658 Sir John Winter had devised a special grate for burning coal. This took the form of an iron box which had a tube for the intake of external air which when opened 'marvellously accelerated the action of the fire'.[78] A similar device was made in 1678 for Prince Rupert of the Rhine (1619–82) by a bricklayer named Bingham.[79] Ham House in Surrey contains some of the earliest surviving coal grates; they are well documented, being mentioned in the inventory of 1679. Meanwhile various improvements were taking place in France, where Nicolas Gauger published his treatise which was translated into English by J. T. Desaguliers and published in 1716. The book contains a useful glossary with information on 'The Mantle-piece' which it describes as 'the ornamental Frame of Timber or Mason's-work', a term which the book compares with the French '*Chambranle* . . . an ornament in Masonry and Joyners-work which borders the sides of Doors, Windows & Chimneys'.[80] Perhaps the most remarkable recommendation in the book is the proposed adoption of 'The Vent-hole', a tube of between 3 and 4 ins (7.6 and 10.2 cm) in diameter designed to draw in air directly from outside the house and deliver it direct to the fire and 'contribute to remedy the inconvenience of Smoak'.[81] The book goes on to state that 'those Persons who have neat Apartments, and valuable Household-Goods . . . are very sensible of these inconveniences [of smoke] . . . especially on account of

59 Chimney board, first quarter of the eighteenth century, oil on pine, 38.5 by 30.75 ins. Very few such chimney boards have survived in Britain where, with the widespread use of coal, narrow-throated chimneys and registers provided the necessary draught-proofing in fireplaces when they were not in use. Victoria and Albert Museum, London.

their Linen, Lace, Headdresses, Cloaths, &c.'[82] The provision of such air tubes did much to prevent rooms being draughty and have only recently been adopted with much enthusiasm. However, when Sydney Smith built himself a parsonage at Foston le Clay, Yorkshire, in 1813, he installed such a device.[83]

The more efficient stove of earthenware or cast iron was always more favoured in those Continental countries where the climate demanded more efficient heating.[84] The same conditions were found in America, but the English tradition there seems to have for long remained stronger than the desire for comfort in the cold winters of a 'continental climate'.[85] The exception was to be found in the

German communities of Pennsylvania where cast-iron stoves were in use in the early eighteenth century. They were probably the inspiration behind the ingenious Dr Franklin's stove. He describes his invention in his autobiography: 'Having, in 1742, invented an open stove for the better warming of rooms, and at the same time saving fuel, as the fresh air admitted was warmed in entering, I made a present of the model to Mr Robert Grace, one of my early friends who, having an iron furnace, found the casting of the plates for these stoves a profitable thing, as they were growing in demand. To promote the demand, I wrote and published a pamphlet, intitled *An Account of the new-invented Pennsylvania Fireplaces &c.*'[86]

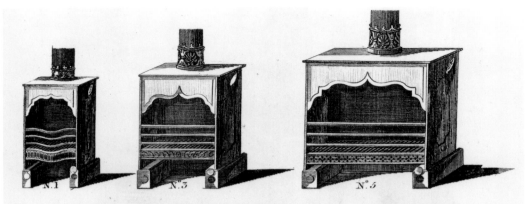

60 'American Stoves', from James Sharp's *Account of the Principle and Effects of the Pennsylvanian Stove-Grates*, London, *c.* 1781. British Library.

61   *John Vine Hall Snr. – Maidstone or district in the small room he called his office* by Arthur Vine Hall (1824–1919), watercolour on paper, *c.* 1840. The Franklin or American stove is seldom seen in Britain but the one illustrated here is of a type identical to that described and illustrated by Loudon (see Fig. 62) in the 1830s as having been introduced to farmhouses in Kent. Private Collection.

Franklin's stove incorporated many European ideas derived from Bingham of England and Gauger of France. Nevertheless, Franklin obtained a patent for his device from George Thomas (*c.* 1693–1774), the Royal Governor of Pennsylvania and the Lower Colonies (now Delaware). Despite the patent the autobiography goes on to say that 'An ironmonger in London, however, assuming a great

deal of my pamphlet . . . got a patent for it there, and made, as I was told a little fortune by it.' The offending 'ironmonger in London' may have been J. Durno of Jermyn Street, Piccadilly, who published a pamphlet in 1753 describing a stove much of which was constructed of brick. Some of his 'Machine Grates' were adapted to burn coal. In his pamphlet Durno makes no reference to

Franklin but does say that he (Durno) ignored the fire-places devised by Gauger 'on account of their expense'.[87] As Franklin's unfinished autobiography ends with the year 1757, Durno is the likely culprit, but there was at least one other possible candidate active in England before Franklin's death in 1790. James Sharp of Leadenhall Street published in about 1781 an '*Acccount of the Principle and Effects of the Pennsylvanian Stove-Grates* (which warm Rooms &c. by a continual Introduction and Exchange of dry fresh air) commonly known by the name American Stoves' (Fig. 60). Sharp claimed to have made 'Additions and Improvements' to these stoves 'For which his Majesty's Patent is obtained'. His factory was at 133 Tooley Street, Southwark. In the pamphlet he gives full credit for 'the Invention [to] the celebrated and ingenious Dr Benjamin Franklin', an acknowledgement that doubtless did little to dampen his opportunism. How successful this side of Sharp's business was however, is doubtful; he only cites two examples of his stoves in use (in the Drapers' Hall and in St John's Church, Southwark). These stoves were undoubtedly very efficient. William Cobbet describes being 'most happily situated' on his visit to Chiddingfold, Surrey, on 13 November 1825, 'by the side of our American fireplace' made by 'Mr. Judson of Kensington' – a third English manufacturer of this trans-Atlantic innovation.[88]

These stoves were probably more effective than the Continental stoves which produced heat exclusively by radiation. The Franklin stove transmitted heat by radiation and by the circulation of warm air. Despite these advantages they were little used in Britain, perhaps because at the turn of the century the designs of another American, Sir Benjamin Thompson (Count Rumford), were adopted more energetically. In London one hundred and fifty homes were fitted with fireplaces to his design which reduced the throat of the chimney to 5 ins (12.7 cm) or less, set the cheeks of the fireplace at 135 degrees to its back and brought forward the fire itself. Unlike Franklin he believed, erroneously, in avoiding the use of iron (except for the actual grate) as a wasteful absorber of heat.[89]

In describing the Franklin stove, Loudon refers to the 'great benefits [that] have been experienced from the introduction of the American stove into some farm houses in Kent' (Fig. 62).[90] A drawing by Arthur Vine Hall (*c.* 1840) of a room in a house near Maidstone, Kent, remarkably enough illustrates a wood-burning stove of this type, and the example illustrated in Loudon's book is identical to it (Fig. 61). A number of these stoves made by the Carron Ironworks of Falkirk in Scotland remain in use in Kent (Fig. 63). Despite these examples the real

62 J. C. Loudon's illustration of an 'American Stove' in his *Encyclopaedia*. Benjamin Franklin invented this type of stove in 1742.

63 An American stove (overall height 32 ins), made by the Carron Ironworks, Falkirk, Scotland, in Yew Tree House (built 1840), Benenden, Kent. Collection: Charles Lenox-Conyngham.

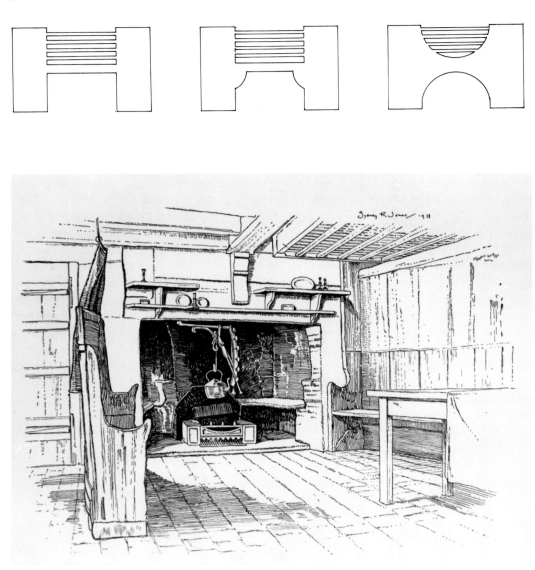

64   The evolution of the hob grate. In its final form, shown on the right, these were known as 'Bath grates' as they were widely used in the spa. Most were manufactured in such iron-founding centres as Ironbridge, Shropshire.

65   Farmhouse interior, East Hendred, Berkshire, 1911 drawing by S. R. Jones. By the nineteenth century the down-hearth gave way to the grate – as here with this 'duck's nest' or 'Sussex grate'. Note the settle with its additional draught-proofing curtain.

importance of the stove in Britain was to be as a cooking 'range'.

In the last quarter of the eighteenth century the coal-burning hob grate became general and these were manufactured in great numbers, principally by Carron in Scotland (which had the advantage of having both Robert and James Adam as directors) and the Dale Company of Coalbrookdale in Shropshire. When it became necessary to reduce the width of a wood-burning fireplace to accommodate coal this was done by filling up the unwanted space to left and right. In cast iron this arrangement resulted in a fireplace constructed of three elements, two hobs linked by a central basket. In time the two cheek pieces were united forming an hourglass shape, the top part of which held the coal whilst the lower half held the ashes (Fig. 64).[91] A variant on this type of hob grate was the 'duck's nest' or 'Sussex grate' (Fig. 65).[92]

Although hob grates are often of extreme sophistication in their decoration they were cheap to produce and were therefore used at many social levels. They were generally known, even in far-off Colonial Williamsburg, as 'Bath grates' simply because they were ubiquitous in houses in the spa.

Towards the end of the eighteenth century the cast-iron cooking range developed (Fig. 66). Early examples often carry the name of the iron foundry that made them; later specimens are likely to bear the name of the company that sold and installed them. There were many such foundries in England and Wales. In the Yorkshire Dales such ranges carry the names of Spence of Richmond, Iveson of Hawes, Manby of Skipton, and Todd Bros. of Summerbridge, Nidderdale, though the latter two once had their own foundries as well.[93] Such objects may appeal to today's catholic tastes, but they were not always designed

66   The kitchen in the Apprentice House at Quarry Bank Mill, Styal, Cheshire. The Apprentice House was built in 1784, the probable date of the kitchen range, although it may be a decade later as the coal tax was not abolished until 1793.

67   Various lighting devices. Left to right back row: a wrought iron cruisie, a rushlight holder, an adjustable candlestick and a rushlight holder and candlestick combined. In the front is a sample of Kimmeridge shale, the natural oil-bearing rock which was burnt in houses on the Dorset coast for both light and warmth. The fish oil lamp contrived from a mussel shell is from Wales. In this case the shell is so exceptionally large (7 ins 17.8 cm in length) that it was probably regarded as something of a trophy. Various collections.

for elegance: by this date the kitchen/living-room was declining in middle-class houses although it remained in farmhouses and cottages, where the kitchen range expressed the handsome, rather than pretty, qualities of engineering which characterise the Age of Steam.

ARTIFICIAL LIGHT

Before the introduction of electricity, and certainly before the appearance of gaslight, the darkness which descended at night was every bit as terrible and total as is described in Genesis. At night rooms were much darker, a moving candle ascending a stair resulting in animated shadows more frightening than we like to recall until confronted by an immobilising power cut. As we have seen, many

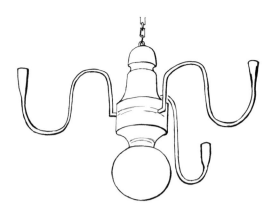

68   An eighteenth-century candelabrum of turned wood and wrought-iron from Stanton Harcourt, Oxfordshire. Such an object would have been well within the capabilities of a wheelwright and may have been made by such a craftsman – it is painted in the sorts of reds and blues used on a hay wain. Oxford City and County Museums.

69   Earthenware candle-trough, seventeenth or eighteenth century(?). Rush lights were traditionally left to 'dry in a bit of hollow bark' – the possible inspiration for this crock. Ashmolean Museum, Oxford.

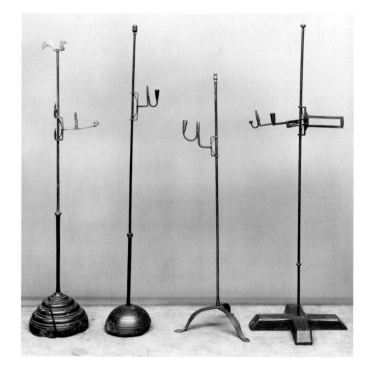

70   A group of eighteenth-century standard rush-light holders. The tallest measures 56 ins. Devices of this kind may account for the rush-light burns often found on the face of the timber bressummer or mantel-tree over a fireplace. Victoria and Albert Museum, London.

houses were lit by little more than the fire on the hearth. In parts of Scotland where peat was burned this source of light was so feeble that in areas with textile 'out-workers' the introduction of coal could be paid for by the extra hours of work that it illuminated. In the north of England Howitt tells us that knitting, a craft that may be performed in almost total darkness, was done communally in one house which was both more friendly and more economical in terms of fuel burnt (see p. 17).[94]

There were, in general, three basic sources of artificial light: fat and wax (rushlights and candles), oil (burned in a lamp) and fir-tree splints (a resinous fuel) (Fig. 67). Lamps, known in Scotland as *cruises*, in the Shetlands as *collies*, in Cornwall as *chills* and in the Channel Islands as *cressets*, were not much used in England. This may have had something to do with the duty payable on wax candles, a tax which was reinforced by a (theoretical) prohibition on the use of oil lamps from 1709 to 1831. This tax may account for the use of oil lamps in outlying regions and islands far from the excise men. Furthermore in more polite urban households fish oil was not much used being unpleasant, smelly and dirty; although the demand for clean-burning whale oil (which was classed as a fish oil) was later to be used in fashionable circles for oil lamps and candles.[95]

The provision of artificial light was expensive, wax candles especially so. The cheapest candles were made of tallow and Sir Hugh Platt in his *Delights for Ladies* (1605? edition) gives a recipe for *A delicate Candle for a Ladies Table*: 'Cause your Dutch candles to bee dipped in Virgin waxe' thus giving a veneer of elegance to candles made from rushes (horse tail: *equisetum hiemale* known in the seventeenth century as 'Dutch rushes'). Until the end of the eighteenth century wax candles cost 30s a pound and with the development of whaling, spermaceti candles were a better but even more expensive form of illumination. In 1758 a dozen of these candles derived from sperm whale oil cost £1 7s.[96] This sort of expenditure was beyond the means of cottagers and even the yeoman class severely rationed their use.

As we have seen, Kimmeridge shale was used to provide fires and lighting for those living on the Dorset coast. The early and often multiple cressets of stone later gave way to the more general type of oil lamp, common in coastal areas where fish oil was available.[97] This was the wrought-iron 'cruisie', sometimes equipped with a secondary container to catch the drips. On the Gower Peninsula and on the Aran Islands[98] the simplest type of lamp was a twisted rag in an oyster, scallop or mussel shell containing either fat or oil.[99] In terms of illumination oil lamps were inefficient, labour intensive and smelly but those patented in 1783 by the Swiss chemist Argand burnt colza oil derived from rape seed and are far too grand to fall within the scope of this book. In central Scotland and in Co. Antrim, where fish oil was not available, splinters of resinous fir wood, or for preference fir knots, were used as 'fir candles' which were sometimes held aloft by a child or old person rather than by means of a peerman, as the holder for fir candles was known in Scotland. As recently as 1951 it was estimated that only one in every six crofts in Scotland had electric light.[100]

Rushlights may have produced a meagre light but they were all that most cottagers could generally afford although rushlight holders sometimes incorporate candle holders for use on special occasions (Fig. 67). The rushes were collected in late summer or autumn. 'You peels away the rind from the peth, leavin' only a little strip of rind, and when the rushes is dry you dips ''em in grease, keepin' 'em well under; and my mother she always laid hers to dry in a bit of hollow bark. Mutton fat's the best, it dries hardest' (Fig. 69).[101]

In 1673 John Aubrey recorded that 'the people of Ockley in Surrey draw peeled rushes through melted grease, which yields a sufficient light for ordinary use, is very cheap and useful and burns long.'[102] Gilbert White in his *Natural History and Antiquities of Selborne* (1789) argued that 'watch lights', rushlights coated with tallow, did little more than make 'darkness visible'. He calculated that a good rush, 28½ ins (72.4 cm) long, would burn for fifty-seven minutes and that rushes costing 3s per pound went 1,600 rushlights to the pound of tallow.[103] The grease for the rushlight was melted in a special elliptical pan (with a handle running at right angles to the axis of the ellipse) known as a 'grisset'. Various devices were made, usually of wrought iron with oak bases to hold

71 A mid-eighteenth-century Liverpool delft candle niche. As particular towns and cities developed specialist crafts, like pottery, it is possible that articles such as this enjoyed a wide social distribution within the locality where they were made. In stone-built walls a candle niche could be masoned within their thickness. Bristol City Museum and Art Gallery.

rushlights. The tall standard rushlight holders (Fig. 70) may well account for the rushlight scorch marks so often found on the centre of timber chimney bressummers.

In stone-built houses candle niches will sometimes be found as in the flint-built basements of the early Tudor houses excavated at Pottergate, Norwich, in 1963. Such

72   Brass candle sconce of the mid-eighteenth century. In gentry houses very similar sconces of silver were used. Private Collection.

niches had to be reasonably large so as to avoid the development of an unsightly stain of candle soot. In eighteenth-century Liverpool and Bristol, delft candle niches, designed to be built into an internal wall, were made which, being glazed, were easily wiped clean (Fig. 71). More rudimentary wall lighting was used at a dance held in a granary in far-off St David's, Pembrokeshire, in 1772 which was illuminated by farthing candles stuck in balls of clay fixed to the wall.[104] Although elaborate carved wood and silver sconces are not relevant here simple brass and pottery wall lights were probably fairly widely used (Fig. 72).[105] Amongst the peasantry in Ireland tables were rare and where they existed at all did not usurp the pre-eminence of the fireplace as a focus of living. For this reason the hob lamp rather than the table lamp evolved there.[106] In all parts of the British Isles various types of standard and pendant devices were in use to hold rush-lights, fir 'candles', tallow, wax and spermaceti candles, as well as oil lamps (Fig. 68).

So that certain crafts could continue after nightfall a costly wax candle was a necessity and, when even this expensive light was insufficient, it could be magnified by means of a water-filled, clear glass globe known in England as a 'flash'.[107] The earliest reference that I have found to this device appears in Sir Hugh Platt's *The Jewel House of Art and Nature* (1594): 'one candle [magnified by a 'flash'] will give a great and wonderful light, somewhat resembling the Sun beames.'[108] He ascribes the invention to the Venetians and mentions that it was particularly useful to a jeweller in Blackfriars. John White's description of this gadget in *A Rich Cabinet with a Variety of Inventions* (1651) clearly derives from Platt. 'How to make a glorious light with a Candle like the Sun-Shine.' White also recommends this source of light for 'Jewellers, Ingravers, or the like', a tradition that continued until the nineteenth century for wood engravers,[109] but they were also adopted by lace-makers in England, as in Denmark by cobblers who used them in conjunction with daylight.[110]

The limitations of artificial light conditioned the crafts that people did in the evening and tended to confine the working day to the hours between sunrise and sunset, except when the harvest moon permitted longer working.

Chapter 3

Walls

Walls may be divided into two main categories: load-bearing and non-load-bearing, both external and internal. Where full crucks were employed in the construction of houses (Fig. 73) the external walls were not load-bearing but were necessarily more substantial than internal partitions. For example, wattle hurdles would provide adequate sub-divisions within a house, at a time when privacy had not elevated itself to the status of a human right, but would do little to help keep out the wind and rain if used on external walls. In a mud cottage at Llithfaen, Pwllheli, Gwynedd, recorded at the end of the nineteenth century, the partition was 'made of cloth' and in 1847, in a cottage at Tal-y-llyn, Gwynedd, the sleeping end was 'separated from the rest of the hut by wisps of straw forming an imperfect screen'.[1] In 1798 John Evans saw a one-room house near Barmouth, Gwynedd, 'divided by a partition of lath and reeds'[2] and in the twentieth century similar partitions were used as party walls between cottages at Rumney, Gwent.

With non-load-bearing external walls the wattle hurdle was often considered adequate for farm buildings and provided useful ventilation. For domestic purposes these hurdles received their due portion of daub or mud. The wattle consisted of vertical rods with horizontal split rods of ash or hazel interwoven.[3] Various names were given to such hurdles including 'freeth' or 'vreath', and perhaps 'wreath' in the west of England and parts of Wales. Before the Reformation, hurdles used as platforms or windbrakes by builders on wooden scaffolding were known as 'flakes'. All these words may be associated with the Danish verb *flette*, to plait.[4] In the late nineteenth century a carpenter from Caernarvonshire recalled that in the Llyn district interior partitions were once made of ropes of twisted rushes or straw woven in and out of

upright poles in the same manner as wattle work.[5] The more usual wattle screen is known to have been widely used in this way.[6] The daubed surface was often plastered both inside and out, and became on both sides a surface to decorate with scribed lines and with paint. Decoration incised in plaster imitating masonry even occurs in stone-built structures such as the thirteenth-century plastered wall surfaces of Hinton Priory, just south of Bath. Plaster used externally afforded some protection from the weather, and in the case of cob walls, or those of 'clay lump' (unfired clay bricks), a plinth of stone and a roof with strongly projecting eaves (e.g. thatch) were essential – hence the saying 'all cob needs is a good hat and a good pair of shoes'.

Structural walls with square panels of timber frame or of stud and mud[7] were important long before the 'Great Rebuilding' whenever and wherever that occurred.[8] C. F. Innocent (1916) quite firmly states that there were 'probably few locations where the use of stone as a principal material for the walls of minor buildings is of any antiquity'. The tradition for the use of timber is therefore of considerable age and importance in the study of vernacular architecture.

One of the most remarkable examples of early walling in England are those of 'stave'-built construction at Greensted Church, Essex (Fig. 74). These have recently been dendro' dated to 1063–1100 AD.[9] This example consists of a series of vertical split oak logs joined by means of splines (tongues) of oak let into grooves worked down their sides, each half log providing a flat surface on the inside face, the corners being of three-quarter logs. The walls at Greensted prove that Scandinavian methods of building in timber were once used in parts of England and point to an early manifestation of what might be

73   Cruck-built barn from Strytlydan as reconstructed at the Museum of Welsh Life, St Fagans, Cardiff. In structural terms the roof in such a building is supported on the paired 'blades' of crucks rather than on the external walls.

74   (*left*) Detail of the corner of the stave-built Anglo/Scandinavian church at Greensted-juxta-Ongar, Essex. These hewn-timber walls have been dendro'-dated to 1063–1100 AD (after Jane Grenville, *Medieval Housing*, 1997).

75   (*right*) A typical stud and plank partition of late fifteenth or sixteenth-century date. See also Figs. 86, 201, 203.

76   Mural scheme of *c.* 1610 in the George and Dragon, Church Street, Beaumaris, Anglesey, as reconstructed in this drawing by A. J. Parkinson. Despite the iconography of this mural there is no evidence that this building was occupied by a recusant. At its apex the two 'struts' (that form the lozenge containing symbols of Christ's Passion) are entirely fictitious. The colour scheme is dependent upon the use of Anglesey ochre.

termed a 'North Sea culture'. Such lavish use of timber produces a formidably powerful and magnificent effect which makes the use of stud and plank partitions seem almost delicate (Fig. 75)!

The internal treatment of timber-framed walls with plaster infill varied. When not covered with hangings or panelling such walls were often given decorative painted schemes which ran arbitrarily across their structural elements. At other times decorative painting was confined within the plaster panels and/or within the timber components with which they were framed.[10] In some examples the complexity of the timber frame was exaggerated, both internally and externally, by the addition of bogus painted-in timbers (Fig. 76).[11] In one very rare, and possibly unique survival in Sandwich, Kent, the rectangular

panels of plaster, and thus the encompassing timbers, is visually asserted by a (sunk-raised) relief border design which has been impressed into the wet plaster in the manner of an Assyrian cylinder seal (Fig. 77). This work appears to have been done in the third quarter of the sixteenth century although the rowel die that was used may well have been somewhat earlier. Such a (boxwood?) stamp may, very tentatively, be associated with the school of craftsmen that worked on the creation of that, long since destroyed, royal confection known as Nonsuch Palace (1538). Certainly the use of such a die would have enabled the aristocratic idioms of a previous generation to be stamped, quite literally, into a vernacular context. In this particular house the next room has painted mural decoration on one wall

which overrides the structural carpentry (Fig. 78) but on another wall in the same room (Fig. 79) this embellishment mostly conforms to the plaster panels or is contained within the limits of each timber member: stud, rail or windbrace.

The various forms of lining used for interior walls – textile hangings, wood panelling or lime plaster – had one feature in common, they all reduced the problems of condensation. This was a less serious issue with timber-frame walls with wattle and daub infill, than with brick or stone – and the harder the stone the greater the problem. It was for this reason that dwellings built of the Kentish rag-stones of the Maidstone district were given

77 Plaster decoration of the walls in a first-floor chamber in the Long House, 62 Strand Street, Sandwich, Kent. In this scheme the square-frame plaster panels have been emphasised by an Italianate border (about 2 ins 5 cm wide) composed of griffins and foliage. This repeat pattern has evidently been done by means of a roller die impressed into the moist plaster in the manner of an Assyrian cylinder seal. It is possible that the original die dated from the early sixteenth century although the work here was probably carried out in the third quarter of the century.

78 Distemper mural scheme of the third quarter of the sixteenth century in a large chamber adjacent to the room in which Fig. 77 is located in the Long House in Sandwich, Kent. The wall measures 17 ft 7 ins by 7 ft 6 ins. In this case the design runs arbitrarily across the timber studs, rails, braces and the plaster infill.

an inner skin of the soft Hassock stone quarried in the same area.[12] Panelling, which only became common in the sixteenth century, was used for one of two reasons: to line a wall as an alternative to tapestry or, more commonly, to provide a partition 'spur' or 'spere' for which purpose it has had a longer history.[13] These partitions could be made in a number of ways out of a variety of materials. A 'spur' or screen of one slab of slate separating the sitting area from the draught of the door may be seen in the one-room cottage dated 1762 from Llainfadyn, Rhostryfan, Gwynedd (Fig. 80). In South Yorkshire thin slates were sometimes slotted between grooved studs.[14] Slates for this purpose were known as 'grey slates' and were plastered over between the studs. The same technique is also recorded at Stamford, Lincolnshire.[15]

The evolution of the screen is difficult to assess as there are very few in small domestic settings that survive from before 1500. However, by looking at medieval rood screens in churches and at the surviving examples in Tudor houses it is possible to draw a few tentative conclusions. The use of edge-to-edge horizontal plank partitions was rare, but examples have been found at Milton Regis Court Hall, Kent.[16] For internal use vertical boarding has had a long and continuous history.

By means of the tongue and groove it was possible to present a flat face on one or both sides of the work. The most usual and one of the simplest, and therefore earliest, methods of creating a timber screen was by means of a series of vertical boards set into a cill and a lintel (Fig. 75). In high-class stud and plank work the studs (posts) were chamfered or worked with mouldings, but in many instances they were scarcely thicker and certainly almost as wide as the 'panel'. This chamfer was often 'stopped' some feet from the floor implying the presence of a fixed bench.[17] These screens simply divided an open space within a house which was otherwise open to the roof.

To reduce the amount of grooving in the stud it became usual to bevel the back of the plank that formed the panel. This process probably suggested the ribbing that is a feature on some surviving examples in which the bevel has, in effect, migrated to the front of the panel (Fig. 81). Indeed the so-called parchemin panels (a nineteenth-century term referring to parchment which they could be seen to resemble) may almost be arrived at by bevelling a rectangular panel on four sides. When such a panel is moulded on one axis the 'stop' of ogival curves is an inevitable by-product. From these humble beginnings the rich effects of the high Tudor linenfold developed.

79   Mural decoration coeval with, and on the opposite wall (in the same room) to, the scheme illustrated in Fig. 78. In this instance much of the design conforms to, and emphasises, the structural components of the wall.

80   Interior of a single-roomed cottage built in 1762 at Rhostryfan, Gwynedd as reconstructed at the Museum of Welsh Life, Cardiff. The 'spur', 'spere' or 'screen' is of a single slab of slate and provides a draught-proof sitting area by the fireplace (partly visible to the right). The edge of a hanging timber food tray or flake can just be seen top right. Another view of this interior is reproduced in Fig. 272.

81   (*bottom left*) Late fifteenth-century plank and muntin panelling of oak in Wilsley House, Cranbrook, Kent. The chamfering of the planks and their central ridge suggests the possible origin of the so-called parchemin and also linenfold panelling.

Early examples such as may be seen in the magnificent setting of Compton Wynyates, Warwickshire, or Paycockes at Coggeshall, Essex, are worked in panels which are noticeably taller and narrower than later examples, perhaps a silent acknowledgement of their origin in plank panelling. Certainly 'linenfold' is another nineteenth-century term, although Tudor documents sometimes describe it as 'drapery pannell'[18] but the more usual term was *lignum undulatum*, wavy woodwork. Linenfold panels are often found in association with early Renaissance carving (known as 'Romayne work') but in themselves they may be regarded as neither Italianate in origin nor medieval in spirit. Such work was expensive and is generally outside the scope of this book – except where this opulence was counterfeited in paint (Fig. 82).

As we have seen, plank panelling stressed the vertical, and the horizontal only existed at the lintel and the cill, equivalent in some ways to the base and cornice of classical architecture. With the addition of more horizontal members or rails the vertical axes declined. Even in the simplest schemes the stiles (as relatively lightweight vertical members are known in distinction to heavyweight studs) and rails are chamfered. Because of the nature of such construction the 'stops' of the chamfering could only be completed once the work was 'made up' and it was here that the mason's mitre was employed (Fig. 83). This method of

82   Oak panel and stile, the panel painted (*c.* 1530–50) to resemble carved 'linenfold'. From a derelict house in Coggeshall, Essex. In counterfeiting expensive carved work the decorative painter was able to introduce high fashion to more lowly interiors, although such work will also be found at a much higher social level as at Sutton House in East London – which has similar faux linenfold painted on plaster. Private Collection.

83   Stone window showing the cill worked with a mason's mitre, a visual effect imposed by a structural solution – also worked in timber.

84   An oak-boarded partition wall, carved to resemble framed-up panelling, in the first-floor corridor of the High House, Stafford – built 1595. This type of work would have been more expensive than conventionally framed-up panelling – which doubtless accounts for its rarity.

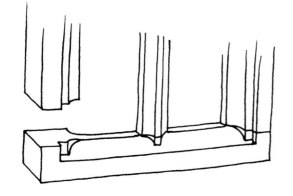

construction and finish was expensive, and later (i.e. early seventeenth-century) panelling used the cheaper 'run out' stop and the scribed cill. As with parchemin panels such features of design evolved as a natural function of crafts-manship. As the design process moved from the bench to the drawing board, from artisan to architect, such organic evolution in design was doomed, but lingered longest at the vernacular level (Fig. 84).

In his *Description of England* William Harrison describes the internal treatment of walls in Tudor England: 'The wals of our houses on the inner sides in like sort be either hanged with tapistrie, arras worke, or painted cloths,

85   Late sixteenth-century polychromatic mural scheme running arbitrarily across a stud and plaster wall from Hill House, North Hill, Essex as recorded in watercolour by Francis W. Reader in 1938. This design perpetuates the tradition for a wall to be divided into two unequal zones, the lower area being panelled, and the larger upper zone being decorated with a mural, a woven tapestry or a stained hanging. A fragment of this scheme is preserved in the Castle Museum, Colchester. Watercolour drawing: Victoria and Albert Museum, London.

86   An internal jetty, over a stud and plank screen, giving emphasis to the dais end of the hall in a late fifteenth-century house at Spaxton, Somerset. The internal jetty, used in this way, is characteristic of east Devon and west Somerset. See also Fig. 188 showing an upstairs room in the same house.

wherein either diverse histories, or herbs, beasts, knots, and suchlike are stained, or else they are seeled with oke.'[19] In the context of Harrison's observation this implies that neither panelling nor hangings were general until the Tudor period (Fig. 85). Woven tapestry was exceptional until the sixteenth century and so it was to remain, – a medieval feature of comfort and social prestige which not even the Renaissance could displace. John Milton uses a reference to tapestry as emblematic of luxury in *Comus, a Mask*:

> . . . honest-offer'd courtesie
> Which oft is sooner found in lowly sheds
> With smoky rafters, than in tap'stry Halls
> And Courts of Princes.

By the end of the sixteenth century stained cloth hangings are referred to quite often in houses of many social levels.[20] In yeoman houses in Sussex the dais reredos was either panelled or hung with tapestry under the coved reredos bressummer.[21] That feature also occurs in Halifax and Huddersfield on a much larger scale to become a canopy so that the hanging on the dais reredos may be regarded as a 'cloth of estate'.[22] In east Devon and west Somerset, as elsewhere, an internal jetty sometimes oversailed this screen to enhance the dais end and emphasise the presence of a solar (Fig. 86).[23]

By the early seventeenth century panelling had become quite usual in farmhouses but was constructed of less substantial oak scantlings, and by the last quarter of the century imported softwoods became more common (Fig. 87). The influence of Classicism was often felt rather than seen. For example, it was Jacobean custom to terminate panelling with a top row of horizontal panels, two panels wide – thus implying a frieze. These panels were often carved in a vaguely classical way and greater emphasis was achieved by 'punching' the ground. In general it was usual

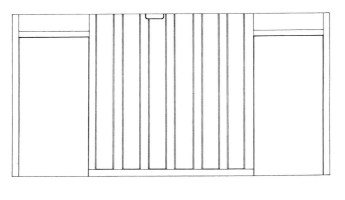

4·5 in (11·4 cm)

87   Early eighteenth-century stud and plank partition in a house at Bury, West Sussex. Although the treatment is much lighter this partition shows the persistence of the medieval structural tradition.

88   (*below*) Early eighteenth-century panelling in the main reception room of Silver Street House, Bradford on Avon, Wiltshire. The garbled knowledge of Classical architecture would often produce charmingly ridiculous details such as the triglyphs in this room.

to 'offer up' sections of panelling about six panels wide. These were then fixed with no attempt being made to mask the joins although sometimes these joins were hidden by pilasters. Because panelling was fixed very simply it could easily be removed and testators had to make it clear when it was to be regarded as a fixture. In 1581 John Manninge of Maldon, Essex, a shoemaker, left 'to my wife Elizabeth my tenement in the parish of All Saints, called by the sign of the Spread Eagle, during her life, provided she shall not remove any of the wainscot nor the glass' from the windows.[24] Originally much of this panelling must have been painted, and nearly all the examples that I have seen reveal, when cleaned, if not actual areas of pigment, grains of paint or gesso in the interstices of the carved or moulded elements.

At the vernacular level, the half-knowledge of Classicism usually associated with the period of Elizabeth I and James I survived into the early eighteenth century in areas distant from London such as the West Country and Westmorland. This is especially true of interiors (Fig. 88), perhaps because most early books on architecture were concerned primarily with the basic structure and planning of buildings and their external elevations. In the panelling of rooms, as in the panels of furniture, this is particularly noticeable, not only in the detailed carving but also in the overall size of the panels. Despite the use of glue, size and gesso by medieval craftsmen, they did not rely on such substances for the structural integrity of joinery. The mortice and tenon was not primarily, or at all, held together with glue (as was usually considered adequate for furniture in the eighteenth century), it was firmly dowelled. Similarly, panels were not made that were larger than the tree was capable of producing. Lightweight scantlings were always quarter sawn, not because this produced the finest 'figure' in the medullary rays of oak, but because such boards seasoned best and warped least. With painted panelling any 'figure' or 'flash' in the grain of timber would not be visible – it was 'quarter sawn' for practical reasons. By the time the centre of the log had been removed (the boxed heart being very strong but very temperamental) the maximum width of such boards was usually about 18 ins (45.7 cm) but for practical purposes 9 ins was typical. This conditioned the width of panels although, as with plank panelling, their length (i.e. height) could be considerable. For these reasons panels, in schemes of panelling, generally remained narrow until the second half of the seventeenth century.

In the first half of the seventeenth century, perhaps coinciding with the emergence of the architect-theoretician rather than the craftsman-architect, the once proud master joiner succumbed to the whim of a master not himself. It was at this time that large panels and the decadent mitre were first introduced, to become common in

89   Painted decoration on a panelled wall at Oakwell Hall, Kirklees, West Yorkshire. Vernacular painting could produce startlingly original schemes which are difficult to date. The joinery appears to be of the late seventeenth century – the probable date of this 'Cubist' scheme.

the second half of the century. Panels surrounded by stiles and rails with mitred joints had probably first come into England in the late sixteenth century as the 'frenche panell'.[25] In late Stuart Britain large panels were made up by means of glueing. In other words, the proportions ordained by Classicism and drawn on paper by the interpreting architect (or the fashion they introduced) had to be arrived at by the craftsman without respect for his craft but out of obedience to the new orders. Certainly most medieval and early post-medieval panels in a scheme of panelling are small (at least in width) so that they may conform to the sizes available in quarter sawn boards (Fig. 89).

90   *A flute player, c.* 1735, attributed to James Cole the younger. Panelling of the simple unadorned character shown in this room was traditionally intended to have canvas stretched over it on which wallpaper would be 'hung' (i.e. pasted on). Sometimes, if funds were short, panelling of this type was painted – as shown here. Upton House, Warwickshire.

It is just possible that the late seventeenth and early eighteenth-century fashion for large panels emerged from their use for the 'hanging' of silk, leather or paper (Fig. 90). In such a circumstance the wood of the panels could split or the joints 'give' without being a visible disaster. Panelling of this type, not usually designed to be seen, may be found in some of the houses in Grove Terrace, Highgate (begun 1769; Figs. 91, 92). Here the walls separating entrance hall from parlour, or bedroom from staircase, are pine partitions constructed in this way. Being designed to take hangings, neither the panels nor the 'framing-up' are embellished with mouldings of any kind and in some instances consists of battens without panels (Fig. 292).[26] When this type of very simple panelling was left visible it was generally painted (Fig. 90).

In medieval and Tudor England oak was the favoured timber but some softwood was also used, although very little has survived. The large panels preferred in the second half of the seventeenth and into the eighteenth century were usually of fir, but in better quality work of pine. These timbers were usually imported from Norway or the Baltic. Best of all was oak panelling but by this time it was left unpainted. According to Celia Fiennes, Irish oak was sometimes selected as in 'this wood no spider will weave on or endure'.[27] At the top of the social scale various exotic woods, such as cedar, brought in at great cost by trade with distant lands, were in use by the late seventeenth century. Such valuable materials were also left unpainted as is confirmed by surviving examples of simulated painted graining (see Chapter 9). In the *Complete Body of Architecture* (1756) Isaac Ware states that in 'general, the stucco rooms . . . are cold; those wainscoted are naturally warmer;

and those which are hung warmest. The stucco room, when heated becomes hottest of all . . . a wainscoted room, painted in the usual way, is the lightest of all; the stucco is the next in this condition, and the hung [with paper, silk, tapestry, etc.] room the darkest of all.'[28]

After planing (and even carving), the final smoothing of wood was done by means of 'a skin called hundys fish-skyn [dogfish skin] for the carpenters'.[29] I have myself used arenaceous shark-skin for this purpose. Unlike glass-paper or sandpaper, shark-skin does not leave a gritty deposit which could blunt edged tools or disrupt paint-ing or gilding. With carved work the proportion of time spent sharpening tools is so high (particularly when 'working' the softwoods which demand sharper tools than, say, oak) that glasspaper should be avoided at all costs, despite the difficulty of obtaining dried shark-skin. Another natural abrasive available to craftsmen and used within living memory, is the so-called 'Dutch rush'. These were used by gilders in establishing a particularly smooth surface on gesso or by house-painters when smoothing their final coat of paint before the application of varnish.[30] The Dutch rush is known by non-craftsmen as the 'horse's tail', *equisetum hiemale*, and it contains a certain amount of silica. The third type of abrasive in common use was pumice stone which was shaped (or

shaped itself through use) to the sections of the mould-ings being worked.

So unimportant was the mitre considered for struc-tural purposes that Joseph Moxon in his *Mechanick Exercises or the Doctrine of Handy-Works* (1677), alludes to the use of a 'Mitre Square' only for 'Picture Frames and Looking-Glass frames'.[31] Although much of Moxon's writing refers back to earlier standards of craftsmanship he is quite clearly of his time when describing the wain-scoting of rooms:

> In Wainscoting of Rooms there is, for the most part, but two heights of Pannels used; unless the Room to be wainscoted be above ten foot high . . . Heights of Pannels are used: As . . . The *Lying Pannel* above the *Base*, . . . The *Large Pannel* above the *Middle Rail*, And . . . The *Friese Pannel* above the *Friese Rail*.
>
> The *Friese Rail* is to have the same bredth the *Margent* of the *Stile* hath; the *Middle Rail* hath com-monly two bredths of the *Margent* of the *Stile* viz. one breadth above the *Sur-base*. And the *Upper* and *Lower Rails* have each the same breadth with the *Margent* of the *Stile*.
>
> Sometimes (and especially in Low Rooms) there is no *Base* or *Sur-base* used, and then the *Middle* and

91, 92   Entrance passage and detail of carved wood pilaster capital in 23 Grove Terrace, Highgate, London (begun 1769). The scale of such details is beautifully adjusted to the small size of these houses, the entrance hall by the front door being a bare 3 ft wide.

93   Early eighteenth-century panelling in Holland House, Barnstaple, Devon. The fielded panels, the 'tabernacle frame', possibly intended to carry an overmantel picture, the dado which marked the extent of the plinth on this Classically conceived interior give a solemn dignity to this relatively small room.

94   Fireplace wall of *c*. 1800 in 57 Upper Brook Street, Winchester, Hampshire. Provincial joiners were quite capable of adapting the more frivolous aspects of the Classical Revival to a scale which met more down-to-earth needs. The projection in the ceiling is caused by the hearthstone of the fireplace in the room above.

Lower-Rail need not be so broad. . . .

You may if you wish adorn the outer edges of the *Stiles* and *Rails* with a small Moulding: And you may (if you will) Bevil away the outer edges of the *Pannels* and leave a Table in the middle of the Pannel.[32]

Most of the terms used by Moxon are recognisable except for the word 'Margent'. Fortunately he includes a glossary and defines this word as 'the flat breadth of the stiles besides the mouldings'.[33] Moxon's proportions for the panelling of rooms is very much a 'rule of thumb' method (Fig. 93). By the mid-eighteenth century various publications had given architects and joiners a deeper appreciation of the Classical Orders – the panelling of a room was after all nothing less than the proportions of a Classical building turned inside out from plinth to cornice, from floor to ceiling. This awareness went further than the elite publications of Colen Campbell and others. In Batty Langley's *Builder's Jewel* (1741) may be found 'Rules . . . To find the breadth of the dado of the Tuscan order', and similar 'Rules' for 'Dorick', 'Ionick', 'Corinthian' and 'Composite'. These rules extend to such details as the 'division of the mouldings'.[34] The 'sur-base' is defined in Peter Nicholson's *New Practical Builder* (1823–5) as the 'upper base of a room, or rather the cornice of the pedestal of the room, which serves to finish the dado, and to secure the plaster against accidents from the backs of chairs and other furniture on the same level.'[35]

The bevelling of the panels with 'a Table in the middle' in Moxon's description is a clear and early reference to the 'fielded panel'. It was and is usual in the assembling of panelling to glue and dowel the mortices and tenons of stiles and rails firmly together leaving the panel loose so that it may expand and shrink without splitting. William Salmon makes this very clear when describing the timberwork panels for painted sundials:

. . . let the edges [of the panel] be shot true, and all of a thickness, that they may fit into the Rabets of the Mouldings, put round it just as a panel of Wainscot doth in its Frame.

This will give the board liberty to shrink and swell without rending, whereas mouldings nailed round the edges, as the vulgar way is, doth so restrain the motion of the wood, that it cannot shrink without tearing.[36]

This explains why panels, when congested with generations of paint, often split. It was found at an early date that if the panels were bevelled it not only made the work lighter but guaranteed that they had 'liberty to shrink'. Medieval panels are bevelled on the back. As we have seen, this necessary feature had migrated to the front where it was often used for decorative effect to create the familiar linenfold and later the 'fielded panel'.

As the use of panelling declined in the eighteenth century (quite when is related to status and geographical location), the skirting and dado, or chair rail, persisted not so much as vestigal remains of panelling, or as fundamental elements of the architecture of a Classical room, but rather as practical ways in which the plaster walls were protected from chairs and brooms (Fig. 94). It was in this spirit that seventeenth-century Dutch interiors (as represented by contemporaneous artists) were given delft tile 'skirtings'. This feature may also be found represented in some interiors in Britain where timber skirting boards are much the most common.[37] Once again the techniques employed in this woodwork persist down to the present day. The simplest method of fitting a skirting board round a room is by means of the despised mitre and in poor quality work this is what is done. However, the dictates of good craftsmanship demand that in the receding angles in the corners of a room such junctions should be butted, the mouldings being accommodated by sawing their sections around scribed lines (Fig. 95). Wood shrinks almost entirely in its width and a mitred skirting board tends to shrink away from the joint, a hazard to which a 'scribed skirting' would not be visibly subject. In the nineteenth century this problem was sometimes overcome by 'running' the skirting in plaster by means of a brass or zinc template, but this contradicted the raison d'être for a skirting board – the protection of a plaster wall from brooms. An alternative was a painted skirting, usually a dark tone, that would make marks from brooms less visible.

Strictly speaking, the making-up of panelling was the province of the joiner, an 'art and mystery' that has been

95 A scribed skirting board.

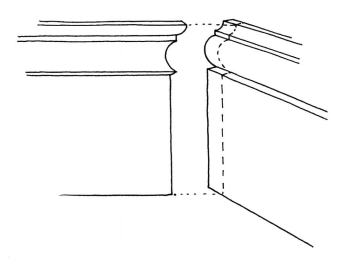

96   *Trompe l'oeil* panelled scheme contrived in distemper on the plaster walls of the main room on the first floor of a house on the east side of St James's Square, Bath. Although these houses were designed by John Palmer in the late eighteenth century, this distempered scheme is evidently twenty or thirty years later and is close to J. C. Loudon's recommended method of 'panelling in . . . colours' (*Encyclopaedia*, Vol. I, 1846 edition, p. 277).

by means of applied mouldings or could be plastered in imitation of panelling. Loudon states quite categorically that 'walls and ceilings of "Plain Cottages" are seldom panelled on account of expence other than by painted lines or coloured papers' (Fig. 96).[40]

Elaborate plasterwork was more common in vernacular interiors on walls or ceilings in the seventeenth century than in earlier or later periods. On late medieval daubed walls a design was often simply scratched onto the surface. With more elaborate 'pargetting' the first layer of daub was applied to the riven laths of beech, oak (sometimes identified in accounts as 'sap and heart' suggesting the use of branches) or softwood.[41] Relief decoration, where it existed, formed part of the final coat of plaster. In the seventeenth century, ornamental plasterwork appeared in smaller houses, the focal point of the chimney breast forming one favourite surface and the frieze between the top of the panelling and the ceiling another. An example of the latter is in the Old Croft, Washford, near Minehead, Somerset (Fig. 97), and a somewhat earlier frieze survives in a house at Six Wells, Llandow, Glamorgan . Examples of plasterwork overmantel decorations, which are such a feature in seventeenth-century houses in Cumbria,[42] are also to be found elsewhere in Britain as, for example, at the Old Manse, Beckington (Fig. 98), and a house at Penwrlod Chapel, Llanigon, Powys, both dating from the first half of the seventeenth century.

John White's *A Rich Cabinet With A Variety of Inventions* (1651) contains an extraordinary conglomeration of facts which the author excuses on the grounds that: 'the laborious Bee gathereth her cordiall Honey, and the venemous Spider her corroding poysen many times from one Flower.' Among White's 'Variety of Inventions' is: 'Receit LX *A dainty strong and glistering Mortar or Plaistering for Seelings, or for Walles.* It is said, that in *Italy* they much use this Conceit for the Plaistering of the Seelings, Floors or Walls, which is by mixing and well tempering together Oxen and Carves blood with fine Loame or Clay, and it will be very strong and binding substance, and being well smoothed it will glister, and become very hard.'[43] This may be the so-called 'black plaster' quoted in the 1340 accounts at Westminster.[44] Plaster of Paris or 'French plaster' may well have come into use in Britain in the middle of the thirteenth century possibly as a result of Henry III's many building projects. Certainly it was only used as a finishing coat and the lime plasters were much the most commonly used. Nevertheless, a couple of centuries later many substitutes were used as William Horman (1519) makes clear. 'Some men will have thyr wallys plastered, some pergetted, and whytlymed, some roughe caste, some pricked, some wrought with playster of Paris.'[45]

distinguished from carpentry by the former's use of the plane,[38] but the demarcation between the two crafts was by no means clear. A more satisfactory distinction would be that the joiner works at a bench (generally in a workshop) in contrast to the carpenter who works on buildings *in situ*.

In the nineteenth century the use of wood panelling declined although, like much else, it would appear in pretentious interiors as a revival. Loudon recommended that 'For the plainest description of cottage the walls may be completely finished with one coating of plaster' when in best work three-coat plaster was general.[39] In larger rooms the walls might be 'thrown into compartments'

97   Late sixteenth-century plaster frieze in a house at Washford, near Minehead, Somerset. Note the tenter hooks along the lower edge of this frieze. These would have been used to hang a stained cloth (see Figs. 192–6).

Whitewash was widely used both inside and out, hence the name of the White Tower of the Tower of London. Evidently whitewashing was considered as much a responsibility of the plasterer as the painter. *The Practical Plasterer* by Wilfred Kemp, first published in London in 1893 (and as recently as 1926), states that 'Whitewashing and the application of coloured washes to walls, technically known as "distempering", fall usually within the province of the plasterer, although often done by painters and decorators.'[46] Kemp's book also clarifies the terms 'pargetting', 'pergetting' or 'parge-work' which 'were and are applied somewhat loosely, and are used in several distinct senses, sometimes for plain plastering on walls, but usually for that of an ornamental character'. However, later in the same chapter he adds: 'The word "pargetting" although now but little used, except by bricklayers for the coarse plastering of the inside of chimney flues, often occurs as applied to ornamental work in ancient records', examples of which he goes on to cite.[47]

At York the plasterers joined with the bricklayers and tilers to form a united guild thus establishing officially

98   Plaster overmantel decoration in the Old Manse, Beckington, Somerset.

their long-standing association.[48] In Bristol, *Sketchley's Directory* for 1775 lists no fewer than twenty-three 'tylers & plasterers', an association which was probably born of the need to 'torch-up' the underside of roof tiles to make them wind-proof and watertight. Plaster of Paris, being white, was often left as the final finish. This was something of a convenience for it was generally agreed that 'Walls should not be painted until finished one year.'[49] Nevertheless, when Sydney Smith was building his parsonage at Foston le Clay, Yorkshire, this process was speeded up by keeping fires burning in each room for two months before the family moved in on 20 March 1814.[50] The following year Sir John Soane used braziers to dry the new plasterwork in the Bank of England.[51]

Tapestries were once hung on bare walls not only for purposes of decoration but also to reduce the condensation which would otherwise have appeared on hard stone interior walls. Lime-plastered walls provided an alternative solution to this problem, indeed it was its raison d'être. Unfortunately most commercial manufacturers of plaster today seem to have forgotten this sound principle. In the restoration of old property it is advisable to retain as much of the original soft lime plaster as possible, or to use the lime plasters *and* lime washes that some specialist manufacturers have begun to produce. This is particularly important in small kitchens and bathrooms which, despite the presence of good ventilation and central heating, will otherwise be greatly at risk from the effects of condensation.

Chapter 4

Doors and Doorways

Doors and doorways, like gates and gateways, are the overture that establishes the mood of what is to follow. From the Gate of Virtue (1567) at Caius College, Cambridge, to Rodin's Gates of Hell (1880–1900) the emblematic importance of an entrance is self-evident; it stands at the frontier between the exterior and the interior (Fig. 99).

At a practical level doors, like the walls they intrude upon, were constructed to face the elements and address the outside world, or they met the less rigorous but more intimate needs of internal spaces. Necessarily, the primitive one-room house only required the former type. In their earliest manifestation, doors were not side-hung on hinges but were simply placed in the doorway when required. The first side-hung doors swung on 'harres', an ancient species of pin hinge that lingered in primitive houses on the northern and western fringes of the British Isles until the end of the nineteenth century (Fig. 100).[1] There are exceptions where such hinges are found in the context of an elegant house; some of the magnificent mahogany doors of the state rooms in the majestic Hagley Hall, Worcestershire by Sanderson Miller (built between 1754 and 1760 at a cost of £34,000) are unaccountably of this type.

Houses constructed of wattle hurdles plastered with mud were lived in by much of the population until the sixteenth century. Such dwellings had wattle-hurdle doors and these persisted in use until the end of the nineteenth century. In Ireland they were still used on farm buildings in the last century where the most rudimentary 'door' consisted of nothing more substantial than a bundle of brushwood (Fig. 101).[2] In the 1890s a derelict cottage at Great Hatfield, Mappleton, East Yorkshire, was recorded as having 'doors' and indeed 'windows' of 'harden', a kind of coarse sack-cloth which 'could be lifted up like a curtain'

(see 'Stained Hangings', pp. 132–3).[3] At about the same period on the Isle of Lewis in the Outer Hebrides 'a straw mat or a cow's hide on a frame might be used as a door', and as recently as the 1960s wickerwork doors were reported as being in use in Wester Ross.[4] In Wales, where the door-hurdle was known as the *dorglwyd*, an example was recorded in 1888 in use in a ruined farmhouse at Strata Florida, Dyfed.[5] J. Evans, in his *Letters . . . in North Wales* in 1798 says of the cottages in Caernarvonshire: 'Door there is none: but this deficiency is supplied by a hurdle, formed of a few wattlings and rushes, which in bad weather is raised perpendicular to stop the gap.'[6]

The whole question of hurdle doors has been most thoroughly studied in Ireland by A. T. Lucas. They seem to have been more usual in the northern and western parts of the country. The Irish examples were either made of woven wattle or wicker and sometimes of brushwood, the latter being generally reserved for outbuildings. What was probably the last brushwood door to be made in Ireland was constructed for a cowshed in 1955 by Sean Fitzgerald of Kilcrohane Parish. It was of birch branches held between two pairs of split halves of 3 ins (7.6 cm) diameter ash, tied with bog-fir rope. In Irish cabins with the typical cross passage one wattle door (or half-door) and one wood-batten door was quite common. The wood door was hung on strap hinges and it was usual to place it in the doorway facing the prevailing wind – if the wind changed the door was simply lifted off its pintles and hung in the other doorway. This custom probably represents a transitional stage in modernisation. To wind-proof the wattle door a straw mat was customarily hung on the inside (Fig. 102). A description of such a door was recorded in 1942 from an informant aged seventy-four:

99 A late seventeenth-century door (64 by 29 ins – 162.5 cm by 73.5 cm) from a room used as a dairy in Hulvertree Farm, Suffolk. Collection Timothy Easton. The incised marks, recently enhanced with white chalk, were made to deter witches, a safeguard which was regarded as particularly important in relationship to food. The same superstitious reasoning accounts for the similar occult devices that have been found on ceilings above areas where culinary activity was likely to take place. Although apotropaic marks have been found in houses, barns, stables, churches and even on furniture throughout the British Isles, east Suffolk boasts a remarkable concentration of seventeenth-century examples. These magic emblems were believed to be particularly important at openings in a building such as doors, windows and chimneys (especially the bressummer). The principal authority on this subject, Timothy Easton (see p. 125 and notes Chapter 2, notes 40, 41), has found that the most common emblems are variations on the initials V, W, M, R and AMR (Ave Maria) invoking the protection of the Virgin Mary, a tradition that continued long after the Reformation (see also Figs. 37–9). Here the inscribed 'spectacle mark' has been interpreted as a device to avert the evil eye.

100 Oak harre-hung door from Langsett, South Yorkshire. The boards are pegged to the battens with chamfered heads, a feature evolved in wood and later copied in iron. Drawing by J. A. after C. F. Innocent, *The Development of English Building Construction*, 1916.

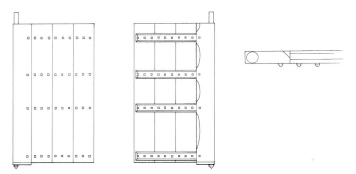

The door consisted of four [superimposed] hurdles. The innermost was made of rods: it had ribs and the rods were woven as in a basket and it was square in shape like the frame [of the door]. There were three others outside that with three-sticks tied [transversely] with withies on them. They [the hurdles] were fixed to each other . . . and the four were fixed so tightly together that a person would find it very difficult to pull them apart . . . The innermost one, which was made like a basket, was plastered with yellow clay, and no wind could penetrate it then. There was a [separate] cross bar to put across the middle of the door [when it was in position in the doorway] and two holes in the wall into which the ends [of the bar] were entered.[7]

Sometimes such doors were hung on hinges of plaited straw, but these wattle or straw 'shields' (*sciatheogai*) were more often simply placed in the doorway, although the straw lining mats were sometimes hung by means of hooks from the inside wall. For this reason the doorway required no framed surround of wood onto which hinges could be fixed. Indeed the same held good when the ancient harre was used. The harre could be made by extending either one outer stile in a framed-up door, or

101 Nineteenth-century Irish hurdle and brushwood doors – after A. T. Lucas, 'Wattle and straw mat doors in Ireland'. National Museum of Antiquities, Dublin.

102 (*below left*) Woven straw door lining from Portacloy, Co. Mayo, Ireland. The hurdle doors of Ireland were often wind-proofed internally by means of straw-mat hangings. National Museum of Antiquities, Dublin.

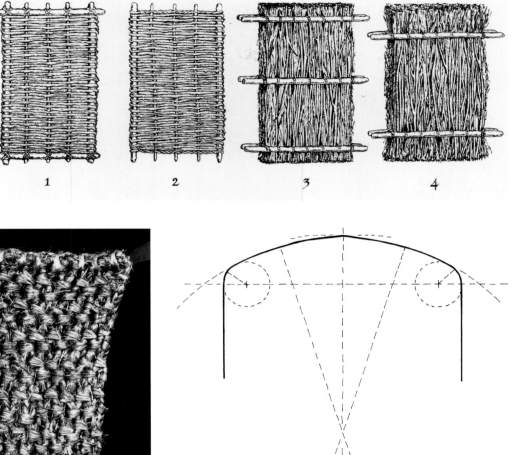

1   2   3   4

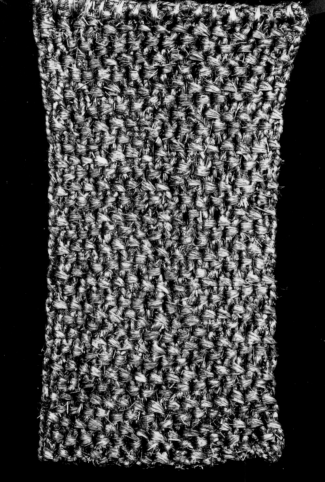

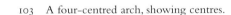

103 A four-centred arch, showing centres.

one plank in a ledge door, to provide a pair of 'horns' on which the door could swing.[8]

In the trabeated form of a timber-frame building the jamb, lintel and often the cill, existed as a necessary part of the structure, but in stone houses the door frame of wood had to be introduced, a feature that had not been necessary with either the wattle or the harre-hung door. The introduction of the timber door frame made possible the use of various types of metal hinge. The square-headed door is usual for timber-frame buildings as a natural consequence of their structure. In fine fifteenth-century yeomans houses in the Weald and elsewhere door-heads are sometimes given a two-centred arch by means of naturally curved jambs (Fig. 188).[9] As timber was customarily used with the natural growth inverted such members were easily obtained from the trunk and the point near the ground where the girth of the tree widens – the 'stamm'. The use of these naturally 'jowled' timbers for two-centred arches in vernacular houses contrasts with the 'four-centred arch' favoured for grander buildings of the Perpendicular period (Fig. 103). The four-centred arch came into use in vernacular houses of the sixteenth century and was to persist. It could easily be cut out of a solid lintel of wood or stone. However, in timber this was more often done by a shaped door-head

104   The sixteenth-century north–south screens passage of Hines Farm, Earl Stonham, Suffolk.

housed into the jambs below the lintel as in the screens passage at Hines Farm, Earl Stonham (Fig. 104). The door-head illustrated in Figs. 105–6 is of this type and the simple carved feather design would probably have been visible from the screens passage while the elaborate tracery would have enriched the hall. It is rare to find such pure tracery combined with such exact Renaissance detail as the guilloche, two features which point to a date between about 1530 and 1550.

Batten doors for internal and external use are constructed of a series of vertical boards held together by means of horizontal boards or 'ledges', usually four in number. The best external doors of this type are composed of two layers of boards (which are sometimes

105, 106 Front and back of an oak door-head, second quarter of the sixteenth century. Such a component probably occurred over one of the doors in a screens passage with the more elaborate side facing into the prestigious hall. It is rare to see such pure Perpendicular blind tracery combined with a no less accurate representation of the Classical guilloche. Private Collection.

lapped) with the vertical boards on the outside, so as to shed water, and the horizontal boards on the inside (Fig. 107). The two layers are united by nails driven through from the front of the door and cleated over on the inside. Many nails were needed for this purpose and these are generally arranged to form patterns which are given emphasis by lines scribed in the wood. 'Batten' doors were, in their simplicity, similar to plank panelling and, on occasion, were also worked with mouldings such as a 'bead and quirk'. In Ulster, despite the deforestation of the country for the purposes of agriculture, doors made up from generously wide planks were sometimes grooved in imitation of narrow boards.[10] The half-door in Ireland sometimes consisted of two doors, one full length, the other half its height. With the full-height door open this had the effect of providing an extra (unglazed) window with the half-door closed and high enough to keep farm animals out of the house. In Britain most half-doors are divided horizontally so that in summer the upper half may be left open with the lower half remaining closed for much of the time. In some parts of England another type of half-door may occasionally be found where the door is divided vertically and hinged in the middle (Figs. 108, 109).[11]

The 'strap and pintle' hinge and the 'cross garnet' (as Moxon describes it)[12] had the advantage of providing a door with additional strengthening. The cross–garnet is a hinge in which the strap is permanently looped into the plate which provides the means of securing the hinge to the door frame. Strap hinges of wood, which dispensed with the luxury of iron, were made and in use on the Isle of Lewis in the middle of the last century.[13]

107 Elm (?) door at Newhouse Farm, Llanfapley, Gwent, early seventeenth century. Doors constructed by carpenters of two layers of boards set at right angles to each other were held together by numerous nails cleated over on the inside. The resulting decorative arrangement of these nail-heads was often emphasised by scribed lines.

108, 109   The front door (external and internal view) of Cross Street Farm, West Burton, West Sussex. The masoned doorway here is dated 1634.

Throughout much of the seventeenth and eighteenth centuries the 'H' and 'HL' hinge of iron were widely used largely because they conformed well to the stiles and rails of a framed-up door. Moxon describes various types of hinges and their use: joiners should

> consider what sort of Hindges are properest for the Door they are to *Hang*. When they have a *Street door* (which commonly is to take off and lift on) they use *Hooks and Hindges* [strap and pintle]. In a Battend-door, Back-door or other Battend-door, or Shop windows, they use *Cross-Garnets*. If a *Frame'd Door, Side Hinges*; and for *Cup-board Doors* and such like Duf-tails [butterfly hinges].'[14]

The well-known 'cockshead' hinge used on furniture and internal doors is an elaboration of the 'H' hinge. In pre-industrial Britain it is noticeable that door furniture, locks and hinges, being made of metal (a valuable resource before industrialisation) are planted on the face of doors for maximum visibility – conspicuous consumption. As industrialisation reduced the cost of metal products such hinges were later superseded by the far less visible 'butt' hinge which was in turn displaced by the 'rising butt' made necessary by the widespread use of carpets from the late eighteenth century – textiles being the other important product of industrialisation.

One of the earliest methods of locking a door was by means of a horizontal beam sliding in large iron staples fixed to the internal face of the wall. Alternatively this beam slides into holes cut in the thickness of a stone wall as at Steyning Manor Farm, Stogursey, Somerset. An example of the latter has also been found in a stone house in Dalkeith, Scotland.[15] In both cases this slot is masoned in the stonework which is lined with timber, presumably to make the beam slide more easily and be less liable to wear. In late Stuart and early Georgian London an alternative method of securing a door from the inside was by means of a chain (Figs. 110, 111, 112). Wooden latches and bolts have a wide distribution in the British Isles (Fig. 113). In the Scottish Islands as well as in Devon and Cornwall the simple wood 'pin lock', as old as Ancient Egypt, remained in use in the nineteenth century, a possible legacy of trade with the Phoenicians.[16] Moxon refers to '*Lock*s for several purposes, as *Street-door Locks*, called *Stock-locks*, *Chamber-door Locks*, called *Spring-locks*',[17] a distinction which survives to this day except that 'Stock-locks' have generally been replaced by 'rim locks' and mortice locks. Stock locks, having wood 'stocks', tended to use less metal and were therefore cheaper than rim locks. As with hinges, rim locks were highly visible being planted on the face of a door. In contrast, mortice locks, a product of industrialisation, are housed in the

110 Eighteenth-century door secured internally by means of a wrought-iron chain. Similar examples. survive in London in 17 Gough Square, 36 Craven Street and 3 Great Ormond Street (see Figs. 111, 112).

111, 112 Chain and worm-catch of wrought iron in 3 Great Ormond Street.

thickness of the door and are all but invisible – locks, like hinges, had ceased to be a visible consumer durable that celebrated conspicuous consumption.

Locks were once items of great value and in medieval and Tudor times were decorated in accordance with their status. It is thought that the Beddington lock (now in the Victoria and Albert Museum) was carried from palace to palace when Henry VIII, whose arms it bears, was on a 'progress'.[18] In nineteenth-century Scotland locks were still considered as tenant's property and the numerous keyholes in many old doors bear witness to this, a feature seen elsewhere in the British Isles. George Hope, recalling the dwellings at Fenton Barns, Scotland, in the year 1861, spoke of 'a door covered with key holes, made to suit the size of the lock of each successive occupant'.[19]

The framed door is probably older than the widespread use of 'framed-up' panelling but its use increased as framed panelling became more common. The two-panelled door of the early seventeenth century, embellished with applied mouldings, became simpler towards the end of the century in keeping with the restraint of Classicism. Internally the two-panel door persisted to the reign of Queen Anne. The proportions of the door surround was to feel the impact of the Renaissance as interpreted by Palladio: '*Doors* within the House, in the least

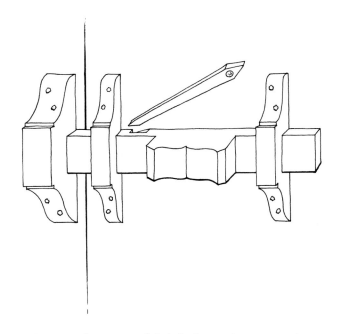

113 Seventeenth-century oak bolt/lock on a door to an attic bedroom at Green Farm, Bushley, Worcestershire. Overall measurements 8 by 12 ins (20.3 by 30.5 cm). In pre-industrial Britain metal goods and textiles were expensive.

Building, ought not to have less than two Foot and a half in breadth, and five Foot and a half in height: Those from three to four Foot broad must have in height twice their breadth; and to great Buildings you may allow ev'n to five or six Foot in breadth and the height double.'[20] As this description demonstrates, the resulting door-height could be very low in small houses (say 5 ft 6 ins – 167.7 cm) – despite which this was recommended in Godfrey Richards's edition of Palladio (1663) and by Richard Neve (1707),[21] but not by Isaac Ware (1756).[22] Externally the doorway in a timber-frame house was, in essence, part of its framing, but in a brick or masonry structure it reflected the stylistic features of its time, such as a four-centred arch or (in stone) a bolection moulding. The pediment was also widely used externally, particularly at the point where vernacular building moves close to the stylistic concerns of 'polite' architecture. It was favoured virtually throughout the eighteenth century. Internally, ceiling heights could limit the use of the pediment although, for this reason, the frieze was sometimes omitted (Figs. 288, 289). In general the pediment was not used in vernacular interiors and even in gentry houses it was found to be too powerful and 'architectural', which was why its impact was often reduced by being 'broken'. More often the architrave was continued round the door-head and simply headed by a cornice. In the second half of the seventeenth century the transome light over a front door provided natural illumination for the entrance hall, a particularly valuable device in the terraces of the fast-expanding towns (Fig. 110). The lunette, fanlight or transome light of cast iron became widespread as a decorative feature in the late eighteenth century when they could be cheaply produced with delicate astragal mouldings by manufactories in Coalbrookdale and elsewhere.

For much of the eighteenth and well into the following century the standard door was framed-up to produce six panels. On external doors it was considered best practice for the top four panels to be 'fielded', but the lower two panels to be finished flush with the stiles and rails marked out with a bead. This simple treatment of the lower panels helped to repel rain at the most vulnerable part of the door. In small houses the ceiling height was insufficient to accommodate six panels and four-panel doors were quite

usual. With the advent of the Classical Revival these panels were given emphasis by the use of an astragal moulding marking its margin. This fashion was all but universal by the early nineteenth century, at which time the edge of the panel was sometimes given 'colour' by carved flutes running at right angles to the astragal and with patera in the corners. Through all these changes in fashion simple ledge doors continued to be made.

Many woods were used in the making of doors and doorways. Early examples are mostly of oak and in the eighteenth century more pretentious establishments favoured mahogany. Hardwood doors certainly occasion fewer problems with fluctuating levels of humidity. By the early nineteenth century Loudon considered only one wood appropriate for smaller houses and cottages: '*Specification Joyners Work*: All inside framing, and all the outside work, to be of sound, well seasoned, dry yellow deal . . . To put proper door-cases (door cases are called proper when wrought, i.e. planed, framed and beaded) of fir (fir is generally applied by builders to Baltic timber; what they call pine generally comes from America . . .)'.[23] Loudon is here using the term 'deal' to imply softwood rather than its exact meaning: a 'scantling' – standard cross-sectional dimensions of timber and stone.

The ledge door was the product of carpenters and remained, in its essentials, unchanged for centuries although its reliance on the use of nails made it liable to split. In contrast the joiner-made framed door was constant in its adherence to sound principles of construction whilst remaining receptive to changing stylistic concerns. Similarly the architrave continued to respect the fashion of the day, but also served a fundamental, practical function in covering the junction between a wood door, or window frame, and its surrounding masonry. By this means the architrave masked the gap that would inevitably result when the timber door frame shrank away from its surrounding masonry. These architraves, from the simplest bolection moulding of the late seventeenth century to the austere reeded forms of the early nineteenth century, reflect not just the architectural styles of their time but also, by their precocious adoption or persistent use, their social background and geographical location.

Chapter 5

Windows

No feature is of such importance to both the interior and exterior of a house as is the judicious arrangement and proportion of its windows. Many eighteenth-century houses have such plain astylar façades that their quality and distinction is dependent upon their proportion and fenestration. Not that serious thought over such matters was confined to these simple, even austere, elevations of the Georgians. The Elizabethans and Jacobeans were similarly aware of the importance of windows and glazing in their often elaborate frontages. The opening sentence of Walter Gedde's *Sundry Draughts Principaly Serving for Glaziers and not Impertinant for Plaisterers and Gardiners* (London, 1615–16) is primarily concerned with the arrangement of lead cames and the pattern that they create: 'As the principal beautie, and countenance of Architecture, consists in outward ornament of lights, so inward partes are ever opposite to the eies of the beholder, taking more delight in the beauty thereof, being cuningly wrought, then in any other garnishing within the same.'

Primitive houses were both lit and ventilated by their doorways. The type is well represented by the so-called black houses of Scotland, the stone-built beehive huts of the Isle of Lewis and elsewhere (see p. 1 and Fig. 5) and by the somewhat similarly constructed pigsties of Wales which are also of stone. The tepee-like, conical shelters of turves laid on a timber framework made by charcoal burners also lack windows, as do the Saxon houses excavated at Erringham-above-Shoreham in Sussex which are similar in type to those which were recorded as still in use in Athelney, Somerset in the mid-nineteenth century (Fig. 1).[1] The Athelney example, being late in date, included a short funnel (made from a cider barrel) to take away the smoke from the fire. This 'smoke-hole', being wide in diameter and short in length, served as an auxiliary window. Another method of admitting light and air was, as we have seen, by means of the half-door, the lower part of which, when closed, served to keep farm animals out of the house. In Ireland double doors were used, one full-height and one half-height. In 1937 an octogenarian native of Cloganeely, Co. Donegal, remembered that in his youth 'The large door was always open, except in a storm; and the little door was always kept shut. It [the latter] kept out the hens and ducks and let in enough air and light.'[2]

Small wonder that when windows were introduced such unglazed orifices were known as the wind eye, the origin of our window (Fig. 114). The insertion of windows also caused problems of security, and Richard Carew in his *Survey of Cornwall* states that the 'ancient' houses of the county had windows that were 'arched and little, and their lights inwards to the court'.[3] In timber-frame buildings there was no structural necessity for the insertion of mullions but clearly such bars would serve to keep out intruders (Fig. 115). In stone buildings the mullions reduced the stress on the lintel which in turn was often assisted, especially in soft freestone districts, by a 'relieving arch'. The presence of these mullions also did away with the need for a monolithic lintel. With random stone walls, commonly 2 ft 6 ins (76.2 cm) in thickness, it was usual to splay the internal reveals to maximise daylight. This splay was generally symmetrical but, for practical reasons, where a window was off-centre to the space it illuminated, the splay could be asymmetrical.

The insertion of mullions divided a single window into a number of 'lights' or 'days'.[4] The top-floor windows in timber-frame houses in wool towns and cities such as Norwich are often very long and divided

into numerous lights. These are weavers' windows, as is frequently confirmed by the presence of shuttles found under floorboards in these rooms. In tall windows it was necessary to divide the void additionally by the introduction of horizontal members known as 'transomes'. In more important houses, of either timber or stone, the upper portion of the window, defined by a horizontal transome, was often reserved for tracery which is usually referred to in medieval documents as 'forms', 'form-pieces' and occasionally 'moulds'.[5]

Mullions, transomes and tracery were masoned, or hewn from wood, with sections of varying complexity. At their intersections these mouldings were worked, in wood as in stone, with the mason's mitre so characteristic of the medieval tradition. In the simplest windows of wood the mullions are square in section but set diamond-wise in the cill and lintel (Fig. 115). The plain rectangular opening is common, whilst the elaboration of 'plate tracery' or the 'fretted slab',[6] in either wood or stone, employs the rudimentary technique of simply being cut out of the solid. Such openings were often used

114   Window in the seventeenth-century gable of an otherwise nineteenth-century tollhouse at Freshford, near Bath. The window opening in this 2 ft-thick wall is a mere 1 ft by 1 ft 6 ins but the wide internal splay, the high lintel and the low cill maximise daylight.

115   Ground-floor mullioned window in a deserted house at Llwynau Mawr, Llanfihangel Cwm Du, Powys, Wales. Simple wood mullion windows such as this were common throughout England and Wales down to the early seventeenth century. Note the survival of the early internal shutters.

to provide 'borrowed light' within a house by piercing a screen or partition wall (Fig. 116).

Having made these apertures of various kinds it was necessary to find some means of reducing or suppressing the draught so created. Despite the presence of window glass in Roman Britain, its subsequent use in window openings was exceptional until the late sixteenth century. In remote parts of the British Isles glass long remained something of a luxury in domestic circumstances until the nineteenth century. This was true of the west of Ireland where many peasants made do without glass in their windows until comparatively recently. In 1939 an eighty-year-old in Feakle, Co. Clare, remembered 'scores of old houses that had neither glass nor doors. A sop o' hay took the place of glass and the doors were made of woven rods.'[7] Part of the reason for the slow introduction of glass in windows was the excise duty imposed on the basis of its weight. The process which resulted in the thinnest and therefore lightest material was crown glass, which is why it was far more widely used than either cylinder glass (labour-intensive production methods) or

plate glass (much the heaviest and most labour intensive). There were six qualities of crown glass of which the third rate, often used in glass houses, was known as 'Irish'.[8]

The draughts from unglazed windows were, at first, excluded by means of shutters which also eclipsed the light. With unglazed windows the shutters could be adjusted to help control the smoke in a house with a central hearth. In contrast to much of post-medieval Continental Europe shutters in England were usually hung on the inside walls. Fourteenth-century accounts use the word *fenestrae* to describe shutters and the translation of this word as 'window' has been generally considered incorrect or at least imprecise.[9] On the other hand a translucent shutter (i.e. panelled with waxed paper) would reasonably be described as a fenestral. In halls where windows occur on both sides of the room the shutters were closed on one side to exclude the prevailing wind, leaving the leeward side open to admit light and permit smoke from the central hearth to escape through this opening and through the roof. Various types of shutter were used including those that slid (horizon-

117　Detail of *The Annunciation* (*c.* 1425) by Robert Campin. The window is typical of an aristocratic house in early fifteenth-century Europe. The glazing is confined to the two lights above the transome and the lower part of the window is fitted with lattice. All these features were typical of lesser houses once glass became more available in late Tudor England. The modernisation of windows by the addition of glazing was a gradual process: window by window, room by room. Metropolitan Museum of Art (Cloisters Collection), New York.

116　'Borrowed light' was often an important feature inside houses. This example is pierced into a stud and plank screen and comes from Eyarth, Ruthin, Clwyd, Wales.

118   Mid-seventeenth-century oak shutters which open out into the reveals of this brick-built house known as 'Fulvens' at Abinger Hammer, Surrey. The mullions and transomes are worked from scantlings measuring 3½ by 3½ ins (8.75 cm), with battens added to form rebates.

tally or vertically) and others that were hung on hinges. Numerous types of hinge were devised, including the primitive pin hinge or its successors the strap, butterfly, and 'HL' hinges.

In higher status houses in which large windows were divided by transomes it was customary for the shutters to seal off the lower lights leaving the upper ones open at a level where the light would be advantageous but the draught would cause least discomfort. This feature may be seen in many early paintings such as the central panel of the altarpiece in St Pierre, Louvain, showing *The Last Supper* (1464–7) by Dieric Bouts. The slightly earlier *Marriage of Arnolfini* (1434) by Van Eyck shows that in some instances the upper lights were glazed, a feature which is also shown in the still earlier panel (*c.* 1425) by Campin (Fig. 117). In America this tradition persisted in the courthouses of Tidewater, Maryland, where the Oxford Courthouse of 1808 had 'wooden shutters for the lower part of the windows and glass for the upper'.[10]

In thick-walled stone or cob houses, shutters could simply be folded back within the splayed reveal of the window (Fig. 118). Where, however, thin walls and wide windows made this impossible the shutters were housed flat on the interior face of the wall (Fig. 119). In the Perley Parlor from an eighteenth-century timber-frame house from Boxford, Colonial Massachusetts (reconstructed at the American Museum in Britain) the shutters slide back into the space between the inner and outer skin of the wall. This simple expedient permits pictures to be hung on the piers between the windows. Sash shutters

119   A first-floor room in the late fifteenth-century lodging at Burwell, Cambridgeshire. Stone is a rare and valuable commodity in much of East Anglia which probably accounts for these remarkably thin walls: expensive in terms of labour, cheaper in terms of stone. Generally speaking, stone-built walls are thick enough to accommodate shutters in the reveals of windows. Where this is not possible they are opened flat into flanking recesses (as here) or into joiner-made boxes constructed for this purpose.

such as the early nineteenth-century examples in the old kitchen at Castle Bank, Appleby-in-Westmorland, similarly leave the intervening wall visible and therefore useable to stand furniture against or to hang pictures or curtains upon (Fig. 120). Shutters retain warmth and provide additional security. However, Charles Kingsley found conventional wooden shutters insufficiently secure in the parsonage at Eversley, Hampshire, and had steel ones fitted following the murder of a neighbour.[11]

The introduction of glazing later combined with the use of sashes encouraged the development of larger windows, despite which shutters remained in use. These larger windows demanded larger shutters which had to be housed when not in use. The problem was usually met by dividing the shutter vertically one or more times, enabling it to fold into the reveal of the window. By George III's reign shutters were required in such prodigious quantities that they, like sash windows, were produced in bulk by specialist joiners. For this reason they seem to have been made to standardised heights, for their variable width is usually accommodated by a central leaf which is not framed-up but comprises a single board which may be cut to a width appropriate to a particular window. Such shutters were designed to open out across the entire window, but in some instances oval apertures were cut in the upper panels for purposes of ventilation. Throughout history shutters have been constructed with the design and constructional elements found in the doors and panelling of their period.

We have seen that glazed windows were a considerable luxury in post-Roman Britain until the late sixteenth century, and William Harrison, writing shortly before 1577, describes the alternatives that were used:

> Of old time, our countrie houses, instead of glasse, did use much lattise, and that made either of wicker or fine rifts of oke in chekerwise. I read also that some of the better sort, in and before the times of the Saxons . . . did make panels of horne in steed of glasse, and fix them in woodden calmes. But as horne . . . is . . . quite laid downe in everie place, so our lattises are also growne into less use, bicause glasse is come to be so plentifull.[12]

The lightweight 'lattise' referred to by Harrison has seldom survived (Fig. 117) except where used internally as in the Kediminster pew (1613) at Langley Marish Church, Slough, Buckinghamshire, and in the 'new' chapel at Ightham Mote, Sevenoaks, Kent. On the other hand, the diaper of wooden laths that Harrison refers to was a feature that persisted, for domestic buildings, much later in remote parts of the British Isles and was used for even longer in workshop windows. Francis Stevens in *Views of*

120   Early nineteenth-century sash shutter shown in William Henry Hunt's (1790–1864) watercolour painting of *A Lady Reading* (detail). Yale Center for British Art: Paul Mellon Collection.

Cottages and Farm Houses in England and Wales (1815) includes a lithograph of a farmhouse at Seaton in Devonshire with lattice windows on the ground floor, and lattice doors were sometimes used for cheeserooms as they provided effective ventilation (Fig. 121).[13]

In his *Letters . . . in North Wales in 1798*, Evans describes 'lattices for the admission of light, formed of interwoven sticks'[14] which provided the ideal armature for carrying paper or linen, waxed to admit light. Windows were treated in this way from a very early date. In 1217 the town of Witney, Oxfordshire, spent 9d on 'linen cloth for the windows of the church'.[15] Such a feature was described by William Horman in his *Vulgaria*, published in 1519: 'Paper, or lyn clothe, straked a crosse with losynges, [to] make fenestrals in stede of glasen wyndowes' (Fig. 122).[16] Thomas More, whilst making sarcastic reference to the opulent use of glass windows in *Utopia* (1516 – 'They keep out draughts by glazing the

121   A wood lattice door in Widbrook Farm, Bradford on Avon, Wiltshire. The window lattice tradition survived best where ventilation was required as in dairy windows and doors. Widbrook Farm was built as late as the 1830s.

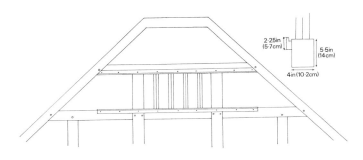

122   Fenestrals were constructed of such lightweight scantlings that the sliding rails that supported them are often remarkably slender. This example survives in an attic window in Leabridge Farmhouse at West Burton, West Sussex.

windows – oh yes, they use a great deal of glass there') also considered paper fenestrals to be perfectly adequate, for 'sometimes [they fit] screens of fine linen treated with clear oil or amber [gris], which has the effect of making it more transparent and also more airtight.'[17] Sir Hugh Platt in *The Jewel House of Art and Nature*, published in 1594, describes how to make parchment opaque for this purpose:

> . . . then straine: . . . [the finest, thinnest parchment] upon a frame . . . and when it is drie oile it all over with a pensill [brush], with oile of sweet Amonds, oile of turpentine, or oile of spike [lavender], some content themselves with linseed oile, and when it is thorow dry, it wil shew very cleere, and serve in windowes in stead of Glasse, especially in such roomes as are subject to overseers. You may draw anie personage, beast, tree, flower, or coate armour upon the parchment before it be oyled, and then cutting your parchment into square panes, and making slight frames for them, they will make a prettie show in your windowes, and keep the room verie warm. This I commend before oyled Paper, because it is more lasting, and will endure the blustring and stormie weather much better then paper.[18]

In 1937 an eighty-year-old in Glencolmcille, Co. Donegal, remembered that 'The houses in those days were not half the size they are now . . . There was a strip of sheepskin in the window instead of glass.'[19] Until the end of the nineteenth century 'harden', a kind of coarse sack-cloth, was used for many mud-built houses in East Yorkshire[20] (see Chapter 9, pp. 132–3 for the use of 'harden' or 'hurds' for stained hangings). On the Merionethshire/Denbighshire border some houses in the nineteenth century had but one window which the occupants contrived to fill with fixed glazing. This solitary glazed 'window' was traditionally broken on the death of the occupant to permit the soul to escape.[21]

As Thomas More's comments in his *Utopia* imply, glazed windows, in early Tudor England, were largely confined to the houses of the wealthy. Consequently they were often fitted into easily detachable casements and were not regarded as fixtures.[22] Even in the seventeenth century they were only to be found in the houses of the well-to-do. Aubrey states that 'Glass windows, except in churches and gentlemen's houses were rare before the time of Henry VIII. In my own remembrance before the Civil Wars, copyholders and poor people had none in Herefordshire, Monmouthshire, and Salop: it is still so.'[23]

Ancient methods of casting window glass in large sheets were (except for plate glass confined to a few windows in royal palaces) dispensed with in favour of blown glass. Because of the relatively small size of each piece of glass it was only possible to fill a large window opening by assembling many pieces within lead cames. The word 'pane' describes such an assemblage of small pieces to form one unit and was often applied to textiles as in 'counterpane'.[24] A sketchbook in the C. A. Buckler Collection in the British Library[25] shows that the designs used were almost as numerous as those for patchwork quilts. Walter Gedde's *Sundry Draughtes Principaly Serving for Glaziers* (London, 1615–16) illustrates no less than one hundred and eighty designs for leaded windows. In general, the diaper pattern was most commonly adopted (Figs. 121, 123) and continued the tradition established by the 'fenestrals' of split oak, in which the diagonal arrangement shed rainwater more effectively so that the wood laths, of which they were composed, were less liable to rot. Sir Hugh Platt, writing in the late sixteenth century, refers to Sussex window glass of adequate quality,[26] but much of the glass made in England then was produced by craftsmen from the Low Countries. In the late seventeenth century, when Dutch influence was at its height, great improvements were made in glass production in England partly as a consequence of an influx of Huguenot refugees some of whom were skilled glassmakers.

In late Elizabethan England there was a fashion, in both stone and timber building, for rather abrupt bow windows.[27] In terms of glazing these were possible because the small glass quarrels and the malleability of their lead cames permitted sufficient flexibility for them to be bent to conform to a given radius. With the introduction of sash windows in which the larger glass panes were held together with wood glazing bars, in place of lead cames, the bow window became, at first, impossible. The introduction of the vertically sliding sash window was closely associated with the emergence of a specialist class of joiner – the moulding-plane-maker.[28] It was only as their products gained in sophistication and the compass moulding plane was devised (probably in the late eighteenth century) that it was possible for the bow window to return to fashion. Sash windows at this date were generally made by specialist joiners who were 'tooled-up' to do this type of work.

In early sash windows the glazing bars are notable for their bulk – indeed they may measure as much as 2 by 2 ins (5 by 5 cm). Towards the close of the eighteenth century and particularly in the early nineteenth century this measurement had changed to $\frac{5}{10}$ by 1¾ins (1.59 by 4.45 cm). In early sashes the counter-balancing lead weights are hung in grooves hollowed out of the solid wood frame of the window, which itself is visible externally and is all but flush with the face of the building. Later cast-iron weights were hung in boxed-up frames.

123 Pierced lead ventilation quarrel, probably seventeenth century, from Witham, Essex. The best leaded windows were set in casements of wrought iron, inferior ones in wooden frames. For cheapness leaded lights were permanently fixed into position with occasional lead quarrels of this kind providing some fresh air.

To prevent the spread of fire from room to room, and in terraces from house to house, legislation was introduced for London in 1709 which stipulated that window frames should be set at least 4 ins (10.2 cm) back from the external face of the wall into which they were rebated so as not to be visible externally.[29] In a pre-bureaucratic age this was not easily enforced and in timber-frame buildings was all but impossible. Ultimately it would be the power of fashion which would eventually see the widespread adoption of these measures. Internally this external recessing of windows had the effect of reducing the apparent thickness of walls whilst giving a greater sense of bulk to the façade.

Simple sash windows dispensed with weights and relied solely on pegs or some similar device to hold the window open or closed. One British traveller in early Federal America complained that the room he was dining in had been built so rapidly that 'there had not been time to place any counterpoises, nor even any bolt

124   Group of three windows (not quite a Venetian window) in the first-floor front room of Ames Cottage, Freshford, near Bath. Note the wide glazing bars. Only the lower halves of these very early eighteenth-century sashes are movable.

or button to hold it up' so that the waiter was compelled to prop it open with a chair. The earliest know extant counterbalanced sash window dates from 1670. It was discovered walled-up in the surviving fragment of Charles II's house in Newmarket. This oak mullioned window has double-hung sashes in each of its two 'lights' and, whilst the sashes themselves are oak framed, the glazing is leaded. Furthermore the mullion is too narrow to house sash weights and cords which are confined to the hollowed-out oak jambs. This 'dug-out' approach evidently preceded the made-up construction of 'sash boxes' in subsequent decades.[30]

Due to lack of height, sash windows are sometimes divided horizontally into two unequal parts. In Holland this unequal horizontal division was usual and the upper section was generally immovable (a *chassis dormant*).[31] Many surviving late seventeenth or early eighteenth-century English sash windows share this feature (Fig. 124). In the first decade of the eighteenth century when

125   Early seventeenth-century vertically sliding shutters in the Old White Hart, Newark, Nottinghamshire. Although not counter-balanced such shutters may be seen as the precursors of the sash window.

Celia Fiennes visited Ashtead Park, Surrey, she noted the 'double sashes to make the house warmer for it stands pretty bleake'.[32] This almost sounds like a reference to double glazing but she is more likely referring to the double hung sash which is composed of two window frames of equal or approximately equal size, both hung and counter-balanced by means of pulleys and weights. Horizontally sliding sashes, where one half of the window slides across the other half, are found throughout the country but seem to be especially favoured in Yorkshire where they are known as 'Yorkshire lights'. M. W. Barley suggested that this may be a native version of the sash window and states that it is found all over the Midlands and the north where one of the earliest examples is at Moss Farm, near Doncaster, which was built in 1705. Late eighteenth-century examples set in seventeenth-century stone houses may be seen as far south as Cornwall. This very wide distribution owes much to economy, such windows were cheaper to make than counter-balanced sashes and, unlike casements, did not require expensive metal hinges.[33]

The whole question of the development of sash windows has been very fully examined by Hentie Louw but their ancestry in Britain remains obscure.[34] The early seventeenth-century vertically sliding shutters in the Old White Hart at Newark (Fig. 125), although not counter-balanced, suggest that the glazed sash window may derive from such precedents. C. F. Innocent has drawn attention to William Horman's reference (as early as 1519) to 'many pretty wyndowes shette with louys goynge up and downe',[35] which may refer to a sliding sash window. Certainly both the horizontal and the vertical-sliding shutter (or evidence of their presence) may be found in timber-frame houses in the south of England. The Metropolitan Museum possesses an interesting window with a 'guillotine' shutter (Fig. 126) which, being American, is late in date but early in character and, with its louvres, is close to Horman's description cited above.[36] The view that sash windows evolved in timber-frame buildings remains a matter for debate. Barley suggests that they 'must have originated in a region of brick building with wooden window frames'[37] – and yet the timber-frame White Hart Inn with its sash shutters would seem to contradict such a view. Sash shutters continued to be used in domestic buildings down to the late nineteenth century. A watercolour by William Henry Hunt (1790–1864) entitled *A Lady Reading* shows a late eighteenth or early nineteenth-century example in use (Fig. 120). In certain circumstances, for example by the sea, provision could be made in this way for security from the elements. For example No. 13 Brunswick Square, Hove, Sussex (built *c*.1823–34) designed by Charles A. Busby (1786–1834) has windows some of which carry as many as five sashes in one box,

the outermost layer being storm shutters.[38] Whatever the basis for the history of the evolution of the sash window they certainly appeared at Whitehall as early as 1669.[39] Celia Fiennes, in her journals (which were written between about 1685 and 1703), makes constant reference to this new fashion. Writing in 1697 about Blyth Abbey, which was rebuilt in 1684, she says that it was 'a very sweete House and Gardens and Grounds, it was of brick coyn'd with stone and the Windows with stone all sashes'.[40]

126   Late seventeenth-century window which may be from Plymouth Colony, Massachusetts. Its string-operated 'guillotine' shutter (just visible) may cover either the lower half of the louvre or the upper leaded light. Being partially glazed this window perpetuates the tradition exemplified in Fig. 117 whilst its shutter relates to Figs. 120, 125. Metropolitan Museum, New York.

127   *A farm kitchen at Clifton, York* as recorded in 1834 in a watercolour by Mary Ellen Best. Despite the presence of some up-to-date furniture, such as the dresser on the right, this interior exhibits many of the traditional features of 'the hall' in a vernacular farmhouse. These features include the casement window and its sparse curtain but above all we are shown the way in which such a living room also served as a place of work. Victoria and Albert Museum, London.

128   Casement window in the central pediment of Prior Park Buildings, Bath, *c.* 1821. Despite the very general use of the sash window in the eighteenth century, the casement was never completely displaced.

In eighteenth and even nineteenth-century houses sash windows are often only found on the principal floors and elevations of the house, attics and other less evident parts retaining casements. Indeed the casement window was never utterly outmoded and its use was generally retained for cottages (Fig. 127). In a few instances they appear as a significant motif in a scheme of sash windows as in the central pediment of the terrace of houses known as Prior Park Buildings, Bath (Fig. 128), which were built in 1821 almost certainly to the designs of John Pinch.

The familiar bull's-eye window of bottle glass now so popular in some suburban developments, was once considered 'the coarsest kind in common use'.[41] Whilst the use of such glass is today but unalloyed sentimentality the continued employment of casements is based on historical fact. The persistence of the casement window, glazed with small pieces of thin blown glass held together by

129   Designs for transparent blinds from Nathaniel Whittock's *The Decorative Painters' and Glaziers' Guide* (1827).

means of lead cames, may be entirely attributed to cheapness. Loudon, writing in the 1830s, makes this very clear: 'We do not like latticed windows because they are generally cold and gloomy; but as they are much cheaper than sashes hung with cords and pulleys, where economy is the main object, recourse must be had to them, or to iron windows. Windows cast of iron very fit for cottages are now made of different forms, and very cheap.'[42] Although casements had for long been made of wrought iron, the use of cast-iron window frames and glazing bars was an innovation of the later eighteenth century.[43] Such cast-iron windows were used by William Strutt for his cotton mills and for the cottages of his workers.[44]

No doubt because windows were few in number in poorer houses where the occupants could not afford glass, the window tax was seen as a method of taxing the rich, but in fact it fell most heavily on the middle classes. The Reverend John William, curate of Lincoln, paid 13s in window tax in 1751 on a house which he rented for £7 11s 4d per annum.[45] It was first levied in England in 1697 in an attempt to defray the cost of making up the deficiency caused to the Exchequer by the clipping of silver coinage. This tax, in addition to the duty payable on the purchase of glass, was assessed according to the number of windows on houses worth more than £5 per annum and with more than six windows, the maximum

130   Detail of a window blind
62½ by 102 ins, mid–nineteenth
century, stained onto Scotch
cambric using dyes bound in
isinglass. Ex Collection:
Judkyn/Pratt.

dimensions of each taxed window being 11 ft (3.35 m) in height and 4 ft 9 ins (1.45 m) in width.[46] Windows in dairies were exempt, which is why buildings or rooms serving this purpose were commonly labelled as such. The window tax was increased six times between 1747 and 1808 but was reduced in 1823. It was abolished, appropriately, in 1851, the year of the Crystal Palace. Many windows were blocked in response to this tax. However, not all 'blind' windows are examples of this. The classical concern with symmetry often necessitated the use of bogus windows to give balance to a facade and/or to reduce the weight of the masonry over voids such as doors and windows. One way of distinguishing

between blocked windows and those which were intended to be 'blind' is that in the latter the stonework or brickwork is 'bonded in'.

In addition to shutters, windows were sometimes furnished with blinds (shades) although curtains were rare in vernacular dwellings until the second quarter of the nineteenth century. Only with industrialisation would textiles, such as carpets and curtains, become cheap enough to be within range of most householders. Economic historians like Lorna Weatherill have shown, through the statistical analysis of probate inventories, how seldom curtains are listed in the century between 1660 and 1760. Furthermore the production of an inventory suggests a degree of prosperity – despite which only about 13 percent of her sample of inventories list curtains, although the figure was higher in London.[47]

By the nineteenth century Nathaniel Whittock in *The Decorative Painters' and Glaziers' Guide* (1827) (Fig. 129) gives instructions for the making of painted window blinds. These may be seen as the successors to the 'fenestrals' of waxed and painted paper or cloth and which, in the techniques used to decorate them, relate to the work of the 'stainers' (see pp. 130–8). In the eighteenth century silk was used for such blinds (see Appendix III 8 April 1786) but in the following century Scotch cambric was favoured (Fig. 130). These 'transparencies' were primarily designed to be used during hours of daylight to reduce the tendency of the sun to bleach both wood and textiles (Fig. 131). Holland and Venetian blinds are sometimes painted in *trompe l'oeil* on external elevations where blank or blocked windows occur.[48] Manufacturers of window blinds in London are mentioned in Ambrose Heal's *The London Furniture Makers* and I have found others in the Heal Collection in the British Museum, Department of Prints and Drawings. The following list is not comprehensive but serves to indicate how widespread the use of window blinds was in eighteenth-century London:

Thomas Atkinson, 1755
John Brown, 1730. Took over the business of
    William Rodwell who advertised in 1727
Henry Buck, 1741–50
James Cox, 1753–62
William Darby, 1760 and 1770
Richard Elliot, *c.* 1780
William Gwinnell, 1741
John Hatt, 1759–79 (successor to John Arrowsmith)
William Kirk, 1749
Landall and Gordon, *c.* 1750
Charles Legg, *c.* 1750
John Newman, 1755
Francis Pyner, 1765–92
Benjamin Rackstrow, 1738
William Rodwell, advertised 1727
Nathaniel Skinner, 1730
John Whitcomb, *c.* 1760
John White, *c.* 1750

Manufacturers of window blinds were even more numerous in the nineteenth century and they were often made, or at least provided, by jobbing builders and undertakers (funeral directors) such as W. Thompson of Chenies Street, Tottenham Court Road, London (*c.* 1860) or I. O'Brien who made 'Venetian, Parlour, Spring, Roller and Outside Blinds in Cases' (*c.* 1820).

John White's label listed above reads: 'Pictures Painted, Mended, Cleaned, and Framed, Blinds for Windows Painted on Canvas or Wire . . . At the Golden Head, Shoe Lane, Fleet Street, London.' Quite what form such wire window blinds took in the eighteenth century is uncertain but reference to them is rare and often confined to one important room in an imposing house. When Robert Walpole, 1st Earl of Orford's home in Chelsea was sold in April 1747 following his death in 1745, 'his Lordship's dressing Room, on the Ground floor' included a lot containing 'A walnut tree corner cupboard, a frame of a cabinet and 2 brass wire window blinds'.[49] This was apparently the only room in the house to have such blinds and the lot fetched the not inconsiderable sum of 15s, a figure which may be attributed to the blinds rather than the other items in the lot because, like textiles, all metalwork was expensive in pre-industrial Britain. The '10 pieces [of] flywire 3 feet 1 inch square' listed in the 1770 'Inventory of the Personal Estate of his Excellency Lord Botetourt', the Colonial Governor of Virginia, were valued at £10–15, more than the cost of two hundred panes of window glass in the Colony. The dimensions of these 'flywires' or insect screens show that they were intended for use in sash windows as does their location in the inventory together with 'pullies for sashes' and 'brass jointed rings for shutters'.[50]

131   A transparent blind shown in use in this detail from E. L. Henry's painting *Totally Absorbed* of 1874. Such blinds were intended for use during hours of daylight which is why they were treated as 'transparencies'.

132a,b 'Drapery' (*left*) and 'festoon' (*right*) curtains produced a rich effect with a frugal use of cloth. The dotted lines indicate the points along which the cords would travel through rings between the curtain and its lining.

These wire-gauze blinds were often painted decoratively, a feature that would not be visible from indoors by daylight. Only in rich households where candles were used in abundance would this decoration be seen clearly at night. John Brown in the 1730s made and sold all sorts of chairs and cabinet work and also stocked 'Blinds for Windows made and Curiously Painted on Canvas, Silk or Wire'.[51] The application of paint to brass wire must have presented numerous problems as the paint would tend to peel off such a surface in a position as exposed as a window. This problem is implicit in the following information given in another label dated 1729 in the Heal Collection:

> made and sold Window Blinds of all sorts, painted in Wier Canvas, Cloth, and Sassenet, after the best and most lasting manner ever yet done so that if ever so dull and dirty they will clean with sope and sand and be like new; where may be seen great choice of the same being always about them. Likewise at the same place is made the new fashion Walnut Tree Window seat cases to slip off and on.

No wire-gauze blinds or window screens appear to have survived from the eighteenth century although a satirical print of *Byng's Ghost* of 1757 seems to illustrate a folding room screen with gauze panels.[52] By the nineteenth century Loudon alludes to 'short inside wire blinds, [which] are not unsuitable for the better description of cottages'.[53] In late nineteenth-century towns and cities wire-gauze window screens were used in ground-floor rooms and painted externally to advertise the commercial nature of the premises they occupied.

Despite the prevalence of painted linen or cotton blinds in the nineteenth century few seem to have survived.[54] Certainly Nathaniel Whittock gives elaborate instructions on how to apply decorative painting to blinds of 'Scotch cambric or lawn'. Small blinds were apparently painted with pigments held in a medium of isinglass dissolved in boiling water, 'but for large blinds the dimensions of a common sash window parchment size' was used. Designs for blinds of this type are illustrated in Whittock's book, one splendid example showing a classical landscape with architectural fragments. Another illustration shows a 'blind properly strained on a framework resembling a quilting frame'. Whittock states that such work was well within the abilities of the housepainter who, when he has 'succeeded in painting landscapes in distemper on walls or in water colour on paper, will find he has acquired the power of painting transparent blinds' (Figs. 129, 130).[55]

The abundant use of metalwork and textiles for interiors before the industrialisation of Britain was evidence of wealth. The use of billowing drapery in a seventeenth and eighteenth-century portrait may thus be seen as more than an artistic device but as an example of 'conspicuous consumption'. As John Fowler and John Cornforth have pointed out, it was for these reasons that the 'upholder' (upholsterer), as the main specialist in one of the most expensive household commodities, generally became the principal contractor in the furnishing of a house of high social standing: he was the interior decorator. In small houses no such specialist would be summoned or required, for curtains were used in such contexts either sparingly or not at all.

It was probably the frugal use of textiles that made window blinds so popular – a simple width of cloth with nothing lost in folds: 'The roller blind, being much the cheapest, may be considered the most suitable for common cottages.'[56] The draw curtain was used sparingly in the eighteenth century as it was inclined to require lavish amounts of cloth. 'Festoon' curtains where drawstrings pull the curtain up vertically, and 'drapery' curtains where the drawstrings pull the curtain up diagonally and apart into a pair of swags, were also relatively economical in the use of fabric (Fig. 132a,b). This meant that although they were sumptuous in appearance when pulled up, and despite the fact that they were relatively complicated to make, householders could afford to fit them to more windows. This is confirmed by Loudon who describes a type of venetian curtain consisting of 'a piece of dimity, or other material . . . [nailed] to a flat piece of wood, in one end of which are inserted two pulleys; while two others are let into it, one in the middle and the other at the opposite extremity. Three pieces of tape are sewed down the curtain, one on each side, and

133   An interior at 14 St James's Square, Bristol in *c.* 1806. The watercolour may well be by a member of John Pole's family as he is known to have lived in the house at this time – perhaps a self portrait of the artist (his daughter?) is included in the composition. Even in a fine middle-class interior such as this the curtain is lavishly deployed although textiles are not abundantly used. Note the fashionably-narrow glazing bars of the early nineteenth century. Bristol City Museums and Art Gallery.

one in the middle, to which are affixed small rings, at regular intervals.'[57] Cords passing through these rings and up and over the pulleys raised the curtains when pulled.

Once the mechanisation of the textile industry was accomplished textiles could be used more lavishly and the draw curtain became general in the mid-nineteenth century, by which time they were known as 'French curtains'. In general the smaller, simpler and earlier the house the fewer the textiles that would have been used (Fig. 133).

Chapter 6

Floors

Beaten earth floors are so basic as to be timeless and universal. In some parts of Britain they have been found in houses within living memory and doubtless are still in use. They were the rule rather than the exception in much of Ireland, Wales and Scotland until the early 1900s, despite the use of tiled floors at a high social level in thirteenth-century England.[1] The 'ground floor' was justly named.

The farmer Henry Best of Elmswell in the East Riding of Yorkshire, writing in the second quarter of the seventeenth century, gives instructions on making such floors.[2] The earth was first dug and raked and then mixed with prodigious quantities of water, the resulting mixture being as soft as mortar. After about two weeks *in situ* the mixture was sufficiently 'leather hard' to be beaten smooth with broad, flat pieces of wood, and blemishes were mended with clay or 'clottes from the faugh field'. Local knowledge played its part in the selection of the type of clay and Best remarks that 'wee use to digge and leade clay for our barne from John Bonwickes hill'. In Armagh, Ulster, the floor was sometimes simply dug up and trampled down again and according to Binns in *The Miseries and Beauties of Ireland* (1837), 'They sometimes have a dance for that purpose.'[3]

The experience of the Weald and Downland Museum in Sussex has shown that such floors would have to be remade fairly regularly. In an attempt to prevent them breaking up, bones were either mixed with the mud or driven into the floor to form a pattern, as is described by Dean Aldrich (a contemporary of Wren's) in his *Elements of Architecture*.[4] An example of this type of floor used as external paving in Broad Street, Oxford, consisted of 'trotter bones laid in a pattern of squares arranged angle-wise within a border. The pattern was defined by bones about 2 in. square, rubbed or sawn to an even surface, and filled in with small bones of sheep's legs, the knuckles uppermost, closely packed and driven into the ground to a depth of from 3 in. to 4 in.'[5] This interesting pavement was destroyed in 1869 but similar floors survive in eighteenth-century grottoes. So long as this type of surface remained undamaged it had a long life but (as with parquet) the removal of one bone resulted in the successive and rapid collapse of its neighbours. In these floors the mud was not so much the floor as the matrix which held its components together.

True mud floors generated much unwelcome dust. The rushes that were laid over them also caused problems with pollen which the regular use of earthenware watering 'cans' served to mitigate (Fig. 134). The use of rushes underfoot remained traditional in Caernarvonshire where, up to the early years of the last century, 'rushes and fern would be strewn on the floor'.[6] In 'Norwegian farmhouses where so many of our ancient customs still [1862] exist' juniper twigs were spread on the floor.[7] Sir Hugh Platt in *The Jewel House of Art and Nature* (1594) recommended that floors should be made of a composition of fine clay tempered with ox blood.[8] Such a mixture would also serve for rendering an internal wall and, so Platt claimed, resulted in a smooth, glistening and hard surface. In some parts of Caernarvonshire earth floors were washed with water containing soot which produced a hard, shiny surface.[9] In Snowdonia a very different alternative to soot was to give earth floors a coat of whitewash, although this was more usually applied only to the perimeter of the room.[10]

Erasmus, in his well-known description of houses in England, was obsessed with the filth that he found underfoot in English interiors:

134   Earthenware watering pot used for gardening but also, in interiors, for laying the dust caused by rush-covered floors.

Again almost all the floors are of clay and rushes from the marshes so carelessly renewed that the foundation sometimes remains for twenty years, harbouring there below spittle and vomit and urine of dogs and men, beer that hath been cast forth and remnants of fishes and other filth unmentionable. Hence, with the changes of weather, a vapour exhales which in my judgement is far from wholesome for the human body.[11]

Not for nothing was the area below the dais in larger houses sometimes known as the 'marsh'.[12] In fact, the interesting conglomerate of matter which such floors absorbed was of great importance to the 'saltpetre man'. In the search for nitre much inconvenience and friction was caused by this official whose officers pulled up the floors of cottages and even churches looking for this important ingredient in the manufacture of gunpowder.[13]

The so-called grip floor (composed of a mixture of lime and ash) was a great improvement on mud or clay. Thomas Rudge describes this in a cottage in Gloucestershire in 1807. A moist mixture of lime and ash was laid to a depth of between 4 and 5 ins (10 and 12.7 cm) and worked and rammed with a heavy slab of wood; and to this, Isaac Ware (1757) recommends the addition of 'smith's dust'.[14] William Marshall describes similar floors in his *Rural Economy of Yorkshire*, published in 1787. In Derbyshire such 'plastered' floors were laid in upper rooms on laths and, further south, on straw.

In Leicestershire and other districts, where good lime is to be had, many of the old floors were formed altogether of plaster. In place of floor boards laid on the

layer of reeds 2 ins or 3 ins well-tempered plaster is spread and thoroughly floated over and brought to a smooth surface. This gets almost as hard as cement concrete, and the under surface of the reeds is plastered to form the ceiling.[15]

A good example of a plaster floor in an upper room is to be found in the attic of the fifteenth-century George Inn at Norton St Philip, Somerset. Isaac Ware suggests that at least some floors of this type were for 'good houses' and that by adding other ingredients to plaster of Paris they 'may be coloured to any hue . . . some of it looking like porphiry'[16] – but this must be a reference to scagliola and is thus beyond our present concerns.

It could be supposed that the use of tiles for flooring was most widespread in the eastern counties where, thanks to influence from the Low Countries, bricks first made their reappearance in post-Roman Britain (discounting the reuse of Roman bricks in such structures as St Alban's Cathedral). However, in Norwich beaten clay floors remained in common use in domestic buildings throughout the sixteenth century until clay 'pamments', fired to a yellow or orange colour and measuring 12 by 12 ins (30.5 cm) or 9 by 9 ins (22.9 cm) and between 1½ and 2 ins (3.8 and 5 cm) thick, began to be introduced.[17] Very similar tiles were used in Ulster in the nineteenth century, but examples in Northern Ireland had a series of parallel holes drilled horizontally through their thickness which served to insulate the floor from the cold ground in winter. An example of a floor with these 'English tiles' may be seen in the 1717 Lismacloskey House from Co. Antrim now at the Ulster Folk and Transport Museum (Fig. 135). The use of the word 'pamment' in East Anglia for clay tiles is paralleled by the word 'pennant' (a blue stone paving slab used in the Bristol/Bath area and South Wales), from the Welsh for 'head of the valley'.

In the eighteenth century and onwards paving bricks for both internal and external use became popular in those districts that did not have access to suitable, which is to say hard-wearing, stone. The colour of these bricks was conditioned by the nature of the available clay and the temperature at which they were fired, but red was the most common. In and around Norwich they were of an orange or yellow hue and measured about 8 by 4 ins (20 by 10 cm) and about 1½ to 2 ins (3.8 to 5 cm) thick. Such bricks lacked a 'frog' (Fig. 36).

The use of stone for flooring seems to have been less widespread than its employment in the construction of walls. Undoubtedly the reason for this must be that much of the stone of these islands is soft freestone which, once masoned, is case-hardened by the silica or 'quarry sap' which comes to the surface to form a protective skin.

When used in flooring this skin would soon be worn through so that the extra expense of the paviour's work could not be justified unless the resulting floor was long lasting. Bath stone has been used for flooring which, as it wears, produces an often disastrous undulating surface. However, in some instances these freestone floors have lasted reasonably well, a tribute to the local knowledge of the hard 'beds'. Today insufficient quantities of stone are quarried (in the skilled meaning of the word) for adequate selection to be possible or this knowledge acquired.

Roach bed Portland and Purbeck stone was used, the abundant fossils providing, so to speak, a hard-wearing aggregate through the stone. Floors in the larger houses with which we are concerned were sometimes composed of slabs, measuring about 18 ins (45.7 cm) square, set diamond-wise in the floor. Their corners were cut leaving a space for small squares of Tournai marble (also known as Belgian Black) or even slate. The hall floor at Chippenham Park, Cambridgeshire, was of this type and described by Celia Fiennes as 'paved with freestone a squaire of black marble at each corner of the freestone'.[18] Whilst in Cornwall in 1698 she made the following notes in her journal:

Bastable [Barnstable] and the north sea [sea to the north of Cornwall] which conveys the stone or rather marble [in fact slate] which they take from hence a

135   The living room in the late eighteenth-century Lismacloskey House from Toome Bridge, Co. Antrim, as reconstructed in the Ulster Folk and Transport Museum. This two-storey farmhouse is typical of a 'planters' house, as are the 'English' tiles on the floor which are alternate grey-blue and buff. The hanging cup-hooks (right) and the folding table fixed to the wall (left) are typical of the Province.

Bole [Delabole] . . . remarkable Quarrys for a black stone exceeding hard and glossy like marble very durable for pavements; this they send to all parts in tyme of peace and London takes off much of it.[19]

In Sussex a hard white stone was often used in the eighteenth century for floors and occasionally the Sussex 'winkle stone' may be found. This material resembles Purbeck 'marble' (in fact a hard limestone which will bear a friction polish – it was made popular, by William of Sens, in the late twelfth century for internal architectural use).[20]

In her journals Celia Fiennes gives particular credit to those towns which are well paved. In Dorchester, Dorset, for example, 'the streets are very neatly pitch'd and of good breadth'.[21] Such paving was composed of wedge-shaped pieces of stone rammed edgewise into the ground by means of a beetle. The stone was in fact 'pitched', which is to say it was 'pitched off' a block of stone with a 'pitcher' and a 'pitching hammer'.[22] Paving of this kind was also used inside houses, and examples have been recorded in Wales (Powys (Fig. 136) and Dyfed),[23] and in England (Cheshire, Derbyshire, Devon, Hampshire and the Isle of Wight, Herefordshire, Lancashire, Northamptonshire, Somerset and Wiltshire).[24] Pitched stone paving was often arranged in patterns and sometimes incorporated white pebbles with the initials of the paviour.[25]

The great problem with stone floors was that they were not only hard underfoot but they were also cold and often damp. Modern damp-proof membranes (polythene sheeting) can be laid under paving to solve this problem. Some materials, such as slate and granite, are themselves supreme damp-proofing materials by comparison with which most contemporary products are mere substitutes. A traditional slate floor is dry, except at the joints, although it will cause condensation to form in cold weather. In Gwynedd, Wales this damp-proofing feature was put to good effect by paving the perimeter of a room with slate so as to protect the furniture that stood on it (Fig. 272).[26] Transport was always a problem, especially with heavy materials unless they were 'water-borne', but in slate-producing districts the size of flooring slabs could be truly gigantic, as at the Penparcau Tollhouse (now at the Museum of Welsh Life, Cardiff) where a number of the slates are about 5 ft (1.5 m) square (Fig. 137).

In most humble houses mud long remained in use for floors, except for the hearthstone and the threshold (Fig. 138). Stone was reserved for these two features which retained a semi-mystical significance and survived the brutalising impact of repetitious rows of back-to-back houses in the industrial heart of England where, against all the odds, housewives continued to whiten or redden their doorsteps daily. For this purpose street traders pro-

136 'Pitched' stone floor in a house at Penrhyiw, Trefeglwys, Powys, Wales. Pitched paving of this kind, indoors or outside, was done segment by segment, each segment being contained by timber forms – which were then replaced by larger 'pitched' stones. A practical requirement put to decorative effect.

vided the lump whitening or the yellow material made in Bridgwater, Somerset and known as 'Bath brick', or another version called 'Flanders brick'[27] which was often bartered in exchange for empty bottles.

> As through the streets I takes my way
> With my bag at my back so gay,
> Crying out 'hearthstones' all day,
> 'Hearthstones!' and 'Flanders brick!'
> A penny a lump, a penny a lump!
> Who'll buy, buy-y-y-!?[28]

The tradition for decorating doorsteps and hearthstones with designs of a calligraphic character is known in Scotland where it is recorded in Strathclyde, Lothian, Dumfries and Galloway, Central Region, Fife and Grampian (Fig. 139).[29] This type of decoration was also applied to floors in the north of England, and in Yorkshire milk was used to darken the stone floors on which curlicues were drawn around the border of the room 'with a piece of light coloured sandstone after each week's cleaning'.[30] Because the designs were fugitive they were generally renewed every Saturday in anticipation of 'Sunday best'. In Wales, white clay was dug in the Holyhead district and in Llyn, and sold in dry balls for the decoration of floors and hearthstones. The patterns were mainly confined to the perimeter of the room with par-

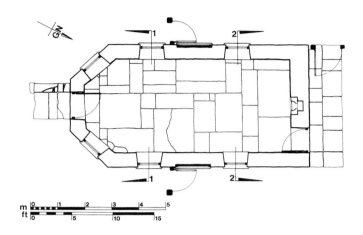

137 Plan of the Penparcau Tollhouse now moved to the Museum of Welsh Life. Note the large dimensions of some of the slate paving slabs.

138 Farmstead from Ostenfeld, Schleswig-Holstein, dated 1685, as reconstructed at the Frilandsmuseet, Copenhagen. The 'house-part' is approached from the barn across the threshing-floor, or threshold. The whole complex is under one roof.

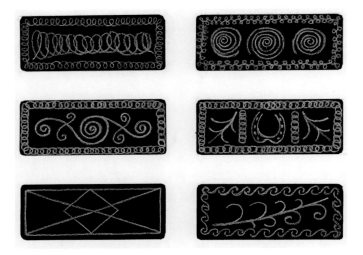

139   Scottish designs for decorating doorsteps (after Lyons 1935). Similar patterns were used on hearthstones and floors in England and Wales and may have originated from apotropaic marks – Figs. 37, 38, 99. Peter Brears (*North Country Folk Art*, 1989) records examples in Yorkshire.

ticular emphasis being accorded to the dresser and long-case clock.[31] In his seminal book *The Evolution of the English House*, first published in 1898, Sidney Addy gives a good description of such work in Derbyshire where

> 'pot moul' and 'rubbing stones' are used for the decoration of floors. Some women make spots on the hearth. This is done by dipping a piece of rag into a basin of 'pot moul', or pipe-clay, moistened with water. Either the whole or part of the stone floor is covered by squares drawn by means of a sharpened piece of pipe-clay used like a crayon, and sometimes a small flower is drawn in the middle of each square.[32]

Sand was another material that is sometimes referred to as having been swept into patterns, but information on this is rather vague, and there is even doubt as to whether sand or sandstone was used. In Lancashire, stone doorsteps, both tread and riser, were dampened, 'and to the damp surface . . . [was] applied dry sand or sand-stone'.[33] According to some accounts the red, yellow or white sand was strewn in patterns around the perimeter of kitchen floors and passages in Yorkshire and a similar tradition existed in New England. These patterns were very similar to those employed for floors, doorsteps and hearthstones.[34] In sculleries the wash tub was often sur-rounded by such decoration as evidence that the week's washing was finished and the 'copper' would not be used for another week – an embellishment as a mark of triumph. Addy describes the use of sand in this way in

Derbyshire as follows: 'The threshold is usually sanded, and a serpentine line or letter S made in the sand. This decoration is done by a brush, and women rarely omit it. They are very particular about keeping patterns clean from one Saturday to another, on which day they are renewed.'[35] In many regions this sand became an article of trade commemorated in the old 'round' song:

> White sand and grey sand!
> Who'll buy my white sand?
> Who'll buy my grey sand?

Certainly in the north of England (and in America) it was customary for the floor of farmhouse kitchens and the public bar of inns and ale houses to be strewn with sand just as in the south of England such establishments favoured sawdust. The last such floor known to the author was in an eel and pie shop in Greenwich in the late 1950s. Today many butchers continue to spread sawdust on their floors to absorb blood from the car-casses, and damp sawdust, like used tea-leaves, has of course long been employed to suppress rising dust when sweeping floors.

The decoration of floors with sand or whitening was exceedingly temporary and paint was used on timber floors with more permanent yet still ephemeral results. It is known that in aristocratic and gentry houses floors were decorated in this way, and examples survive at Belton House, Lincolnshire, Crowcombe Court, Somerset, and the Lindens, Washington, DC (removed from Danvers, Massachusetts, in the 1930s by the late Judge and Mrs George Morris).[36] Louisa Goldsmith's watercolour drawing (*c.* 1818) of the White Room at Aubrey House, London, shows a floor painted or stained with a series of pale octagons arranged at intervals (not touching) on a darker ground. Each octagon occupies three 6-in (15.2 cm) boards (Fig. 140).[37] In settings of grandeur such floors may have been conceived as fleeting pleasures, as were those decorated with whitening in humble households. Such a possibility is indicated by Wordsworth's lines:

> These all wear out of me, like Forms with chalk
> Painted on rich men's floors for one feastnight.[38]

Despite the widespread use of painted and decorated floorboards in small domestic interiors in America I have not succeeded in locating surviving examples, in which the entire floor is treated decoratively, in small houses in Britain.[39] However, I have found early nineteenth-century floors painted with one colour. Loudon refers to this as follows:

> When a parlour carpet does not cover the whole of the floor, there are various ways of disposing of the margin between it and the wall. Some recommend oil-

cloth, others baize, drugget, coarse broadcloth, or brown linen; for our part, we greatly prefer to any of these, painting that part of the boards of the floor which is not covered with the carpet, of the same colour as the woodwork of the room.[40]

John Claudius Loudon (1783–1843) was born at Gogar near Edinburgh, and a particularly good example of one of these borders, with a Greek key pattern, has been recorded by Ian Gow at 3 Mansfield Place, Edinburgh (Fig. 141).[41] Sometimes the whole of the floor was painted if not decorated. In one early nineteenth-century example at Tollhouse, Freshford, Bath, the floors of the upper rooms were painted with a yellow ochre glazed over with a red ochre. Time and wear gave these surfaces a beautiful variation in colour. In America, yellow or red ochre were the colours favoured by the Shakers for their painted floors. It is tempting to see in these colours the influence of the earth floors treated with ox blood.

Ground-floor rooms were boarded in quite early times and there is even evidence for the use of split-timber floors in the Iron Age lake villages of Glastonbury.[42] These ancient examples, however, scarcely established a trend. A writ of Henry III orders a room on the ground floor of Windsor Castle to be 'boarded like a ship',[43] which implies the exceptional use of this feature. Even Richard Carew's *The Survey of Cornwall* of 1602 states categorically that the houses of the 'Yeomanrie of Cornwall' had 'no planchings [plankings]'.[44]

In general the central hearth made the roof space unusable for anything but storage. With the introduction of the chimney flue it became possible and useful to floor-in the attic for human occupation. As has been seen, plaster floors were sometimes used for upper rooms; doubtless they were cheaper. In the *General View of the Agriculture of Ayr* of 1811 William Aiton writes that 'the generality of farmhouses' in the late eighteenth century had attic floors of brushwood covered with divots of moss or grass.[45] Some authorities have seen the word 'solar', signifying a private upper room, as deriving from the Norman French *sol*, floor, and *solive*, a beam – which implies a timber floor.[46] Floorboards were clearly more suitable for upper rooms, but oak or elm was expensive and for this reason such boards were not always fixed, neither were they regarded as 'fixtures', as is confirmed by surviving wills. Testators like Gilbert Isaac of Rayleigh, Essex, found it necessary to state that he regarded various items as fixtures that are today accepted as such: 'all the glass in the windows of my house, the windows, doors, locks, bolts, benches, shelves, all the boards and planks in the garrets and upper chambers and floors beneath, nailed and unnailed, the gates and pales of my yard and iron work, as they now stand, to remain to

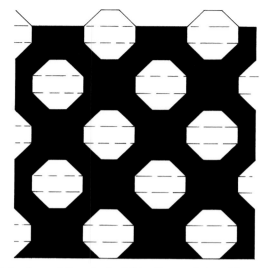

140 Stained wood floor in the White Room, Aubrey House, Kensington, London as recorded by Louisa Goldsmith in *c.* 1818 (John Cornforth, *English Interiors 1790–1848*, 1978, fig. 110).

141 Early nineteenth-century Greek key design painted on floorboards from a room at 3 Mansfield Place, Edinburgh.

the house' (1597).[47] The removable nature of floorboards that were not nailed in place may account for the term 'naked flooring' for the floor frame of joists, etc. (i.e. unclothed by boards or by a plaster ceiling beneath). By 1677, when Joseph Moxon began to publish his *Mechanick Exercises*, it was usual for boards to be nailed 'an Inch or an Inch and a half within the edge of the Board'.[48] In contrast to modern practice, he recommends that alternate boards should first be fixed and the intervening boards pushed into position by two or three men jumping on them assisted by 'Forcing Pins and Wedges'. The oak boards to which Moxon implicitly refers were used in substantial widths and thicknesses, 12 by 1 in (30.5 by 2.5 cm) being common, though in Norwich boards measuring as much as 16 ins (40.6 cm) wide have been encountered.[49] Hand-sawn boards often differed in width and thickness, a problem for carpenters on which Moxon gives advice:

> If the second Board prove thicker than the first, then with the adz (as aforesaid) they hew away the under side of that Board (most commonly cross the Grain, lest with the Grain the edge of the Adz should slip too deep into the Board) in every part of it that shall bare upon a Joyst, and so sink it to a flat superficies to comply with the first Board. If the Board be too thin, they underlay that Board upon every Joyst, with a Chip.[50]

The use of parquet floors was confined to grand establishments, but Celia Fiennes describes 'Mr. Ruths' (Rooth's) house in New Inn Lane, Epsom, a substantial house befitting Lady Donegal's husband. Its interiors were seen by Miss Fiennes between 1701 and 1703 and she states that instead of parquet 'the half paces [landings] are strip'd, the wood put with the graine, the next slip against the graine, which makes it looke pretty as if inlaid'.[51] This was a cheap way of achieving a rich effect in hardwood and may well have been employed in smaller houses.

Because of the natural strengths and weaknesses of timber it was usual, and is now general, for floorboards to be arranged so that they run at right angles to the joists that support them. This is true even where the use of a dragon beam in a house, jettied on two adjacent faces, results in the joists meeting the dragon beam at an acute angle; in such instances the floorboards above meet in a mitre or, for preference, are placed in echelon. However, what was usual and logical was not at first universal, and some fifteenth and sixteenth-century floorboards are placed on the same axis as their supporting joists, although these boards are extra thick for strength. In these cases the boards are rebated into the joists so that the upper faces of these joists serve also as alternate floor 'boards' – as was the case with the fifteenth-century floor (now destroyed) from 6–8 High Street, Bromsgrove (Fig. 142) and a surviving floor (with new boards) at Chester House, Knowle, Warwickshire. A related but later example of this type, once in Dove Hill Houses, Endcliffe, Sheffield (now destroyed), is recorded where alternate boards were sufficiently stout to double as joists.[52] Floorboards were often lapped and also tongued and grooved.

From the eighteenth century onwards softwood floors became more common, but oak was always preferred, with elm (very liable to warp) as a less good alternative to softwood. Henry Best refers to the purchase of 'firredeales' in Hull in 1641. He states that they were 'brought from Norway' and recommends 'reade-deale which is allmost as durable as oake, and will not worme-eate so soon as white deale; besides they are handsomer and better, both for smell and colour; and (for the most parte) better flowred'. The word 'deal', now used as a vague term for second-rate softwood, once referred to the cross-sectional dimensions (the scantlings) of planks. Best describes the boards he used as 'full twelve foote longe, full twelve ynches in breadth, somewhat more than ynch thicke'.[53] By the middle of the nineteenth century deal floorboards were commonly about ¾ in (2 cm) thick and from 7 to 9 ins (17.8 to 22.9 cm) wide, 'but for better floors a width of only 3 inches to 5 inches [7.6 to 12.7 cm] is used. The advantage of the narrow boards is that the shrinkage and warping have not so much effect on the spaces between.'[54]

142   Oak floor/ceiling of the late fifteenth century from a house demolished in 1962 at 6–8 High Street, Bromsgrove, Worcestershire. Whilst the summer beam is at right angles to the joists in the customary way, the thick floorboards are on the same axis to the joists into which they are rebated. A similar example survives (with restored floorboards) at Chester House, Knowle, West Midlands. C. F. Innocent (*The Development of English Building Construction*, 1916) recorded a much later example of a floor framed in this way in Sheffield in which thick boards alternated with still thicker ones.

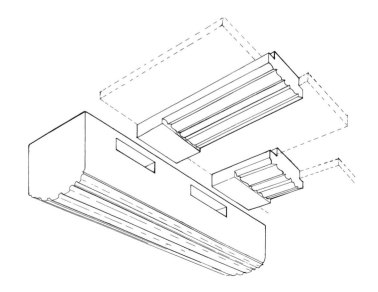

To some extent it was possible, by the late eighteenth century, to gauge not only the importance of a house but also the status of individual rooms according to their type of flooring. In 1787 John March, carpenter of Stoney Middleton, Derbyshire, submitted an estimate for demolishing and rebuilding the parsonage at Godington. The parlour was to have an oak floor, the bedrooms white deal and the garrets elm, whilst the dairy was to be paved with stone or brick.[55]

In France, where parquet floors achieved astonishing elaboration, wood floors in large houses were polished, in the eighteenth century, by a specialist servant known as a *frotteur*.[56] Caroline Halsted writing in 1837 states that 'even in the present day in France . . . parquets . . . [are] kept constantly rubbed with wax, by men who have brushes affixed to their shoes for the purpose'. She also mentions 'highly-polished oak, as is still visible in many an ancient picture gallery, and in staircases, libraries, and best apartments of old manor houses'.[57] Despite these observations it seems that, in the eighteenth century, floors were dry-rubbed with sand and sometimes swept over with herbs to give rooms a clean scent. This was certainly recommended by Hannah Glass in her *Servants Director* of 1760. At a more modest level it is likely that a mixture of beer and sand was used for scrubbing floors. This had the effect of giving wood a bleached appearance with the soft grain cut back to reveal the full 'figure' of the timber. In 1772 this was described as giving floors in English houses 'a whitish appearance, and an air of freshness and cleanliness'.[58]

Eighteenth-century genre paintings by artists such as Arthur Devis show that even the inhabitants of gentry houses were content with bare floorboards in their interiors. In medieval and Tudor England carpets imported from the east, as well as from Brussels, were reserved for use as 'table carpets' or for press cupboards. There are a few exceptions to this rule as in Isaac Oliver's portrait of Richard Sackville, 3rd Earl of Dorset (1589–1624), in which a rich oriental carpet is shown ostentatiously on the floor.[59] However, even at this social level it is carefully placed upon a woven straw mat and indeed such mats were the more usual way of furnishing floors at this date (Fig. 143). Matthew Paris graphically describes the indignation of medieval Londoners at the sight of the youthful Archbishop Elect of Toledo and his entourage. 'They remarked that the manners [of the Spanish] were utterly at variance with English customs and habits; that while the walls of their lodgings in the Temple were hung with silk and tapestry, and the very floors covered with costly carpets, their retinue was vulgar and disorderly; that they had few horses and many mules.'[60] This 'extraordinary' custom of placing carpets on floors was noted when Eleanor of Castille arrived at Westminster where she found her apartments adorned (through the care of the ambassador) with rich hangings 'like a church and carpeted after the Spanish fashion'.[61]

143   The parlour at Kennixton Farmhouse, *c.* 1630, from Llangennydd on the Gower Peninsula as reconstructed at the Museum of Welsh Life. The rush mat on the floor is modern but is of a type once common before the introduction of carpets. The typically Welsh tridarn on the right is dated 1702.

144   Marram-grass mat, twentieth century, of a type once commonly made on the Welsh coast. In the late seventeenth and early eighteenth centuries they were also made in Cornwall. This example is about 2 ft 6 ins (76.3 cm) in width. Museum of Welsh Life, Cardiff.

Inventories, wills and sale catalogues reaffirm what the eighteenth-century pictures suggest – floor coverings were rare. When the contents of the Earl of Orford's house in Chelsea were auctioned in April 1747 not one carpet was included, but there were a number of references to mats which may well have been of a type described by Carew in *The Survey of Cornwall* (1602):

> The women and children in the West of *Cornwall*, doe use to make Mats of a small and fine kinde of bents there growing, which for their warme and well wearing, are carried by sea to *London* and other parts of the Realme, and serve to cover floores and wals. These bents grow in sandy fields, and are knit froom over the head in narrow bredths after a strange fashion.[62]

Mats of marram continued to be made using grass from Newborough Warren, Anglesey, North Wales until the 1980s (Fig. 144) and rush mats are still made in East Anglia (Fig. 143).

Floor cloths or oil cloths, like mats, probably had a wide social distribution, especially before the introduction of linoleum in 1860. In Britain the earliest reference to floor cloths so far discovered is in the Temple Newsom papers in which payment was made in 1722 for 'a Bed Tent and Markee £38.8s' and for a floor 'oyled cloth to lye in the tent 19s'.[63] Of the seventy-five American inventories of 1758 cited by Rodris Roth only three mention floor coverings of any kind, and by 1777 the proportion had increased to only nine out of seventy-five, of which four included floor cloths.[64] When William Burnet (Governor first of New York and New Jersey and later of Massachusetts) died in 1729 he left 'two old checquered canvases to lay under a table' and 'a large painted canvas, square as the room'.[65] Many of the floor cloths in use in the colonies were imported from the mother country. By 1739 John Carwithen had published his *Floor-Decorations of Various Kinds . . . Adapted to the Ornamenting of Halls, Rooms, Summer-houses &c . . .* In some editions of this work, which was published in London, the author, who was an engraver by trade, explains that the designs are suitable 'wither in Pavements of Stone, or Marble, or wth. Painted Floor Cloths'.[66]

145   Floor cloth, oil paint on canvas, probably late eighteenth-century English. Henry Francis du Pont Museum, Winterthur, Delaware.

146 The trade-label of Alexander Wetherstone, *c.* 1763, 'at ye Painted Floor Cloth & Brush' Portugal Street, London. Ambrose Heal Collection: British Museum.

to be painted on the back of floor cloths. The earliest of these was a design which consisted of a series 'of discs of brown and cream in simple diagonal patterns' found on the back of the 1833 hatchment for Francis Gregory in St James's Church, Styvechale, Coventry. Two further, but later, examples have been found on the back of hatchments, and no doubt others will be identified. The eighteenth-century association between the painting of hatchments and floor cloths is also known through the trade-label of B. Philpott of Great Carter Lane near St Paul's, London. The label, which dates from the third quarter of the eighteenth century, states that Philpott painted 'Escutcheons, Trophies & all Requisites for Funerals. . . . Coach, House, Sign & Floor Cloth Painting at the Lowest Rates.'

The Henry Francis du Pont Museum in America possesses what may be the earliest floor cloth to have come to light so far (Fig. 145). It is composed of dark and light lozenges which though now dark brown and yellow may once have been black and white. A very similar design occurs on the trade-label of Alexander Wetherstone (*c.* 1763) 'at ye Painted Floor Cloth & Brush in Portugal Street', London (Fig. 146). In this example the design is centred by a 'compass rose' in which the initials of the cardinal points are omitted. As houses in the eighteenth century were often planned on the north/south or east/west axis, with the rooms inevitably following this plan, it is likely that floor cloths with such a feature were aligned with the compass when in use.

Undoubtedly the nautical connection with oil cloth was long established. John Smith mentions oil cloth in 1676, not for use on floors but for water-proof clothing.[69] 'An Experiment relating to Oyl Colours of great use to

Another source was Batty Langley's *The Builder's and Workman's Treasury of Designs* of 1750. The plates, mostly bearing the date 1739, are of 'Decorations for Pavements &c . . . Irregular Octogons & Geometrical Squares . . . Trapezoids [and] Parallopipedons and Cubes Erect'. Carwithen illustrates twenty-four designs in his book showing each on plan and in perspective demonstrating their effect *in situ* in a room. All his designs are geometric in character with the strong tonal contrasts found in marble floors of the period.

The utilitarian nature of floor cloths would make the survival of early examples unlikely, although the sample books of Nairns (now at Kirkcaldy Museum, Fife) go back to the 1840s.[67] A potential source for eighteenth-century examples has been discovered by Coventry City Art Gallery and Museum.[68] Conservation work by this museum on a number of funerary hatchments or escutcheons in churches in the Midlands has shown them

147 Early nineteenth-century floor cloth, showing both the top and the underside, at Audley End, Essex. Simple floor coverings of this kind had a very wide social distribution but have inevitably survived best in the houses and even the carriages of the élite.

Travellers of Some kinds: To the chief Officers of Camps and Armies, to Seamen and such like.' Smith's book went through a number of editions in the eighteenth century and in 1821 was reissued with additions by W. Butcher who simply states that oil cloth is 'now used for umbrellas, hat-cases, and many other uses' without specific reference to floor or table covers. Whilst geometric designs were favoured (Fig. 147) it is clear from contemporary descriptions and paintings of interiors that plain colours were also common. The use of plain colours was probably inspired by John Smith's description of how to make water-proof cloth for clothing – the probable origin of floor cloths. The following is taken from Butcher's edition of 1821: 'Take drying or burnt linseed oil, set it on the fire, and dissolve in it some good rosin or gum-lac . . . you may either work it by itself, or add to it some colour; as verdigris for green, or umber for a hair colour, white-lead and lamp-black for gray or indigo and white for light blue.'[70]

Aside from painted geometric designs more elaborate patterns were printed using wood blocks. A mid-nineteenth-century manuscript concerning the Barnes family oil cloth business categorically states that 'between the years 1766 to 1773 . . . the first block was cut for the purpose of printing floor cloth.' Joseph Barnes was in business as a general house and sign painter and floor-cloth manufacturer. From 1762 his address was in Basinghall Street, London (Figs. 151, 152).[71] Floral patterns were employed in addition to geometric designs, and many illustrations that appear on trade-cards show floor cloths with the favourite design of lozenges surrounded by a 'fluid' border. A characteristic range is listed on a mid-eighteenth-century label: 'At Biggerstaff's & Walsh's, Floor-Cloth Warehouse Behind the three Wheatsheaves at Islington, Are Made and Sold all Sorts of Painted Floor Cloths, Such as Plain, Ornamented, Check, Matt and Carpet Patterns, Entirely New. The Cloth Prepared so as not to Crack or Peel. Old Cloths new Painted and Repair'd' (Fig. 148).[72]

Cracking and peeling was something of a problem when floor cloths were exported and it was recommended that they should be dispatched when the paint was thoroughly dry with 'some slight woolen Rolled up with the floor Cloths to Prevent their Rubbing so as to be Defaced by Getting the Paint off'.[73] The importance of this was recognised by Messrs Crompton and Spinnages (in about 1769) whose warehouse was at Cockspur Street but who also 'Painted Floor Cloths of all Sorts and Sizes, Painted in Summer at their Manufactory at Knightsbridge, dry and fit for immediate use'.[74] A number of floor-cloth manufacturers were located in this part of London so it is possible that Crompton and Spinnages simply 'bought in' their stock.

Floor cloths are known to have been fitted to rooms in the eighteenth century and to have been placed under dining tables but over woven carpets to protect them from spilt food. They were tough enough to be mopped over with water.[75] In Britain their use was probably less exclusively elitist in the eighteenth century, but early in the next century Loudon, whilst conceding that floor cloths are among 'the kinds of carpets most suitable for cottages', gives some cautionary advice concerning their use:

Painted Floorcloths may sometimes be used in the lobbies and passages of cottages; but they are not economical articles, where there is much going out and coming in of persons generally employed in the open air, and of course wearing strong shoes, probably with nails in the soles. When they are used in cottages, the most appropriate patterns are imitations of some materials usually employed for floors, such as tessellated pavement, different coloured stones, wainscot,

&c.; but, for the better description of dwellings, where oilcloths are considered chiefly as ornamental coverings, there seems to be no reason why their patterns should not be as various as those of carpets.[76]

Charles Eastlake in his *Hints on Household Taste*, however, quotes a trivial example of a floor cloth 'intended to represent the spots on a leopard's skin'. He strongly believed that 'a floor-cloth, like every other article of manufacture . . . should seem to be what it really is, and not affect the appearance of a richer material. There are endless varieties of geometrical diaper which could be used for floor-cloth without resorting to the foolish expedient of copying the knots and veins of wood and marble.' He stresses that the design should not 'attempt to indicate relief or raised ornament in the pattern.'[77]

Along with the more widespread use of carpets in wealthier houses in the opening years of the nineteenth century, floor cloths remained in use. An advertisement in the *Salisbury and Winchester Journal* of Monday 1 January 1827 lists items to be sold at auction, including 'Brussels and Turkey carpets, bed round and stair-case ditto, hearth rugs, painted floor cloth'. By Loudon's day, floor cloths had moved downwards in social importance and were only found in the utilitarian areas of grand establishments. As a result manufacturers found that their business was mainly confined to 'Exportation, & Country Dealers', or the making of 'Prepared Cloths for Verandah's &c.'[78] Nevertheless, the deck of Queen Victoria's royal yacht was covered with oil cloth painted to simulate planking.[79]

These floor coverings were variously described as floor cloths, oil cloths, painted canvas, canvas and combinations of the above. They were made, or at least sold, according to eighteenth and early nineteenth-century trade-cards, by a variety of shops, most important of which were those which undertook ornamental painting; as well as oil and colourmen; turners and, strangely enough, Leghorn-hat sellers. An example of the latter was 'James Cox at ye Hat & Star near St Martins Lee Grand in Newgate Street, London', whose card for 'The Hatt & Floor Cloth Warehouse' dates from the third quarter of the eighteenth century.'[80] He is listed in the London directories for 1760 and 1762 at Blowbladder Street, as the east end of Newgate Street was then known. It is possible that the sale of straw hats and floor cloths may have originated in a similar market for straw mats. Certainly Cox was no exception, as Gatfield and Co., listed in the directories in 1777 and 1784, also made and sold 'Painted Floor Cloths, Leghorn and Straw-hats'.[81] Others included Thomas Iliffe and 'John Shepherd at the Straw Hat and Floor Cloth Warehouse opposite St Clement's Church in the Strand, London' (*c.* 1751) (Fig. 149).

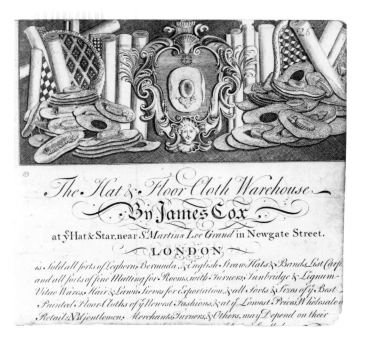

149 The trade-card of Thomas Iliffe of London, mid-eighteenth century. Floor cloths or oil cloths were sold by Leghorn-hat merchants. This card illustrates the two principal types of oil-cloth design – the chequered and the painted representation of a woven carpet. By the nineteenth century the tessellated pavement had been added to the repertoire. Ambrose Heal Collection: British Museum.

By the early nineteenth century many floor cloths were sold by those who specialised in 'Awnings and Portable Rooms', such as Hare and Co. of Newington Causeway, and John Samuel Hayward of the same address.'[82] There may be a connection between Hare of Newington Causeway and Messrs John Hare and Co. of Bristol, the manufacturers who exhibited at the International Exhibition of 1862 a remarkable copy in floor cloth of a Roman mosaic from Cirencester.[83] The Bristol company employed the technique of printing in oil on canvas to produce 'prints' (which resemble oil paintings) of the *South East View of Redcliffe Church, Bristol* (Fig. 150). This technique of printing designs in oil paint on floor cloth is described by the Bristol easel-painter, Rolinda Sharples, in her *Diary* for 1816 (see Appendix I). The paint for all these floor cloths was applied on only one side of the coarse canvas. The earliest reference to Hare of Bristol occurs in a Bristol directory of 1787. The firm is also mentioned in the *National Commercial Directory* for Gloucestershire in 1830 (published by Pigot and Co.). It is the only company listed under 'Floor Cloth Manufacturers' and the address is given as Temple Gate, Bristol. The Heal Collection includes a number of receipts which mention floor cloths, among them one to Mr

150   *South East View of Redcliffe Church, Bristol*, a 'picture' printed on floor cloth by Hare's of Bristol, 28 by 20 ins (71.2 by 50.8 cm; sight), mid-nineteenth century. Ex Collection: Ian McCallum.

John Wallis from James Cox, dated 1753, which refers to '16 yds of Check painted floor cloth . . . a pole and packing Mat . . . a pair of Window Blinds [for a total of] £1 15s od.'[84] Another receipt, dated 1818, records that Frederick Booth of Spring Gardens paid H. Buckley £2 17s 6d for 'floor cloth No. 129' which implies a catalogue number.[85]

By consulting the hundreds of labels in the British Museum I have drawn up a list of at least some of the shops, warehouses and manufacturers active in London in the second half of the eighteenth and the first quarter of the following century (see Appendix VIII). Allowing for the fact that many publicly stated that they were involved in 'exportation'[86] or supplying 'country dealers' it is clear that in London at least such floor covering was widely used.

The great problem for the manufacture of floor cloths was that the basic fabric should be seamless because any ridge would produce uneven wear. The introduction of John Kay's fly shuttle, patented in 1733, made it possible for canvas to be woven in reasonable widths. In the early nineteenth century the floor-cloth manufacturers Buckley and Son congratulated themselves on making 'Canvas 7 yds wide without a Seam'.[87] By the middle of the century these problems had been overcome. *Chamber's Encyclopaedia* of 1862 speaks of the canvas basis which was manufactured in Dundee (also well known for its sailcloths) where it was woven from 18 to 24 ft (5.5 to 7.3 m) in width, and in lengths of from 100 to 113 yds

(91.4 to 103.3 m). The canvas was stretched on frames some of which measured 100 by 24 ft (30.5 by 7.3 m). The back, as well as the front, was primed with size and pumiced to keep it smooth. The object of this was to prevent the paint penetrating the canvas and making it brittle. The paint itself was mixed with linseed oil, with little or no turpentine, making it thicker than ordinary oil paint. It was first applied with a brush and then smoothed with a steel trowel (Fig. 151) and allowed to dry for twelve to fourteen days. The process was repeated with a second coat after the first coat had been smoothed with pumice. The final coat of paint was then carefully applied with a brush. This was the surface upon which a pattern could be printed by means of wood blocks cut in pear tree backed by two layers of deal (Fig. 152), the three layers having the axis of their grain opposed for strength (as in plywood). Stencils were also used to paint decorations onto floor cloths.[88] The best quality floor cloths were allowed to dry for several months in a drying room and to be really durable it was important that the product should remain with the manufacturer to cure for three or four years.

'Narrow floor-cloth, 18 ins, 24 ins and 36 ins [45.7, 60.9 and 91.4 cm] wide, for staircarpeting, passages &c.' was made in the same way but was cut in strips before being decorated. The designs employed in decorating floor cloths usually involved 'a large pattern in the middle and

151 Eighteenth-century implements for floor-cloth manufacture including clout-nails and tacks for stretching the canvas, a stone muller and ledger for grinding paint together with a voiding knife and a trowel for spreading the paint on the canvas. From the notebook of Joseph Barnes whose firm claimed to have been the first to print designs on floor cloth. The National Art Library, London.

152 Wood block for printing floor cloths, 10 by 9½ins (25.25 by 24 cm), late eighteenth century. Kirkcaldy Museum and Art Gallery.

a border of a smaller design'.[89] The basic commodity in the manufacture of floor cloths was canvas, and it is probably for this reason that in the second half of the nineteenth century the two great centres for their manufacture were ports where sail cloth was important. As we have seen, Bristol, where John Hare was in business, was one of these centres but the other was Kirkcaldy, Fife, where the still-prospering firm of Michael Nairn and Co. was established in 1847.

As 'American cloths', oil cloths to cover kitchen tables remained in use until the mid-twentieth century, but as floor coverings their use rapidly declined in the late nineteenth century as a result of industrialised methods of producing linoleum (their direct successor), ceramic tiles and carpets.

> The laying of lobbies and passages with encaustic tiles has lately led to the superseding of floor cloth in such situations, while . . . [for the] covering of floors in churches, reading-rooms, and waiting-rooms at railway-stations it is superseded by the newly invented material called kamptulicon, or vulcanised India-rubber cloth. This new material is made plain or figured to resemble painted floor-cloth.[90]

Kamptulicon was patented in 1844 by E. Galloway[91] and linoleum, as we would now call it, was patented in 1860 and 1863 by F. Walton. It is very similar in composition to floor cloth except that the oxidised linseed oil is mixed with ground cork as well as pigment which is why 'lino' is thicker and bulkier than traditional floor cloth. A related material was Lincrusta-Walton which was embossed and used as wallpaper.

While floor covering of any kind was rare in the eighteenth century, there were several alternatives to floor cloths – 'list' carpeting, 'hair' cloths and straw mats. In the 1760s Alexander Wetherstone sold at his shop near Lincoln's Inn 'floor Cloths, Hair Cloths, List Carpets, Royal and other Matting'. English-made straw, rush and grass matting was supplemented in the late seventeenth century, probably through the Dutch East India Company (the source of split cane for chair seats and backs), with grass mats from the Far East. Their popularity was greatest, however, in those countries which suffer temperatures of greater extremes than are found in Britain. Some rather grand households in England are known to have changed their floor coverings for winter and summer but it does not appear to have become a general practice as it did in France.[92] In North America, from Boston south, the arrival of summer was marked by replacing curtains of silk or wool with linen or cotton, and wool carpets were displaced in favour of grass mats. It is known that this household custom dates back in America to the eighteenth century but it was not usual at

that time, even there. Jacques Pierre Brissot de Warville wrote of his *Travels in The United States* in 1788 that, 'A carpet in summer is an absurdity; yet they spread them in this season [summer], and from vanity: this vanity excuses itself by saying that the carpet is an ornament; that is to say, they sacrifice reason and utility to show.'[93] Caroline Halsted's *Investigations or Travels in the Boudoir* of 1837 takes the form of an educational dialogue between mother and daughter and describes 'The floor covering in your papa's study . . . composed of split portions of rattan, or cane, manufactured into a fine matting by the inhabitants of Sunda [Indonesia] and other islands east of China.'[94]

'List' carpets were probably the great alternative to the ubiquitous floor cloth in the eighteenth century, one reason being that they were cheap and they could be made at home (Fig. 153). In architecture a 'list' is a synonym for a 'fillet' (a flat, narrow band or ribbon running along a moulding) and in textiles can be a synonym for selvage.[95] List carpets were constructed of a warp of woollen yarn into which a weft of strips of rag (the 'list') tied together were woven. This strongly textured and indeed rather knobbly carpeting of humble appearance was probably once found in all walks of life before industrialised methods of production brought the cost of textiles down to a level which would increase their use.

By the nineteenth century, list carpets were generally replaced by the so-called 'Venetian' carpets, but hair carpets remained in use from the mid-eighteenth century almost to the present day. Hard-wearing hair carpets, as their name implies, are a twilled material made up of a weft of spun hair (e.g. goat) with a cotton, linen or wool warp – it is not to be confused with the woven horse-hair textile used to cover chairs.[96] Unlike horse-hair fabric, hair carpets were not slippery so they were used on stairs as well as in passages as runners. Stair carpets were something of a luxury well into the nineteenth century. Archdeacon Julius Hare (1795–1855) in *The Story of My Life* describes the rectory at Stoke-on-Tern, Shropshire, in which 'the stair carpet was taken up unless there were visitors, and the drawing-room furniture draped in wrappings' except when 'company' was expected.[97] According to Thomas Sheraton in his *Cabinet Dictionary*, 'Venetian' carpets derived their name from their place of manufacture and were 'generally striped', the pattern being all in the warp. 'Dutch' carpet was a coarser and cheaper version which sometimes contained cow hair.

Perhaps the most decorative of all these simple floor coverings were the 'Kidderminster' and the 'Scotch ingrain'. These carpets, like the Kendal carpet in Fig. 154 and the Barnard Castle carpet in Fig. 155, did not have a pile. The introduction of looms with Jacquard attach-

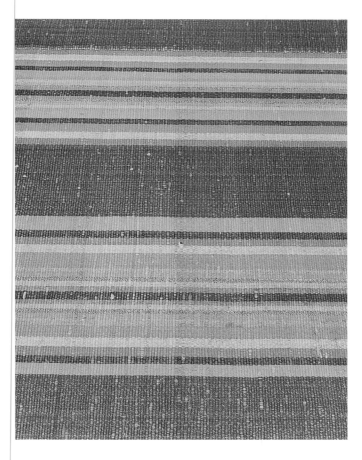

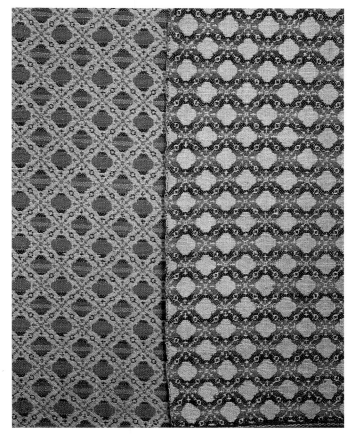

153 A 'list' carpet woven from yarn warps and rag wefts, late eighteenth or early nineteenth century, English or American. American Museum in Britain, Bath.

155 Reversible Barnard Castle carpet, late eighteenth or early nineteenth century. Bowes Museum, Barnard Castle.

154a, b Reversible Kendal carpet, late eighteenth or early nineteenth century. Victoria and Albert Museum, London: on loan from the National Trust.

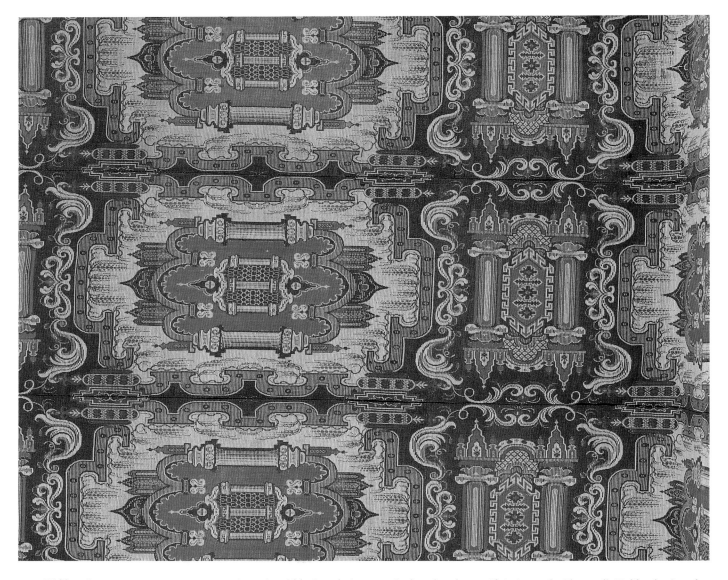

156   Kidderminster carpet *c.* 1835–40, woven in 36-in widths in a design organised so that the motifs in it may be 'dropped'. Unlike the Scotch ingrain carpets, or those from the north of England (Figs. 154, 155) Kidderminster carpets are 'bag' woven, each colour representing a separate yet integrated layer of cloth. For this reason carpets of this kind are very fragile and are now, inevitably, rare. Ex Collection: Judkyn/Pratt.

ments in the early nineteenth century resulted in quite elaborate designs. Sheraton's *Cabinet Dictionary* (1803) describes 'Scots carpet . . . [as] one of the most inferior kind'. Caroline Halsted (1837) provides a very clear 'pecking order' for the different types of floor covering available at that time: 'The carpets usually styled Kidderminster, are an improvement on the Scotch, which are the cheapest and commonest kinds manufactured . . . being within reach of persons of limited incomes, and . . . used also for sleeping-rooms, and offices in larger establishments' (Figs. 156, 157).[98] *Travels in the Boudoir* provides much useful detailed information on Kidderminster carpets, in which 'each distinct part of the pattern is

hollow like a bag' whereas the Scotch carpet is 'not separate in this way . . . carpets, such as we are now accustomed to see were only uncommonly used in England in the early part of the [eighteenth] century; as we read of a Mr [Thomas] Moore having received a premium from the Society of Arts in 1757 for establishing a manufacture in London in imitation of those of Turkey and Persia.'[99]

'Brussels carpets' were made at Wilton in Wiltshire as early as about 1740, and 'Wilton' carpets were made there by 1754. In Devon, Axminster carpets began production in the 1750s.[100] Despite the splendour of these carpets their width was at first restricted to about 3 ft (91.4 cm) which meant that large carpets had to be made up of strips sewn together. Motifs could be organised so that the designs could be 'dropped', thus camouflaging the joins. By 1755 Thomas Whitty of Axminster succeeded in weaving a carpet 36 by 21 ft (11 by 6.4 m). The Royal Society of Arts thought it worthwhile to institute premiums for the best pile carpets measuring not less than 15 by 12 ft (4.5 by 3.6 m). Not unnaturally Whitty won the prize in both years that it was awarded, but had to share it in 1757 (the year mentioned by Halsted) with Thomas Moore of Moorfields, London, and in 1758 with Claude Passavant of Exeter. For the most part, English-made pile carpets of this period were far too grand for the vernacular interiors with which we are concerned.

By 1837, when Loudon published his *Encyclopaedia of Cottage, Farm, and Villa Architecture*, carpets were more generally available. Even so, 'for neither the parlour nor the bed room would we recommend the carpet to be fitted to the room' in cottages. Instead, Loudon suggests for the parlour a

> square of carpet [which] may be changed eight times [by being turned and reversed] so as to be worn equally in every part of both sides. For a cottage's bed-room, we would chiefly recommend one piece of carpeting placed by the dressing-table, and pieces neatly fitted to each other to go round the foot and sides of the bed. Stair carpets give an air of great comfort and finish to a house; and a cottage should never be without one.[101]

In the previous century the use of strips of carpet round three sides of a bed was quite usual in more pretentious surroundings. In 1752 Mrs Delany mentions, in one of her illuminating letters, that her 'candlelight work, is finishing a carpet in double-cross-stitch, on very coarse canvas to round . . . [her] bed'.[102] As carpet became more available such mitreing round of carpet strips tended to be confined to smaller houses and the edges of more important rooms where, with fitted carpets, the border was placed. Sheraton's *Cabinet Dictionary* (1803) states that 'to most of the best kind of carpets there are suitable borders in narrow widths'. He describes the method of laying such carpets, starting at the most conspicuous part of the room – the focal point occasioned by the fireplace hearth.

Loudon makes it clear that home-made carpets and rugs were the answer for many houses and describes how to make '*Paper Carpets*' which were made by 'cutting out and sewing together pieces of linen, cotton, Scotch gauze, canvas, or any similar material &c.', sizing it as necessary 'and carefully pasting it round the margins so as to keep it strained tight . . . When the cloth thus fixed is dry, lay on it two or more coats of strong paper, breaking joint, and finish with coloured or hanging paper, according to fancy.'[103] Clearly a great deal of work was put into making various home-made floor coverings but unfortunately no paper carpets are known to survive. Among the *Substitutes for Carpets* mentioned in the *Encyclopaedia of*

157 Detail of an English vernacular painting of *c.* 1830 showing a Kidderminster carpet fitted to the room. Private Collection.

Cottage, Farm and Villa Architecture are green baize and drugget, but Loudon also describes a 'kind of patchwork' carpet, surviving examples of which have yet to be located. 'Remnants of cloth bought from the woollen-draper, or tailor, and cut into any kind of geometrical shapes, may be sewn together, so as to form circles, stars, or any other regular figures that may be desired; and, when arranged with taste, produce a very handsome and durable carpet at a very trifling expense.'[104] Caroline Halsted's book, which is roughly contemporary with Loudon's, refers to the homemade carpets of the eighteenth century: 'the coverings of ordinary apartments were merely square pieces of painted canvas [i.e. floor cloths], or woollen stuffs, baize, and coarse cloth; the latter ornamented with curious devices figured in the middle, or bouquets of flowers in the corners.'[105]

Just as the carpet was first presumed to be a textile covering for a table, so the rug (derived from the Swedish *rugg*: rough hair) was assumed to be a bed cover rather than, as now, a small textile floor covering. Despite the fact that bed rugs are known to have been used in seven-teenth and eighteenth-century England, no examples have come to light, although a number, dating from a few decades either side of the year 1800, have been found in America. Hooked rugs employ a different technique from bed rugs. They remain popular in the north of England and may be of Norse origin.[106] Most date from the late nineteenth century or later and are made of strips of rag looped through a coarse canvas backing. In parts of Scotland they are known as 'clootie' rugs and in the north of England as 'hookies and proddies', a clear refer-ence to the process by which they are made. 'Stobbies' or 'stobbie rugs' were made in Cumberland 'with the ends sticking out'.[107] In the richer south of England, 'Berlin' woolwork rugs were usual by the mid-nineteenth century, but Flora Thompson, recalling her childhood in the 1880s, mentions 'a superannuated potato-sack thrown down by way of a hearthrug . . . [or] brightly coloured handmade rugs on the floor'.[108]

Whilst it must be accepted that carpets offer much comfort, their excessive use in many old houses today may be out of character with their period.

Chapter 7

Ceilings

Today the word ceiling is used to denote the overhead lining of a room with plaster, but in the past this was termed 'under drawing'. Medieval and Tudor documents generally use the word 'ceiling' to describe the wood panelling on internal walls.[1] In simple, single-storey houses open to the roof the thatch covering was visible from within. This, in most houses, was considered perfectly adequate, but on occasion an attempt was made at greater finish. This 'finish' was always most easily installed first, before the roof was thatched. One quite simple method, adopted in parts of Wales, was to lay a series of straw mats over the rafters which formed a base for the thatch and a lining to the roof space (Fig. 158). Heavy-duty mats were laid on the principal rafters and the purlins, from the ridge to the eaves. This procedure had the further advantage of making secondary rafters unnecessary. A still earlier method involved the use of hazel sticks in place of the mats (Fig. 177) – in both cases such provision did much to prevent stray straws or reeds falling into the house. In those parts of Scotland where turf roofs were the tradition a trickle of earth or even mud could be an annoyance and it became customary to line such roofs with divots of moss or grass laid on the rafters. The use of a canopy over the dais in the hall or over a bed established high status but may have had its origins in practical necessity.

In nineteenth-century Ulster the inside of the roof of the bed outshot was lined with layers of newspapers pasted together and tacked in position across the underside of the rafters and whitewashed. This is probably a second-rate version of the use of mats of marram grass in the same position. Some years ago a rare example of such matting was found in a farmhouse at Shantallow, near Londonderry (Fig. 159).[2] Despite the vestigial traces of the long-house in its overall planning, this house is of sufficiently high quality to suggest that it had been built for a 'planter', which would account for its resemblance to houses in the 'Upland Zone' of England.[3] These grass ceiling and wall mats probably owed their survival to being left *in situ* in a sealed loft, the occupants of the house being unaware of their existence. The loft was approached by massive stone stairs concealed behind double doors which had been papered over in about 1900.

Perhaps related to the grass-mat ceiling is the straw roof lining found in Stradbally, Co. Waterford in 1962 (Fig. 160) although a more probable ancestry is the use of a 'base coat' of straw visible on the underside of a thatched roof.[4] On the other hand this example (now destroyed) may be unique and so related to nothing else. It was found only in the bedroom (measuring 13 by 15½ ft (3.9 by 4.7m)) of the single-storey thatch-roofed house. The straw of the lining was attached to boarding on the two sloping sides of the roof, the narrow portion of horizontal ceiling near the apex of the roof, and the gable area on the partition between bedroom and kitchen/living-room. The lining was divided into bands about 15 ins (38 cm) wide and each band was made up of a single layer of wheat straw held in place by laths ¾ in (1.9 cm) wide by ¼ in (0.64 cm) thick. The lowest bands were apparently applied first and held with the bottom lath, and the lath of the next row up then held the top of the bottom row and the base of the next row of straws. 'This successive screening of the projecting upper ends of the straws in one zone, by the lower ends of those in the zone above it, was continued up the slopes of the roof and, presumably, across the ceiling as well.'[5] The ceiling was said to have been made in about 1869 by

158   Bedroom in Kennixton Farmhouse (*c.* 1630) from Llangennydd on the Gower Peninsula as reconstructed at the Museum of Welsh Life. The straw mat resting on the purlins both lined and helped to support the thatch making secondary rafters unnecessary – see also Fig. 177. The wooden plinth on which the right-hand bed is placed is created by the charnel or recess in the ceiling (for hanging bacon, herbs, etc.) of the room below (reproduced in Fig. 255 although this feature above the fireplace is not quite visible).

159   Marram-grass roof lining to the first-floor bed outshot in a farmhouse in Shantallow near Londonderry, Ulster. From the early nineteenth century, bed outshots were more often lined with newspapers and distempered. Marram-grass mats were also used as floor coverings – see Fig. 144.

160 Straw-lined ceiling (now destroyed) in a house in the High Street, Stradbally, Co. Waterford, Ireland. This remarkable ceiling was thought to have been made in the mid-nineteenth century.

a man named Hannigan and despite its age 'was in an astonishingly perfect state of preservation. All the straws were as straight and tubular as if they had just been cut from the living plants. . . . They were, moreover, incredibly clean and retained their original golden colour.'[6]

The steep-pitched roofs of East Anglia indicate that they were evolved for thatch. Because of the proximity of the Low Countries, pantiles probably often replaced thatch in this region at an early date. It is likely that this sequence of events led builders to discover the advantages, in terms of insulation and wind-proofing, of hanging the tiles on a layer of straw or reed. Whatever its origins, such lining was customarily used in East Anglia where it was a traditional practice to plaster the reed-lined ceilings of attic rooms. The plastering of the underside of a tiled roof was a widespread practice known as 'torching-up'. With the uneven stone-tiled roofs, typical of regions like the Cotswolds, torching-up was an effective way of keeping out wind-driven rain and snow. For purposes of insulation roofs in the north of England, in Scotland and in New England were traditionally boarded over their rafters and under the roof covering – these were known as 'sarking boards'.

As we have seen, upper floors could not generally develop until chimneys were installed, and ceilings were in their turn dependent upon floors. It was therefore quite logical that early ceilings consisted simply of the joists that supported the floor above. Most ceilings of this type reduced the span that the joists bridged by means of a 'summer' beam which, for strength, was of considerable girth. Related to the summer beam, indeed often supporting one end of it, was the 'breast-summer' or 'bressummer' which was let into the face of a wall.[7]

In houses that were jettied on two adjacent faces it was necessary that the joists be placed on two different axes at right angles to each other. This was made possible by means of the 'dragon beam' which was, most often, set at an angle of 45 degrees to the joists and which is, in effect, a type of summer beam (Fig. 161). In early houses the joists are notable for their great size and the close intervals at which they are tenoned into the summer or dragon beam. In some examples this interval can be as little as 1 ft (30.5 cm) between the centres of the timbers. Each tenon on each joist was tallied with a particular mortice in the summer beam by the use of a variant of Roman numerals as these were easily stabbed-in with a carpenter's chisel. As we have seen (p. 92), some early floors and ceilings were constructed of alternate joists and planks laid on the same axis so that the upper face of the joist was in effect a floor 'board', and the lower face

161   Dragon beam in Bayleaf, a fifteenth-century yeoman's hall-house as reconstructed at the Weald and Downland Museum, Chichester, West Sussex. The dragon beam supporting two sets of joists was a necessary feature in houses with a jettied storey on two adjacent elevations. The early date is indicated by the close spacing of the joists, which are of heavy scantlings, and by the absence of chamfers or mouldings. Photograph: Weald and Downland Museum, Chichester.

162   Ceiling of 151 Angel Street, Hadleigh, Suffolk. Joists and their supporting summer beams were chamfered or moulded and provided with 'stops' of numerous kinds throughout much of the sixteenth and early seventeenth centuries.

of the board took on the role of a lining to the ceiling (Fig. 142). An example of such a floor has been recorded in a house, now demolished, at Dove Hill Houses, Sheffield,[8] but similar floors have also been located in Norwich and Co. Durham.[9]

In simple medieval buildings, joists are usually found squared by means of the adze or broad axe with no further attempt made to finish them. In Tudor and later buildings it became usual to chamfer these timbers and in important houses from the fifteenth century the joists were given elaborate sections. The magnificence of Paycocke's at Coggeshall (1525) is emphasised by the exceptional quality of these features. The degree of elaboration or simplicity of the joists often provides a clue not only to the likely age of the house, but also to its relative importance and the status of the individual rooms

163 A movable wrought-iron crane (early nineteenth century?) attached to the summer beam in a room in Hononton Farmhouse, Brenchley, Kent. As the principal girder the summer was a convenient timber on which to attach hooks and other lifting devices associated with butchery.

(Figs. 162, 163). The mouldings and their 'stops' also provide clues as to the size and shape of the rooms where later partitions have confused the original planning. In timber-frame houses to which stone or brick fronts have been added it is sometimes possible to find stops buried in the masonry indicating that the rooms have been reduced in size to the extent of the thickness of these later walls.

With these methods of construction it was inevitable that the underside of the boards of the floor above should be visible from below. For this reason these boards between the joists were sometimes decorated with painted designs (Figs. 164, 165). This feature is often associated with Scotland and the north-east of England, but a late sixteenth-century example recorded in Wickham, Hampshire, suggests that this form of decoration may have been widespread. In seventeenth-century East

164 Painted ceiling and mural scheme in the 'Painted Chamber' at Gladstone's Land, Edinburgh, a house built 1617–20, the probable date of the decoration.

165   Painted timber ceiling from Owengate, Durham, mid-seventeenth century.

Anglia apotropaic symbols from the black of a candle flame have been found on the plastered surfaces between the joists or, with a fully plastered ceiling, scratched-in designs may be present which are strategically placed at vulnerable points by doors or windows and over areas where food was prepared (see Appendix VI).[10]

Where an upper floor was made of plaster (rather than boarded with timber) it was the plaster that was visible and this may have given rise to the 'under drawing' of wood floors with plaster panels which could then be painted decoratively (Fig. 166). In Derbyshire, plaster floors were laid upon laths, but further south reeds were commonly used.[11] In Norfolk, 'The floors were solid, and were formed in this way: joists 4 inches by 3½ inches [10.2 by 8.9 cm] were laid flatwise on the main beams and were covered with a layer of reeds about an inch in thickness: on this again were laid wide oak floor boards nailed to the joists through the reeds. This being done, the underside of the reeds was plastered between the joists, giving a good, sound-proof floor and yet barely 3

166   Stencilled decoration applied between the joists of a ceiling in a farmhouse at Basing, near Cowden, Kent. This Yeoman house was built in 1597, the probable date of the decoration. Watercolour drawing by Martin Hardie, July 1936. Victoria and Albert Museum, London.

167   A framed oak ceiling of the late fifteenth century in the hall of Reeds Court Farm, Lydiard St Lawrence, Somerset. The subsidiary joists have been covered with lath and plaster as is usual for a ceiling of this type.

inches [7.6 cm] thick.'[12] When reed is used in place of laths it was known by plasterers as 'speer'.

Plaster on reed was very common in Norwich in the eighteenth and nineteenth centuries,[13] but I have also found an example of reeds used as laths attached to the underside of joists for a plastered ceiling in a derelict seventeenth-century house by the west end of Shepton Mallet Church, Somerset.[14] In the town of Stamford, which has access to the fenland of East Anglia, plaster floors of between 1 and 2 ins (2.5 and 5 cm) thick were 'run' on a layer of straw or reeds which were laid directly across the joists. The plaster for this purpose was usually mixed with a little crushed brick or ash so that in 1700 one hundredweight (50.8 kg) of lime plaster was considered sufficient to make 1 sq yd (84 sq m) of flooring.[15]

According to William Harrison, writing from Radwinter, Essex in the 1570s, reeds were widely used as a base for plastering, but he draws attention to a hazard that was considered to be attendant upon their use:

In plastering likewise of our fairest houses over our heads, we use to laie first a laine [layer] or two of white morter tempered with haire, upon laths, which are nailed one by another, (or sometimes upon reed or wickers more dangerous for fire, and made fast here and there with saplaths, for falling downe,) and finallie

cover all with the aforesaid plaster, which beside the delectable whiteness of the stuffe it selfe, is laied on so even and smoothlie, as nothing in my judgement can be doone with more exactnesse.[16]

The hair that was traditionally mixed with plaster was either cow or goat with white hair being favoured for the final coat of plaster.

A variant of the joisted floor/ceiling was the framed version in which the ceiling (the support to the floor above) was divided into a series of rectangles by principal bridging beams into which subsidiary joists were tenoned. To reduce the bulk of these bridging beams, both physically and visually, they were customarily worked with elaborate mouldings. The joists between were sometimes underdrawn with plaster (Fig. 167). The earliest domestic ceilings of this type date from the mid-fifteenth century.

In East Anglia where wool wealth was combined with close contact with Continental Europe through the Low Countries, a number of timber-boarded ceilings have been located. In Norwich a wood lining of boards about ¼ in (0.63 cm) in thickness was used, running parallel to the joists and lying between them and the floor boards above (whose axis they opposed).[17] In very rare instances the joists were covered by narrow boards running

168   Boarded ceiling of the late fifteenth century in Garrad's House, Water Street, Lavenham, Suffolk. The boards are a mere ³⁄₈ in. thick and cover the joists but not the summer beam. The ribs and bosses help to prevent these thin boards from sagging.

parallel to the summer beam which remained visible. In the example at Lavenham, Suffolk (Fig. 168), the edges of the boards are 'V'-jointed and only about ¼ in (0.63 cm) thick, which means that the narrow ribs planted on their face, together with the bosses at the intersections, serve a structural function and prevent sagging.[18] Gwilt quotes a fifteenth-century example at Wingham in Kent and adds that this type of ceiling was usually decorated with distemper.[19] The Lavenham ceiling shows traces of such paint in the interstices of the moulded ribs and the carved bosses. In the 1990s a late fifteenth-century ceiling of this kind, retaining much of its painted decoration, was discovered in a 1430s merchant's house in Abingdon, Oxfordshire (Fig. 169).

The use of plaster between joists probably gave rise to plastering the joists themselves, a fashion that was at its height in the first half of the seventeenth century. A number of examples of such plaster-clad timbers survive (Fig. 170). A particularly good example was preserved in a ground-floor room in a house at Merchants Barton,

169   Boarded ceiling of the late fifteenth century in a ground-floor room in the Merchant's House in East St Helen Street, Abingdon (built *c.* 1430) (see also Fig. 168). The boards are about ½ in. (1.2 cm) thick and the ribs help to prevent any tendency to sag. Whilst the joists are covered with boarding the finely moulded summer beam remains visible. The painted decoration is probably original. Ceilings of this type may have been inspired by the framed ceilings that preceded them (see Fig. 167) and later provided the inspiration for the ribbed plaster ceilings which followed them – see Fig. 191.

170 Plastered timber ceiling in Brickhouse Farmhouse, Hitcham Street, Hitcham, Suffolk, early seventeenth century.

171 Seventeenth-century plaster ceiling in 1 Duke Street, Hadleigh, Suffolk.

Frome, Somerset, until the house was demolished by the town council in the late 1960s.[20]

The plaster ceiling obscuring, and indeed attached to, the joists was not general in vernacular houses until the seventeenth century (Fig. 171). The double layer, created by the floor and a ceiling of this kind, provided better sound insulation and, on occasion in East Anglia, this was improved by filling the cavity with chaff or, in the Cotswolds, with chopped straw[21] – a technique sometimes used in partitions.[22] From the sixteenth century, plaster ceilings, on occasion, carry richly moulded ribs, probably in imitation of the timber ribbed ceilings described above (Fig. 191). However, as a plastic material, plaster was more easily worked than oak and ribbed ceil-

172   Signature in the attic of the Merchant's House, Marlborough which reads '1656/William Brunson/October 3'. The top of the collar (beneath the inscription) measures 3 ft 6 ins wide. Whilst the 'logo' in the apex, and the standard of this plasterwork, is of reasonable quality this house does not include a single surviving example of decorative plasterwork. This is in marked contrast to the high standard of decorative painting (see Figs. 183, 210–212). The explanation may be that, since plasterers combined their trade with work in distemper, it was Brunson who was the author of the decorative painting cited above – see Fig. 210.

ings, divided into panels of considerable complexity, were to become fashionable by the end of the century. This type of work was referred to in Rees's *Encyclopaedia* (1786) as 'fretwork', which is defined as 'a kind of knot or ornament consisting of two lists or fillets, variously interlaced'. At an earlier date Sir Balthazar Gerbier (1663) has much to say about 'Playsterers work in Fret seelings.'[23] Similarly John Rea's *Flora* . . . (1665) illustrates plans for knot gardens which he describes as 'frets'. Thus the definition of a 'fret' relates to the design rather than the material and, as we have seen (pp. 69, 74–5), these designs, if not the term, could just as easily be used for the lead cames in a window.

Whilst elaborate decorative plaster ceilings were a feature of vernacular buildings in the early seventeenth century they became less common in the latter half of the century, except in certain counties like Devon and Somerset (Fig. 93). In contrast the Merchant's House (1653–70) at Marlborough, Wiltshire has no such ceilings, at least none that survive, despite the elaboration of its joinery and painted decoration (see pp. 121–2, 147–9). Certainly William Brunson, the plasterer who was employed on this house, was probably capable of such work judging by the quality of his signature (Fig. 172). In Devon and Somerset the work of Robert Eaton and no less than three generations of the well-known Abbott family of plasterers were capable of remarkable levels of elaboration.[24]

Despite the popularity of decorated plaster ceilings in vernacular houses in the seventeenth century they seldom occur in minor domestic buildings of the last

173   In both sacred and secular contexts, the notion that ceilings should be 'clouded' by 'decorative painters' was probably inevitable. This very fragmentary example evidently occupied a 'tray' ceiling. It probably dates from the second quarter of the seventeenth century judging by the decorative Baroque plaster ceiling beneath it which made the painted scheme redundant by about 1700. This decoration survives in the attic space of a large farmhouse at Stockland Lovell, Fiddington, Somerset.

174   Plaster ceiling in a two-room cabin (since destroyed) in Freshford, Co. Kilkenny, Ireland. Despite the provincial grandeur of this ceiling, its location and date (late eighteenth century) are surprising, to say the least. A Classical Revival ceiling in the next room was doubtless installed at the same time. Note that the cherubs near the perimeter of the ceiling are the wrong way round and will therefore always be viewed upside down, a very provincial detail.

three-quarters of the eighteenth century. The extraordinarily elaborate though provincial plasterwork discovered in the 1960s in a cabin at Freshford, Co. Kilkenny, must be regarded as an amusing aberration; it has since been destroyed (Fig. 174).[25] The cottage no doubt provided the lodgings for the craftsmen employed on a neighbouring 'big house'.

The apparent lack of decorative plaster in lesser houses of the last half of the eighteenth century is the more remarkable in view of the introduction of *carton-pierre*, an oriental innovation, which reached England via France. A rare instance of its use in a 'lesser' house occurs in Smith's *Nollekens and His Times* (1829):

Upon an investigation, in consequence of a report that there was a very fine copy of this work [the painted ceiling at Whitehall] of Rubens, as a fixture in a house on the south side of Leicester-fields, I found that the curiously ornamented *papier-maché* parlour ceiling of No. 41 had been painted, though very indifferently by

some persons who had borrowed groups of figures from several Rubens designs which they had unskilfully combined.[26]

Smith goes on to quote a conversation concerning the manufacture of papier-maché between Twigg, the well-known Covent Garden wit and fruiterer, and Mrs Nollekens.[27] Twigg is alleged to have remarked, 'I recollect the old house when it was a shop inhabited by two old Frenchwomen who came over here to chew for the papier maché people.'

Because cornices were seen as an integral part of the wall in Classical architecture, Loudon asserted that without them 'no Room can have a finished Appearance'.[28] The mores of Classicism demanded a cornice but in smaller houses they were often left out on the grounds of cost. On the other hand ceiling decoration could be omitted without any sense of betrayal, consequently '*Plaster Ornaments on Ceilings* have not hitherto been much introduced in cottages on account of expense.'[29]

There were alternatives to the use of such plasterwork, and Loudon goes on to say that ornaments for ceilings could be obtained which were 'manufactured by Messrs Bielefelds and Haseldon at a very low price, of a description of papier maché'. Gwilt observed that '*carton-pierre*, a species of *papier-maché* has been re-introduced for cornices, flowers, and other decorations. . . . They have not all the delicacy of plaster cast . . . but their lightness and security with which they can be fixed with screws render them preferable to plaster ornaments.'[30]

It was not until the second half of the nineteenth century that decorated ceilings began to assume a popularity comparable to that which they had enjoyed in the seventeenth century. The question of weight was always a problem for plaster 'stick and rag work' and it became a saying in the trade that 'if it stays up wet it'll stay up dry'.[31] Fibrous plaster became more popular than papier maché in the second half of the nineteenth century and Gwilt states that 'Mr Owen Jones has extensively used this material in his interior decoration.'

Chapter 8

Stairs

In 1595 William and Mary Chapman completed the modernisation of Hunt Street Farm, Crundale, Kent. The porch of their house commemorated the event with the inscription 'WC 1595 MC'. The work included the insertion of a fine brick flue and a framed oak staircase to replace the ladder that had previously been used.[1] As a consequence of this the upper floor was to become more accessible and therefore far more useable as an integral part of the house. Another early example of this kind of modernisation is the floored-over hall of Kite House, Monk's Horton, Kent, where the alteration carries the date 1574, although the fireplace is dated 1578.[2] It should be noted that in the traditional Wealden house the hall was placed centrally with floored-in rooms on either side, a feature reflected by the façade with its pair of jettied storeys. For this reason such houses needed two stairs or ladders but one of these could be dispensed with once a chimney flue was inserted and the hall was floored-over (Fig. 284).

Other house types might include lofts for storage, access to which could easily be provided by means of a ladder, but in general it was not until the widespread introduction of flues that the upper spaces of the house were sufficiently free of smoke for living purposes, and thus that upper floors, and the consequent need for stairs, became common. Exceptions to this include, as we have seen, the typical Wealden house (not confined to the Weald of Kent and Sussex) and the first-floor hall sometimes found in the Midlands and the north of England.

The whole question of the twelfth-century 'first-floor hall' reached by internal stairs or external steps has, of recent years, been considerably revised.[3] It is now thought that high status domestic buildings such as Boothby Pagnell Manor, Lincolnshire, are the surviving remnant of a larger complex which once included, in addition to the extant 'chamber block' with its upper rooms, an adjoining (if not always attached) 'ground-floor hall'. Such an arrangement survives in some twelfth-century domestic buildings in Normandy although, as a type, this house plan is probably Anglo-Saxon in origin – an instance of the victors being influenced by the conquered. Despite these revised interpretations, the first-floor hall, even if now understood as a semi-private space, offered its occupants a defensible stronghold. With a spiral staircase rising clockwise, only a defender would have his right sword arm unimpeded by masonry. Whatever the truth of the matter, it was possibly their home-grown origins and their strategic value which account for the persistence of steps or removable ladders. In this way the first-floor hall occupied a strategic location. In much of the upland zone of Britain this building type may have continued for reasons of tradition, but in the far north of England on the borders with Scotland the peel tower offered refuge for both cattle (on the ground floor) and people – in the first-floor hall.[4] It should be added that some external steps to the first floor provided access to rooms which, although part of the main body of the house, could remain separate from it. At Old Farm, Youlgrave, Derbyshire, of 1650, these rooms were the quarters for the farm servants (which is to say labourers, etc.).[5] In Scotland Dr Johnson described old houses approached 'by a flight of steps [outside] which reach up to the second storey; the floor which is level with the ground being entered only by stairs descending within the house'.[6] The dwelling (built c. 1490) known as John Knox's house in Edinburgh is of this type.

Because ladders occupied very little space they long remained a popular alternative to stairs. Furthermore

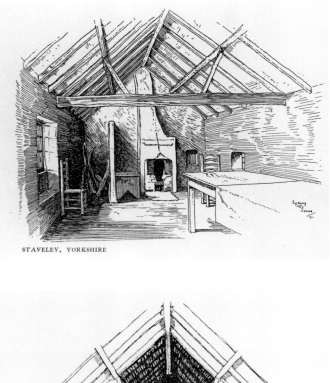

STAVELEY, YORKSHIRE

ENTRANCE TO SLEEPING LOFT OF ABOVE COTTAGE

175, 176   Single-cell house with a sleeping loft at Staveley, Yorkshire (S. R. Jones, 1912). From such simple beginnings the first floor developed in vernacular dwellings – as did the need for a ladder to gain access to this space. The loft is positioned in the gable opposite the fireplace; the latter has a chimney which would preserve the loft from smoke.

they could be slanted in several directions providing access to different rooms. A mud-built house which survived at Great Hatfield, East Yorkshire, until the late nineteenth century had a broad 'stee' or ladder to give access to the floored-over half of the house. This chamber in the roof was barely 5 ft (152 cm) in height and was approached via the 'stee' through a hole in the floor which was covered by a trapdoor known as a 'throp hetch' or 'trap hetch'. The 'chaamer' in this instance was not created until the early nineteenth century and so is a very late example of what was probably an early form which persisted longest in the north of England.[7] A similar feature is recorded by S. R. Jones's drawing (Figs. 175, 176).

The use of the ladder long persisted in Wales. Abern-odwydd Farmhouse was originally built in the sixteenth

century and modernised a hundred years later when the wattle and plaster flue was made and two attic rooms created. These two rooms are accessible by one ladder which may be sloped to reach either room (Fig. 177). The centrally placed flue probably occupies the site of a cross passage so that on one side of the fireplace a 'baffle' entry has been created whilst the other side of the flue provides space for the ladder. This reuse of the cross passage is also found in most parts of England.[8]

The problems of exchanging a ladder for a stair of some type was as much a matter of space as of cost (Fig. 178). The timber stair, which at first consisted of nothing more than treads set into 'stringers' and without 'risers', was simple to make but occupied a considerable amount of room. If space permitted, a straight flight constructed out of triangular baulks of timber laid on a pair of raking beams provided an effective and, in the days before carpet, relatively silent stair.[9] Addy recorded a most remarkable variant of the type at Hawkesworth House, Upper Midhope, near Penistone (dated 1671) (Fig. 179) which occupied very little space at the expense of being awkward to use. He describes it as being made of 'triangular blocks of oak' with gaps between them like a ladder: 'The first five steps are perpendicular and the remaining steps incline slightly towards the top.'[10] According to Addy the handrail, which was round in section, was original and the stairs were placed in a corner of the buttery backing onto the stud and plank panelling of the hall. The top of the stairwell was made safe on one side by a timber-framed partition wall and on the other by 'an immense ark or meal chest'. (Fig. 234). Another type of stair occupying very little space consisted of a series of elements comprised of two 'treads' (one for each foot) for each riser – an example of the type, in stone, survives in the ruins of Glastonbury Abbey – and Loudon recommends a wooden version of this 'economical staircase' (Fig. 178).[11]

As we have seen there were many parts of the country in which the chimney and the stairs were both placed in the area once reserved for the cross passage. However, there was not always room for this arrangement so that either the stairs or the flue or both were located elsewhere. In general the axial central flue was at first favoured, being a more efficient use of the heat it transmitted than one placed on an outside wall. If, alternatively, the staircase was placed on an outside wall, a turret was built for the purpose, a feature often added to houses as part of their modernisation. In Somerset and Devon the winding newel stair, at first of solid-oak baulks and later in high-status buildings of stone, is placed in the back wall in its own projection of stone or cob.[12] In Lincolnshire the Priory at Haydor has stairs approached from the hall but housed in a wing rising to the attic. The

177 Bedroom in Abernodwydd Farmhouse from Llangadfan, Powys as reconstructed at the Museum of Welsh Life. This farmhouse was probably built in the sixteenth century and floored-in at some point in the seventeenth century. The horns of the ladder which provided the means of reaching this chamber, and the one the far side of the chimney, are just visible. The timber-frame flue is infilled with wattle and daub which the heat from the fire has burnt to a crisp. Note the wheels on the simple truckle bed and the hazel rods which serve as minor rafters in supporting the thatch – an alternative to the use of straw mats shown in Fig. 158.

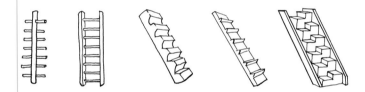

178 Various types of ladder and steps used to reach upper floors in simple vernacular buildings. The example shown on the right is illustrated by J. C. Loudon (*Encyclopaedia*, 1846, fig. 137) and a stone version of this type survives in Glastonbury Abbey. Steps of this kind, which offer two steps for each riser, are particularly useful in confined spaces.

179 Timber stairway in which the first five treads rise vertically. This stair was recorded by S. O. Addy (*The Evolution of the English House*, 1898) at Hawksworth Farmhouse, Upper Midhope, West Yorkshire.

newel stairs in this example are of stone which, although remarkably old fashioned for their date (1620–30), are nevertheless characteristic of other stone regions such as the Cotswolds.[13]

In Essex where the simpler houses of the late sixteenth and early seventeenth century were of two rooms chambered over (creating four rooms in all), the upper floor was reached by a winding stair alongside the axial stack, the traditional solution in many parts of the country. At this time the staircase wing in the yeoman houses of East Anglia, and notably in Essex, was generally at the rear of the houses in which the cross passage was insufficiently generous to accommodate both a chimney and a staircase.[14] The central flue was easily added to existing structures, but whilst it provided an efficient source of heat it

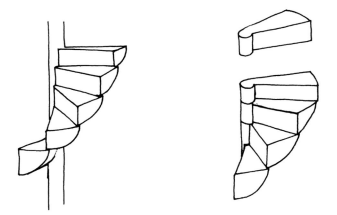

180   Spiral staircase worked from baulks of timber morticed into a central post and a masoned spiral in which the central post is an integral part of each step.

occupied a great deal of space. In a new house fireplaces built into the gables permitted the central staircase to expand in size and become, not only an object of beauty, but one that provided better circulation to more rooms. It should be added that such a staircase occupied no less, and frequently more, space than the flue that it had displaced, but with a new building the house could be made larger to compensate. Although the Palladian 'piano nobile' was not fully applicable to smaller houses,[15] the importance of such ideas was the emphasis accorded to the first floor which, in practical terms, offered a means of escaping rising damp. This resulted in a first floor reached by an ostentatious staircase or external steps, a fashion which, when adopted, was built on whatever scale the owner could afford. Furthermore, the central staircase and gable flues brought with them that other great tenet of classicism, symmetry. By 1700 small farmhouses were built with symmetrical façades, a central door flanked by a window on each side with the whole ensemble bracketed by a pair of chimney stacks.

Winding or spiral stairs occupy less room than any other type and therefore have a longer history than most. The earliest spiral stairs were probably built of wood (Fig. 180), the central newel or post of which was sometimes a single log of oak. When they were imitated in stone this feature continued to be employed, each masoned step incorporating a segment of the newel.[16] A remarkable spiral stair which survives in the dovecote of the thirteenth-century Priory at Hinton Charterhouse, a few miles south of Bath, has the lower components of stone and the upper sections of wood.

Both the dog-leg staircase and the staircase rising round three sides of a well occupied, respectively, about three or four (or five) times more space than the spiral

stair.[17] Nevertheless, after about 1625 (by which time staircases were standard fixtures in houses in the lowland zone) the framed staircase was usual but it often incorporated some 'winders' to save space (Fig. 181). In the north the staircase became a standard fixture somewhat later. In a house known as The Gables in the hamlet of Little Carlton near the Trent, two or three miles north of Newark, there is evidence for the use of ladders until the installation of the staircase in about 1700[18] and, as we have seen, ladders remained in use in place of stairs in Yorkshire and Wales in the nineteenth century.

In the south-east the open newel may have evolved from stairs with a closed well. In an aristocratic establishment like Penshurst, the stairway (*c*. 1341) leading from the great hall to the solar rises round a walled-in well.[19] In many vernacular houses this well is sealed by stud and plaster, as at Rayne Hall, Essex (*c*. 1550), Cookes House, West Burton, West Sussex (*c*. 1580), Fulvens House, Abinger Hammer, Surrey (*c*. 1660) and the sixteenth-century Augustine Steward House, Tombland, Norwich.

181   By the use of winders a staircase could be formed which was in part a dog-leg and in part winding, as here in 84 St Aldates, Oxford – the stair dating from the second quarter of the eighteenth century.

A similar type of stair at Gaythorne Hall, Ashby, Cumbria, has the well walled-in with stone reminiscent of the Penshurst example.[20] Barley, when discussing an example of this type of stair at Rake House, Whitley, Surrey (*c.* 1630), argues that it is a 'new type'.[21] However, as it dispenses with the problem of counter-balancing the stairs it may well be the precursor of, rather than the successor to, the open well, and examples of the latter are certainly more numerous. With both the dog-leg (when not walled off) and the open newel it became necessary to provide some form of balustrading (Fig. 183). This was an opportunity that the turners, a specialist branch of the woodworking trades, met with some enthusiasm. Occasionally balusters or finials may be found that are square turned. This was achieved by attaching the scantlings for the individual balusters securely to the outer face of a giant wheel. The wheel was then revolved at speed and one face of the balusters 'turned'. This process was repeated four times thus completing a set of 'square-turned' balusters. Such work may be identified by means of a straight edge as each face of the baluster is slightly bowed.[22] Very often, and especially if balusters were worked on a raking plane, these were carved by hand and eye but sometimes examples may be found that were truly 'thrown' on a lathe.

At the vernacular level, an alternative to the expensive work of the specialist turner was the pierced flat baluster (Fig. 182) which could easily be made by the joiner. It is common to find cut and pierced balusters at the less visible top of the stairs, with the much grander turned variety at their foot. Such balusters continued to be made well into the eighteenth and even the nineteenth century. Their silhouette could more easily be given a raking plane than their more sophisticated three-dimensional cousins. At the élite level the substitution of carved and pierced panels in place of balusters had a brief vogue in the mid-seventeenth century and was followed by a longer-lasting and more widespread fashion for balusters turned with the well-known barley-sugar design. The status of a house is often established by the density of these balusters with fourth-rate and third-rate houses having two to a tread, second-rate and first-rate houses boasting three or four to a tread. In provincial Britain and Colonial America such turned balusters persisted until the close of the eighteenth century at a time when the most splendid establishments in England preferred wrought iron.

The introduction of the staircase resulted in the need for dog gates – just as dogs in church resulted in the Laudian requirement for altar rails. The well-known dog gate at Hatfield House (1607–11) is one of the most famous of the breed. On a much smaller scale the dog gate at Collinfield Manor, Kendal, Cumbria, is a good example (Fig. 182). Generally such gates were fixed at or near the foot of the stairs and the Kendal example may well have

been moved to its present position to become a 'child gate'. This possibility is indicated by comparison of the balusters of the gate with those of the landing for although they are of the same design their scale is different.

The great staircase at Knole, Kent (*c.* 1605), and another somewhat later example at Boston Manor, Middlesex, have the walls that encompass them painted with a 'reflection' of their handrails, balusters and newel posts. These very splendid examples inspired a later generation to have similar decoration applied in a less exalted vernacular context – as in 24 High Street, Colchester, Essex (*c.* 1670–80) and the Merchant's House, High Street,

182 Staircase in Collinfield Manor, Kendal, Cumbria. The dog gate may have been moved from the foot of the staircase. Flat balusters were far cheaper to produce than turned or thrown ones.

183   Staircase, *c.* 1660–70, the Merchant's House, Marlborough, Wiltshire. The painted 'echo' of the balustrade on the opposing plaster walls records the finials which are now missing from the staircase itself.

Marlborough, Wiltshire (1653–70) (Fig. 183).[23] This notion was later adopted for the ramped staircases of the early eighteenth century in which the opposing walls have ramped panelling to dado (handrail) level which responds to the ramped handrail supported by turned balusters.

Because the turner was a specialist, and turning mechanical, it is sometimes possible to locate work in dif-ferent houses (and even in different materials[24]) which may point to common authorship. Certainly the details of the staircase (second quarter of the seventeenth century) at Hassage Farmhouse, Wellow, near Bath, bear a striking resemblance to the stairs of the Old Manse at Beckington, Somerset, ten miles away. Another instance of stylistic relationship is the staircase of 1658 in the farmhouse at

Brant Broughton, Lincolnshire, which is 'identical' to the one at Auburn Hall five miles away.[25] The example immortalised by Beatrix Potter in *The Tale of Samuel Whiskers* at Hill Top Farm, Sawrey, Westmorland, has balustrading and a handrail which, though smaller in scale, are to the same design as the main staircase at Castle Bank, Appleby-in-Westmorland, which is forty-one miles (66 km) away by road, or thirty miles (48 km) by road and ferry across Lake Windermere. These two Cumbrian staircases are of late eighteenth-century date but in many ways their wide, flat handrails would place them at least eighty years earlier if found in the south-east.

Until the opening decades of the eighteenth century, framed stairs were generally built by carpenters, a tradition that is evident from their construction. For example, the central bearing string found in the carriage of the stair of the High House, Stafford (*c.* 1595; Fig. 184) is a carpentry detail that was also found during restoration work in *c.* 1992 on the staircases in No. 9 Beaufort Square, Bath (1727), although hidden beneath the plaster ceiling on the underside (Fig. 185). The stair was transformed into the stair 'case' once it was made by joiners. In the course of the eighteenth century the staircase builder was becoming the specialist that he undoubtedly became in the nineteenth century; certainly many of the houses in Georgian Bath seem to have employed the same firm of staircase joiners, with their signature crossbanded mahogany handrail.

Batty Langley's *Builder's Jewel* (1754) is largely concerned with joinery and carpentry, containing sections on panelling and roofing timbers as well as Chapter 5 of the Supplement, 'Of Stair-cases'. He gives '11 different designs for stair-cases, from which the ingenious workman may form such others as his occasions may require'. These were 'circular', 'semicircular', 'octangular', 'triangular', 'trapezia', 'geometrical square' and 'elliptical', whilst his 'parallelograms . . . may be fit for any nobleman's palace'. Generally speaking it was only in larger houses that the space occupied by the staircase was sufficiently generous for pictures to hang on the surrounding walls.

In the century following Langley, Joseph Gwilt defined the 'Geometrical Staircase' as one 'whose

184   Some staircases are carried by a central bearing 'string' (as here) in addition to the flanking strings. This example is in the High House, Stafford which was built in *c.* 1595.

185   Although, in the course of the eighteenth century, staircases began to be made by joiners, carpentry details like the central bearing string persisted as here in No. 9 Beaufort Square, Bath (built from 1727) – a detail which only became visible when the lath and plaster was removed in the course of restoration.

186 'Toads back' section to a handrail (after Joseph Gwilt *Encyclopaedia*, 1842).

187 Staircase with an open string, a scroll to terminate the mahogany handrail and a corresponding 'cur-tail' on the bottom step. The fret-cut brackets are applied to the face of the open string. This early nineteenth-century example is in a house at Bottisham, Cambridgeshire.

opening is down its centre, or, as it is called, an open newel, in which each step is supported by one end being fixed in the wall or partition, the other end of every step in the ascent having an auxiliary support from that immediately below it, beginning from the lowest one, which; of course rests on the floor'.[26] Gwilt was here describing the structure of a wood stair but in masonry

the problem was even more acute: 'one of the edges of every step [should be] supported by the edge of the step below, and formed with joggled joints . . . The principle upon which stone geometrical stairs are constructed is, that every body must be supported by three points placed out of a straight line [which triangulate].'[27]

All writers on the subject of stairs make the point that the ideal ratio of riser to tread (which establishes the 'pitch' of the stair) should first be decided and that these should later be adjusted to the circumstances of the house and the distance between the floors. Batty Langley urges that the '*headway* be spacious': 'That the breadth of the ascent be proportional to the whole building . . . The height of the steps should not be less than five inches [12.7 cm], nor more than seven inches [17.8 cm], except in such cases where necessity obliges a higher rise. The breadth [horizontal depth from front to back of tread] of steps should not be less than ten inches [25.4 cm], nor more than 15 or 16 [38 or 40.6 cm], although some allow 18 inches [45.7 cm], which I think too much. The light to a stair-case should always be liberal.'[28] In some regions, such as the Lake District, tall vertical windows rising over a couple of stories were used, by the eighteenth century, to light staircases. At Hill Top Farm, Westmorland (see above) this window is protected, at the level of the landing, by a timber balustrade matching that used to support the handrail. Batty Langley was of the opinion that a staircase should not be less than 3 ft (91.4 cm) in width but Gwilt felt that for better houses 4 ft (122 cm) was the minimum, whilst conceding that 'want of space in town houses often obliges the architect to submit to less in what is called the going of the stair'.

Even in quite small cottages, Loudon considered that stairs ought to open into the entrance lobby. In our age of low relative mortality his main reason for this seems quite grotesque. He points out that if the stairs rise from the entrance lobby 'the bedrooms may be communicated with without passing through the back; or front kitchen. This in the case of sickness, is desirable, and also in the case of death, as the remains may be carried down stairs while the family are in the front room.'[29] From the second half of the seventeenth century onwards the dog-leg stair has been usual in third and fourth-rate town houses and smaller houses elsewhere. The handrail is frequently formed into a simple cross-section in mahogany or oak, but the more elaborate 'toad's back' rail (Fig. 186) was also used.[30] By the nineteenth century the balusters are often square in section with two to a tread, but in better houses three is usual. From the late eighteenth century the handrail was terminated by a scroll which is reflected by the bottom step, both being united by a cluster of balusters. This bottom step is known as the 'cur-tail' and is especially apt for dog-leg stairs (Fig. 187).[31]

Chapter 9

Paint and Painting

MATERIALS AND TRADE ORGANISATION

It may seem wayward to begin a chapter on paints and distempers with a few brief lines on the place of textiles in interior decoration. The dominant role that fabrics (and wallpaper) have played in furnishing the average home with colour and pattern dates back little further than the nineteenth century. Only in late Georgian Britain did the products of industrialisation begin to bring textiles (and metal goods) into more general use. By then it was possible for the less affluent to afford carpets, curtains and upholstered furniture in their homes. For this reason soft furnishings are of little relevance to the vernacular interior until the second quarter of the nineteenth century or later. So long as textile production remained unmechanised only a very small privileged minority used fabrics, on any scale, for interior decoration. The abundant use of furnishing textiles served to reinforce social distinction to the extent that the deployment of opulent drapery in an aristocratic portrait is more than a compositional device, it is an emblem of status. So costly were textiles that the upholder (upholsterer) was to become the principal contractor in fitting-up the rooms of the aristocracy – the interior decorator.

For most people, paints and distempers offered the means by which interiors could be enlivened (Fig. 188). This would include the simple all-over colouring of walls, ceilings and floors as well as their decorative treatment with pattern. House-painters also ornamented such items as oil cloths, chimney boards and window blinds (or shades). Although there are a few surviving examples of polychrome decoration on vernacular furniture, this was rare in post-medieval Britain as compared with much of Continental Europe. More often a single colour

would be applied so as to unify a piece of country furniture made from a mixture of native woods. A stick-back chair was traditionally assembled from woods such as elm, beech and ash; paint gave such an object visual unity (Fig. 244). The paints, stains and distempers that were traditionally employed involved the use of a bewildering variety of pigments, numerous media with, in addition, a surprisingly diverse number of trades involved in their application. These are matters of considerable technical complexity which have been very fully examined by others elsewhere.[1]

In essence the various media used by the relevant tradesmen were composed of a 'vehicle' (for example water or a volatile oil) and a binding agent (e.g. size or resin). Robert Dossie (1758) gives the following definition of media stating that it 'answers the double purpose of reducing the colours [pigments] to a state fit for being worked with brush or pencil, and cementing them [the grains of pigment] to each other and the ground they are laid upon.'[2] There was also what I will term the 'prospective media' in which the ground was prepared in advance to hold the pigment, leaf metal or ground glass. This was the case with true fresco (*fresco buono*), with both water and oil gilding and for the 'strewing of smalt'. In these instances pigments, leaf gold, or ground blue glass were held by mordants like damp plaster, or various oils or sizes.

In terms of trade organisation the story is no less complex. In London the stainers were united with the painters to form the Painter Stainers Company as early as 1502.[3] However, plasterers were permitted by the Painter Stainers to apply distemper, but they were confined to very few pigments: white (chalk), black, red ochre, yellow ochre and russet. An early nineteenth-century example

of this linkage between plastering and distemper is to be found in the trade-card of P. Summers of 3 Bartholomew Street, Birmingham, who advertised his services as a 'Stucco Colourer and Ornamental Plasterer'.[4]

The third trade to be involved in the application of pigments was that of the plumber and glazier. These tradesmen, unlike the plasterers, were officially granted the dispensation to apply oil paint but not distemper. There are several possible explanations for this. They may, for example, have been responsible for making lead-based paints and dryers. A more probable connection is to be found in the plumber's traditional role of making lead cames for the leaded lights which they also glazed. With the introduction of sash windows, with wood glazing bars, these tradesmen found themselves fixing the glass with sprigs and putty. To retain its flexibility (for structural reasons) putty was coated with oil paint. Thus oil painting became, by extension, one of the activities of plumbers and glaziers, a tradition that persisted well into the nineteenth century and beyond. In 1837 Joshua Whitaker of Bratton, Wiltshire employed N. Taylor of Westbury, 'Painter, Plumber and Glazier', to redecorate his parlour for £5. Similarly Joseph Desilva (1816–c. 1875) of Liverpool advertised his services as a 'Painter, Plumber and Glazier . . . Paint, Oil and Colour Dealer', adding that he painted 'Portraits of Ships taken in any situation'.[5]

Although those who used distempers and paints were responsible for their preparation the ingredients were purchased from dealers. In far-off Devon the late-Stuart plasterer John Abbott purchased his brushes, media, colours, leaf gold, and silver as well as shell gold (i.e. powdered) from the 'Iremonger'. At about the same time the decorative painter John Martin obtained 'Most of the Collours' he needed 'in Little Bladders and the rest in powders with oyles, Shilles [shells] and varnish at Mr. Coopers at the sign of the three pidjohns in Bradford Street, [London], a print shop'.[6] Mussel shells were used as containers for paints and varnishes (hence shell lac, shellac).[7] The bladder colours, in use since the mid-seventeenth century, were pre-prepared oil paints. In effect they were precursors to the later collapsible metal tubes for paint and other commodities (patented 1841).[8] The powder colour mentioned by Martin would have been ground in water or, for quicker processing of small quantities, with a volatile oil. Pigments were not ground dry although they were reduced dry in a pestle and mortar. By the second quarter of the eighteenth century the Emertons of London were producing paints on a large scale using horse mills. As a result, house-painters in the capital were deprived of an important aspect of their work – the manufacture of paint. By direct reference to the Emertons, Campbell (1747) alludes to the 'low ebb' to which painters were by then reduced with the result that they were: 'the dirtiest, laziest and most debauched set of Fellows that are of any trade in or about London [and that] no parent ought to be so mad as to bind his child Apprentice for Seven Years, to a Branch that may be learned in as many Hours, in which he cannot earn a Subsistence when he has got it [and] runs the Risk of breaking his Neck every Day and in the end turns out a mere Blackguard.'[9]

As the mechanisation of paint production increased, in London and other cities, so house-painters were compelled to offer an ever widening range of services. This situation is confirmed by a number of sources including the letter-books and ledgers (1763–85) for the Bristol painter Michael Edkins[10] (see Appendix III) and by a trade-label of some fifty years later for Meggitt & Son (active 1779–1860) of Kingston upon Hull. Amongst their many activities the Meggitts did marbling and graining, gilding and bronzing, varnishing and japanning whilst for their more aristocratic clients they list 'Room Floors Chalked for Balls'. This degree of diversification was in no way uncharacteristic as Nathaniel Whittock's *The Decorative Painters' and Glaziers' Guide* (1827) confirms. Whittock was, by trade, a printer so the true author of the *Guide* is something of a mystery – but the book is certainly authoritative.[11]

Beyond the large centres of population, in the provinces and in the colonies, the range of skills undertaken by craftsmen was, for practical reasons, very wide. For example, in rural Devon the notebooks of the tradesman John Abbott (1639/40–1727)[12] suggest that, in addition to his work as a decorative plasterer, he also undertook painting (oil), staining,[13] and work in distemper (size) as was accepted for plasterers. In cities and large towns the various crafts were defined and regulated, with varying degrees of vigour, by the relevant guilds until the second half of the eighteenth century.[14]

In the empirical understanding of paint and distemper these tradesmen could be reassuringly unconcerned with matters aesthetic. Not only would a plumber apply oil paint to putty for structural reasons, but limewash was brushed onto a mud floor for purposes of consolidation, onto interior walls as a disinfectant and externally and internally distemper was applied to thatch as a fire retardent.[15] Above all, distempers and paints were applied

188   (*facing page*) Interior of an unrestored, late fifteenth-century house at Spaxton, Somerset (see also Fig. 86). Survivals of this kind present considerable problems and opportunities if they are to be rescued and brought into use. On the one hand the nineteenth-century distemper has great charm, but it also highlights the one-time presence of an inserted ceiling.

to almost every conceivable surface in addition to the envelope – the walls, floors and ceilings – that defined a given room. These craftsmen added colour to transparent blinds, to oil cloths, chimney boards and furniture. Whilst the tax on printed wallpaper made this commodity far too expensive for the sort of rooms with which we are concerned, stencilled decoration provided an effective alternative. Not that house-painters were confined to pattern, for their repertoire included pictorial work with figure compositions and the kind of landscapes found on overmantel panels and mural schemes. For good reason the house-painter was also termed a 'decorator'. Their work was remarkable for its diversity and, at times, for its artistry.

The Pigment and the Medium

Painting has been described as 'the art of covering the surfaces of wood, iron and other materials with a mucilaginous substance . . . acquiring hardness by exposure to the air.'[16] In the world of interior decoration nothing is so fugitive as paint and textiles nor so ephemeral in terms of fashion. Much of the evidence from the past has been either destroyed or obscured and that which has survived has either darkened or faded with age. With such an elusive topic it is perhaps appropriate, whilst avoiding the complexities of chemistry and optics, to look briefly at some of the fundamental facts concerning the painter's craft; and a craft it undoubtedly was before the introduction of such technical 'advances' as plastic emulsion paints (PEP) of recent years.

All paints consist of two basic ingredients, the pigment and the medium. Pigments may be natural or artificial, organic or inorganic, but they may not be soluble in the medium, for then they would be dyes such as those used by the stainers or by painters in glazes. In general the binding agents used in the various media have been derived, until recently, from animal or vegetable sources. In addition to the pigment and medium, house paints usually include ingredients to help with the drying process as well as a basic 'covering' material to give more 'body' to the paint. Oil paints are made up of four parts: the base (e.g. white lead), the pigment (colour), the vehicle (turpentine) and the binder (linseed oil). To these a 'drier' is sometimes added. A thickening medium known as 'megilp' was added by painters engaged on graining and marbling. For oil paint this megilp included ingredients like beeswax and rotten stone, but for distemper, soap and stale beer as well as wax were used. For most distempers the base is usually whitening, the medium water, and size provides the binding agent; to basic whitewash may be added numerous pigments to

provide a colour wash. Although true distemper (from the French *détrempe*) was bound with size, limewash, with its water vehicle, was closely related to it.

The techniques used in employing these materials varied according to the surface to be painted and the medium to be used. With wood it is necessary to 'prepare' the surface with size, and with softwoods it is important to 'kill' all resinous knots. For oil painting undercoats were often executed in paint with a medium that was 'lean' in character, with the final coats being of a progressively more 'fatty' nature, a sound principle which is still followed. This approach necessitated a minimum of three coats.

The complex character of the chemistry of paint and the numerous methods concerning the craft of painting are endless and cannot be dealt with in detail here. Many books have been published on the subject in the past. One of the earliest in Britain is probably William Salmon's *Polygraphice: Or The Arts of Drawing, Engraving, Etching, Limning, Painting, Varnishing, Japanning and Gilding &c* (1672) which, whilst emphasising the crafts of the fine arts (being dedicated to 'SR Godf. Kneller, Kt.'), does touch on aspects of house-painting.[17] John Smith's manual *The Art of Painting in Oyl* first appeared in 1676, (but it went through no less than six further editions or impressions and in 1821 was revised and reissued by Butcher). This was followed in 1685 by the anonymous *A Short Introduction to the Art of Painting and Varnishing* published by George Davies. Another seventeenth-century publication that includes relevant information on painting is John Stalker and George Parker's *Treatise of Japaning and Varnishing* (Oxford, 1688). Relatively few such trade manuals were published in the seventeenth century largely because of craft secrecy. In 1704 John Elsum prefaced his *The Art of Painting* with the plea that it should not cause 'offense to the Masters of the Mystery'.

As the power of the guilds waned in the eighteenth century such manuals became quite common but one of the best known is probably Robert Dossie's *The Handmaid to the Arts* of 1758. Dossie is particularly withering in his reference to Salmon who 'took upon him to give instructions for the practice of almost all the arts and mysterious trades . . . His collection would indeed have had considerable merit at the time it was published, if the valuable parts had not been confounded with such a heap of absurd stuff and falsities.'[18] In the nineteenth century authors of such books abound but one of the most instructive of these manuals is Nathaniel Whittock's *The Decorative Painters' and Glaziers' Guide* of 1827. In addition to these publications the numerous encyclopedias are also a useful source of reference, among them *The Complete Dictionary of Arts and Sciences* edited by T. H. Croker and Others (London, 1764).[19]

The early painters and decorators not only mixed their own paints, they also ground their own pigments. John Smith recommends 'A Grinding stone and Mulier; the stone it self ought to be Porphyrie, which is the best',[20] but any hard close-grained material that would not itself crumble and contaminate the pigment being ground was used. In the 1705 edition of his *The Art of Painting in Oyl* the muller is described as 'a pebble Stone of the form of an Egg' (Fig. 189).[21] Dossie describes 'The operation subservient to the making and preparing of colours [as] sublimation, calcination, solution, precipitation, filtration, and levigation'.[22] It was levigation, the grinding of pigments with a medium, a volatile oil or water, that necessitated the use of mullers.

Contrary to popular belief, oil paint was well known to medieval craftsmen.[23] However, it was but one of a variety of media known to them among which were lime-water (limewash), size (distemper), milk and wax – the latter being an emulsion rather than the wax encaustic of classical antiquity. The details of their methods are not certain as they, unlike later craftsmen, did not in general commit their knowledge to writing. As Elsum indicated, secrecy was vital. Despite these difficulties it is possible to infer the methods used by medieval and early modern craftsmen by reference to later publications and even living craftsmen where it is clear that the use of materials and tools has been passed down by word of mouth and example over many generations.

Oil paint must always have been valued for outdoor use, but before the Reformation it was less favoured for interiors, perhaps because of its frequently harsh appearance, but also because it darkens with age. In comparison the alternatives are remarkably stable, although with an occasional tendency to fade – a particular problem with the pigment known as russet. The use of oil paint was paralleled by gilding where only oil-based gold size is suitable for exterior work; for interiors 'water gilding' has always been considered best for those surfaces that will accept it – but water gilding was beyond the competence of most house-painters whose skill in the application of leaf gold was confined to oil gilding.

One of the most timeless of materials is distemper: in post-Roman Britain it was certainly in use by the twelfth century.[24] While ordinary whitewash consisted of whitening bound with size, for preference the 'binder' used was starch as it did not impair the colour. Blue (which in the nineteenth century was made by Reckitts) or 'blueblack', a carbon made from vegetable matter, was often added with a small quantity of turpentine to make the white less 'cold' in appearance. Limewash, the alternative to distemper, was generally made from slaked lime mixed with 2½ lb (1134 g) of rock alum, in place of size or starch, for every pail of limewash. Another type of white

189 Three mullers for grinding paint. These examples come from (left to right) Sussex, Shropshire and Somerset. Private Collection.

finish was 'stucco whitewash' made from unslaked chalk lime slaked in boiling water and mixed with ground rice (although other cold water pastes were no doubt used).[25] To convert 'whitewash' into 'colour wash' a variety of pigments were used, including red ochre known as 'rodel',[26] 'Oxford ochre' (yellow) from Wheatley,[27] verdigris which produced a pale greenish-blue which was apt to fade, and lime-blue made by precipitating sulphate of copper by means of milk of lime, using some heat.

The oils mixed with pigments to form paints included linseed, olive, walnut, poppy seed,[28] rosemary and oil of spike (lavender). For most house-painting purposes linseed oil was commonly used as the other oils were far too expensive. The great problem with using linseed oil was that its yellow 'cast' turned blue pigments green – hence the importance of strewing smalt in which the grains of blue glass lie on top of the binding agent. The turpentines used included those listed by Dossie which were 'the Common Venetian, Strasburg, Cyprus and Chio', of which 'Venetian', an exudate of larch, was most recommended.

Related to the turpentines were the lacquers, and Salmon lists

> *Gum-Lac* called *Shell-lac*, *Gum-Animi* (it is either Oriental, coming from the *East Indies* or Occidental, coming from the West Indies . . .), *Gum-Copal* (. . . from Hispaniola, Cuba and other places in the Spanish West Indies), . . . *Gum Sandarack* (. . . brought from *Barbary* in long Tears or Drops . . .), *Benjamine* . . . *Rosin* . . . *Mastiche* (. . . Gum of the Lentisk-Tree

growing in Chio, Ægypt and Syria . . .), *Gum-Elemi* [and finally the mysterious] *Olibanum* [which was] . . . the true ancient Incense but from what tree it is produced, Authors have not agreed.

However, Salmon goes on to say, 'but for myself being in the West Indies, I gathered it [olibanum] plentifully from the Floridian Cedar which is the Cedrus Baccifera'.[29] All of these lacquers were used in a variety of ways in paints and for both varnishing and japanning.

Wax as a medium, like milk, goes back to antiquity, and both were used in the Romano-Egyptian world. Wax is mentioned by Edward Edwards in his *Anecdotes of the Painters* (1808) in connection with the Swiss artist J. H. Müntz who 'had a landscape painted in *encaustic* a process of which he seems to have considered himself the inventor; for he published a small octavo volume [1760] in which he demonstrated the operation, but it certainly does not deserve the attention of an artist'.[30] The wax emulsions used by medieval craftsmen were altogether different. The great virtue of this type of painting was its luminosity which gives a sense of the underlying material. The medieval version of this process was particularly effective for polished interior woodwork which, when treated in this way, reveals its ligneous character despite the gesso ground used for this type of work.[31] The wills of medieval craftsmen/painters show that wax was used in place of, and certainly in greater quantities than, egg tempera.[32]

Casein, made from curds of milk,[33] tended to produce an unpleasant smell which Butcher, in his edition of John Smith's *The Art of Painting in Oyl*, claims to have overcome by means of a new recipe.[34] The traditional means of solving this problem was by the addition of ammonia – usually in the form of urine. By reference to Butcher's book, 'The very offensive and injurious smell . . . may be obviated by the following recipe – [which] will answer for inside work.' The materials used in this concoction were 2 qts (2.3 l) of skimmed milk, 6½ oz (184.3 g) of fresh slaked lime, 4 oz (113.4 g) of linseed oil and 3 lb (1360 g) of whiting.

Put the lime into a stone [stoneware] vessel, and pour upon it a sufficient quantity of milk to form a mixture resembling thin cream; then add the oil a little at a time, stirring it with a small spatula; the remaining part of the milk is then to be added; and lastly the whiting. The milk must on no account be sour. . . .

The whiting, or ochre is gently crumbled on the surface of the fluid which it gradually imbibes, and at last sinks: at this period it must be stirred in.

The paint may be coloured like distemper or size colour, with levigated charcoal, yellow ochre etc . . . the quantity here prescribed is sufficient to cover twenty-

seven square yards [22.6 square metres] with the first coat, and will cost about three halfpence per yard.

These instructions make no allusion to the need for preparing this limewash over a low flame but this was probably necessary. Today's plastic emulsion paints (PEP) are very similar to the casein paints of the past, and produce similar results, and when waxed resemble wax emulsion paint. Of recent years, a number of specialist manufacturers have begun to produce traditional distempers.

Various other paint-like substances apart from those outlined above were in use, many of which date back a long way. Medieval timberwork is often found bearing traces of a reddish, stain-like pigment which has not been applied on the usual foundation of gesso. This is probably the same as the mixture brushed onto the South Door of York Minster as late as 1861 which consisted of rud (red ochre) and bullock's blood.[35]

THE WORK OF THE STAINERS

Originally 'The Painters and Staynors were two companies [guilds], the one for painting with colours in oil and size upon timber, stone, iron and such like, and the Staynors for cloth, silk and such like'.[36] When these two guilds united in 1502 it was perhaps inevitable, as is so often the case in such circumstances, that one party to the merger would be subsumed by the other.[37] In this instance it was to be the Stainers who were to be eclipsed. Indeed, as early as 1530 the Stainers are not mentioned in the grant of arms issued to the joint company. Consequently the once ubiquitous stained hangings are now very rare and in only a couple of instances in England do they hang in their original context. They have been the subject of a recent monograph by Nicholas Mander which builds on the earlier work of Elsie Matley Moore.[38]

The primary source of employment for stainers was in the production of their eponymous hangings which, in terms of technique, were a cheap alternative to woven tapestry – although in artistic terms they could be very imposing. The most magnificent surviving examples in an English house are a set of *c.* 1600–1 attributed to John Balechouse, a Continental artist working in Derbyshire. These hang in the High Great Chamber at Hardwick Hall.[39] At a less exaulted level inventories regularly refer to stained hangings as 'hallings', indicating that they customarily hung in the halls of yeoman and gentry houses.[40] In a very modest labourer's cottage it is possible that a single hanging provided the one note of colour in the home. Such a view is supported by the continuation of this tradition in early nineteenth-century Sweden

190   Late seventeenth-century stained hanging from Munslow Farm, Munslow, Shropshire (see also Figs. 196–8).

where the colourful Dalecarlia *bonad* were often shown in whitewashed, but otherwise unpainted, interiors.[41]

In 1558 this form of decoration was so common in England that a French visitor, Etienne Perlin, categorically states that: 'The English make such use of tapestries of painted cloths [tapisseries de toiles pinctes] which are very well executed . . . for there are few houses you could enter without finding these tapestries.'[42] A few years later, in 1564, William Bullein would describe a fictitious, and therefore presumably ideal, inn as having 'a comlie parlour, verie netlie and trimlie apparelled, London like, the windowes are well glased, and faire clothes with pleasaunte borders about the same, with many wise saiynges painted upon them.'[43] This 'London

like' high standard of living with glass in the windows and hangings in the parlour recalls William Harrison's *Description of England* of 1577 which gives an account of 'The Walls of our houses on the inner sides in the like sort be either hanged with tapesterie, arras worke, or painted cloths, wherein either divers histories, [or] herbs, beasts, knots, and such like are stained.'[44]

Numerous references to these furnishing textiles are to be found in probate inventories. For example the 'paynted cloths about ye chamber' in an Oxfordshire farmhouse which, in 1579, were valued at 6s 8d.[45] In Warwickshire it is known that William Shakespeare's grandfather, Robert Arden, owned eleven sets of stained hangings, whilst, Henry Field, a tanner and neighbour of the playwright's father in Stratford-upon-Avon, owned several in both his hall and his parlour.[46] In these circumstances it is perhaps inevitable that Shakespeare, through the pugnacious Falstaff, makes reference to stained hangings in *Henry IV*, Part I (1590–1?), *Henry IV*, Part II (1590–1?) and *The Merry Wives of Windsor* (1597) whilst they also occur in *As you Like It* (c. 1594), *Love's Labours Lost* (1594–5?) and his epic poem *The Rape of Lucrece*.[47] It might be added that the Elizabethan stage employed stainers to paint the modest back cloths that served as scenery and also stained banners and similar 'props'. The continued popularity of hangings at this time is confirmed by the fact that 56 per cent of late Tudor inventories in Nottinghamshire list painted cloths or tapestry.[48]

The reasons for the popularity of hangings extended beyond their decorative qualities to their practical function. In timber-frame buildings, traditionally constructed of green oak, the wood shrank away from the wattle and daub infill. Stained cloths suppressed the inevitable draughts, whilst in stone buildings they did much to reduce problems of condensation. Despite these practical considerations the production, but not the use, of stained cloths went into sharp decline in late Tudor England. As early as 1483 the threat of imports from the Continent, particularly the Netherlands, was such that merchants were prohibited by statute from importing 'painted glass, painted papers, painted images, painted cloths, etc.'[49] These measures were evidently ineffective for by 1598

191   Fireplace in a first-floor chamber of *c.* 1603–13 in a house known as The Lockers, near Hemel Hempstead, Hertfordshire. The fireplace is constructed of brick, plastered to counterfeit stone. This has been painted with a representation of a pair of Ionic columns, embellished with ribbons and bows, which support a painted moulding. The overmantel carries a canvas hanging *stained* to resemble woven tapestry – in contrast to the *painted* hanging (Fig. 192) which was once used elsewhere in the same house.

John Stow, in describing the Painter Stainers hall in London, concludes 'that [the] workmanship of staining is departed out of use in England.' This observation is confirmed by a bill, introduced in Parliament in 1601 on behalf of the Painter Stainers which refers to the 'Painting of Cloths' a trade 'much decayed and not an hundred yards of new painted cloth [is] made in a Year here by reason of so much Painted Flanders pieces brought from thence.'[50] The fact that stained hangings were imported to this extent may have contributed to the decline in their use in Britain, although the rising fashion for imported 'pentados' or calicos from the Far East, and the increased use of framed pictures and wood panelling (also largely imported) are more likely explanations. It should, though, be remembered that stained hangings and wood panelling could happily coexist. Indeed, such an arrangement is recorded in a late sixteenth-century mural from Hill House, Colchester in which a stained hanging, or painted wall, occurs over a panelled dado, the whole ensemble being represented, in this instance, in distemper (Fig. 85).[51] John Aubrey (1626–97) describes a similar arrangement in the dwelling of a 'widow woman' at Eton, Berkshire which was 'a handsome darke old-fashioned house. The hall after the old fashion, above the wainscot, painted cloath, with godly sentences out of the Psalms etc., according to the pious custome of old times.'[52]

Since so few hangings survive, the descriptions of them are valuable but probably give undue prominence to those which had a story to tell. It therefore seems reasonable to assume that many stained cloths were decorated with a repeat pattern similar to those seen on wall paintings (Fig. 204). Even where Classical and biblical themes are illustrated they were often 'carried' by the sort of verdure one is familiar with in woven tapestry (Fig. 190). For figure subjects Tessa Watt has demonstrated that popular prints were the exemplars.[53] She has, for example, drawn attention to the Painter Stainers' searches of 1632 which revealed that this connection was commercial in that several stationers were involved in the stainers' trade.[54] With the Puritan compulsion to white-wash the interiors of churches their visual richness was transferred to domestic settings. Old Testament narrative scenes were acceptable to a Protestant clientel whereas New Testament portraits could be seen as Catholic and idolatrous.[55] There were no such ideological hazards for those who sought refuge in Classical mythology. Both biblical and Classical themes were popular as in Shakespeare's description of stained hangings which depicted 'the story of the Prodigal [son]' in both *Henry IV*, Part II[56] and in *The Merry Wives of Windsor*[57] whilst allusion is made, in jest, to 'Alisander the conqueror' being 'scraped out of a painted cloth' in *Love's Labours Lost*.[58]

As will have been noted the documentary record describes these canvases variously as 'stained' or 'painted'. Surviving examples and documentary evidence (cited below) indicate that, in order to resemble a woven tapestry and its prestige, it was important that the weave of the canvas should remain visible (Fig. 191). Deception of this kind seems to have been intentional since the Scottish decorative painter, John Mellin or Melville (fl. 1587–1604), was well known for his 'imitation tapestry'.[59] For this reason emphasis was given to staining rather than painting – as is implied by Shakespeare's reference to 'The German water work' cloth hanging.[60] An exception to this approach may be seen in a fragment of such a hanging dating from *c.* 1600 in the Victoria and Albert Museum (Fig. 192). This is painted in solid colour which obscures the weave of the canvas and thus the surface more closely resembles the polychromed panelling which it imitates (W.41–1952). Most of the existing examples seem to be on a coarse unbleached linen or hempen canvas made from *hurds* or *hards*.[61] In the late seventeenth century chapmen continued to sell brown osnabrucks and hemp canvas for 'ordinary painting'.[62] It is unlikely that the fine linen canvas known as 'holland' was employed for this purpose although it was certainly used in the early nineteenth century for stained window blinds (Fig. 130).

There are two very different surviving descriptions concerning the methods used to stain canvas for hangings of this kind. The earliest of these is quoted in Eastlake's *Materials for a History of Oil Painting* (1847).[63] It derives from the copy of a manuscript made in Bologna on 11 February 1410 and lent to the copyist by Theodoric of Flanders, 'an embroiderer who had obtained the recipe in London from the artists involved in that work.' This suggests that, in the early fifteenth century, the Stainers of London were far ahead of those in the Low Countries who would later become their competitors. The transcript reads as follows:

The aforesaid Theodoric, from whom I had these receipts, said that in England the painters work with these water colours on closely woven linen saturated with gum water. This, when dry, is stretched on the floor over coarse woollen and frieze cloths; and the artists, walking over the linen with clean feet, proceed to design and colour historical figures and other subjects. And because the linen is laid quite flat on the woollen cloths, the water colours do not flow and spread, but remain where they are placed; the moisture sinking through into the woollen cloths underneath, which absorb it. In like manner, the outlines of the brush remain defined, for the gum in the linen prevents the spreading of such lines. Yet, after this linen is

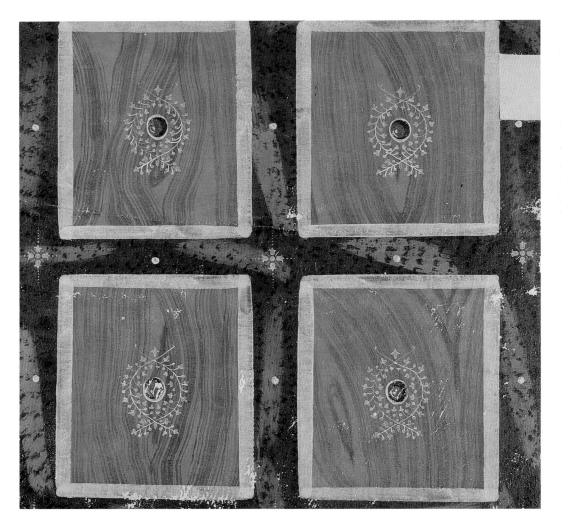

192   Painted hanging (*c.* 1603–13) from The Lockers, Hemel Hempstead, Hertfordshire. Although this hanging was recently moved (from elsewhere in the house) to the same room as the canvas in Fig. 191 its treatment is very different. Here the canvas has been *painted* (rather than stained) to more closely resemble the surface of wood panelling. Victoria and Albert Museum, London.

painted, its thinness is no more obscured than if it was not painted at all, as the colours have no body.

The 'gum' referred to is, of course, the size used as a preparation on the canvas and in the medium. The finest size for small-scale work was made from boiled parchment, but in this procedure rabbit skin (cony) size was probably used. Theodoric's allusion to stretching the canvas may be related to the will of 1581 of the widow of Thomas Gammige of Essex: 'all my frames [probably straining frames] with painted pictures or stories on them, together with all my [grinding] stones, colours and frames [possibly picture frames], and all other things belonging to the mystery, science or occupation of a painter.'[64]

The second recipe giving procedures for this type of painting is from the 1662–3 manuscript of the Devon plasterer, John Abbott (1639/40–1727).[65] It reads as follows:

To painte upon Cloth either with water colours or oyl colours

Off Water Colours
ffirst spread abroad your cloth, with nailes against the wall, or the like, very plaine and smooth, or upon a frame made for ye purpose, then strike it all over with starch boiled and let it dry.

Then prime it: that is strike it all over with a brush made of piggs haire with Spanish white, or with ledd [white], being well ground as shall be here after shewed, then lett itt dry & it is ready to work upon – If it be upon wood or stone or the like then you need not use any starch.

Take glew and disolve it into hot water and with it some what claimay [clammy], which you may try between your fingers this all.

Size then with this size, grind your white led or chalke; if it be grose worke your paint you may temper all youre clear collers with this size also.

Note

All sorts of pencels [brushes], and collouers for painting and lynseed oyle, are to be soulde at the Iremongers; Alsoe leafe gold, Shell gold and leaf Silver.

The notebook goes on to give advice on how 'To Temper gum water' and 'To make a gleare [glair]'. Significantly

193, 194   The hangings at
Owlpen Manor,
Gloucestershire, are stained
onto a coarse linen canvas 42
ins wide. They appear to be by
the same hand, or derive from
the same workshop as those
from Munslow Farm (see Figs.
196–8). Hangings such as these
enjoyed a very wide social
distribution.

Abbott advises that these hangings should be stained vertically whereas Theodoric categorically states that this
was best done with the canvas stretched flat on the floor
– the most likely procedure. Whilst most of this work was
done freehand with brushes, stencils were used, particularly for the repeat pattern in borders. The use of stencils
was seen as something of a threat to the Painter Stainers
of London who, in 1581, forbade deceitful work 'wrought
with stencil pattern'. Indeed stencils have probably always
been seen as a way of counterfeiting true artistry. In 1836
Mrs Phelps in her book *The Female Student* warned that
although 'handsome [theorem, i.e. stencilled] pictures are
made' in this way 'they are almost wholly mechanical
operations.'[66]

A considerable number of stained hangings still hang
in the great country houses of Continental Europe[67]
although in Britain the Hardwick Hall series are exceptional. Of those with a vernacular character few survive
and in the British Isles only three or four remain in the
houses in which they first hung.[68] Others exist which
have long since been removed from their historical
context.[69] Perhaps the finest to remain in their original
house (although removed from the room in which they
hung until *c.* 1963) are those at Owlpen Manor, Gloucestershire (Figs. 193, 194, 195). At the time of their installation these were in a 'gentry' setting but they are close in
character to, and may be by the same hand as, the set
which hung, until recently, in the principal bedroom

195   These stained 'cloths' were hung in the bedroom of the east wing (built *c.* 1720) of Owlpen Manor, Gloucestershire. Despite the late date of their installation it is possible that these hangings were made only a few decades earlier, a possibility confirmed by the character and housing of the Munslow series. Here in their original setting the Owlpen hangings, with their border top and bottom, measured 8 ft 4 ins (254 cm) in height.

in Munslow Farm, Munslow, Shropshire – a dwelling on a much smaller scale (Figs. 196, 197).[70] As with the Munslow cloths, the Owlpen hangings originally graced a principal bedroom in the east wing which was rebuilt in about 1720. The Owlpen examples probably date from twenty to thirty years earlier although Christopher Hussey ventured 'not to rule out the first decade of the eighteenth century'. They are stained onto strips of canvas 42 ins wide sewn together and, with their borders top and bottom, were originally 100 ins (8 ft 4 ins, or 254 cm) high.[71] The Munslow canvases are, unusually, framed into contemporaneous panelling, with bolection mouldings so typical of the period. Unlike the Owlpen examples which are animated with Old Testament themes, like Joseph and his multicoloured coat, those at Munslow apparently offer no narrative 'story-line'.

Hangings of this general kind were probably mass produced in strips of considerable length in specialist workshops. This is implied by the Painter Stainers of London, in 1601, when, as noted earlier, they bemoaned the fact that 'not an hundred yards of new Painted Cloth [had been] made in a Year here'.[72] Certainly the Munslow examples may have been produced in this way with some figures (the ghostly outlines of which survive) being painted *in situ* (Fig. 198). This might account for the contradiction between the two methods of working given by Abbott and by Theodoric (see pp. 133–5 above).

From medieval times, and possibly even earlier, stained hangings remained fashionable until the early seventeenth century, and popular for a century thereafter. They provided an effective means of embellishing rooms in households of nearly all degrees, whilst at the same time

196   (*above*) The stained hangings of Munslow Farm, Shropshire. These were incorporated into a scheme of panelling which, judging by such details as the bolection moulding, date from the decade around 1700.

197   The Munslow Farm hangings occupied the upper chamber in the brick-built wing on the left.

198   Hangings were generally mass-produced but may have been 'customised'. The outline of a figure of a man with a staff is just visible in this detail of one of the Munslow hangings – the figure appears to have been added *in situ* as an afterthought.

being important for their draft-proofing and insulating properties.

Although not a direct descendant of the stained hangings of the past, the Georgian enthusiasm for transparencies may have been a Franco-Dutch fashion introduced to Britain by the Huguenots from *c.* 1685.[73] The principal use for these was in conjunction with glazed windows and as such they were akin to the decorated waxed paper or linen fenestrals described by Sir Hugh Platt in 1504 (see above, Chapter 5, p. 74). These decorations were also used for both public and private celebrations. On 27 April 1749 a festivity took place in St James Park to celebrate the peace of Aix la Chapelle of 1748. This occasion was graced by transparencies which were illuminated by 'a great number of Lampions' and fireworks all of which provided a backdrop for 'a grand Overture of Warlike Instruments composed by Mr.

Handel' – his 'Firework music'.[74] Eighteenth-century transparencies such as those illustrated by James Gillray in his engraving of the *Exhibition of a Democratic Transparency . . .* of 1799 were 'stained' onto finely woven textiles like 'Sarsenet', 'Scotch Cambric' and even silk rather than the coarse canvas used for stained hangings.[75]

In 1807 Edward Orme published his *Essay on Transparent Prints, and Transparencies in General* in which he claimed to have invented a special method for doing this type of work. He argued that his transparencies would 'supply the place of painted glass' and that, in addition to their use in windows they could be employed to make lanterns, lampshades and fire screens. It was, however, as window blinds that transparencies would be used to shade interiors from the fading effects of the sun (see pp. 81–2). It is for this purpose that they were described by Nathaniel Whittock (1827) and illustrated in use by the American artist E. L. Henry in his painting *Totally Absorbed* (1874; Fig. 131).

THE PAINTERS

Some historical and visual imagination is required if one is to summon up a picture of the polychromatic decoration that once helped to establish the prestige of a medieval cathedral within the hierarchy of ecclesiastic architecture. The external elevations of Wells Cathedral, no less than its interior, were once embellished with gilding and painting so that, from a distance, it must have resembled a jewel box set down in the green hills of Somerset, a magnet for pilgrimage.[76] Similarly, royal palaces were no less gaudy internally. Even somewhat smaller buildings such as the Longthorpe Tower, Cambridgeshire, has fine murals of *c.* 1330 which combine secular and sacred themes.[77] The great strength of all this colour was that, metaphorically, and possibly literally, the paint came off a palette rather than out of a pot. A blue or a red colour was gloriously inconsistent, like those in a good old Persian carpet. In contrast to a house of god, or those of the aristocracy, most small domestic buildings were white limewashed in late medieval or early modern England but colourful hangings could enliven interiors. The effect was probably similar to the rooms recorded visually by artists of the seventeenth-century Dutch school, painters such as Vermeer and de Hooch. White distempered walls, cool spaces, animated by people and colourful plenishings.

In post-Reformation English houses 'biblical themes continued to be used for murals and hangings but secular, often Classical, subjects were also employed together with abstract designs and foliate pattern. The recently discovered, mid-sixteenth-century wall paintings, in the Merchant's House, East St Helen Street, Abingdon, may be ideologically neutral but retain a pre-Reformation sense of colour (Fig. 199). Their subject matter, flowers on sods of grasses, could well be taken from a medieval herbal.

In those periods of history noted for their archaeological zeal the use of colour is usually restrained. This was largely because exhumed sculpture and fragments of architecture had generally lost their original paint and distempers. Probably for this reason the Renaissance rejected the notion of the polychromatic painting of architecture and sculpture; although in countries like Germany, where medieval traditions permeated later idioms, the use of colourful painted decoration lingered. Sir Henry Wotton in his *Elements of Architecture* (1624) referred to this situation with ambiguous emotions appropriate to the period of aesthetic change in which he lived: 'various colours on the *Out-walles* of *Buildings* have always in them more Delight then Dignity; therefore I would there admit no *Paintings* but in *Black* and *White*, nor even in that kinde any *Figures* (if the roome be capable) under *Nine* or *Ten* foot high, which will require no ordinary *Artizan*; because the faults are more *visible* than in small *Designs*'.[78]

In 1601 the Stainers of London and, by extension, elsewhere in England, were believed to be losing business as a result of the importation of 'painted Flanders pieces' – in other words stained hangings. As a consequence members of the Painter Stainers Company had 'nothing to live on but laying of Oyl-Colours on Posts, Windows, etc.'[79] This confirms that, at this time, whilst there was adequate work for house-painters, the activities of the stainers in England were in terminal decline. The following pages will look primarily at the decorative work of the painters in distemper and in oil paint whilst not losing sight of the reality that plasterers were also permitted to apply distemper (size-based media, see pp. 125–7) and plumbers used paint (oil-based media, see pp. 125–7).

It is clearly advisable, as Wotton acknowledges, that the treatment of interiors should be related to their scale which, in my opinion, he confused with their dimensions. Furthermore, the aspect of a room should, ideally, influence the colours selected to adorn it – dark tones in a room facing north (in the northern hemisphere) would be sombre indeed. Similarly, in small rooms white paint or distemper is often advisable for the way in which it reflects light. Loudon recommended 'the colouring of the Walls of rooms with water colours, or what is called distemper . . . All the different colours are used for the walls of rooms but the most common after white are some shades of yellow, red, green or grey. As a general rule the ceiling should be of a lighter colour than the walls.'[80] The primacy of white is clear in this passage,

199   Sixteenth-century mural decoration in the Merchant's House, East St Helen Street, Abingdon (built *c.* 1430). The motifs may derive from the woodcuts in a herbal.

but in one town, Norwich, it seems to have been used until the nineteenth century to the exclusion of all others – perhaps because of the city's proximity to Holland.[81] The primacy of white in Norwich is possibly confirmed by Celia Fiennes who, writing in 1698, states that every year 'on Holly [Holy] Thursday when the Major [Mayor] is sworne in . . . they [the inhabitants] newe washe and plaister their houses within and without.'[82] It should be noted that limewash provided a welcome disinfectant and that such 'decoration' was probably but an extension of 'spring cleaning'. An Act of Parliament of 1802 concerning apprentices stipulated that an apprentice's room should be whitewashed twice a year although the Apprentice House at Quarry Bank Mill (Fig. 66) was only whitewashed internally once a year.[83]

Before the Reformation surviving records concerning the internal treatment of walls is largely confined to the

200   The lion and the griffin of Tudor England painted in distemper on plaster at Synyards, Otham, Kent – early sixteenth century.

palaces of prince or prelate. Salzman quotes the fashion, in medieval interiors, of marking out white walls with red lines to resemble masonry, and also mentions the treatment of the interior walls of the Tower of London, which in 1337 were given a coat of whitening contrasting with the timber posts and beams which were distempered with 'size and okkere' – an early instance of colour being used to give emphasis to structural timber.[84] In late medieval England the range of pigments available to the rich was quite considerable. The remainder of the population probably had to make do with decorating their houses with nature's pigments, chalk being the most common, with ochre, both red and yellow, as possible alternatives in some districts (Fig. 76). Even in a Kentish yeoman's house of the quality of Synyards, Otham, the painting on plaster over the fireplace, showing the lion and griffin of Tudor England, is confined to earth ochres and lamp black on a white ground (Fig. 200). In New England the late Nina Fletcher Little found 'little evidence for paint or distemper in interiors during the seventeenth and early years of the eighteenth centuries',[85] a situation born of the high cost of importing pigments and media from Britain. Although the circumstances of Colonial America did not obtain in the mother country – lesser interiors in Britain were most often decorated with distemper and the palette was restricted; yet another reason for the popularity of stained hangings.

With the dissolution of the monasteries came the concomitant redistribution not only of wealth and lands, but also of materials and skills. One of the most remarkable survivals of a painted screen in a relatively modest domestic interior was discovered in the 1970s at Cross Farm, Westhay, Meare, Somerset (Fig. 201). Sixteenth-century paintings at the domestic level can be difficult to place for period. In this instance the presence of the guilloche pattern suggests a date no earlier than about 1540. Meare, a few miles from Glastonbury, was an important centre for the Abbey estates with the abbot's country house and the Fish House located there. The last abbot, Richard Whiting, and two of his monks were executed on Glastonbury Tor on 15 November 1539.[86] It is therefore probable that the Westhay mural dates from shortly after the disposal of the Abbey estates. It is painted on plank and muntin panelling which probably pre-dates the Reformation by some fifty years. The chamfer stops occur near the cill but by the time the distemper decoration was applied, a bench was apparently placed against the screen, and it is at seat level that the mural decoration ceases. It was the clear intention of the artist to produce a rich effect by giving a subsidiary role to relatively common pigments like red ochre (used as the background) whilst affording a central place to exotic pigments like verdigris green (employed for the principal motifs). Lamp black and chalk white are used to delineate the design and to provide internal drawing. Thus all the colours were relatively easily obtained but the most expensive were deployed ostentatiously. It will be noted that the design is painted quite arbitrarily over the panelling despite its high relief and strong shadows. A similar disregard for the underlying surface may often be found in walls of stud and plaster where the design runs easily over either surface (Fig. 78).

The room in which this remarkable survival stands measures 173 ins (439.4 cm) by 120 ins (304.8 cm) and

201 Painted timber screen (12 ft 9 ins by 7 ft or 388 by 213.5 cm) at Cross Farm, Westhay, near Glastonbury, Somerset, second half of the sixteenth century. This painted scheme stops 1 ft 6 ins (45.75 cm) above the floor, presumably to allow for the presence of a bench. The screen itself is probably earlier than the painting, which has been applied arbitrarily without regard to the stud and plank panelling.

includes a fine fireplace similar to the example in the Priest's House some sixteen miles away at Muchelney. The room at Cross Farm was apparently the 'hall' of the house and was originally open to the roof, which is of raised cruck construction (as defined by Eric Mercer).[87] The screen divides the hall from the parlour, which served until recently as a dairy. The back of the screen is unchamfered and undecorated save for the whitewash which has probably been applied regularly over a considerable number of years (Fig. 202).[88] A similar screen on

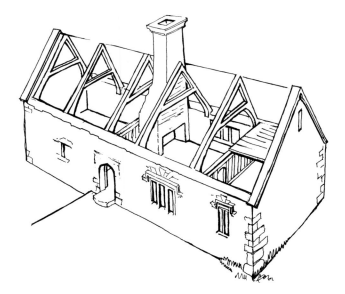

202 Sketch reconstruction of the possible original form of Cross Farm, Westhay. The 'bottom end' originally served as a byre. The screen separates the hall from the parlour which may have functioned as a service room – of recent years it was used as a dairy.

the first floor of the Gate House at Glastonbury Abbey, six miles (9.6 km) from Westhay, bears traces of painted decoration including a guilloche similarly treated to that at Cross Farm. Apart from these details the design of the painted screen at Westhay is an exception, an aberration even. More characteristic of its period, if a couple of decades later than the Westhay painting, is the screen at Markers 'cottage', a yeoman house in Devon (Fig. 203).

With the building of Nonsuch Palace, Surrey (1538) a new idiom, brought over by craftsmen from abroad, would move outwards across England to influence all aspects of decoration in rooms which otherwise remained determinedly medieval in their planning and character (see pp. 45–6). Woodcarving, textiles, plasterwork and painting all employed this new 'antick' or 'Romaine' fashion as this Classically-inspired style was then known. Mural decora-

203   Detail of a late sixteenth-century painted screen in a yeoman house known as Marker's at Broadclyst, near Exeter, Devon. This scheme is far more typical, even conventional, compared with the Westhay screen (Fig. 201).

tion of this type is characterised by florid, all-over patterns that run arbitrarily across structural timbers and other features.[89] One example of the sort is to be seen in an upstairs chamber in the Long House, 62 Strand Street, Sandwich, Kent (Fig. 78). In contrast another wall in the same room carries designs which conform to the plastered wattle and daub panels, with a secondary pattern used to decorate and emphasise the timber stiles, rails and wind-braces (Fig. 79). The difference in treatment may be due to the greater visibility of these structural elements on this wall. To unify these two distinct approaches, the two schemes share the same Vitruvian scroll, which forms the frieze, whilst just above the painted skirting there is a 'run' of informal arcading. The colour scheme is restricted to lamp black and ochres on a white ground. A second room on the same floor in this house (described on p. 45) has decoration impressed into the plaster which serves to emphasise the rectangular panels into which the timber stiles and rails divide the interior wall surfaces (Fig. 77). The painted decoration in the Sandwich house possesses much the same uninhibited, yet accomplished flowing quality, which could appear when figure subjects were introduced. A superb example of this can be seen in the freely drawn and sophisticated fragment from the painted chamber at Queen Hoo Hall, Hertfordshire.[90] Mural decoration of the Queen Hoo Hall kind does not seem to have extended down the social scale lower than the yeoman class.

Another type of mural scheme, which was probably more widespread, is typified by the example recorded by Martin Hardie in July 1936 (Fig. 204). This decoration was found on the east wall in an upper room in a farmhouse at Basing, near Cowden, Kent. It probably dates from the late sixteenth century and is similar in kind to work of the same period in Cornmarket Street, Oxford, in a building that was formerly the Crown Tavern.[91] In both cases the design consists of a repeat pattern with texts placed in panels in the frieze. This pattern was probably executed with the assistance of stencils although this was expressly forbidden in the Painter Stainers' Company Charter of 1581. By 1626 the Lord Chamberlain condemned the use of stencils as 'a great hindern of ingenuity and a cherisher of idleness and laziness in all beginners in the said art'[92] (see p. 135 above). In the Basing mural the distemper decoration extends to the fireplace bressummer and to the door. The texts remained a popular feature into the seventeenth century and there were two prime locations for these 'black-letter' inscriptions: the chimney breast or, as here and in the Oxford example, in cartouches in the frieze.[93] These brief phrases or aphorisms were more easily brushed onto smooth plaster or timber than onto the rough woven surface of a stained hanging, although the written record is inclined to contradict this practical consideration. In 1564 William Bullein describes 'faire clothes

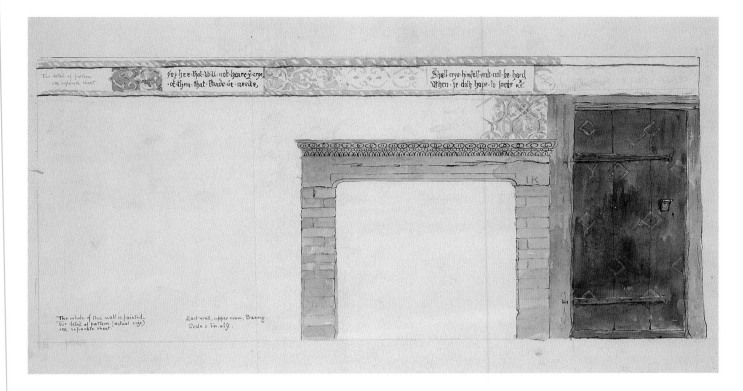

204   The east wall of an upper room in a yeoman's house at Basing, near Cowden, Kent. The house was built in 1597, the most probable date of this mural scheme recorded in watercolour by Martin Hardie in July 1936 – see also Fig. 166. Victoria and Albert Museum, London.

with pleasaunte borders about the same, with many wise saiynges painted upon them.'[94] Certainly Shakespeare must have had such a cloth in mind in his lines:

Who fears a sentence in an old man's saw
Shall by a painted cloth be kept in awe[95]

The farmhouse at Cowden, Kent, also included a ceiling with painted decoration, described in Chapter 7 (Fig. 166). This comprised a Vitruvian scroll of alternately reversed stencils applied to the plaster 'underdrawing' under the floorboards (of the room above) and between the joists. This type of ceiling painting was also done in the north-east of England (Fig. 165) but it was a fashion that was most fully exploited in Scotland in the houses and castles of the aristocracy and gentry, and is generally beyond the scope of this book (Fig. 164).[96] In early Stuart England the burgeoning use of plaster ceilings was to obscure the joists, and the spaces between them, two zones on which painters had previously bestowed so much of their artistry. However, in view of the exalted households in which this type of decoration is often found in Scotland some explanation for the disparity between the two neighbouring countries is called for. It may well be that the strong cultural links with Scandi-

navia, where painted decorative ceilings long remained a significant element in interior decoration, may account for their persistence in Scotland.[97] This hypothesis is perhaps confirmed by the fact that most Scottish examples of this kind are found towards the east coast,[98] as indeed is the case in England (Fig. 165). Numerous Scottish artisan artists have been recorded who painted ceilings, among other activities like portrait painting.[99] Amongst these tradesmen was the Englishman Valentine Jenkin who was working in Scotland by 1633. Had he, one is inclined to speculate, moved north of the border as the fashion for this work declined in England?

The conceit for painting clouds on plaster ceilings in both ecclesiastical[100] and domestic settings was popular in the seventeenth century and has a long history (Fig. 173). Examples have been recorded at Alderman Fenwick's house, Newcastle upon Tyne, and a fragment of another exists above a later Baroque plaster ceiling (the ceiling of *c.* 1700) in Farm Estate House, Fiddlington, Somerset (Fig. 173). As late as 1805 a provincial drawing master, Robert Dixon, placed an advertisement in the *Norwich Mercury* in which he announced that he had established a 'house painting business . . . Drawing-rooms, Vestibules, etc. ornamented in the newest and

most approved stile. Clouded and ornamental ceilings, Transparencies and Decorations in general.'[101] (I have discussed the question of 'transparencies' above – see p. 138).

For some fifty years from the last decades of the sixteenth century the fashion for blackwork embroidery on clothes was reflected by the use of linear patterns in black on white for the decoration of interiors (Figs. 205, 206). A good example of this type of work came to light in the 1970s in Ivy House, Fittleworth, Sussex (Figs. 207, 208), and some sections of this painted plaster are now preserved in the Weald and Downland Museum. The scheme seems to relate closely to the patterns in Thomas Trevelyan's manuscript books of designs. His *Miscellany* dates from 1608 and his later manuscript was completed on 12 September 1616. Curiously enough this later book has a Sussex provenance having been in the Leconfield sale of 24 April 1928 (Petworth House, the Leconfield seat in Sussex, is but two miles from Fittleworth) (Fig. 209). One section of this manuscript states that it was intended 'for ioyners and Gardeners, as knotes and Buildings' which brings Trevelyan's aspirations close to those of Walter Gedde in his book of 1615 (see pp. 69, 75).[102] It

205   Detail of painted door decorated (*c.* 1600) with 'blackwork' panels and stiles and rails which have been 'grained' to resemble no known timber. This door came from Hyde Abbey House, Winchester but bears little relationship to the existing structure. Victoria and Albert Museum, London (W123, 1937).

206   Painted timber from an upper hall in a house in Bishopric, Horsham, West Sussex, late sixteenth century. Before this house was floored-in the powerful zigzag design would have been viewed from a distance in the shadows of the roof timbers.

207, 208   Decorative 'blackwork' painting of the early seventeenth century from Ivy House, Fittleworth, West Sussex. Similar designs were also applied to early wallpaper, furniture lining paper and to embroidered work on clothes.

209   'Blackwork' design by Thomas Trevelyan. Two manuscript volumes of his designs survive – one dated 1608, the other 1616. The later compilation belonged (until 1928) to the Leconfields of Petworth House, just two miles from Fittleworth. Trevelyon's designs may well have inspired the Fittleworth blackwork decoration – see Figs. 207, 208.

210   Mural scheme (restored) in the dining room of the Merchant's House, Marlborough. The work may be tentatively attributed to William Brunson (see Fig. 172). This remarkable interior was created sometime between 1656 and 1670 when Thomas Bayly, the owner of the house, died. The painted plaster fireplace lining is typical of south-west England and certain other locations – see Figs. 45–50. Despite the apparent richness of the striped decoration the pallet is simple, just three colours, indigo, red and yellow ochre, on a white ground (plus combinations of these).

should be noted that many of the examples of wallpaper and lining paper (in furniture) which survive from this period are of the 'blackwork' type.[103]

By the early seventeenth century a greater variety of pigments had become available to more people so that despite what Entwisle has described as 'the "Black and White" vogue', and notwithstanding the rising influence of Classicism (as expressed by such as Wotton), polychrome decoration came back into use. Indeed it was employed throughout the seventeenth century, even for garden sculpture.[104] A good example of *c.* 1632 is a fragment of plaster painted with an image of Mary Frith (1584–1659), now in the Victoria and Albert Museum. Mural painting with figure work persisted at the higher social levels but for the most part died out elsewhere in

the course of the eighteenth century. War may tend to suspend aesthetic development but it was at the vernacular level that post-Commonwealth England retained much the same visual language for interior decoration of the preceding half century. This was in sharp contrast to the élite for whom a lavish lifestyle included the new fashions brought in, at the Restoration, from Continental Europe.

By way of example we will now turn to a series of interiors which have remained remarkably intact since they were created in the third quarter of the seventeenth century. They are to be seen in the Merchant's House, in the High Street, Marlborough (Fig. 210).[105] In 1652, the third year of the Commonwealth, this small Wiltshire wool town suffered a disastrous fire. As the citizens had sided

211 Built-in cupboard at the top of the stairs in the Merchant's House Marlborough (see also Fig. 183). The panels appear to be an attempt to imitate the decoration found on imported Italian cedar-wood cassones – except that the panels may be of native yew and are decorated with paint rather than with a heated stylus.

with Cromwell during the Civil War the republican government ordered a national collection to help meet the losses of goods and property estimated at some £58,623.[106] In the following years Thomas Bayly, a silk merchant, built himself a new timber-frame house and shop which was completed by the year of his death in 1670. In many ways this building, and its interior treatment, demonstrates the continuity of design from much earlier in the century – but in one respect it is altogether exceptional. The staircase (Fig. 183), which has been discussed in Chapter 8, has an echo of its balustrade rendered in distemper on the opposite walls. This was a notion which had appeared at Knole, Kent as early as *c.* 1605,[107] at Boston Manor House, Middlesex at about the same time,[108] at Sutton House, Middlesex some twenty five-years later,[109] and at 24 High Street,

Colchester some years after the Marlborough example.[110] The Merchant's House staircase, and its painted mirror image, is at least half a century behind the times. Similarly the built-in cupboard at the head of the stairs is distinctly *retardataire* (Fig. 211). Although constructed of oak there seems to have been an intention in the panels to recall the imported Italian cedar-wood *cassones* which had been fashionable with an earlier generation. These panels counterfeit the 'look' of such expensive imports except that the floral design is painted, rather than burnt-in with a heated stylus, and the panels may be native yew rather than alien cedar.

If these features are backward-looking then it is the 'Dineing Roome' which offers a truly original mural scheme, one that is almost without precedent and totally

212   The Merchant's House murals at Marlborough, *c.* 1656–70.

without successors (Fig. 212). This room occupies the upper floor of a wing which runs at right angles to the High Street frontage. It has windows on both sides facing west and east – suitable for both breakfast and dinner. Because the light levels in this room are high it was possible to introduce a fairly dark colour scheme. The room measures 16 ft 5 ins (5 m) by 21 ft 6 ins (7 m 50 cm) but its length was probably once curtailed by a screen to obscure a service area. The ceiling height to the soffit of the summer beams (a cruciform arrangement) is 7 ft 4 ins (2 m 32 cm) and the oak floorboards are an average of 14 ins (35.5 cm) wide.

The mural decoration here is in a milk (casein) -based distemper with ammonia (urine) added to prevent the medium turning sour. Recent conservation work has established the sequence in which these coloured distempers were added. Despite its apparent richness the palette is simple, just three pigments: indigo, red and yellow ochre, on a white (chalk) ground which gives considerable luminosity. Once this white undercoat had been applied the next colour to be added was the green (indigo and yellow ochre) leaving the pilasters as white vertical stripes. Further polychrome stripes were then added to these pillasters. At some point, whilst the work was in progress, it was decided to widen these to an average of 13 ins (33 cm) at the top and an average of 13¾ ins (35 cm) at the base. This has had two effects. First, the outer stripes are darker in tone than the inner ones (the former being on top of the green ground). Second, the spaces between these pillasters have been reduced to an average of 14½ ins (37 cm) at waist level. Thus, despite the conscious use of an entasis, the pillasters have become less visible so that the room fails to achieve the Classical 'look' that was evidently intended at first. In this confusion of intention a thoroughly original scheme has been achieved, one that anticipates the striped, 'hard-edged' paintings of twentieth-century artists of the New York school like Barnett Newman (1905–70).

As we have seen, the Marlborough Merchant's House was built for a silk mercer. The mural somewhat resembles an interior in *Amsterdam Town Hall* as recorded by the artist Peter de Hooch in 1652, although in Amsterdam the stripes may well have been contrived by strips of different coloured cloth.[111] It is possible that this was the inspiration for Bayly's painted dining room. The sgraffito fireplace is

213 Mural scheme in the George Inn, Chesham, Buckinghamshire, 10 ft by 4 ft 6 ins – as surviving in the upper half of the room.

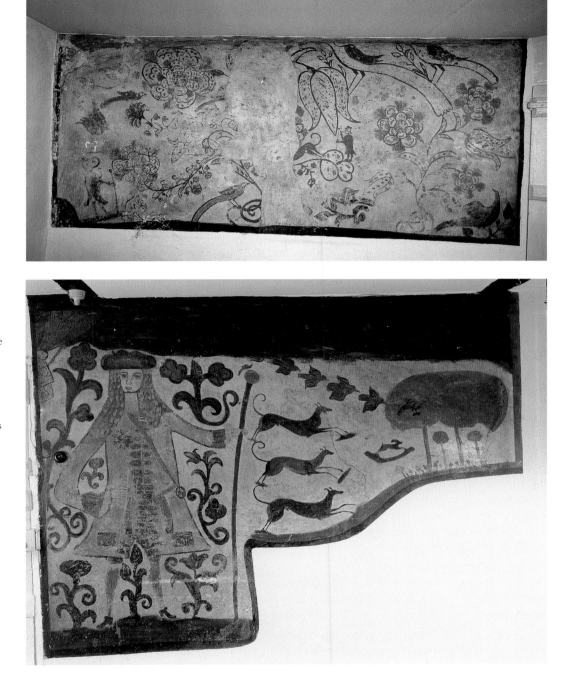

214 Mural in an upper chamber (the same room as that in Fig. 213) of the George Inn, Chesham, Buckinghamshire. It is possible that the mural may have been painted to celebrate the accession to the throne of George I which would give a date for the work of 1714. The overall dimensions of this mural are 7 ft 6 ins (wide) by 6 ft (high).

typical of those found elsewhere in south-west England (see pp. 26–8, Figs. 45–50). To complete the picture a surviving inventory of Thomas Bayly's goods and chattels, including his 'Dineing Roome', is given as Appendix II.

In the decades either side of the year 1700 mural painting, at the vernacular level, was either a continuation of earlier traditions (medieval in origin) or it was something altogether new (often Dutch in its immediate inspiration). As for the older traditions, the murals in the George Inn at Chesham, Buckinghamshire, may be amongst the last of their kind (Fig. 213). These may well have been painted in 1714 to celebrate the accession of George I, whose image seems to be included in the composition (Fig. 214). This type of wall painting was presumably the kind that Daniel Defoe had in mind when describing 'the [medieval] painting in the choir' of Salisbury Cathedral as more resembling the 'common drawing room, or tavern painting, than that of a

215   Overmantel mural in distemper on plaster at 2 Wardrobe Place in the City of London. Note the simulated carved wood frame which surrounds the composition. The strong Anglo-Dutch character of this work suggests a date shortly after 1689 when William of Orange came to the throne (with Mary).

church'.[112] By comparison with the Chesham scheme most late Stuart overmantel and overdoor paintings appropriate to 'common drawing rooms' are positively avant-garde. The 'landskips' and still lifes found in these locations are painted in distemper on plaster, as at 2 Wardrobe Place in the City of London (Fig. 215) or in oils on panels built into a scheme of panelling. Writing about 1712 Celia Fiennes describes 'the very good pictures' at Durdens, Surrey, which were 'in all the roomes over chimneys and doors fix'd into the wainscoate.'[113] A great exception to these two basic types is the overmantel painting at Sundial House, Corton, Wiltshire, which, being apparently a true fresco, is probably unique in Britain (Fig. 216). Although these paintings may sometimes be seen in rather important houses their quality is variable. As 'furnishing' pictures they most often remain part of the vernacular artisan tradition and thus possess formal, even abstract, qualities which are probably more widely admired now than at the time they were painted.

Coinciding with the Restoration of the monarchy a new type of panelling emerged (see Chapter 3) which owed more to the drawing board than the joiners bench. Large panels made up with a glued 'rub joint' were framed by bolection mouldings. Joinery schemes of this kind are divided horizontally by a dado with smaller square panels beneath and tall vertical ones above, the whole composition surmounted by a coved cornice. With the finishing of this type of work we are con-

fronted by a curious contradiction. In aristocratic houses the joinery in the state apartments is generally left unpainted whereas elsewhere in such establishments, and in the vernacular interiors of the period, the panelling is painted. In the former the wainscot was left in its natural state so as to reveal the quality of its quarter-sawn oak, or the exotic character of expensive imported woods like cedar – not to mention the pale delicacy of lime-tree woodcarving of the school of Gibbons which was often applied to it. In this way the consumption of this expense, skill and effort was left all the more conspicuous. In contrast, in smaller rooms and lesser houses the panelling at this period is generally constructed of Baltic softwoods. To unify the variation of colour and texture found in these timbers, and mask unsightly knots, the joinery was generally painted. It should be added that this was done with considerable care. Following the 'killing' of resinous knots[114] and the use of a primer, the mouldings of the stiles and rails, and the bevel of the fielded panels (an eighteenth rather than seventeenth-century feature), were rubbed down after each coat of paint was dry, using pumice stones shaped to the relevant section. In this way successive coats of paint (most commonly three or four) did not obscure the quality of the joinery.[115]

The large panels that characterise this type of work were an innovation and, as such, provided decorative painters with new opportunities. The pictorial treatment which they sometimes applied to these surfaces either covered the whole sequence of panels, both above and below the dado[116] or, as was more common, was confined to significant points within a room such as the overmantel or overdoor. A George II room at the Manor Farm, Hughenden, contains a particularly successful example. Here the panels below the dado contain complete individual landscapes while those of the larger upper panels may be 'read' as individual compositions or as a continuous landscape. Wilsey House, Cranbrook, Kent contains a room which reverses this idea by showing in the lower panels hounds chasing a hare and in the upper ones ships at sea.[117] The stiles and rails of the panelling in this room are painted in imitation of marble. The lowly status of such painting may have had something to do with the fact that it was 'built-in' and not easily available as part of the currency of art. Furthermore, paintings of this kind were often exposed to the smoke and heat of the fire, or they were 'skyed' beyond visibility. In short, they were not in locations that were considered appropriate for 'real' works of art. George III placed his collection of Canalettos in just such a position.[118]

In response to this demand for furnishing pictures a whole school of artisan artists emerged. In general it has not proved possible to unite known works with known painters partly because many of these artisan artists worked through dealers. One such middle man was the print-seller and engraver Regnier of the Golden Ball, Newport Street, Long Acre. His trade-cards of *c.* 1759 advertised that he supplied 'Hunting Pieces, Battles, Landskips, Shipping, Fishes, Flowers, Gardens . . . etc.'[119] There is some suggestion that these paintings were produced on speculation since the artist, Nathaniel Maister, working in Hull in about 1760, argued that a commissioned overmantel picture would cost more than one ready painted.[120]

In some regions, the survival of these vernacular works *in situ* suggests the presence of a particular painter or

216   Overmantel mural in Sundial House, Corton, Wiltshire, dated 1775. The landscape measures 2 ft 9½ ins by 3 ft 7½ ins (85.1 by 110.5 cm) within the *trompe l'oeil* frame. This conceit occurs elsewhere in England (e.g. Fig. 223) and also in Scotland as in the library at Woodside House, Beith, Ayrshire. What makes the Corton overmantel so exceptional is that it appears to be a true fresco – a great rarity in Britain.

217   Overmantel painting in a wood-panelled bedchamber at Urchfont Manor, Wiltshire. This house built between 1678 and 1688 boasts overmantels in no less than six of its rooms. Gentry houses accepted vernacular paintings in hazardous (over the fire) or near invisible locations (overdoor pictures) within a room.

school of painters. Thus the set of six overmantel paintings of *c.* 1688 at Urchfont Manor, Wiltshire (Fig. 217),[121] the overdoor panels at Melrose House, Frome (seven of *c.* 1700) (Figs. 55, 56) and at Tredegar House, Gwent (series in the Baroque Room *c.* 1680)[122] and a single panel painting of, and probably from, Treworgan House, Monmouthshire,[123] all have a close 'family' resemblance. Certainly Horace Walpole refers to several artisan artists who specialised in this kind of work. Among these was John Stephens (d. 1722) who was 'mostly employed for pieces over doors and chimneys'[124] and Luke (Marmaduke) Cradock 'who died early in the reign of George I'.[125] Cradock was born in Somerton, Somerset and was apprenticed to a house-painter in London. His paintings of birds were particularly 'strongly and richly coloured, and were much sought as ornaments over doors and chimney pieces.' He worked 'by the day [day wage] for dealers who retailed his works' at a profit to themselves. At this point, Walpole generously suggests that this arrangement enabled Cradock to maintain a certain distance from those who purchased his work, clients who might otherwise have been expected to have 'confined his fancy and restrained his freedom'.

Despite the decline in the use of bolection mouldings in the second and third decades of the eighteenth century and the displacement of the coved cornice in favour of the more regular use of modillioned cornices (plain or enriched), large panels remained in favour and demanded embellishment. Such joinery was also elaborately marbled and grained (Fig. 219) sometimes combining both treatments in the one scheme without regard to the structural impossibility of such a concatenation. Even with the decline of panelling, and the growing popularity of wallpaper and its cheaper cousin stencilling, overmantel paintings remained popular.[126]

John Stalker and George Parker quote, with some misgivings, the use of paint to simulate on wood, materials other than wood:

> Before Japan was made in England, the imitation of Tortoise-shell was much in request, for Cabinets, Tables, and the like; but we being greedy of Novelty, made these give way to modern Inventions: not, but that tis still in vogue, and fancied by many, for [mirror] Glass-frames, and small Boxes; nay, House Painters have of late frequently endeavoured it, for Battens, and Mouldings of Rooms; but I must of necessity say, with such ill success, that I have not to the best of my remembrance met with any that have humour'd the [tortoise] Shell so far, as to make it look either natural, or delightful.[127]

Surviving examples of this work appear to have been intended to be 'delightful' rather than 'natural', a notion confirmed by Loudon who argued that all woodwork should if possible be 'grained in imitation of some natural wood, not with a view of having the imitation mistaken for the original, but rather to create an allusion to it and by diversity of lines to produce a kind of variety and intricacy which affords more pleasure to the eye than a flat shade of colour'.[128] A remarkably good and early example of such an 'allusion' to graining is to be found on a fragment of a door of *c.* 1600 from Hyde Abbey House, Winchester, and now in the Victoria and Albert Museum (Fig. 205). The panels in this fragment are painted in a linear 'blackwork' design on a red ground so characteristic of its period. The stiles and rails have been painted a yellow ochre on which a most informal and calligraphic rendering of crimson graining has been superimposed.

Celia Fiennes, describing Newby Hall near Ripon, Yorkshire in 1697, remarks that 'the best roome was painted just like marble'.[129] Despite the presence of such painting in the finest room in an aristocratic house, it was probably employed in houses of many social levels, especially as the fashion declined in the early eighteenth century. Graining, marbling and even japanning was used to embellish quite small houses in eighteenth-century

America and the practice must have been quite common in England where Stalker and Parker's instructions on how 'To counterfeit Marble' would have been invaluable (Fig. 218).[130] Salmon's *Polygraphice* also gives instructions on the painting 'Of Marble and Tortoise Shell Japan' which should be finished

> before it is too dry, with a smaller pencil [brush] and one degree darker gently touch in the lesser veins and variety of Marble endeavouring as much as may be, to imitate, the exact foot steps of Nature, after this with a small pointed feather, and the deepest Colour, touch and break all your smaller Veins making them irregular, wild, and confused as they appear in real stone: let it

dry for a day or two and wash it over with isinglass Size, or Parchment [size] . . . Let it dry [again] for 2 or 3 days and then Varnish it over with the best white varnish.[131]

The treatment may be seen on the stiles and rails of an early eighteenth-century folding screen in the Victoria and Albert Museum. The naive drawing of the female figures in this screen and the accompanying landscapes imply that its original home was less than grand. It would however be a mistake to suppose that such an object derives from very far down the social scale.[132]

The graining and marbling of wood panelling provided the setting for walnut furniture in which the forms

218   The panelled fireplace wall from the Joseph Pitkin House (1723) from East Hartford, Connecticut was marbled in a particularly flamboyant way which is, nevertheless, consistent with similar work in Britain.

219   Detail of a grained and fielded scheme of panelling in which the whole effect is achieved in paint – a remarkable early eighteenth-century *trompe l'oeil* in a room at Cogges Manor Farm, Oxfordshire.

220   Early eighteenth-century painted panelling in Ugthorpe Hall, North Yorkshire (built *c.* 1586). By comparison with vernacular houses of its status in the south of England Ugthorpe is of modest size but high quality. This painted scheme may distantly relate to John Stalker and George Parker's designs for '*Japaning*' (1688) but in its light-hearted charm is closer in spirit to Scandinavian painted decoration.

were simple so as to reveal the 'figure' of the wood (Fig. 219). With the rise in the importance of mahogany, in which (except in Honduras mahogany) the grain is more noticeable by its absence, fashion shifted from simplicity of form to complexity, with an abundance of carved detail on high quality furniture. Furthermore, the influx of Huguenot weavers to England in the late seventeenth century had brought about the lavish use of richly patterned brocades at a time when wallpaper was also available to the wealthy. This resulted in the deployment of incidental 'pattern' as had previously been provided by, but no longer demanded of, paint in upper-class households. These trends taking place in the higher reaches of society were only later passed down the social scale where furniture continued to be made of walnut and oak rather than mahogany for rooms in which stencilling would be deployed in place of wallpaper. In other words, the *effect* on design took root in vernacular interiors without its material *cause*, but in imitation of patrician taste. Within these conditions fashion for wainscoting declined amongst the élite. At the vernacular level its use continued, but whatever features the joiner added, the walls were either painted in simple colours or were given 'interest' by means of painted decoration (Fig. 220). In general the colours used at this time were considerably less pungent than those used in marbling, graining or japanning. In New England 'pumpkin yellow' and 'Indian red' (as Dossie described it in England) continued the ancient use of easily available ochres.[133]

In the cleaning of 'Wainscotting, or any other Joynary or Carpentry Work that is painted in Oyl', John Smith recommended a mixture of water and 'well sifted' wood ash (i.e. potash) but added that 'if your painting be more Curious, whether Figures of Men, Beasts, Landskip, Fruitage, Florage, or the like, then let your picture be gently scoured, and then cleanly washed off with fair Water: after it is well dry, let it be run over with Varnish made with white of Eggs, and you will find the Beauty and Lustre of your Picture much recovered.'[134]

Where wide open spaces of coloured distemper were used on walls, notably in the first forty years of the reign of George III, a less finite surface was sometimes created by means of distressing the distemper with dry brush strokes and 'scumbling'. With oil paint on the other hand, the importance of glazes to give lustre to the surface cannot be over-emphasised. Dossie described the virtues of glazing in his own inimitable way. 'The property of *glazing* . . . is of so much importance . . . that no other method can equally well produce the same effect in many cases, either with regard to the force, beauty, or softness of the colouring.'[135]

The use of decorative painting was never totally out of fashion. In the third quarter of the eighteenth century,

221   Painted 'dado' in one of the service corridors at Calke Abbey, Derbyshire. Such distempered walls served a practical function in that the lower part of the wall, being darker in tone, was less likely to reveal finger marks, etc. The one concession to visual pleasure is the wave pattern that marks the two zones into which the wall is divided.

however, the archaeological researches of the Adam brothers brought about a reassessment of the 'antique' and an awareness that, contrary to the notions of the Renaissance, the Greeks and Romans used painted decoration. The Classical Revival was about to reveal itself to the world in all its effete and painted details.[136] In a desire to obtain ever more exotic woods even painted marbling and graining were back in a big way. By the early nineteenth century, with the publication of Whittock's *The Decorative Painters' and Glaziers' Guide* (1827), painters were simulating Oak, Pollard Oak, Spanish Mahogany, Satin Wood, Rosewood, Bird's-Eye Maple,[137] Coral Wood (from Celon), Watered Damask Coral Wood, Red Satin Wood, Veined Marble, Sienna Marble, Verde Antique, Black and Gold Marble, and Porphyry.[138] Whittock gives instructions for all of these to be imitated in either oil or distemper. However, the eclecticism, the fickle liking for a succession of idioms, so characteristic of Victorian taste, is foreshadowed in this volume and, despite his observation that Ancient Greece reached a 'high state of civilization and refinement', this is what Whittock perceives to be an historical statement rather than an aesthetic sentiment. He goes on to describe the 'Gothic' as 'The most beautiful and varied style of decoration.'[139]

Some forms of decoration were rudimentary in the extreme. In Ulster this amounts to little more than a high dado of chocolate-brown distemper or paint with a paler tone above; a practical measure rather than an aesthetic experience.[140] Indeed so utilitarian was this feature that it can also be seen in the service corridors of Calke Abbey, Derbyshire. In North Yorkshire the walls of attic bedrooms were painted a drab colour, but where they joined the slant of the roof wavy lines of dark blue marked the

222   S. O. Addy (*The Evolution of the English House*, 1898) describes and illustrates walls which, in the north of England, were decorated internally, and sometimes externally with an 'archil' or 'orchil' limewash giving it a deep-blue colour. Addy goes on to state that in Yorkshire this design is applied internally to the junction between a sloping attic ceiling and a vertical wall and that in Derbyshire this pattern was known as a 'witch worm' – see Fig. 221 for comparison.

junction of the two planes with a spot of the same colour placed within each undulation (Figs. 221, 222).[141] This use of spots may relate to the tradition for 'spotting' in North America where eighteenth-century examples have been identified in Massachusetts and Pennsylvania.[142] Another example of the use of colour in North Yorkshire is the custom of decorating 'the inner walls of houses, and occasionally the outside stonework, with a colour obtained from the plant liver-wort. This substance, known as "archil", or "orchil", is mixed with limewash to give it a deep blue colour . . . In the north of Yorkshire yellow-ochre sometimes competes with archil . . . In Derbyshire the ceiling and the walls were sometimes decorated by a light green colour. This was done by putting copperas into limewash.'[143]

Pictorial mural-painting on plaster at the vernacular level seems to have persisted in Britain, as on the Eastern Seaboard of North America[144] for a hundred and fifty

223   Mural (*c.* 1770–80) in the principal bedroom of Hall Green Farm, Action, Cheshire. The panelled dado, the picture frames and even the rings from which they are 'hung' are all fictitious.

years down to the middle of the nineteenth century. However, in Britain so little has survived, or been discovered, from that century and a half that it is not possible to develop an overview on the basis of such fragmentary evidence. Certainly very few of these murals, floral or pictorial, have come to light in post-Stuart, pre-Victorian interiors other than those cited here. In the Lake District two have been found, one at Wood Farm, Troutbeck, the other at Low Tock How, Hawkshead. The Hawkshead wall-painting has been dated to 1680–1730 and consists of free-flowing flowers and foliage executed in yellow, red and dark blue-black.[145]

In relationship to these rather simple schemes, the mural of *c.* 1770–80 in the principal bedroom of Hall Green Farm, Acton, Cheshire, is a precious survival. As a faux picture gallery including *trompe l'oeil* picture frames, and the rings from which they are supposedly hung,

224   Mural in 39 Grosvenor Place, Bath. This terrace was begun in 1791 to designs by John Eveleigh but was not finished until 1819. The interiors were completed by John Pinch the younger. This house was not occupied until 1828 when it was taken by the architect and painter Thomas Shew to whom these murals have been ascribed.

225 Mural painting of the Montpellier Pump Room, Cheltenham. This painting is in a four-roomed urban cottage once occupied by the decorative painter Thomas Vick, the probable author of these paintings (see also Fig. 226). They date to about 1826 when the architect, J. B. Papworth, completed the rotunda and dome on the Pump Room.

226 Mural attributed to the decorative painter, Thomas Vick, *c.* 1826. This work occurs in the same room as the painting illustrated in Fig. 225.

together with the painted shadows, the whole scheme gives a sense of veracity which is entirely fictitious – except that the paintings are painted (Fig. 223). This particular mural is reminiscent of a number of Scottish examples of this kind such as those at Woodside House, Beith, Ayrshire, in which paintings of pictures are surrounded by representations of 'swept' frames with shadows giving a sense of reality to a fictive gallery of landscapes.[146]

A number of murals painted in distemper survive from the early nineteenth century and I show one (Fig. 224) that was rediscovered in the 1970s in the first-floor front room of 39 Grosvenor Place, Bath. This terrace was begun in 1791 to designs by John Eveleigh but the

interiors designed by John Pinch the younger were not completed until after 1819. No. 39 was not occupied until 1828 when it was taken by Thomas Shew the architect and painter, and it was he who was probably responsible for creating this mural (Fig. 224).[147] Whittock gives instructions for painting such murals in his *Guide* of 1827. A further example comprises two fragments in one of the four rooms of an urban cottage in Cheltenham, Gloucestershire (Figs. 225, 226). This house is known to have been occupied, in the early nineteenth century, by the decorative painter Thomas Vick so it is probable that he was their author. The Montpellier Pump Room is the subject of one of these paintings so the murals probably

227   Mural in the main bedroom of Phippens Farm, Butcombe, North Somerset. This scheme runs right round the room and, on the window wall, is signed Walters – almost certainly the Bristol-based decorative painter, Thomas Walters, listed in an 1830 *Directory* as living at Upper Maudlin Street.

date from *c.* 1825–6 when the architect J. B. Papworth added the rotunda and dome.

All of the painted decoration mentioned above is in distemper. At Phippens Farm, Butcombe, North Somerset, two rooms with complete mural schemes were rediscovered in the 1970s having been wallpapered over in *c.* 1920 (Fig. 227). The murals are probably in distemper although the highlights appear to be in an oil-based paint. Both schemes are executed in a blue grisaille on a dirty-pink ground. The wall-painting in the drawing room (which measures 177 by 150 ins, or 449.6 by 381 cm, height 102 ins, 259.1 cm) is of simple pastoral and decorative subjects carried out with a fairly subdued tonal contrast, probably to allow for the intrusion of tall furniture and the arbitrary

hanging of mirrors and pictures which have caused some damage. The artist has painted a *trompe-l'oeil* dado imitating blue marble. The wall-paintings in the principal bedroom (232 by 152 ins, or 589.3 by 386.1 cm, height 100 ins, 254 cm) are of a higher quality and in a better condition than those in the drawing room. They contain much more activity, principally a stag hunt, and in the background may be seen a rather generalised view of nearby Blagdon church. It is painted on a dirty-pink ground and there is greater chiaroscuro here, but the treatment of the chimney breast is low in key, probably so as not to compete with a mirror or framed picture that may well have hung in such a position. The artist considered this mural worthy of his signature which appears painted on a representation of a rocky outcrop on the window wall as 'Walters' and very probably once included his address. The *National Commercial Directory* for Gloucestershire, published by Pigot and Co. in 1830, lists Thomas Walters, Upper Maudlin Street, Bristol, under '*Painters*: House, Sign &c' but significantly he is not listed under '*Artists:* Portrait, Landscape and Miniature'. As a house-painter he was undoubtedly responsible for the stencilling found in the dining room and for the marbled fireplaces, and the pilasters in the entrance passage.

The drawing room mural, which is of a different quality, may be by one of the sons of Thomas Walters who were first referred to in the 1831 Bristol directory. By 1832, 'Geo. Walters, Ornamental Painted Baize manufacturer for table covers, mats, etc.' and 'Thos. Walters, Sign and ornamental Painter' are listed in the directory at 15 Narrow Wine Street. The earliest reference to the family occurs in the 1819 directory (as 'Walter') and the latest is in the 1847 edition, by which time paper-hanging had been added to their range of skills. Bristol Art Gallery possesses a delightfully innocent shipping picture signed 'Walters' and including the date 1827. The Phippens Farm murals are probably some five years later. The size of the windows in the bedroom in relation to the ceiling height is such as to have given little or no space for curtains which would also have obscured part of the mural on the flanking walls. The reveals of the windows house shutters, but there is also evidence for the use of spring blinds. If these were used it is possible that they were painted as transparencies *en suite* with the mural. The whole scheme is probably typical of wall-painting of this period and status although surviving examples are now exceedingly rare in Britain. Such wall-paintings were made in imitation of the contemporaneous, though more expensive, imported scenic wallpapers.

How widespread these nineteenth-century murals were in Britain has yet to be established. The scenic wallpapers produced by Zuber of Rixheim (from *c.* 1804) and Dufour of Paris (from *c.* 1815) were certainly far less popular here than in North America where they were widely emulated at the vernacular level by many house-painters including the polymath Rufus Porter.[148] In early nineteenth-century Britain it was probably more common to perpetuate an old tradition for dividing an interior wall into zones of distemper which resembled panelling. Loudon is explicit on this point: 'The Panelling of the Walls or Ceilings of Rooms of plain Cottages is seldom attempted otherwise than by lines painted on the wall.'[149] A decade or so earlier work of this kind remained relatively fashionable, examples having been located in houses in St James's Square, Bath (Fig. 96) and in Spitalfields, London.[150] Writing in the early nineteenth century, Edward Pugh noted that in his youth in Welshpool it was 'general . . . to paint the walls of the rooms of public houses in size (distemper), with decorations of fes-

toons, and in panels ornamented with various devices strongly mimicking the present mode, so prevalent among the fashionable world.'[151] Pugh was to reveal the aesthetic prejudices of his time by concluding that these murals were only 'executed by sign painters' and that they consequently revealed 'a want of taste' — an attitude which was to persist to the 1930s.[152]

Stencilled decoration in medieval England is well known. The word seems to have originated from the verb 'estenceler', to sparkle or cover with stars. It is known that Henry III favoured green walls scattered with gold stars.[153] Salzman, in referring to work on St Stephen's Chapel, Westminster, quotes the purchase of '6 dozen and 8 foils of tin for pryntes'. 'Pryntes' or 'doublettes' were apparently medieval terms for stencils although Salzman only found one instance of the use of these words.[154] Numerous examples of such work survive from medieval times to the seventeenth century. Addy states that in Derbyshire 'Before the introduction of wallpaper it was usual to decorate walls with patterns, such as green leaves with rather indistinct stems. This was done by means of a contrivance resembling a large stencil plate. The practice is ancient, whether the stencil plate was used anciently or not. The regulations of the *Feste de Pui* in London stipulated that the room for the feast was not to be hung with cloth of gold, or silk, or tapestry, but decorated with leaves and strewed with rushes', a tradition that seems to have formed the basis for many freehand (Fig. 228) and stencilled designs.[155]

Walls were the main areas for stencilling but so long as the technique was popular it was widely used on many other surfaces. The earliest-known example of English wallpaper bearing a pattern dates from 1509 and carries a design rendered by stencil.[156] Indeed, although other

228 Decorative painting, probably late sixteenth century, in the Merchant's House, Tenby, Pembrokeshire, Wales.

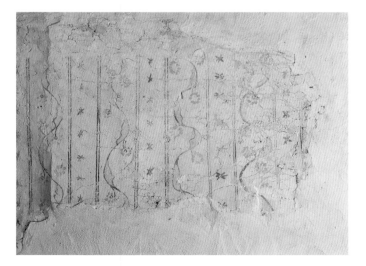

229   *John Middleton with his family*, c. 1796–7 by an unknown artist. Middleton was one of the most successful artists' colourmen of late eighteenth-century London. This interior is probably above his shop in St Martin's Lane. Despite Middleton's contact with numerous artists only one painting is shown hanging on the wall. Furthermore, and notwithstanding his commercial success, he could not afford, or did not want, printed wallpaper on the walls of this room. The duty imposed on printed papers (including newspapers) was levied on both British and imported products – a feature confirmed by a brass stamp (in the National Museums of Scotland, Edinburgh) which reads 'KIRKWALL DUTY PAID ON FOREIGN STAINED PAPER' surmounted by the Royal Cypher GR – probably George IV (NM 206). Despite the duty on printed paper Middleton has invested in a wallpaper border which runs round the room immediately below the cornice, above the dado and round the fireplace. This border also runs around the perimeter of the plain chimney board (the presence of which suggests that this picture was not painted in the winter months). Museum of London.

methods such as wood blocks were used for printing wallpaper, stencilling long remained a popular method of producing quite complicated designs. Robert Dossie in his *The Handmaid to the Arts* (1758) recommends for wallpaper the use of 'thin leather or oil cloth stencils'.[157] However, the type of stencilling with which this book is concerned was generally executed *in situ* directly onto the sized surface of wood or plaster, as in most of the examples that I have located so far – although it was occasionally applied to lining paper. Edward Batling's

trade-card (at the sign of the Knave of Clubs, Southwark) of about 1690 makes it clear that wallpaper was then available 'in lengths or in Sheets, Frosted or Plain: Also a sort of Paper in Imitation of Irish Stitch,[158] of the newest Fashion, and several other sorts, viz Flock-work, Wainscot, Marble, Damask, Turkey-Work'.[159] If paper 'Hangings for Rooms' were available in London by the late seventeenth century, why was stencilling direct on walls so popular in both America and Britain about a century later? Taxation appears to be the explanation.

Plain paper had been dutiable since 1694, but in 1712 an Act was passed which imposed a duty of 1d (½p) later increased to 1½d on every square yard (.84 sq m) of paper 'printed, painted or stained'.[160] These taxes made patterned wallpaper expensive (Fig. 229, 292) and most surviving examples of 'direct' stencilling are to be found in relatively small houses or in the lesser rooms of larger ones. Again and again references to stencilling, although it is a labour-intensive method of working, emphasise its cheapness. Robert Dossie refers to stencilling paper hangings as 'a cheaper method of ridding coarse work than printing'[161] but unless worked *in situ* this was still liable to attract excise duty (Fig. 230). Loudon observes that 'This mode of ornamenting walls of rooms is not unsuitable for cottages of the humblest description on account of its cheapness and because in remote places or in new countries, it might be done by the cottager himself, or by the local plasterer or house painter (Fig. 231).'[162] It is clear that Nathaniel Whittock in *The Painters' and Glaziers' Guide* (1827) regarded stencilling as part of the house-painter's craft. Certainly a craftsman such as George Evans would have been capable of such work. He is described by Edward Edwards in his *Anecdotes of the Painters* (London, 1808) as follows: 'George Evans . . . practises as a house painter but fre-

230 Stencilled wall decoration in the first-floor front room of No. 1, Camden Terrace, Bath (*c.* 1820–30). The tax on printed paper made patterned wallpaper far too expensive for the occupants of most third and fourth-rate houses. This was certainly true in the fashionable spa of Bath and, very possibly, in London (see Fig. 229).

231 (*below*) Although stencilled wall decoration could achieve a sophistication comparable to wallpaper (see Fig. 230) it could also have a charm that was all its own, as here in a house at West Pentire, Cornwall, early nineteenth century.

quently painted portraits . . . Much cannot be said of his powers as an artist, nor will his portraits be much in request with posterity.'

A number of instruction manuals by writers like Dossie survive from the eighteenth century although many are of much more recent date. *The Modern Painter and Decorator* by Jennings and Rothery, published (in three volumes) as late as 1920, includes a chapter on 'Stencils and Stencilling', an art 'that deserves more attention than it usually receives'. It goes on to say that cartridge paper and occasionally 'thick lead foil is often used'; and 'Willesden paper which being specially treated in order to make it waterproof, is specially recommended for stencils as it does not require the application of either linseed oil or knotting shellac.'[163] Linseed oil was particularly recommended as it made the paper translucent, enabling the craftsman to place each stencil with greater accuracy. The cutting of stencils demanded considerable skill, and Jennings and Rothery recommended 'A very sharp knife, not unlike that used by shoe-makers, and called a "clicker's knife"', but they underline the importance of 'the use of various shaped punches' and surviving examples attest to the prevalence of these. The stencils, once cut, were held on the wall 'by means of specially made pins. These have handles sometimes of wood.' Distemper was apparently usual for this work but oil paint was sometimes employed. In either case it was important that the paint should not be 'so liquid as to find its way underneath the stencil'. Guidelines were drawn on the wall surface and with designs that were 'spotted or diapered, such as, for example, a fleur de lis . . . it will be a help if these guidelines are not only drawn vertically and horizontally, but also diagonally'. The instructions in *The Modern Painter and Decorator* are comprehensive and include recipes for suitable distemper: 'the use of dry colour ground in water . . . and thinned down with equal parts of turpentine and gold size . . . in order to improve the lasting qualities of distempered work, beeswax may be added with advantage . . . the best wax is that to which a small quantity of cannuba wax has been added to stiffen it. One gallon [4.5 l.] of distemper will require about three ounces [85 g.] of wax dissolved in about half a pint [.28 l.] of turpentine or less.' Although these instructions were first published in the 1920s they clearly hark back to much older traditions. However, a final paragraph in this chapter concerns the innovation of 'spraying through stencils' which 'in addition to the great amount of time saved, . . . a gradation of colour may be obtained . . . [and] there is practically no risk of colour spreading beneath the surface of the stencil'.

It is clear from documentary sources and from surviving examples that stencilled wall decoration was widespread in both Britain and America from about 1790 to 1840 and it is likely that further research will show that the tradition did not completely die out between 1700 and 1790 (on either side of the Atlantic).[164] However, it is noteworthy that Robert Dossie's account of stencilling refers to its use exclusively as a means of decorating paper hangings and examples of this type of work can be seen in the collections of the Victoria and Albert Museum, London. In both England and America wallpaper remained a superior form of wall decoration so long as it remained expensive. The City of Bath, as a fashionable spa, was closely in touch with London fashion, and yet wallpaper was apparently confined to first and second-rate houses in the spa throughout the eighteenth and early nineteenth centuries.[165] Poorer households had to make do with stencilled walls such as the Manchester millworker's living-room so perfectly described by Elizabeth Gaskell in *Mary Barton* (first published in 1848):

> The room was tolerably large, and possessed many conveniences . . . On the opposite side to the door and window was the staircase . . . The other door, which was considerably lower, opened into the coal-hole – the slanting closet under the stairs; from which, to the fireplace, there was a gay-coloured piece of oil cloth laid. The place seemed almost crammed with furniture (sure sign of good times among the mills), beneath the window was a dresser with three deep drawers. Opposite the fireplace was a table, which I should call a Pembroke, only that it was made of deal, and I cannot tell how far such a name may be applied to such a humble material. On it, resting against the wall was a bright green japanned tea-tray having a couple of scarlet lovers embracing in the middle. The fire-light danced merrily on this and really . . . it gave a richness of colouring to that side of the room. It was in some measure propped up by a crimson tea-caddy, also of japan ware. A round table on one branching leg rarely for use, stood in the corresponding corner to the cupboard; and if you can picture all this with a washy but clean stencilled pattern on the walls, you can form some idea of John Barton's home.

As we have seen, plain paper had been dutiable since 1694 and printed paper since 1712 – but in 1836 this duty was abolished.[166] Furthermore, wallpaper could now be easily produced by the roll on machinery. For these reasons wallpaper ceased to be expensive and therefore exclusive. As a result stencilling became relatively costly and therefore returned to its fashionable status. As in medieval Europe, it reappears as decoration in places of worship – 'churches, chapels, ecclesiastical structures, Masonic temples, etc, where it may be regarded as being in every way appropriate'.[167] In the north of England this transition is somewhat ruefully recorded by Christopher Thomson in his *Autobiography of an Artisan* when, at one

232   *The Drawing Room*, artist unknown, *c.* 1840. Walls painted a single colour probably always remained popular and, in the early nineteenth century when a Greek Revival colour like terracotta was selected, it could also be fashionable. Ex Collection: Judkyn/Pratt.

point in his life, poverty compelled him to resume his 'old trade of stencilling . . . My improved patterns were [in 1828] scarcely equal to many of the paper hangings that are now [1847] sold at one penny per yard. However they were considered superior to the general run of such things then in use, [and] I got several excellent jobs thereby. From the cottages of the poor stockingers, I was elevated to the parlours of the "tradesmen" and the boarding schools.'[168] With the abolition of the tax on printed paper wallpaper became a commodity available to a much wider spectrum of the population. It could now descend the social scale. William Bardwell's *Healthy Homes and How to Make Them* (London, 1854) lists minimum building and decorating standards and recommends that paper shall be hung on 'all the walls of the sitting and

bedrooms of the dwelling with figured paper to the value of one penny per yard of approved designs.'

According to Stalker and Parker (1688), painters preferred to price work by the yard but some customers insisted on asking for prices for the 'job' out of a 'mistaken piece of frugality . . . [thinking], if they can agree with a Painter by the great, their business is done; for by these means, they not allowing the Artist a Living price, he cannot spend both his oyl and labour, nor stretch his performance to the utmost extent of his skill.'[169] The various methods of paying house-painters seems to have been set by convention. In *The Complete English Tradesman* (1727) Daniel Defoe warns shopkeepers not to spend too much money on 'painting and gilding, wainscoting and glazing' because 'the Joyners and Painters, Glaziers and Carvers must have all ready money: the Weavers and Merchants may give credit'.[170] Campbell (1747) states that in London house-painters were 'idle at least four or five months of the Year. Their Work begins in *April* or *May* and continues till the return of the Company to Town in Winter'.[171] For the sort of houses with which we are concerned this was not a consideration. Where it was, the problem could be mitigated by the use of paint made by the Aromatic Paint Company of 439 Strand or 22 Change Alley, Cornhill, London, which was active from *c.* 1820–40. This Company claimed that 'By this invention, Families are not under the necessity of quitting their residence during the operation of Painting; on the contrary, it will be found not only perfectly innocent to the most delicate constitution, but highly fragrant and pleasant in its affect. It dries either with a gloss or a flat surface, in a few hours.'[172]

As commercial manufacturing of paint by mechanised means increased so house-painters undertook an ever widening range of responsibilities. In the past the making of paint had been one of the crafts of this art; one that enabled the best craftsmen to move out of the trade and into the profession of easel painting. Of these Edward Edwards in his *Anecdotes of the Painters* (1808) states that George Evans (see p. 162) and Joshua Kirby were so trained – the latter 'resided in the early part of his life at Ipswich, in Suffolk where he practised as a coach and house painter, and where he formed a lasting friendship with Mr Gainsborough'.[173]

For the careful restoration of early interiors, as historic entities, it is important that every attempt should be made to establish the original colour scheme of a room at a given time in history and then to reproduce the paints and colours that would have been used then. In the United States, and certainly on the Eastern Seaboard, the leadership of various organisations (such as the Society for the Preservation of New England Antiquities) and individuals (like the late Nina Fletcher Little) have made this archaeological approach standard practice. As a result, careful 'scrapes' and microscopic cross-sections of paint are taken in the early stages of planning a restoration.[174] In Britain we have begun to learn from American experience.[175] The great danger with taking scrapes (or indeed with cleaning paintings) is that it is very easy to remove the glaze with the later accretion of paint and dirt. The whole question is a complex matter for which specialist knowledge is available and should be sought.

Chapter 10

Furniture

In *The Boke of Husbandrie* by John Fitzherbert (*c.* 1523) may be found a formidable list of household chores and farming duties under the heading *What markes a wyfe shulde do in a generalytie*. The tasks for the day are listed in order from sunrise to sunset. Thus in the morning the 'wyfe . . . than first swept thy house dress up thy disshboard and set all things in gode order within thy house'. From such references one may infer that a 'disshboard' was more than a utilitarian article for storage – it was a basis for the display of plate, the 'consumer durables' of their day. The furnishing of a home has probably always, and at all social levels, played this dual role. Even with the poor, where possessions were meagre, a few 'treasures' held more than a material significance. Robert Roberts's *The Classic Slum* sums up this seeming contradiction where 'For many in the lowest group the spectre of destitution stood close; any new possession helped to stifle fear.'[1] There was more to consumption than economics.[2] In the course of the eighteenth century a growing desire for social refinement is evident,[3] even if the effects of 'emulation' have been exaggerated.[4] In pre-Reformation England possessions were few. This was partly because the elite maintained for their pleasure, as did the poor out of necessity, an active outdoor life. These conditions long persisted, resulting in furniture designed to fulfil many uses:

> The chest contriv'd a double debt to pay
> A bed at night, a chest of drawers by day.[5]

It would be a mistake to presume that the standard of furniture, any more than the standard of living, was consistent throughout the British Isles before the coming of the railways (Figs. 1, 6, 7). Even in the age of steam, disparities would inevitably remain despite which popular taste became ever less regional. After the intrusion of the 'iron horse' it was only the standardisation of the meas-urement of time that arrived nationally and immediately. Loudon, writing just before the full impact of steam-powered transport, describes 'Two Ploughmen's Cottages in a Village near Salisbury': 'The Interior of these cottages, it will be observed, is very different from that of either the Scotch or Northumbrian ones: irregularity and variety characterise the former much as plainness and simplicity do the latter. The one gives the idea of the cottage of a serf and the other of that of a free man.'[6] This inequality, together with the use of different materials, accounts for certain regional characteristics in the type and design of furniture.

Vernacular furniture in Britain is a formidable subject to look at in a few pages and I shall therefore use this chapter to discuss those aspects which are particularly characteristic such as the placing of furniture within a room, perishable and painted items, built-in cupboards (Fig. 233) and beds, and the persistence of the dowelled through-tenon (Figs. 234, 249).[7]

Much early furniture was either immovable because of its size or weight, or was a fixture which may be 'read' as part of the architecture. The Archbishop's throne of Purbeck 'marble' at Canterbury is a fine Romanesque example of such a 'dormant' object. At the domestic level there are the stone beds and the 'dresser' at the Neolithic settlement at Skara Brae, Orkney (Fig. 235),[8] which are strikingly similar in form to the eighteenth-century fixed wood furniture from Åmlid, Valle, Setesdal, Norway (Fig. 236); a reversal of the classic use of stone in the image of wood. The 'found object' too would on occasion fulfil a household need, such as the vertebra of a whale used as a stool[9] or the log of wood which traditionally provided a seat on one side of the central or 'roundabout' hearths still used in Co. Antrim in the late nineteenth century.[10] Sometimes the basic structure of the house would, in

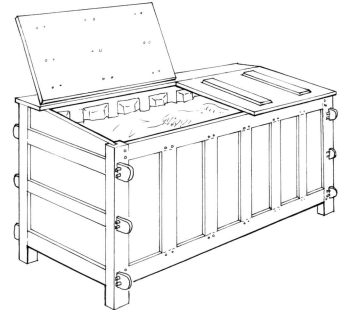

234   Meal chest from the north of England showing projecting and wedged horns. Large furniture of this kind was made to be dismantled so that it could be moved from one room to another. Examples may be seen at the Museum of Lakeland Life, Kendal and at Beamish, the North of England Open Air Museum.

233   Built-in cupboard in a ruined croft in the Scottish highlands.

235   Although some five thousand years old the houses which form the Neolithic settlement of Skara Brae, Orkney retain their stone furniture.

236 Living-room of a farmhouse in Åmlid, Valle, Norway as reconstructed at the Norsk Folkemuseum, Oslo. Although of medieval type, and not too far removed in character from the interiors of Skara Brae, this room is not earlier than the late seventeenth century.

effect, incorporate furniture to serve the needs of its occupants. The single-room mud houses of Athelney, Somerset, were contrived so as to provide a bench around their perimeter created by the central trough which was their floor (Fig. 1).

None of these exotic if rudimentary examples of furniture provided the storage space which only the chest, and its descendant the chest of drawers, could offer. In its earliest form as the trunk, it was, as its name implies, a 'dug-out' tree trunk. The hewn quality of such articles of daily use, sculptured out of the solid, characterises not only the surviving examples of 'trunks' of this type but also the constituent parts of much early carpenters' and even joiners' work (Fig. 237). Quite apart from the influence of the 'dug-out', the sensible use of timber in pre-industrial circumstances (sawing was expensive) encouraged its lavish use, and the influence of the mason confirmed it.

The 'dug-out' trunk was followed by the six-board chest. Most examples of the latter have suffered the consequences of damp floors and are today usually much lower than when first made. In fact the end-boards were traditionally made from the fifth board sawn in half.[11] When seen from its frontal elevation such a chest conforms to a double square, a rather sophisticated visual trick which was probably nothing more than serendipity occasioned by the economical use of materials and labour. The construction itself was far from sophisticated: nails

237 Late eighteenth-century (?) chair hewn from a log of elm.

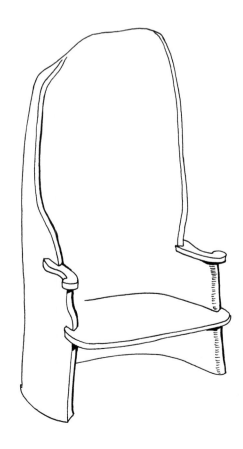

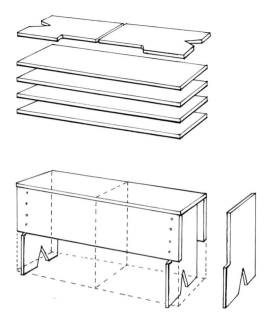

238   Six-board chest, the ends composed of the same scantlings, sawn in half, and partly reduced in width to accommodate the front board. This economy in the use of materials and labour produces a sophisticated double square proportion.

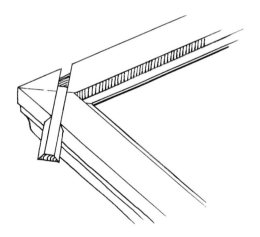

239   Because the mitre is an inherently insecure joint it was sometimes reinforced (as in picture frames) by means of a 'key'.

held the timber fast and prevented its natural movement. Most examples will be found to be badly split (Fig. 238).

Some early types of furniture have persisted longest in those utilitarian roles where they are least subject to the whim of fashion, the butcher's chopping block being a good example. Similarly the meal chest known as the 'ark', with its movable pegged, horned tenons and its roof-like lid, continued to be made in Wales and the north of England into the eighteenth century (Fig. 234).

Early in the thirteenth century a species of chest common to most of Europe, and known in Germany as a *stollen* chest,[12] was devised which had a slab lid, back, front and bottom with panelled ends. The framed-up ends permitted a certain amount of movement in the panels and were therefore found to be structurally more effective than the butt joints and rigid nailing of the six-board chest. This type may be seen as transitional and the immediate antecedent of the fully framed chest made by the joiner rather than the carpenter. The great disadvantage of the chest was that nothing could be put on its surface without impeding access, and having gained access it was often necessary to delve deep to find one small object. These twin problems were overcome by the chest of drawers.

The framed chest was the result of much labour with its many mortices and tenons, and its stiles and rails grooved to accommodate panels. For this reason the top and back, and sometimes the ends as well, often remained as simple slabs of wood and the single element which maintained the sound principles of frame and panel construction was the front. Even the plainest of framed chests has stiles and rails with bevelled edges surrounding the panels thus producing the familiar mason's mitre; elaborate examples were given rich mouldings. The mason's mitre is a subject about which much could be written (Fig. 83). In contrast the true mitre produces that dubious feature in a structure known as the 'feather edge'. A feather edge does not long survive in stone.[13] For this reason all junctions in masonry are kept as near the right angle as possible. The familiar mason's mitre results from the bevel worked on one piece of stone (usually horizontal) being given a 'stop' to provide the 'return' for the bevel, or moulding, worked on another stone member placed at, or near, right angles to it.

In timber the feather edge is possible and therefore the 'true' mitre has been used for wood since the late sixteenth century, but only for non-structural purposes as it is a weak joint. Medieval carpenters and joiners seem to have recognised this weakness and despite the great expense of working the mason's mitre in wood its use long persisted. Furthermore 'end grain' makes a bad glue joint. Throughout much of the seventeenth century the decadent mitre became something of a vice among designers (if not craftsmen) who began to relish the use of a profusion of applied mouldings, whilst significantly resisting its charms for structural purposes. Even the later Louis XIV rooms, elaborately panelled in wood, employ the sound principle of construction of the mason's mitre despite an often frivolous use of ornament. The strength of the mortice and tenon remained important for the framing of heavy mirror glass and the weak mitre was strengthened, in bulky picture frames, by means of a 'key' dovetailed diagonally into the back of the joint (Fig. 239). Moxon, in his *Mechanick Exercises* (1677...), describes the

'Mitre Square and its use' and remarks that 'thus Picture Frames and Looking-Glass frames are commonly made'.[14] The treatment of detail and decoration on chests may be related to the panelling that is contemporary with them. Both obeyed the structural standards of their time and the aesthetic fashion of their day.

Today the words 'plank' and 'board' have, almost unconsciously, retained their historic and distinctive meanings, the plank (as in a scaffolding plank) being considered heavier than the board (as in a floor-*board*). Undoubtedly the cup-*board* uses lighter timber than the plank of a trestle table. In sixteenth-century documents a 'table' was either a movable panel-painting[15] or what we would now call a table top – 'a table lying on two trestles'. In joiners' work it was described as a 'table with the frame'.[16] 'Refectory tables', as they are often now known, were generally considered as fixtures or tables 'dormant'. The use of fixed furniture conformed well to the immutable status of individuals in early modern Britain, and was to remain relevant in remote districts until the close of the nineteenth century. These fixed social positions were probably all the more convenient when, paradoxically, society was more integrated – when different classes lived together under one roof; a situation as true for a farmhouse as for the houses of the gentry. Addy, describing the furnishing of Hawksworth's Farmhouse, Upper Midhope, West Yorkshire, notes that the table, though movable, is so large that it must have been constructed *in situ* when the house was built in 1671.[17] In his plan of the house, Addy located the main long-table in its traditional place alongside the lateral screen (Fig. 240). Against this screen is a fixed bench; on the other side of the table are two long forms and at its head, a joint stool. This arrangement is not just a superficial matter of decor. The regular accommodation of a large number of individuals at table is not simply a reflection of the larger families of the past but indicates the continuation of the ancient tradition whereby the family of the house coexisted with the unmarried farm servants at mealtimes (see pp. 8–9). In the south this would be considered a late survival of an earlier tradition. Even in this example the family, as Addy's plan shows, has deserted the traditional table for a round one near the fire. At this social level it was not until the late nineteenth century that the divorce, albeit under one roof, of family and servants was made absolute.

The actual use of the principal living room in such a farmhouse was confirmed by a farmer in neighbouring Derbyshire recalling his youth in the early nineteenth century:

The master of the house [the farmer] and his servants [the farm labourers, etc.] had dinner in one and the

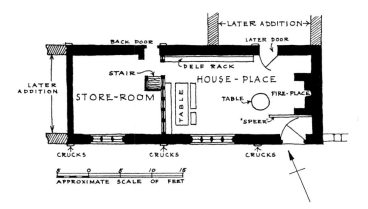

240   Plan of Hawksworth's Farmhouse, Upper Midhope, West Yorkshire after S. O. Addy (*The Evolution of the English House*, 1898) showing the organisation of furniture, and consequently the people who used it. The 'house-place' was used for meals by the farmer and his family. They sat at the round table by the fireplace and the farm servants at the long-table by the screen.

same room – the kitchen – a large apartment. The master and his family sat at a table near the fire, and the servants at a long table on the opposite side of the room. First the master carved for his family and himself, and then the joint was passed on to the servants' table. The head man presided over the servants' table, and always sat at the end of it, and at the opposite end sat a woman. The men sat next to the chair in order of seniority and were very particular about keeping their proper places.[18]

Amongst the gentry this tradition for dining communally, but in defined zones, above or below 'the salt', declined by the mid-sixteenth century.[19] The Upper Midhope example was a rare survival – the physical remains of which lasted until an auction of the contents of the house in 1932.[20]

By the late sixteenth century tables were more numerous and various and in the second half of the seventeenth century the introduction of hot drinks (coffee, tea and chocolate) further encouraged this trend.[21] The rising importance of heated beverages accelerated the importation of porcelain from the East, as it encouraged the manufacture of home-produced ceramics, especially pottery. So as to prevent rooms becoming congested with furniture, the gate-leg table was devised and became common in the late seventeenth century. It may be a development of the so-called credence table of the early part of the century which also has a 'gate' leg, but hinged table tops were also in use much earlier.

In the eighteenth century the tilt-top table (Fig. 16), supported on a column and tripod, possessed a similar

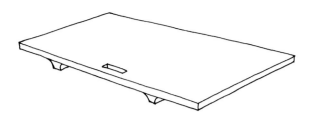

241   Table, 20 by 12 ins (50.75 by 30.5 cm), cut from bog-wood, Co. Armagh. Such tables, lacking legs, were used by being placed on the knee in the manner of a tray. When not in use they were hung on the wall – after Emyr Estyn Evans (*Irish Folk Ways*, 1957).

242   Two Welsh stick-back chairs. Because of uneven floors movable furniture such as tables and chairs were often given three legs. In this instance the left-hand example has been modernised by having the third near leg replaced by two.

space-saving virtue. J. T. Smith in *Nollekens and His Times* (1829) writes of the popular taste of 'the same class of persons, who in my boyish days would admire a bleeding-heart-cherry painted upon a Pontipool tea board [of tin plate], or a Tradescant-stawberry upon a Dutch table.' In a footnote Smith provides further information:

This description of ['Dutch'] table, the pride of our great-grand-mothers, in which the brightest colours were most gorgeously displayed, was first imported from Holland into England in the reign of William and Mary. The top was nothing more than a large oval tea-tray, with a raised scalloped border round it, fixed upon a pillar, having a claw of three legs. They are now and then to be met with in our good old-fashioned family mansions, and brokers' shops. They were formerly considered by our aunt Deborah to be such an ornament to a room, that in order to exhibit them to advantage, they were put in the corner of a waiting-parlour for the admiration of the country tenants, when they brought their rents, or sat waiting their turn for an order for coals in a severe winter.[22]

The 'scalloped border' is today known as a 'pie crust'. Despite Smith's assertion that these painted 'Dutch' tables were found only in 'mansions', they undoubtedly had a wide social distribution. Their basic feature of a tilt-top on a tripod stand continued in use well into the nineteenth century.

Before leaving the subject of tables it should be remembered that not all homes had one. They tend to be absent from the black houses of the Outer Hebrides. Fynes Moryson, writing in the eighteenth century, says that the Irish country people 'have no tables, but set meat upon a bundle of grass as napkins to wipe their hands . . . I trust no man expects among these gallants any beds, much less feather beds and sheets.'[23] In such houses the table was often a simple, thin slab of wood, circular or sometimes rectangular, which hung on the wall when not in use (Fig. 241). At mealtimes the family would sit in a circle and place this board upon their knees.[24] To save on the need to use trenchers some tables in Hertfordshire, Devon and Yorkshire had depressions worked in their tops to contain meals in place of wooden platters. Washing-up was simply a matter of scrubbing down the table top.[25] This cleaning was traditionally done with beer and silver sand, a technique also used for floors (see p. 93).

The upholstered comfort of today's chairs bears little relationship to the past when to have a back, to even a wooden seat, signified status – a cushion being a luxury enjoyed by a minority. With smoke-filled interiors seating was kept low, and with uneven floors three legs were customary for both stools and tables – the so-called cricket table being characteristic (Fig. 246). In fact the word 'cricket' may once have meant 'stool'. Moxon, in describing the use of the draw knife, says that it was 'seldom used about *House-building* but for the making of some sorts of Household-stuff as the Legs of Crickets, the rounds of Ladders, the Rails to lay Cheese or Bacon on &c.'[26] In all these instances the draw knife would be used to taper the ends of small scantlings of wood to produce, what in effect is, a cheap form of tenon, round in section without a shoulder. Since this type of joint is weak it was usually compensated for by means of wedges and was later extensively used for the so-called stick-back chairs made with or without turned members. When these chairs or indeed stools had thick seats the additional support afforded by stretchers was unnecessary and they were often dispensed

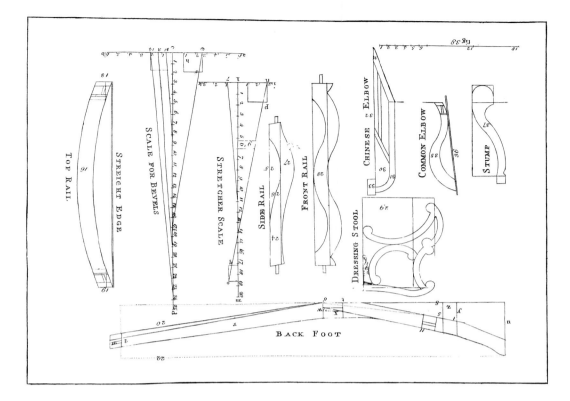

243 Diagram of the components used in making a chair, from Robert Manwaring's *Cabinet and Chairmaker's Real Friend and Companion, or, the Whole System of Chair-Making Made Plain and Easy* (1765). For a chair to be comfortable fluid lines, which depart from the right angle, are important, hence Manwaring's emphasis on the importance of the joinery tool known as the 'bevel'. On the title page of this manual the author makes the very radical suggestion that, by means of this book, 'most ignorant persons' would have sufficient understanding to make chairs just as well as those who had 'served Seven Years to know' this specialist work – i.e. an apprenticeship. Note that the 'Back Foot' refers to the whole length of the back leg, a usage of the term which survives to this day amongst chairmakers.

with. In fact chairs of this kind are nothing more than a stool with a back added, the legs and back being unrelated structurally (Fig. 242). In contrast the 'stool-chair' or 'back-stool', described and illustrated in Randle Holme's *Academy of Armory* (written between 1648 and 1649), have 'back-feet' (as they are traditionally termed)[27] which are continuous, forming leg and back (Fig. 243).

The most common term for the stick-back seat is 'Windsor Chair'. One of the earliest references to them by this name is the 1730 advertisement for John Brown of St Paul's Churchyard, London, who sold 'All sorts of Windsor Garden Chairs of all sizes painted green or in the wood'.[28] Such chairs probably derived their name from those made in the vicinity of the royal borough which were shipped to London via the river Thames in large numbers. Unfortunately very few were labelled or branded until the early nineteenth century, but some bear the name 'Richard Hewitt, Chairmaker at Slough in the Forest'. At that time Slough was little more than a

hamlet in the parish of Upton and it is likely that the chairs from this area became known by the name of the point from which they were shipped by river to London and beyond – Hewitt's workshop was only two miles from Windsor – although some labels make reference to 'Windsor Forest'. This certainly applied to materials like 'Windsor loam' and 'Windsor bricks' destined for the building trade in Hanovarian London.[29]

Just as Hewitt sent his goods via the Datchet road to the Thames for onward shipment to the capital, so the Wycombe makers sent their products to Marlow which is also on London's river.[30] On the basis of this sort of evidence it is logical that a number of dealers (they often claimed to be manufacturers but they may have assembled the components) in these chairs are known to have been located on or near the Thames, downstream, in or near London. The Ambrose Heal Collection of trade-labels provides information on these retailers. A good example is a label dating from the second half of the eighteenth century for 'Lock^n Foulger – Chair Maker at Wallam Green, Makes all sorts of Windsor Chairs, Garden Seats, Rural Settees &c. Wholesale and Retail.' Others include J. E. R. Prior of Uxbridge, Middlesex, and 'William Webb, Near the Turnpike, Newington, Surrey, Maker of all Sorts of Yew Tree Gothic and Windsor Chairs, China and Rural Seats, Single and double angle, and Garden Machines, Childrens Chaises on the most reasonable terms. NB for Exportation.' Newington, today in the heart of London, is just over Lambeth Bridge on the south side of the river. William Webb is listed in the directories there between 1792 and 1823. In 1817 (R.) Webb and Bruce were located in the King's Road, Chelsea, but by 1823 they had moved to Hammersmith, all these boroughs being on the river.[31]

Although chairs of this type are now inseparably associated with the town of Windsor, stick-back chairs were in fact made in many parts of England as well as Scotland, Ireland and Wales (Fig. 244). Certainly the chairmakers in the two neighbouring counties of Buckinghamshire and Berkshire (the latter county being where Windsor is located) were influential not only through their products but also through the craftsmen themselves. It has, for example, been shown that some Windsor chairmakers in the Midlands were born in the Chilterns in Buckinghamshire.[32] The stick-back chair is probably ancient and although none are known to survive from before the eighteenth century, certain types related to them do. By about 1725, chairs of this kind had migrated to America where the use, by colonial crafts-men, of woods such as pine and hickory resulted in a mutation that must be seen as a distinct species (Fig. 245).[33] In England the traditional woods were elm for the seat, beech for the legs and stretchers, with ash for the back. In a 'comb-back' the 'comb' is often of the same wood as the seat – elm. In high quality examples yew was used for the legs, stretchers and back which in excep-tional examples were elaborated with 'Gothick' details.

All chair backs sustain considerable leverage. In some Windsor chairs this problem is solved by seats which have an additional dovetail extension at the back known as a 'fan' or 'bob-tail' from which sprang two extra 'sticks' for support. The addition of arms also provided supplemen-tary support to the back. The sticks at the top of a typical English hoop-backed chair are generally wedged like the legs, but in many American examples, and those made in some English counties like Devon, they will be found to be dowelled with tiny dowels.[34] The use of bent wood in the construction of such chairs required very special skills. One labelled Windsor chair, said to have been used on board ship by Captain James Cook on one of his voyages, bears the label '. . . Pitt, wheelwright and chair-maker'. Recent research has shown that this was an estab-

lished association between the two trades. Examples include Hewett of Slough (see above); the common thread between the two trades being wood-turning.[35] The 'bodgers' of Berkshire worked in the beech woods turning the legs 'green' (unseasoned) on pole lathes. Once seasoned they became slightly elliptical in section which increased their strength when driven into the hole that was drilled through the seat to receive them. The bodger's craft was confined exclusively to producing the turned legs and other turned elements in Windsor chairs. Bodgers, working in the traditional way as a band of craftsmen using the reciprocating action of pole lathes in temporary workshops in the beech forests, survived in the county until the late 1950s, one of the last of the tribe being H. F. Goodchild of Naphill.

Yew-wood chairs were left unpainted and unlike their less exalted brethren more often bear the brand of their maker, for example John Amos of Grantham.[36] Other names that have been recorded date mostly from the fourth decade of the nineteenth century. Those that pre-date 1800 included the large firm of Gillows of Lancaster (c. 1790), two in Lincolnshire (James Marsh in addition to John Amos), and four from Buckinghamshire (Charles and Edwin Skull, Richard Hewett – cited above – and Amos Catton d. 1777). A notable concentration of makers of stick-back chairs have been located in Nottinghamshire and these include John Gabbitass, Benjamin Gilling, George Nicholson and Frederick Walker.[37] These were presumably the Windsor chairs of the type so commonly seen by Loudon (1833) in kitchens 'in general use in the midland counties of England',[38] but also found elsewhere (Fig. 246)

It was probably usual for the more ordinary sort of stick-back chairs to be painted; dark green and blue were popular in England but an earth red was also used in Wales. Windsor chairs were used at all social levels from cottages to impressive country houses where they were found in summer pavilions and gardens. According to pictures by artists such as Thomas Robins (1716–70) they were, when used as garden chairs, painted white. By Loudon's day the fashion for painting Windsors was declining. They were 'frequently stained with diluted sul-phuric acid and logwood; or by repeatedly washing them over with alum water, which has some tartar in it; they should afterwards be washed over several times with an extract of Brazil wood.'[39] This process produced an effect resembling mahogany and the final oiling and rubbing 'with woolen cloths' completed the deception. Loudon credits a 'Mr Dalziel under whose direction most of them have been prepared' with 'preserving the character of simplicity' in these chairs. There is probably some bias in this statement as Dalziel was responsible, together with Edward Buckton Lamb (1806–69), for the furniture

244 A Welsh stick-back chair (*left*) and an English comb-back chair (*right*). The use of a mixture of woods, as here (elm, ash, blackthorn), encouraged the application of paint to hide the disparity of materials.

245 An American (*left*) contrasted with an English Windsor chair. The use of timber native to North America resulted in the exaggerated lines of the Colonial stick-back chair.

246   The kitchen of a house at Compton Basset, Wiltshire, painted in 1849 by Elizabeth Pearson Dalby. Amongst the myriad of household items shown here are chairs, related to the Windsor, of a type illustrated by J. C. Loudon (*Encyclopaedia*, 1846 edition, p. 319) which were stained and oiled to resemble mahogany. Salisbury and South Wiltshire Museum.

designs that appeared in Loudon's *Encyclopaedia*.[40] Other nineteenth-century makers in the region included Thomas Widgington (who set up a workshop in High Wycombe, away from the beech woods, in 1801), Samuel Treacher and, later in the century, Daniel Glenister, Walter Skull and Benjamin North.[41]

Why has the Windsor chair been successful for so long? For a seating type constructed entirely of wood to be comfortable without the benefit of upholstery, the fewer right angles in its design the better – a requirement which resulted in the development of the specialist craft of chairmaker in high-class work. For good reason Sheraton in his *Cabinet Dictionary* (1803) states that 'Chairmaking is a branch [of woodworking] generally confined to itself.'[42] When Carpenters make furniture they tend to create the rectilinear appearance which is also found in most joiner-made rural chairs.[43] Both retain an earlier age of discomfort. But chairmakers were spe-

cialists who could bring the fluid lines so necessary in the production of a comfortable chair (Fig. 243), and the Windsor chair was at first almost alone in providing, at a low cost, the comfort offered by these more 'fluid' lines. The chairs illustrated in Fig. 246 are related to the Windsor and were known as such; they were and are commonly found in kitchens. Loudon's illustration of this type is the earliest that I know of. Also related to the Windsor chair, in some of its details, is the so-called Mendlesham chair of the early nineteenth century. These are named after Mendelsham in Suffolk where its chief makers, Daniel and Richard Day, were located. A simpler variant was also made in Essex, but in either case they were, more often than not, made either of fruitwood (apple or pear) or sometimes of yew (Fig. 247).[44]

Of recent years the regional chair has attracted a considerable body of research,[45] perhaps because chairs in general, and vernacular ones in particular, offer a poignant glimpse of long-since dead personalities – an echo of the human form. This corpus of research has established no less than eight basic yet coherent English regional traditions.[46] Many of these, and others in Wales, Scotland, the Isle of Man and Ireland, relate to the structural imperatives of the stick-back or Windsor chair.[47] That is to say they avoid, where possible, the employment of the expensive square-sectioned shouldered tennon and its corresponding mortice. Whilst these features of joinery are not entirely absent they are (to take one example) used very sparingly, if at all, in the spindle and ladder-back chairs of Lancashire and Cheshire.[48]

In the seventeenth century and before, the chair retained its status as the seat of the master of the house, the 'chairman' – a significance that it has not entirely lost. The majority of people sat on stools or forms. As level floors were introduced so stools and chairs abandoned the use of three legs in favour of four; examples of furniture brought up to date in this way survive (Fig. 242). On simple stools the legs are usually set at an angle to enhance stability. On square-seated, four-legged stools this angle is consistent when viewed from any elevation. However, with forms, their natural stability is greatest on the long axis and it will generally be found that the angle of the leg is more acute when viewed from the end ele-

vation than when seen from the side (Fig. 248). Simple boarded stools and forms made by carpenters were eventually succeeded by 'joint-stools' and forms which employ the shouldered mortice and tenon of the joiner and the legs of the turner. Once one pair of legs was extended upwards to create a back the familiar back-stool was arrived at.

As the joiner deferred to the subtleties of the cabinet-maker, so he in turn gave ground, towards the close of the seventeenth century, to the new breed of woodworkers, noted above, known as chairmakers. Undoubtedly much country furniture continued to be made by general joiners and cabinetmakers, but their wares are noteworthy for their more rectilinear appearance and the persistence of the dowelled through-tenon. Notwithstanding the early character of much provincial furniture in Britain, most craftsmen seem to have responded, with interestingly various degrees of success, to prevailing fashions. The chair illustrated in Fig. 249 is a characteristic example of such a hybrid, with its medieval construction employing dowelled through-tenons and its design merging a 'Queen Anne' back splat within an overall form of the 'Chippendale' period.

Many articles of furniture, and most notably chairs, employ turnery. The turners long remained a separate group of craftsmen, making drinking vessels and trenchers as well as components for furniture. Until the sixteenth century earthenware cups were extremely rare. As late as 1552 the Drapers' Company was still using turners' work at their feasts 'with ashen cups set before them at every mess'.[49] The turners in London received their charter as a guild in 1604 and four years later had extended their activities to include chairs and wheels.[50] A number of 'thrown' or turned chairs and stools survive from this period which were also known as 'buffets' or 'tuffets' – Little Miss Muffet sat on a tuffet, not a 'stump'

247   Early nineteenth-century East Anglian 'Mendlesham' chair.

248   Late eighteenth-century oak form. Forms and benches possess greater stability along their length than from side to side. For this reason legs were given a greater splay in one direction (as viewed from one end) than the other (as viewed from the side).

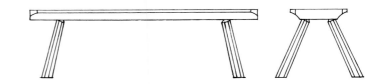

249   An English country chair (with a Sussex provenance), late eighteenth century. This oak chair combines the doweled through-tennon of medieval tradition with the Queen Anne period solid back splat and the overall lines of the age of Chippendale.

of grass.[51] Chairs of this type usually have three legs for stability and are triangular on plan up to the seat level, with the back and arms forming a rectangle above. These two layers of construction are united by diagonal members. Seating furniture of this kind endeavours to counteract structural weakness by multiplying the components of which they are composed. Randle Holme illustrates a stool of this type and states that they were 'Wrought with Knops and rings all over feet. These and the chairs are generally made with three feete.'[52]

It is likely that chairs of this type reached Britain from the Continent via the Low Countries (Fig. 250) but it has also been suggested that they originated in Byzantium and reached our shores via Scandinavia.[53] Whatever the truth of this, they were undoubtedly to be found in fairly large numbers in the Welsh Marches in the mid-eighteenth century. Writing from Strawberry Hill to George Montagu on 20 August 1761, Horace Walpole reported that 'Dicky Bateman has picked up a whole cloister full of chairs in Herefordshire. He bought them one by one, here and there, in farmhouses, for three-and-sixpence and a crown apiece, they are wood, the seats triangular, the backs, arms, and legs, loaded with turnery. A thousand to one there are plenty up and down Cheshire too.'[54] These early seventeenth-century 'thrown' chairs may be considered by some to be too grand for the minor interiors with which we are concerned. However, in Walpole's day it is clear that they were found in 'farmhouses', although from his social position in the eighteenth century he, or Bateman, probably underestimated the status of the early seventeenth-century houses in Herefordshire where they were found. Significantly, these chairs were 'picked up' by Dicky Bateman 'one by one' and each was probably the one and only 'masters chair' in

250   Buffet chair. Detail of a painting by Jan Steen (*c.* 1626–79). Such chairs may have reached the British Isles via Scandinavia but the Low Countries were a more likely source. See also Fig. 36.

251   Francis Hayman, *Thomas Nuthall and Hambleton Custance*, 1748. As a ranger of Enfield Chase Thomas Nuthall and his companion are shown here at an inn or hunting lodge. The rush-seated ladder-back chair was commonly found in such establishments (see Fig. 16). The almanac hanging on the wall is also typical. Tate Gallery, London.

the house. Furthermore Bateman found these chairs on the Welsh borders and many have since come to light in the Principality. The oldest known variant of the kind in England is a bishop's throne, thought to date from *c.* 1200, in Hereford Cathedral.[55] Some of these chairs were relatively simple and without arms such as the example portrayed by Frederick Daniel Hardy (1826–1911) in his (185?) painting of the *Interior of a Sussex Farmhouse* (Fig. 36). These Sussex examples represent a survival lingering down to the mid-nineteenth century but none of this very simple kind are known to survive. In general chairs descended from this type but with four legs, became, in late Stuart England, simpler and were worked from much smaller scantlings. In their scaled-down form they were to proliferate throughout England and the eastern states of Colonial North America.[56]

It is more than likely that the rush-seated ladder-back chair also came into this country from the Low Countries (Fig. 251). Many Dutch paintings show ladder-back chairs in modest interiors, but in *A Tea Party* by Nicolaes Verkoje (1673–1746) they are shown in elegant surroundings.[57] They are described in the late seventeenth-century inventories as 'Dutch matted chairs' or 'Dutch Flagg chairs'.[58] The reference to the flag may suggest the use of irises as a substitute for rushes. In America, Indian corn was sometimes used as an alternative.[59] The front legs of the characteristic chair of this type are sometimes of a form that could be termed a 'suppressed cabriole', but early (i.e. early eighteenth-century) examples probably had simple turned legs such as those illustrated by Grimm in the Saracen's Head, Southwell (Fig. 16). The ladder-back consists of three or four 'rungs' of ash which

252   *The Parlour at Kings Weston, Gloucestershire*, by S. H. Grimm, *c.* 1788. Spindle-back chairs had a wide distribution but were to become more common in the north of England. Note the typical three-legged 'cricket' table on the right.

253   Group of chairs from the Scottish Highlands and Islands. Top row (left to right): Sutherland chair, Invernesshire chair, bog-wood chair from the Isle of Harris; bottom row: Argyle chair, child's chair from Invernesshire and a rush-seated chair from North Uist.

are shaped on elevation and bent on plan. In some examples the back consists of a series of vertical spindles (Fig. 252) and these were particularly popular in Lancashire and Cheshire. The sections of some of the turned members in these chairs is often rich, not to say voluptuous, and this is notably true of their front stretchers.

As has been noted, chairs of the Windsor type were used in Scotland, but in some crofting areas where timber was scarce little more than small trees or driftwood was available out of which to construct furniture. These conditions encouraged the development of chairs made from a 'patchwork' of timbers (Fig. 253). 'Knees' from small trees were used in 'Sutherland' chairs to provide the 'armature' for seat and back. The seat of a simple chair is normally made out of one slab of wood. Not so in some regions of Scotland, such as Argyll, where a 'knee' was used to provide the rear portion of the seat and onto this was 'housed' a smaller, straight section of timber. Birch is a wood that grows well in cold climates and high altitudes and it was favoured in Scotland as well as in Scandinavia. These 'patchwork' chairs use a variety of hardwoods including, in addition to birch, the fruit-woods. Most valuable was ash which, like hickory, has great strength along the grain and was therefore an important component of many country chairs. Another very distinct type is the Invernesshire chair with its unusual protrusion of the seat behind the back, and with front stretchers shaped in a manner reminiscent of late seventeenth-century 'high style' work. The 'Orkney' chair, which combines straw rope and wood, is well known by the many reproductions that have been made of it (Fig. 19).

Rejecting the view that the deforestation of Ireland was an English military strategy which, at the same time, provided fuel for the iron furnaces of Cumbria, Oliver Rackham makes the point that between 1700 and 1840 Ireland experienced a fourfold increase in population. As a consequence woodland gave way to agriculture.[60] Aside from the elegant furniture made from imported mahogany very little Irish furniture dates from before the Famine of the 1840s. Because by the late eighteenth century the native oak forests were largely destroyed, the mass of furniture in nineteenth-century Ireland came to be made from imported softwoods, driftwood or, for special purposes, bog-wood (such as bog oak).[61] In Co. Antrim the successor to the three-legged 'creepie' was a characteristic low, four-legged chair which, like its counterpart in the crofting communities of Scotland, was constructed out of a minimum of timber (Fig. 254).[62] Although apparently in one piece the seat is, in fact, composed of several scantlings. A combination of a very thin top with framed members which provide strength and give an appearance of thickness. The two lateral battens into which the legs are thrust are a structural necessity.[63] Such chairs were usually painted a dark red or green. The repainting of furniture for 'the stations', when the priest came to conduct a service in a chosen house in the village, was an occasion for repainting all the furniture. Consequently accretions of paint bestowed status on the owner.[64]

Many of these chairs from the cabins of Ireland or the crofts of Scotland were made by 'hedge carpenters'.[65] They are invariably low-seated because of the smoky conditions in the simple homes for which they were designed.

> By sitting low, on rushes spread,
> The smoke still hover'd overhead;
> And did more good than real harm
> Because it kept the long house warm.[66]

The medieval tradition of placing or fixing a bench against the lateral timber screen in the hall is the probable origin of the settle. Certainly by the eighteenth century the settle often occupied a similar position in the house. Loudon in fact describes settles as 'benches' and even illustrates a 'Grecian Bench'.[67] Unlike the combined screen and form it was not so draught-proof, a deficiency that was sometimes met by the provision of a curtain. 'On the back there might be a towel roller or, in a superior kind of cottage, the back of the settle might be ornamented with prints or maps in the manner of a [movable] screen . . . there might even be book shelves fixed to the back, and a flap might be hung to it, with a jib bracket to serve as a reading or writing table'.[68] When 'box' seated, the space in the settle was used for storage, with access by means of a lid in the seat or drawers in the front. Occasionally the back took the form of a cupboard, traditionally used for hanging sides of bacon, and in Wales the back of the settle

254 A three-legged 'creepie', a rush pess and chair and three other chairs all from Ulster.

255 The hall at Kennixton Farmhouse from Llangennydd on the Gower Peninsula, built *c.* 1630, as reconstructed at the Museum of Welsh Life. The cupboard-bed, which forms the back to the settle, dates from the eighteenth century. A recess in the ceiling above, and in front of, the fireplace is known as the charnel. It offers a dry space for hanging bacon and herbs whilst at the same time providing a plinth for a bed in the room above – see Fig. 158.

256 Early nineteenth-century 'seise' or settle from a croft in North Uist. This type of bench was also known in Scotland as a 'deece' or 'deas', from the dais of a hall where they originally stood. Museum of Highland Life, Kingussie.

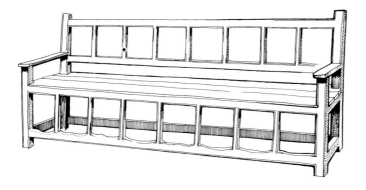

was sometimes the side of a box-bed (Fig. 255). The Scottish equivalent of the settle was the 'seise', which provided no draught-proofing whatsoever (Fig. 256).

The settle-beds of Ireland have been recorded in inventories there from 1640 (Figs. 257, 258) but were not apparently used elsewhere in the British Isles although they are found on the North-Eastern Seaboard of North America in both Canada and the United States.[69] John Fraser describes them in his *Canadian Pen and Ink Sketches* (Montreal, 1910) adding that 'they are to be found in every house more particularly the French and Scottish farmhouses . . . [they] are always nicely painted.'[70] Fraser may well have mistaken the 'Scotch' farmhouses for those of Ulstermen (i.e. the Scotch/Irish) whilst the French-Canadian *banc lit* may have been derived from Irish immi-

257 Settle-bed, painted fir, Ulster, 6 ft by 4 ft 9 ins (height) by 1 ft 9 ins (front to back) (183 by 144.75 by 53.25 cm). The seat folds forward to create a trough in which the bedding was placed. The height of the 'seat', 2 ft 6½ ins (77.25 cm), suggests that when closed this 'settle' may have been used as a sideboard. The medieval character of the design and its construction (sledge feet and primitive dovetails) points to an early date which, in terms of Irish vernacular furniture, means the eighteenth century. Certainly most settle-beds date from the nineteenth century. This furniture type is found in the north-east of North America (USA and Canada) and in Ireland, but not elsewhere in the British Isles. Ulster Folk and Transport Museum.

grant tradition. Kinmonth has argued that in Ireland settle-beds were possibly once reserved for use by servants in the households of the Ascendancy and from thence were transmitted to humble rural dwellings.[71] The planks forming the seat and front of these settle-beds are fixed to one another to form an 'L' section which is hinged to open out forming a trough-like space which usually measures about 72 by 36 ins (183 by 91.4 cm) by 18 ins (47 cm) deep. In principle these settles, when opened as beds, are similar to the ancient stone beds of Skara Brae on Orkney or the related wooden beds of medieval type found in Norway (Figs. 235, 236). In all cases these beds were filled with heather, straw or some such material which would provide a mattress. Rather similar is *la veille*, also known as *la filyie*, of Jersey and the similar *lit-de*

258 Settle-bed from Ulster shown open.

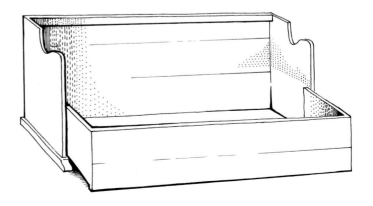

259 Mid-eighteenth-century built-in cupboard-bed in Admiral Blake's House, Bridgwater, Somerset. Although also found in Wales (see Fig. 255) beds of this kind are most characteristic of the north of England and Scotland.

260 (*below*) Cupboard-bed initialled 'D.MP.' and dated 1702 from Badenoch, Scotland – constructed of fir. Softwoods were widely used in Scotland and Ulster. In the absence of a ventilation grille one of the doors was presumably left open when this bed was in use.

fouaille or *la joncquière* of Guernsey in the Channel Islands which, though not beds, were seats in the shape of boxes 'filled with dried bracken, and sometimes covered with a piece of carpet'.[72]

The type of mattress used was related to pocket, class and region. The rich could afford feathers, horse hair or combed wool, but many had to make do with flock or straw. In William Harrison's day (1577) servants were fortunate if they had so much as an undersheet 'to keepe them from the pricking straws that ran oft through the canvas (of the pallet) and rased their hardened hides'.[73] Writing in 1664, John Evelyn recommended beech leaves 'gathered about the fall and somewhat before they are frostbitten'.[74]

The box or cupboard-bed was probably once widespread in the British Isles where surviving examples will now be found only very occasionally in the south of England – for example, an eighteenth century box-bed built into Admiral Blake's house, Bridgwater, Somerset (Fig. 259). A reference to 'Painting a press Bedstead Red' in July 1765 in Edkins's ledger book (see Appendix III) shows that such beds were also in use in Bristol and a Welsh example has already been cited (Fig. 255). Surviving beds of this kind are more common in the north of England but are most characteristic of Scotland (Figs. 19, 260).[75] Such beds were once common in Scandinavia[76] and the Netherlands[77] whilst they are also found in Brittany.[78] The distribution of these beds offers further evidence for a North Sea culture which extended down the English Channel and beyond. These box-beds are either freestanding or built-in and may derive from the bed alcoves that were built into the thickness of masonry walls. Undoubtedly box-beds were kept snug by the warmth of the human body. Some are provided with ventilation, but those that are not gained air, one may presume, through an open door. In those parts of Scotland where wood was scarce such beds were often screened off by curtains rather than doors. In small one-room cottages they were, in effect, bedrooms offering some privacy, and it was probably for this reason that they were made well into the nineteenth century. Loudon illustrates 'An Improvement in the Box Bedsteads used in Scotch Cottages'.[79]

In Ulster the 'bed outshot' was a reasonably standard feature, built into the wall running at right angles to the fire-hood wall.[80] In some examples a proportion of the interior depth of these alcoves is accommodated by reducing the wall thickness (Figs. 30, 34).[81] Despite the generally rudimentary roof lining elsewhere in the house, the *cailleach* or outshot was invariably lined with newspapers pasted together and whitewashed. Judging by the dates of these newspapers this is probably an early nineteenth-century innovation in place of the woven grass mats once used to line bed outshots (see p. 105 and Fig. 159). In Ulster these beds were often reserved for older members of the family (typically a grandmother) or for visitors.[82] The family slept on the floor, with mother and father side by side in the centre, the youngest daughter next to the mother and son next to the father, and so on in gradually increasing ages.

The importance attached to providing some sort of ceiling to the bed outshots of Ireland is analogous to the use of canopies over beds and 'cloths of estate' which ran up behind and over the high chair in the hall. In buildings that were not otherwise ceiled overhead, canopies provided some protection from falling straw and soot. Thus a feature that was once a matter of practical necessity was to become an emblem of status.[83]

From early times many people in mainland Britain slept on half-headed bedsteads. These resemble modern bedsteads except that, as with other beds, the primitive mattress was supported by interwoven ropes that passed through drill holes in the surrounding frame. On these, as on many bedsteads, the mortice and tenon was often held by means of bolts which could be undone to dismantle the bed. In Kennixton Farmhouse from the Gower Peninsula, now re-erected at St Fagans, the divan bed is in fact on top of the recess in the ceiling of the room below (Figs. 158, 255). This recess, known locally as a 'charnel', was near the fire on the ground floor and not only made the bed warm but also, in the room below, provided a dry space in which to hang joints of bacon and bunches of herbs. This feature is also recorded in Yorkshire in Langstrothdale and in the Dales around Sedbergh.[84]

One of the most important uses of the enclosed cupboard was for the storage of food. By building it into the thickness of a stone wall and equipping it with a wooden door, reasonably cool temperatures could be maintained. These cupboards are found in most parts of the British Isles but in the seventeenth century they were particularly popular in Cumbria (Figs. 261, 262, 263). When built into the warm wall of the chimney, cupboards of this kind stored items like salt or herbs in suitably dry conditions (Fig. 28). The use of such a cupboard for valuable herbs may be inferred by their small size and the presence of a lock. Many other foodstuffs are best preserved by means of ventilation and such provision may help to distinguish between a food cupboard and a wardrobe. In early times when these cupboards were known as 'aumbrys' the needs of ventilation were probably met by the use of woven wickerwork. Although the names applied to furniture in the past always related more closely to function than form there can be no doubt that food cupboards were known as 'aumbrys' as the following lines of 1573 make clear:

> Some slovens from sleeping no sooner be up,
> But hand is in aumbrie, and nose in the cup.[85]

261, 262 (*facing page and above*) Tester bed dated 1724 and bearing the initials 'FHA' for Francis and Anne Hall. The Halls were a yeoman family and their bed remained in the first-floor chamber of their stone-built house in Kirkbride, Cumbria until the 1960s. In its original setting the door in the centre of the headboard, painted with the emblem of a tree, opened as a cupboard contrived in the thickness of the masonry wall behind the bed. Whilst painted furniture is known in post-medieval Britain (e.g. Fig. 244) polychromatic work of this kind is very rare (see also Fig. 274). Leeds City Museums and Galleries.

263 Oak cupboard built into the masonry of the central room of Heaning Farmhouse, Windermere, Cumbria. It bears the initials of its owner, 'IDO', and the date 1681 – which may be 'read' as the period of the 'Great Rebuilding' in Cumbria.

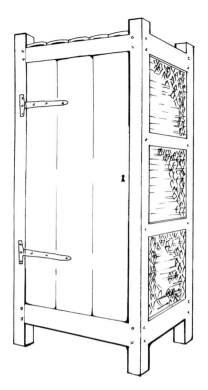

264, 265   Fir and wicker food cupboard from Acharacle, Highland, Scotland. Although dating from the late nineteenth century this cupboard indicates the probable appearance of earlier examples made of similarly fragile materials.

266, 267   Pine cheese cupboard from Strathnairn, Scotland, early nineteenth century. The spacing of the rods suggests that they were probably originally backed with gauze as a fly screen. Museum of Highland Life, Kingussie.

A late example, but of an early type, is the remarkable cupboard from Acharacle, Highland (Figs. 264, 265). The alternative was to frame-up panels of turned spindles, as in the cheese cupboard (Figs. 266, 267) from Strathnairn (a fertile dairy-farming region), or to pierce panels of wood with drill holes, as in the front of a built-in cupboard of the seventeenth century removed in the 1970s

from Blue Barnes, north Essex (Fig. 268). Some rather grand medieval examples employ pierced tracery for this purpose.[86]

As its name implies, the cupboard was a simple board for cups. In aristocratic households they were used for the display of plate (silver) but a farmer might, as Harrison recorded in 1577, display 'a fair garnish of

pewter on his cupboard'.[87] Eventually these 'cup-boards' evolved into the open court-cupboard of the type that stands in the background of Hans Holbein's picture of *The Ambassadors* (1533). Wolsey and Luff have argued convincingly that, in this sense, the term 'buffet' does not seem to have been part of the vocabulary of Tudor England – although it was, as we have seen, used in connection with certain types of seating furniture.[88]

Towards the close of the reign of Elizabeth I the upper half of some court-cupboards were partially enclosed. In the course of the seventeenth century this process was completed with both levels fully enclosed by doors, thus creating the 'press-cupboard', but with vestiges of the original form surviving in the columns or pendentives to the upper section which also retains a narrow shelf (Figs. 269, 270). In Wales these pieces of furniture were taken a stage further by the addition of a third tier – they are

268   (*above*) Mid-seventeenth-century food-cupboard front with pierced oak panels from a house at Blue Barns, north Essex. Ventilation was an important feature. Victoria and Albert Museum, London.

269, 270   (*below*) Two oak press-cupboards built into the north wall of a room in Common Farmhouse, Windermere, Cumbria. The earliest of the two (left) is dated 1628 but the later one (right), dated 1715, whilst part of a continuing tradition in the county, has evidently been designed to be in keeping with the earlier cupboard.

271 Living-room in a house at Drumaghlis (Townland), near Ballynahinch, Co. Down. The pyramids of inverted bowls on the bottom shelf of the dresser and the forward-sloping plates are typical of Ulster. Photograph *c.* 1910 by R. Welch. Ulster Museum.

known as 'tridarns' (Fig. 143). These objects may be seen as the natural predecessors of the ubiquitous dresser without which no home from the eighteenth century onwards was complete.

Loudon unequivocally asserts that dressers are 'essential to every kitchen, but more especially to that of the cottage to whome they serve both as dressers and side-boards'. Most of the late eighteenth and nineteenth-century examples that will be found built into the kitchen of the average town house are made of soft-woods. However, in the country, when the hall served the double function of kitchen and main living-room, oak was favoured and every attention was given to the finish as befitted furniture for such a space. In the north of England dressers of this late period were frequently embellished with mahogany crossbanding and given ivory key-hole escutcheons. Probably the simplest of all the oak dressers was the type made in the region of Bridgwater, Somerset. These were not carcassed-up in the usual way in two sections – shelves and base – but were made in one piece with the sides composed of a pair of boards running from floor to ceiling.[89] Their construction is more akin to the work of carpenters than to joiners. Not all dresser shelves were given boarded backs as the wall of the house was often adequate. In England and Wales the shelves are usually equipped with a groove into which the plates were slotted and leant against the

back. An alternative method, occasionally found in England and Wales but common in Scotland and Ulster, was to fit battens of wood onto the front of the dresser between the shelves so that the plates could be leant forward. The favourite crocks that were displayed on these shelves were willow pattern and other 'Staffordshire blue'. In Ulster the bottom shelf of such dressers was usually reserved for pyramids of inverted soup bowls (Fig. 271). Inverted vessels, like plates lent forward, were less inclined to become dusty in smoke-filled rooms.

In Ireland and Scotland dressers were generally constructed of softwoods. Indeed, the more widespread use of conifer for the furniture in small traditional interiors in these two countries produces an effect markedly different from equivalent interiors in England and Wales. The dresser often occupied the wall facing the fire, and in one-room cottages its position was advanced away from the wall, screening off small bed spaces (Fig. 272). In the so-called black houses of the Hebrides and elsewhere in Scotland the dresser more often stood against an outer wall. So that it could fit in that position the top hood (when viewed from the side) was angled to be parallel to the rafters (Fig. 273). This is characteristic of some late Gothic, south German softwood furniture; a comparison which is coincidental, few surviving Scottish dressers being earlier than the nineteenth century – although the architectural causes of this feature may be similar.

272 Single-room cottage from Rhostryfan, Gwynedd, dated 1762, as reconstructed at the Museum of Welsh Life. The dresser backs onto a partition which creates two small bedrooms with a loft over. Note that the dresser is preserved from rising damp from the earth floor by standing on small slabs of slate; the continuous slate step on the left similarly protects the cupboard which stands on it. See also Fig. 80.

273 Nineteenth-century fir and pine dresser from a croft at Eochar, South Uist, Outer Hebrides, Scotland, 5 ft 9 ins high by 3 ft 9 ins wide and 1 ft 10 ins deep overall (175 cm by 114.20 by 56 cm). Dressers of this type stood against the outside wall of the croft so that the hood was angled to run parallel to the rafters of the low roof. Museum of Highland Life, Kingussie.

Whilst court-cupboards and dressers, when garnished with pewter or crockery, offered a sense of domestic well-being, pride of place was given to the long-case clock, in those households privileged enough to own one. Indeed clocks, together with items like curtains and pictures, have been used by economic and social historians to demonstrate dramatic increases in the standard of living – especially between 1705 and 1715.[90] In the same decade a divide between town and country is revealed in household inventories with a 21 per cent ownership of clocks in urban centres and 7 per cent in rural ones.[91] By 1763 this growth in consumerism was noted with upper-class disdain: 'in a few years we shall probably have no common people at all.'[92]

In England and Wales most furniture for small domestic interiors was made from oak, fruitwood, ash and elm. As we have seen, softwood with some birch was widely used in Scotland and Ireland together with some of the hardwoods common to England and Wales, except that in Ireland bog oak was employed. Compared with Continental Europe remarkably little of this furniture was given polychrome decoration between about 1700 and 1800. The ubiquitous stick-back chairs and the settle-beds of Ulster being simply painted one colour. Decorative multicoloured painting, used to such good and florid effect in much of peasant Europe, is very rare in post-medieval Britain (Fig. 274), though it may have persisted into the seventeenth century as a survival, and is found on the inner side of the lids of nineteenth-century sailors' chests and on the furniture traditionally used in the cabins of canal boats.[93] As Eric Mercer has observed, 'Early timber furniture has survived less well, but its direct successors in eighteenth and nineteenth-century Scandinavian peasant houses reflect its qualities.' Among these qualities was the love of polychromatic decoration, 'The important difference however is that in early years even the best furniture of kings was often painted, while later painting was usually confined to the furniture of lesser men or to the less important furniture of the great.'[94] For these reasons the painted bed dated 1724 from Kirkbride, Cumbria, is an astonishing survival and one that may point to a persistent use of colour in remote areas, into the eighteenth century (Figs. 261, 262), a lingering of the medieval tradition in the post-medieval Lake District. Only under the influence of Robert Adam's neo-Classicism was there a fleeting return to the use of polychromatic painted decoration for 'polite' furniture. In many towns outside London the fashionable materials of the eighteenth century, including walnut and (later) mahogany, were used for furniture which is otherwise provincial in style and construction. Chairs in oak, elm and fruitwood with 'drop in' seats are quite common – but stuff-over upholstery was rare at the vernacular level.

Apart from wood, other materials were used for furniture. As we have seen, the vertebra of a whale provided a convenient stool, but such an object was obtainable only in certain coastal regions. More widespread was the use of woven wickerwork, a tradition going back to Roman Britain if not earlier.[95] In the cathedral on the island of Iona wickerwork coffins were found in the crypt.[96] In areas such as the Hebrides, where timber was scarce, wickerwork chairs (Fig. 275) were much used and where wickerwork was unavailable straw rope provided an alternative which was also used in timbered regions. Loudon (1836) records that 'In Monmouthshire, easy chairs with hoods, like porter's chairs in gentlemen's halls, are constructed of straw matting on a frame of wooden rods, or of stout iron wire; and [some] chairs . . . are made entirely of straw in different parts of England in the same way as the common beehives.'[97] A 'lip-work' chair from

Wales of the type described by Loudon is illustrated in Fig. 276 and they are also well known in the west of Ireland.[98] Chairs of this type were also common in Scandinavia and the word 'lip' is thought to correspond to the Danish *løb*.[99] The word also occurs in English dialects as 'leap', to mean basketwork. A lip-work chair of this kind, indistinguishable from examples in Britain, is exhibited in a farmhouse from Vemb, West Jutland, in the Frilandsmuseet, Denmark. In Wales these seats were known as *cadair telynor* or harpist's chairs. The design, though born of straw rope, has in at least one example been translated into wood (Fig. 277). Rushes were also used to make furniture, and the drum-like 'pess' is still made in East Anglia (Fig. 278).[100] It is a type of hassock. In fact the latter may well be related to the pess as the word 'hassock' has been thought by some to derive from *hesg*, the Welsh for sedges.[101]

The dominance of 'easel painting' must be seen as a product of the Renaissance. Before then the movable panel-painting was the exception and the painter's craft ranged over a wide variety of surfaces integrating the work fully with its public and the buildings in which these skills were deployed. Overdoor and overmantel pictures (described in Chapter 9) were among the last examples of pictorial art to be united inseparably with their architectural setting. However, by the late seventeenth century movable pictures, paintings, maps and prints, were to be found in many interiors. The popularity of maps, usually shown hanging between rollers, can be seen as heralding the decline of limning (the use of solid gouache) and the rise of translucent watercolour which would not obliterate the printed line. The burgeoning use of movable pictures of all kinds is particularly evident between about 1675 and 1725. In that half century some 35 per cent of tradesmen owned pictures although only 4 per cent of yeoman farmers did. This could point to an urban/rural divide contingent upon the cash economics of towns in contrast to the persistence of barter in the countryside.[102]

(facing page)

275 (*bottom left*) Wickerwork chair of a type once traditional to the Isle of Skye, Scotland. This example was made as recently as 1936 in the Highland Homes Industry Factory. It is 30 ins in height. Museum of Highland Life, Kingussie.

276 (*bottom right*) Welsh lip-work chair, possibly early nineteenth century – note the use of leather where straw would wear or be uncomfortable to the touch. Although only late examples survive, furniture made of straw, rush and wicker has been in use in Britain since Roman times (J. Liversidge, *Furniture in Roman Britain*, 1955). Museum of Welsh Life.

274 Chest on stand with polychromatic painted decoration. Guernsey, Channel Islands, mid to late eighteenth century. Such work is probably closer in character to provincial France or even Colonial North America than to England – see also Figs. 261, 262. Guernsey Museum and Art Gallery.

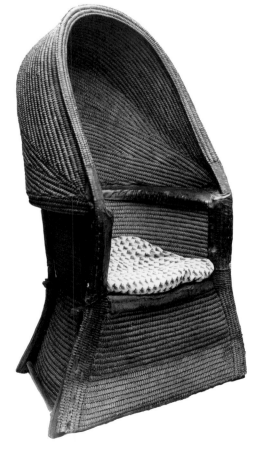

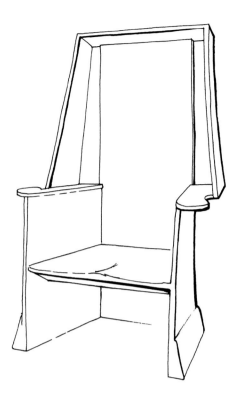

277   Timber chair, possibly made in imitation of lip-work, from Blaencrymlin Farm, Blackmill, near Bridgend, Glamorgan, Wales – probably nineteenth century. Museum of Welsh Life.

278   Two rush pesses from East Anglia. Norwich City Museums.

Early picture frames followed architectural practice and included a cill, as in a window, with the familiar mason's mitre. The general introduction of easel paintings by the early seventeenth century promoted the development of the picture frame as an object, not simply removed from architecture, but intended to isolate a picture from its surroundings. Carved and parcel-gilt (partly gilt) frames of the type described by Sir Balthazar Gerbier (1663) which were 'fifteen inches broad, the ground a fair white (probably gesso) cost five shillings a foot' and are thus beyond the scope of this book in terms of scale and money.[103] An alternative type of frame, also described by Gerbier, was probably more relevant to the smaller domestic interior typical of those with limited means. These were the painted (and sometimes gilded) frames worked 'upon a flat [i.e. uncarved] moulding, and set-off with shading, like carving, one inch broad . . . worth four or five pence a foot'.[104] In the middle of the century, and through to its conclusion, a common and simple type of frame which derived from the Continent employed ebony worked with a 'wriggled' moulding. These Franco-Dutch frames were extensively used in England and are alluded to in Felibien's *Principes* (1699) which also mentions the 'waving machine'.[105] Being worked by means of an 'engine', rather than being hand carved, these mouldings were cheap in terms of labour. However the use of ebony from the distant East meant that these frames (and indeed furniture) were, necessarily, expensive. Quite how this wriggle moulding was achieved is scarcely helped by Moxon's description

Of the Waving Engine . . . And as the Rounds of the Rack ride over the round edge of the flat Iron, the Rack and Riglet will mount up to the Iron, and as the Rounds of the Waves on the under side of the Rack slides off the Iron on edge, the Rack and Riglet will sink, and so in progression . . . The Riglet will on its upper side receive the form of several waves.[106]

By 1688 John Stalker and George Parker were recommending lightweight simulated ebony frames which 'are usually made of stained Pear-tree, with narrow mouldings for little pieces, which increase in bredth, as the size of your picture does in largness; they are made with Rabets, and are afforded for 6, 8, and 12 pence, or more, according to their several dimensions.'[107] These frames long remained popular and today are known as 'Hogarths'. The elaborate, carved wood frames of the seventeenth and eighteenth centuries, with their resplendent water gilding, are generally outside the scope of this book. In the early nineteenth century, frames with a simple section were sometimes painted to simulate bird's-eye maple and at about the same time rosewood and bird's-eye maple veneer was also used. Original examples of the painted bird's-eye maple are now very rare. Another type dating from the second half of the nineteenth century was the 'Oxford' frame; it is described in *The Practical Carver and Gilder's Guide* (c. 1880): 'These

279 *The Harvest* [Festival]
*Children at Prayers, Kirby
Parsonage with the Green Dale
Oak Cabinet* [from Welbeck
Abbey], *Nott*, watercolour
drawing by S. H. Grimm,
c. 1780. Pictures were
commonly hung high in
the eighteenth century.

frames have become favourites within the last few years.
They are made of oak, with cross corners, and are made
up in fancy patterns, some of which are finished with
ultramarine on the bevels. They can be had of the wholesale houses' their sizes ranging from 4¼ in by 3¼ in to
29 in by 21 in [10.8 by 8.3 cm to 35.6 by 30.5 cm].[108] The
Gilder's Guide adds that 'Oxford frames are suitable for
sacred subjects, mottoes, views in the Holy Land, &c., but
are used for portraits, and many other pictures look well
in them.' In the nineteenth century many frames were
made to imitate expensive carved work. Although made
of wood they are in fact embellished with cast 'composition' (a form of gesso), with 'slips' of 'German' or 'Dutch'
gold – a substitute for the real thing.

In the seventeenth, eighteenth and early nineteenth
centuries pictures were generally hung rather high in
relation to the average height of individuals. The interior
of the Reverend Richard Kay's parsonage recorded by
his protégé, the German artist Grimm, shows this feature
clearly (Fig. 279). This apparently enabled pictures to be
viewed more easily when the company was standing. The
excessive height at which pictures were hung was sometimes compensated for by tilting them forward, and the
two methods of hanging often coexisted in the same

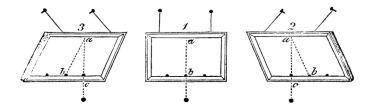

280 The visual distortion caused by viewing pictures obliquely
when they are hung tilting forward. An illustration from Prince
Hoare's *Epochs of the Arts*, 1813.

room as is shown in the drawing of Pepys's library.[109] The
painter Prince Hoare (1813) firmly rejected the method
of hanging pictures so that they tilted forward on the
grounds that everything within a painting was distorted
unless viewed frontally (Fig. 280).[110] In panelled rooms
pictures were sometimes shown hung arbitrarily across
stiles and rails and not kept within panels, a feature which
is well illustrated in the 1762 Irish group portrait of *The
Family of Thomas Bateson*, attributed to Philip Hussey
(1713–83), now in the Ulster Museum, Belfast.

281   *Interior of a Cottage on Boxley Hill, Maidstone*, Kent. Watercolour drawing *c.* 1840 by Arthur Vine Hall (1824–1919). By the nineteenth century the yeoman's house of the sixteenth century was regarded as a 'cottage'. This drawing shows the early tradition for sparse furnishing continuing in early Victorian England. The Queen Anne mirror hanging on the extreme left was clearly intended for a grander setting. Employers in 'the big house' often gave generous wedding presents to villagers 'in service'. Private Collection.

At Newby Hall, Yorkshire, in the late seventeenth century the pictures were 'not set up, the house being in mourning for his Lady and her mother the Lady Yorke',[111] but it is not known how general this practice was in lesser households. In early post-Colonial New England mirrors were certainly covered with a cloth during times of mourning as a means of rejecting the vanities of life.[112] According to Harriet Beecher Stowe there were other reasons for this practice as a shroud of muslin was thought to protect mirrors from 'attack' by flies.[113] On both sides of the Atlantic mirrors long remained expensive because of the very high cost of plate glass, which is precisely why they were so lavishly used by the rich in the eighteenth century (Fig. 281).[114] Their more general distribution did not occur until the nineteenth century.

In the eighteenth century cheap prints became available to many people, but by the following century they were truly ubiquitous. The great advantage of prints was that, unlike easel paintings, they were relatively cheap in themselves, did not need framing and could be stuck on the wall. Furthermore, unframed prints shown in this way dispensed with glazing, glass being an expensive commodity largely because of the excise duty it attracted. For this reason framed prints were sometimes

varnished as an alternative to glass. A mid-eighteenth century painting by C. L. Junker of a tavern interior shows an engraved portrait and a map stuck on the wall whilst 'serious' sporting subjects (a fighting cock and a race horse) are properly framed (Fig. 282).

In the pre-industrial circumstances of late Stuart Britain the craft-based economy of the time resulted in a visually educated artisan class. For this reason the ownership of pictures may have been far greater than might be supposed. John Michael Montias has certainly shown that in seventeenth-century Delft large numbers of pictures were owned by a very wide spectrum of the city's population.[115] In England a successful Doncaster shopkeeper occupying a thirteen-roomed premises had no less than twelve pictures hanging in his 'dineing Roome' in 1674.[116] On the other hand the merchant Thomas Bayly II 'late of Marlborough' only had '2 pickters' in his dining room, one 'lawnskip' in his kitchen and three 'pickters' in his shop according to the inventory drawn up in 1690/91 (see Appendix II).

In terms of subject matter the range of pictures in vernacular interiors was less diverse than that which graced the households of the élite. In large houses particular types of subject are known to have been reserved for relevant rooms. Lomazzo's *Tracte* which was 'Englished' by

Haydocke (1598) went so far as to list those themes suitable for churches, 'Princes Pallaces' and even 'places of torture and execution'.[117] Mercifully, the farmhouse in the country or, more likely, the third-rate house in town was generally adorned by canvases which took more prosaic subjects as their theme. A ship's captain in London might have a 'likeness' of his vessel, perhaps painted by 'Bowen and Fuss, Painters and Glaziers in General [of] 29 Artichoke Lane, near Sampson's Gardens, Wapping.'[118] Similarly a farmer would commission portraits of his prize-winning cattle. From the second half of the eighteenth century the agricultural revolution that accompanied the industrialisation of Britain established a demand for portraits of livestock. Indeed before the gradual introduction of 'stock and flock' books, in the course of the nineteenth century, they were a practical necessity – a form of visual pedigree. These oil portraits of prize cattle, pigs, and sheep, in their engraved form, had a wide distribution. The 'pictures of famous rams, that have fetched

fabulous prices, framed against the walls', described by Richard Jefferies, were probably of this kind.[119]

Portraiture was not confined to the practical needs of shipping or agriculture, but included human subjects. In an age of high infant mortality there was a poignant urgency for representations of children. Not that practical and emotional need was the only motivating force. Even at the vernacular level, 'art for art's sake' maintained a presence in the shape of an overmantel landscape or a framed still life.

It was prints though, hand-coloured or plain, that were most widely available. For example, *The Gentleman's Magazine* for 1789 reported the death of John Hooper Esq. of Walcot, Bath. The obituary goes on to allude to Hooper's 'supposed' income of £3,000 a year 'though his origin was little better than that of a day labourer'. Because of his 'avaricious disposition . . . He lived in a mean house opposite Walcot church-yard, the inside of which the walls were *originally* white-washed, and annu-

282   *Tavern Interior*, mid-eighteenth century, by the amateur artist C. L. Junker (d. 1797). This picture was later engraved by Patrick Purcell under the ironic title *The Sportsman's Hall* – note that the less 'important' prints (a portrait and a map) have been stuck direct on the wall whereas the more significant sporting pictures are framed, although possibly not glazed (varnish being a cheaper alternative at a time when glass was taxed). Patrick Purcell may have been related to the engraver Richard Purcell (*c.* 1736–66) who was described by Samuel Redgrave (1874) as 'depraved in habit and licentious in manner' but was also one of the great 'wags' of his day.

ally ornamented with a Poor Robin's sixpenny almanac.' Early in the following century Edmund Bartell was able to acknowledge that 'Prints, or pictures, though certainly articles of luxury, are such pleasing ornaments, that we should be doing great violence to our feelings not to admit them among the furniture of the ornamental cottage . . . That they should be neatly framed, is all that is required . . . The love of pictures is not confined to persons in the higher situations of life. Do we not see in almost every, the meanest, cottage, ordinary pictures and prints, and . . . even ballads, pasted on the wall with good effect'.[120] If in 1804 Bartell was under some compulsion to justify such a case, it was, by Loudon's day (1836), the conventional wisdom that there was 'scarcely a cottage where its inmates do not look with pride and pleasure upon some humble effort of art, that adorns the walls of their home'.[121]

It was often found aesthetically advisable, with large numbers of small prints, to hang them in 'constellations'. In general there was no objection to picture wire or cord being visible, but in the nineteenth century it was recommended that 'The colour of the cord should correspond with the paper or the paint in the room as much as possible, so as not to be noticed, as it is no ornament to see cords on the walls.'[122] This was in great contrast to the seventeenth century when silk cords, ribbons and bows were used, very visibly, to hang pictures.[123] Picture chain was used in gentry establishments simply because it was essential for the heavy pictures and mirrors deployed in such interiors. Where it was used, chain was kept to a minimum length. Clearly in a matter of this nature there was considerable individual variation: 'much depends on taste; some will have the bottom edge of the frames all round a room to range exactly, while others prefer to see the line broken',[124] often by using a notional horizontal centre line through each picture.

By the early nineteenth century Loudon was writing about 'Pictures, Sculptures, and other internal Ornaments' which were so ubiquitous that 'There is no cottage or dwelling, however humble, in which there will not be found some object purely ornamental.' By the second half of the century this trend was firmly established, to the extent that 'from the artisan to the titled nobility of our land, the work of the artist and engraver is admired and valued.'[125]

However, not all pretty things were necessarily regarded as 'purely ornamental'. Hanging shelves and spoon racks were both decorative and useful, and following the 1851 Exhibition the astonishingly cheap and attractive Connecticut clock found its way into almost every home in the British Isles. Superstitions, often of ancient origin, resulted in household features that were not merely pretty but were of fundamental importance to those who owned them. In *John Ashby of Tysoe* his daughter, M. K. Ashby, describes an interior with its apparently innocuous collection of bric-a-brac: 'On the mantle-piece were china figures of old-fashioned policemen, pale blue-and-white, and small lions with crinkled manes. On the wall above were hung long hollow glass 'walking-sticks', twisted like barley sugar, one of them filled with tiny coloured balls like a confectioner's 'hundreds and thousands'.[126] These walking-sticks were more than Nailsea glass nick-nacks. They were hung in houses by the superstitious to absorb disease which, so it was believed, could be wiped off the glass with a cloth.[127] Such features and objects like the witch-posts of Yorkshire, the Bridget's crosses of Ireland or the mirror glass balls that were thought to repel evil spirits, may have been decorative but their primary purpose concerned the need to assuage primitive fears.

In the general furnishing of the rooms of a house with objects large and small, utilitarian and ornamental, the inventory is long, the possibilities endless. In looking at furniture and furnishing I have endeavoured to illuminate those aspects of the subject that are peculiar to the smaller house, but I must acknowledge that much has been omitted. Clearly the presence of pottery in small houses was important, but no space remains to describe the sgraffito ware of north Devon and Somerset,[128] or the treen love-spoons of Wales,[129] or the universal and ancient tradition for corn dollies, made from ears and stems taken from the last wheatsheaf of the harvest, and hung from the ceiling of the farmhouse for a year, perennial but enduring symbols of the 'staff of life'.[130] All such objects contributed to the appearance of the home, to its spiritual and physical comforts.

Conclusion

The Vernacular Interior in Context

In looking at small domestic interiors detail by detail it is easy to lose sight of wider issues. Furthermore, some elements within an interior are but two sides of the same coin – floors and ceilings for example. I will therefore conclude with a brief overview in an attempt to outline the ways in which these various components relate one to another.

Vernacular buildings are the consequence of historical and social development conditioned by climate and the availability of materials and skills. Dwellings of this kind are less influenced by aesthetic fashion than are the houses of the élite. In a regional building a particular room is but part of a continuum reflecting its time and place. In their use in the present, the interiors of the past accommodate the ebb and flow of ephemeral elements, such as movable furniture and painted decoration, in ways which respond to the needs, emotions, spiritual values and superstitious fears of their inhabitants. These are powerful forces, which is why such interiors have the capacity to be greater than the sum of their parts.

In many ways vernacular buildings evolve and respond to their environment like natural organisms. With some exceptions, like 'territory' and 'display', 'polite architecture' tends to tidy away provision for animal instincts and functions into façades of respectability and plans of discretion. In contrast a traditional and regional house and its interior is less masked by style and symmetry and is therefore more direct in its appearance; a distillation of human need. A large country house dilutes these essential requirements within a much greater volume with more specialist rooms and furniture. The one may offer a series of interiors of impressive sophistication, the other a few rooms with great visual intensity.

Over the last few decades a considerable body of research has advanced our understanding of vernacular building as the horizon of certainty has receded. There was a time, not many years since, when cruck distribution was firmly anchored in Wales and the northern and western regions of England.[1] Similarly the Wealden hall-house was once securely located in Kent and Sussex. Both propositions have been amended as a result of the evidence produced by a growing body of fieldwork.[2] As for the 'Great Rebuilding', that particular notion has been revised out of all recognition whilst remaining a useful analytical device.[3]

Although material evidence has altered and amended our perceptions, revisionist thinking has probably owed even more to students of the social history of housing. For example, in seeing the home as the theatre for human activity Lorna Weatherill and others have compared the 'front of house' to those 'back stage' areas where less attempt was made to impress.[4] This interpretation of the fabric of the past has for long been understood, but social historians have backed this approach with a statistical analysis of probate inventories and have therefore advanced our understanding of the furnishing and use of the home.[5] Despite research of this kind we still know very little about zones of domestic responsibility. Whilst the home may, to some extent, have imprisoned middle-class Victorian women it also empowered them – they assumed responsibility for its management and thus, by extension, made decisions on its furnishing. In pre-Victorian Britain ephemeral details like wallpaper may have been chosen by the lady of the house but its basic architectural planning seems to have been a male preserve.[6]

With these ever shifting positions in our understanding of the material culture and the social conditioning of domestic life, one might be tempted to cling to a belief in a continuation of high standards of craftsmanship in early modern Britain. Even here we are confronted with uncertainty. Matthew Johnson has suggested that 'with the separation between *house as process* and *house as product*' traditions for high quality workmanship were placed under severe strain.[7] The boom in speculative building in late Stuart London certainly put enormous pressures on the tradesmen involved in realising these schemes. It would, though, be a mistake to suppose that speed of execution was incompatible with high quality work: on the contrary, it was a sign of a well-trained craftsman that he could achieve supreme standards in a remarkably short time.[8] The consistency of brickwork depends on fast working and much the same was true for plain plasterwork – even when using the slower-curing lime plaster. The true problem with the *house as product* occurred where commercial pressures encouraged the use of inferior building methods or materials. It was a 'management' issue rather than one that was necessarily within the responsibility of individual tradesmen – although, it must be said, some of these craftsmen became speculative builders. Isaac Ware (1756) gives yet another explanation for poor quality work and explicitly states that in the construction of a typical London terraced house 'the art of slight building' was attributable to 'the nature of the tenures', leases which were, at best, for ninety years.[9]

For the craftsmen of the pre-industrial past, making and designing were simultaneous activities.[10] These men were described, in their own day, as 'artists in their trades'.[11] An apprentice 'served his time' – usually seven years from the age of fourteen – gaining experience in his chosen 'art and mystery'. At the end of his time he submitted his 'masterpiece' to the relevant guild. In this context we are concerned with art as in artisan and masterpiece as in proof piece.[12] In some respects this book has been about the building craftsmen who both made and designed the interiors which have been sampled in the preceding pages. Vernacular buildings were the product of various tradesmen who were specialists in handling a given material such as wood, stone or brick. This is not to say that craftsmen in the countryside were not also engaged in agriculture – they often were. It was, rather, that the converse was seldom true. A farmer might repair a dry-stone wall or help to thatch a rick, but in general even the latter was left to the halliers – a word that identified two aspects of roofing: the trades of thatcher and tiler.[13] I use the word 'craftsmen' with deliberation. Although women were involved with work on the building site as labourers or as employers, they were not permitted, indeed they were rigorously excluded from, direct participation in these crafts. In most cases a woman became an employer as a conse-

quence of her husband's premature death. In this respect the widows of plumbers are statistically over-represented, presumably because of the toxic properties of lead. These were the circumstances in which a widow would run a business until such time as her eldest son completed his apprenticeship and came of age (the two events generally coincided at twenty-one years) or, more often, had spent some time as a journeyman.[14]

The guilds were town-centred organisations which were probably at the height of their powers in the decades immediately following the promulgation of the Statute of Artificers of 1563 which translated localised rules into nationwide regulations.[15] Although there were many village-centred craftsmen the ultimate standards for training and workmanship were defined by urban-based masters at a time when the great bulk of the population lived in the countryside.[16] Furthermore, high quality work at affordable prices is dependent upon a degree of specialisation which may only be sustained where there is sufficient demand, and this is generally contingent upon an adequate population base. Alan Everitt has gone further and argued that it was, in particular, the county towns which were the nurseries of the crafts. He has demonstrated that, in the late eighteenth century, approximately half the population in these urban centres were comprised of craftsmen of one sort or another.[17] If one considers that, of these various skills, about half again would have required considerable training of eye and hand,[18] it is likely that a quarter of the working population of a typical English county town had received a visual education of great sophistication, at a time when the craft guilds are generally seen to have been in decline.[19] It would, of course, be a serious over-simplification to see a direct cause and effect between the decline in the power of the livery companies over their respective crafts and a reduction of skill. Besides, the connections between these guilds and their ostensible trades had, by this time, become tenuous. Certainly the growth of 'pauper apprenticeship' had given this system of training a bad name.[20] Even so, some master craftsmen continued to give individual apprentices a fine education, one that should not be underestimated. After all, as Everitt has pointed out, 'a seven year apprenticeship [was] twice as long a training' as that enjoyed by 'a modern undergraduate' with the result that 'English craftsmen came to be associated with those qualities of deftness and individual ingenuity that we now associate with the Japanese'.[21]

This craft background, shared by a large proportion of the urban population, made the tradesman as a customer no less demanding of others than he was of himself. As a result some artisans were in a position to use their craft skills to provide homes for their families which were far above their apparent social status. The carpenter Thomas

it will have implications elsewhere. This is particularly true of the chimney, the widespread introduction of which, in late Tudor and early Stuart England, may have been a somewhat inadequate response to the arrival of the rigours of the 'Little Ice Age'.[23] Although far from being an innovation at this time, the flue was slow to be adopted and, in remote parts of the British Isles, did not appear until the early twentieth century. At a high social level the great hall boasted a central hearth, open to the roof, where it was long retained as part of the conservatism of ancient ceremony.[24]

In general the introduction of the chimney flue was to have a greater impact on the house and its interior than any other single element in domestic architecture. It was to affect the planning of houses. On elevation the single floor was to be displaced by the storied house, once a chimney rendered upper spaces usable.[25] We should not presume that these improvements occurred first in the south-east since in Kent and Sussex the prestige of the open hall was only reluctantly dispensed with in favour of greater comfort and more rooms. Also the typical Wealden hall-house, wherever it was located, was so arranged as to make flues less of a priority (Fig. 284).[26] In some counties in the south of England, such as Somerset, flues were inserted, in the latter half of the fifteenth century, not only in halls open to the roof in the traditional way but also in stone-built storied houses[27] (see also p. 201 for the chimneys added to Vicars' Close, Wells in 1466).

283   A house in Holywell Street, Oxford. Thomas Holt, a Yorkshireman by birth and a carpenter by trade, lived in a house in this street with three rooms on the ground and first floor with two cocklofts above – perhaps the house shown here. From 1618 to 1624 Holt was in charge of building the School's Quadrangle of the Bodleian Library, so he could afford to live in some style.

284   A medieval three-cell 'cot', a typical home for a landless peasant, and a fifteenth-century yeoman's 'hall-house' characteristic of the Weald of Kent and Sussex.

Holt (d. 1624) lived in a seven-room house in Holywell Street, Oxford (Fig. 283) which comprised a ground-floor hall, lobby and kitchen with three chambers above and two cock lofts in the attic. As for the masons, bricklayers and others who became builder-architects, they lived on a scale comparable to minor gentry.[22]

For these reasons, and despite the economic pressures which sometimes resulted in the use of second-rate methods and materials, the visual qualities of the product could be maintained, in a well-informed market, at little if any extra cost. Nowhere are these somewhat contradictory trends more evident than in the English terraced house, that mid-seventeenth-century innovation which, by the end of the century, was to be the chief manifestation of an emerging consumerism.

For practical reasons the preceding chapters have progressed detail by detail (see pp. viii–ix). However, a house is obviously an entity so that what happens in one part of

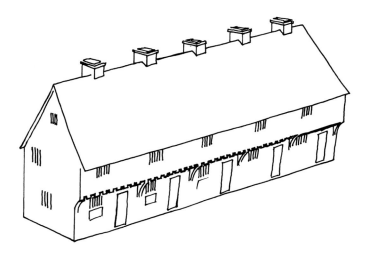

285   A typical sixteenth-century row of houses with their upper floors emphasised by a continuous jetty.

The chimney, and all it stood for, was a cause for celebration. Externally it was made conspicuous by elaborate, not to say ostentatious, chimney stacks while the upper stories it made more possible were underlined by the continuous jetty – floor joists made visible (Fig. 285). Internally, elaborate staircases, ceilings and chimney pieces proclaimed the presence of this single 'mod con'. With the advent of the flue and all that followed in its train, the evolution of the English house was, fundamentally, complete. Consequently houses that were built by the Planters in Ulster,[28] or the Colonists in North America, were at the end of a long evolutionary chain.[29] Nevertheless this general house type was to be amended in the New World by material and climatic considerations which would cause certain mutations, not least a return to the use of timber for 'America's Wooden Age'.[30]

One feature of the wood-burning 'down-hearth' is the need for firedogs to support the logs, and to protect the wall behind the fire. A fire-back met this requirement and also provided radiant heat. For those with access to the products of the iron industry of late medieval and early modern Sussex and Kent, cast-iron fire-backs and wrought-iron dogs provided the best answer to this need. Elsewhere alternative solutions were sought including the construction of an easily replaceable panel of bricks or tiles at the back of the fire, whilst in north Devon pottery fire-backs and firedogs were used on the hearth down to the early eighteenth century (Figs. 21, 41, 42). By the end of the century improvements in transport, most notably the inland waterways, enabled iron foundries such as Carron in Scotland and at Ironbridge in Shropshire to distribute their products all over Britain

and beyond to the eastern states of North America (Fig. 63). The widespread distribution of such products would spell the decline of localised traditions for interior decoration.

In the particular circumstances of early Colonial America craft skill was at a premium and prospective settlers were provided with long lists of tools and materials needed for house building.[31] As a 'control' group (in a scientific sense) these pioneers, and the things they constructed to sustain daily life, have much to tell us about domestic building and craft organisation in the mother country. Take, for example, the question of craft training. In 1660 the Boston Selectmen objected that the 'youths in this Towne, being put forth Apprentices to several manufacturers' completed their term in 'but 3 or 4 years time, contrary to Customes of all well governed places'. As a result these journeymen had become 'incapable of being Artists in their trades.'[32] By the following century the situation was even worse,[33] and by 1806 the Reverend William Bentley concluded that many of those who claimed craft skill sufficient to train apprentices 'taught what they practised, not what they knew'.[34] These were the circumstances in which an English artisan would write back home to a friend about the wonders of America where 'Employment of all sorts is going a-begging, and wages are capital. You have only to chose a trade, Jem, and be it . . . At present I haven't quite made up my mind whether to be a carpenter – or a tailor.'[35] And this was the sort of flexibility that made it possible for a New England house-painter like Rufus Porter (1792–1884) to become, among other things, the founder of a journal like the *Scientific American*,[36] or a carpenter such as Ezra Cornell (1807–84) to make a fortune sufficient to found a university.[37]

In Britain the decline in craft autonomy in the second quarter of the nineteenth century offered no such freedoms. Instead a 'them and us' worker/employer situation developed that was, at first, well suited to serve the interests of industrialists for whom an expanding Empire and a burgeoning population provided raw materials, a workforce and consumers.[38] The building crafts were to be dominated by the architect and the general contractor. The manufactures (manual factories) were to give way to the factories (i.e. mechanised). These trends first appeared in Restoration London and were noted by Nicholas Barbon in *An Apology for the Builder; or a Discourse Shewing the Cause and Effects of the Increase of Building* (London, 1685). Although this was the blatant propaganda pamphlet (37 pages) of an unscrupulous capitalist property developer, many of his observations have the ring of truth. He was at pains to point out that 'Country Gentlemen' had no cause to fear that the growth of the City would 'depopulate the Country' or that rents and property values in the capital would be depressed. On the contrary, the development of London was the consequence of an expanding population which would, in turn, offer a larger market for the products of the countryside whilst rents would, if anything, increase. The whole situation was comparable to the trade in 'Timber, Pitch and Tarr of the cold Countries' which were 'Exchanged for the Wine, Brandy and Spices of the hot'.[39]

With the expansion of towns, from the seventeenth century, the need for an urban form of building emerged. An assemblage of existing house types, typical of many villages, was not good enough and, to use a modern term, neither was it 'cost effective'. Although row houses had been a feature of the medieval town, the timber-frame structure tended to result in a terrace that was, in a sense, a repetition of a free-standing dwelling. This was the consequence of the components used, which is to say, the maximum length/height of an oak tree. Important though the numerous scarf joints were, timber frame construction is modular: length by length, bay by bay. Curiously enough, with smaller components like brick or stone block-work, a more cohesive, more collective approach to individual, yet connected, houses became a natural way of building. This form had been achieved with remarkable consistency of façade in the stone-built Vicars' Close at Wells of 1349, although recent research has shown that the roof was reworked and chimneys added in 1466. In general though, the gable facing onto the street persisted for the good reason that it defined the width of the individual burgage plots.[40]

The first inkling of a new approach to an urban scheme was the Covent Garden Piazza in Westminster which was begun in 1631 under the auspices of the landowner, the 4th Earl of Bedford. By 1640 this rather haughty style had been somewhat modified in Great Queen Street, Westminster but, as a new vernacular idiom, survives best in a group of houses on the north side of Newington Green (c. 1650) in what was then a northern suburb of London (Fig. 14). The Anglo-Dutch character of these early brick terraced houses may be seen as part of a 'North Sea Culture' which owed much to centuries of exchange and, in particular, to the Hanseatic League.[41] This is reflected in the precocious use of brick and also of Baltic timber in eastern England (and Scotland), and in such architectural details as 'crow-stepped' and 'tumbled-in' gables. The box or cupboard-beds and the painted timber ceilings of the early seventeenth century, which are found in the same regions in Britain, are most characteristic of countries neighbouring the North Sea. From this cultural base, housing of the Newington Green type may have retained the gables of tradition but in other respects were harbingers of things to come.

Perhaps this building system would not have taken root had it not been for the Great Fire of London of 1666. In practice, houses of this type and period were to offer the most rapid means of reconstructing the devastated City. Once built they were to influence the design and the planning of towns and cities in many English-speaking communities.

As we have seen (p. 131), as early as 1564 William Bullein enthused about a 'comlie parlour' at Eton, Berkshire which was 'verie netlie and trimlie apparelled London like'.[42] Evidently small country towns, even at this date, aspired to emulate the fashions of the capital. Well over a century later, in 1697, Celia Fiennes was able to describe Nottingham as 'much like London and the houses lofty and well-built'. The following year she referred to Liverpool as 'London in miniature' and she makes similar comments about other towns and cities that she visited.[43] From such descriptions and surviving buildings it is certain that, once established, this urban form became a new vernacular, a dialect of building understood, with some variations, as easily in Philadelphia and Boston as in Dublin and Edinburgh. Even before the first relevant pattern books were published it was to become the lingua franca for urban development. Only after this manner of building was well established were the necessary grammars and vocabularies published for this visual language. Books by writers such as Leybourne (1680) and Moxon (1677–83) may have offered some notion of syntax but there were, at first, no lexicons.[44] The whole situation is the more remarkable when one considers the simpler terraced house with its astylar façade, an astonishingly sophisticated elision of a virtually unpublished idiom – and, so far as the building tradesmen were concerned, relevant books were almost unavailable. Even the learned brick-layer Venterus Mandey (1645–1701), with his library of over five hundred books,[45] owned only a couple of volumes on architecture and none that would have had much relevance to the terraced house.

In these circumstances it was probably the quality of the education received by building craftsmen that made all this possible. Not only were they able to make houses and their interiors, they designed them as well – but then, in many respects the two activities were not seen as separate and distinct. In *The London Tradesman* (1747) Campbell makes numerous references to the importance of drawing in certain key building crafts. Thus masons should have 'Skill in Drawing' and a carpenter should 'know how to design his work'. As for bricklayers, 'they generally know the just Proportions of Doors and Windows [the astylar façade], the Manner of carrying up Vents, and other common Articles in a City House.'[46] The relative absence of appropriate pattern books

286   Following the fire of Warwick in 1694 three houses were built at the crossroads near the centre of the development which were intended, in a rather Baroque way, to exemplify three of the Classical Orders. This house, dated on a rainwater head to 1696, represents the Doric Order. Photograph (*c.* 1900).

enabled the terraced house to evolve without the inhibition of printed precept. Even the Acts of Parliament concerning fire prevention and other public safety issues were less than systematically imposed and, when they were, they were sometimes later abandoned.[47]

Of possibly greater importance, from the point of view of the building trades, was the legislation that was introduced to limit the restrictive practices of the guilds in the interests of rebuilding the City after the Great Fire.[48] It is very probable though that the importance of these measures has been exaggerated since, even before the Fire, the association between a livery company and the craft that it was traditionally designed to regulate, protect and promote was being eroded. One reason for this was due to membership by patrimony rather than as a result of the guildsman having served the relevant apprenticeship.[49] Despite this situation high standards of craftsmanship were maintained – standards which withstood the pressures of speculative building. How was this possible? Could it be that the sense of the eye and the dexterity of the hand were intrinsic habits of mind rather than extrinsic questions of regulation? Certainly a complex craft is learnt by watching rather than listening, by doing rather than reading and by having a basic aptitude for a given skill. In addition craftsmen, over the years, gained a depth of understanding through experience and a knowledge of materials and tools. The building craftsman could memorise the buildings he had seen, or commit them to a drawing on paper. For these tradesmen existing buildings, rather than published engravings of them, were the exemplars.

Evidence for such a view can be found in a number of sources. In 1685 Nicholas Barbon argued that since 'Buildings are now so well finish'd, every house is a Little Book of Architecture.'[50] This notion was taken literally in Warwick following the fire of 1694 which consumed rather more than a third of the town. As in London, the authorities abandoned the use of timber-frame construction in favour of less-flammable materials.[51] At the crossroads formed by High Street, Jury Street, Church Street and Castle Street the new houses that were constructed on three of the corners had façades which represented, in a rather Baroque way, one of the Orders of architecture. Thus Ionic, Corinthian and Doric (Fig. 286) were demonstrated – the fourth corner being now occupied by Francis Smith's Court House of 1725. A similarly didactic approach was adopted by Thomas Jefferson in his University of Virginia, the constituent buildings of which were intended 'to serve as specimens for the Architectural lecturer.'[52] To what extent such buildings inspired emulation is not easily assessed, particularly as the most evident use of the Orders was generally applied to commissioned architecture rather than speculative housing.[53] Neverthe-

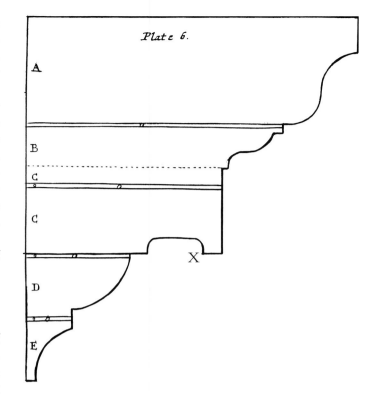

287   The 'drip', marked X, was an important feature on the external detailing of a cornice. Capillarity caused rainwater to accumulate at this point so that it would drip clear of the façade. In 'scholarly' interiors cornices will be found to retain this detail. This is taken from part of plate 6 of Joseph Moxon's *Mechanick Exercises* (edition of 1703).

less, the intention was clear, the Orders of architecture were the basis for design.

This outlook extended to the handling of many interiors. It was these architectural Orders as manifest in pilaster and capital, in plinth and cornice, that are implied though not present in the astylar façade. These were the self-same proportions that were used in a panelled room. Here the zone from the skirting to the dado formed a plinth, the upper panels represented the columns (capitals and bases) with the whole scheme being crowned by an entablature, part of which, in later years, would dwindle to a picture rail with a plain band above serving as a frieze. The classical interior was the exterior turned inside-out, or rather outside-in. With the best examples this conceit went so far as to include such features as a 'drip' – a detail which, one may hope, served no practical purpose (Fig. 287).

These architectural ideas were not always followed to the letter, particularly with regard to furniture and the panelling in a room. For example, the frieze might be omitted from a high style George II mirror which is otherwise complete with a swan-necked broken pedi-

288   Even rather impressive mirror frames of the 1730s, complete with swan-neck broken pediments centred with a cartouche, often omit the frieze – presumably to avoid becoming too 'architectural'. Private Collection.

289   Wordsworth House, Cockermouth, Cumbria. In contrast to the mirror frame (Fig. 288) the absence of a frieze (there is simply a narrow gap) between the architrave of the door and its pediment betrays the provincial nature of this panelled room of 1745 – see also Fig. 88.

ment and architrave (Fig. 288).[54] In a movable article of furnishing a less 'architectural' and consequently more domestic 'look' is often desirable. With a panelled room the omission of the frieze is a serious architectural neologism that punctures the grandeur to which a provincial joiner may have aspired (Fig. 289).

If existing buildings rather than pattern books were the basic way in which artisan/architects (before *c.* 1735)

acquired new ideas then travel must be seen as an important issue. In this respect the documentary record confirms as much. It has been estimated that in England, as early as 1700, as many as one person in six had lived in London at some time, so it is only necessary here to cite a few individual cases to demonstrate the point.[55] In a letter dated 6 July 1752, the builder-architect John Bastard of Blandford (1688–1770) refers to a new type of roof structure introduced to his Dorset firm by 'Mr. John James [1672–1746] of Greenwich . . . as good a carpenter as any in his time [who] was Oaften at ower house.'[56] In this and other examples metropolitan ideas were transmitted outwards but provincial tradesmen also travelled to the capital. Between 1725 and 1727 the joiner John Wood lived and worked in London before returning to his native Bath. As a consequence he would have become conversant with the methods used to finance urban housing schemes, as well as developing his architectural understanding.[57] Similarly, trans-Atlantic migration played its part in the transmission of cultural ideas and business methods. In this way Philadelphia benefitted from an influx of London-trained building craftsmen who migrated to Pennsylvania because of the surplus of skill in the British capital. Even as late as the mid-nineteenth century the house-carpenter-architect William Eyre of Philadelphia travelled to New York City to look at new techniques for cast-iron construction.[58]

If the history of architecture can be used as a way of looking at the structure of history then there were two events in post-Reformation Britain which are very firmly built into the fabric of our past.[59] The first of these events delayed and therefore consolidated existing traditions; the second enabled building to proceed as a secure investment. The Civil War (1642–6) and the Republic which followed it resulted not only in revolutionary social and political change but, in architectural terms, it simultaneously subdued and maintained the status quo. The migratory craftsmen, those who were best placed to transmit new ideas were, it seems, as conservative in their taste as they were radical in their politics.[60] As a result, what had once been high-style fashion persisted for over half a century to become the common currency of the many. The painted staircase in the Merchant's House at Marlborough (Fig. 183) is distinctly *retardataire* when compared with similar work of more than sixty years before at aristocratic Knole (*c.* 1605) in Kent. Aesthetic traditions tend to linger in times of turmoil. In this way the simple brick terraced house of the second quarter of the seventeenth century persisted, consolidating its position to become the 'new' idiom, one that was to gain great importance at the Restoration and afterwards.

No less significant for our theme, although for very different reasons, was the Glorious Revolution of 1688 which, among other things, secured property rights against the claims of the Crown. This was to be an important factor in relationship to property development in general and was fundamental to the rapid expansion of towns and cities at this time – the 'English Urban Renaissance' of the 'long eighteenth century' (1688–1820).[61]

With improvements in carriages, such as the introduction of the leaf spring in about 1670, commuting between a house in the country and work in town became more common. Certainly suburban development became significant at this time in satellite communities around cities like London and Bristol. Nevertheless, the visual divide between town and country was generally abrupt. Many cities retained their defensive walls well into the eighteenth century partly because civic powers were primarily intramural. Despite these physical and corporate barriers, town and country remained quite close, or at least interdependent, in social and economic terms. For urban building craftsmen this was particularly true, after all many of their materials were drawn from rural areas – wood, stone, sand, lime, etc. Similarly, the divide between the 'vernacular' and the 'polite' is *now* more apparent than it *was* real. To a mason or carpenter our preoccupations with the 'little tradition' in contrast to 'patrician culture' would have seemed incomprehensible.[62] A job was a job wherever, or in whatever, it was located. Undoubtedly some craftsmen would have been more appropriately employed in one sort of ambience than another, but otherwise such distinctions are of more use to us than they were relevant to those concerned.

From the building craftsman's point of view demarcations between trades were of much greater consequence than those between the popular and the polite, between town and country or between the exterior and the interior. A mason, a carpenter, a painter-plumber and even a plasterer would work on both the inside and outside of buildings as occasion demanded.[63] More serious were the demarcations which divided one craft from another, although this is not reflected in the structure of this book.[64] In the earlier periods with which we are concerned it was a criminal offence to practise a trade to which one had not been bound.[65] For these reasons the conflicts between related trades, such as between carpenters and joiners, were the most impassioned, not least because in small communities, or Colonial settlements, some of these trades were customarily united.[66] Even in a large town like Philadelphia, the Carpenters Company *Rule Book* of 1786 casually includes the work of joiners.[67]

On the other hand what has since been termed 'the withdrawal of the upper classes' from the 'popular culture' that they had previously enjoyed,[68] was probably less apparent to craftsmen than it was to their patrons. Trends such as this probably began even earlier, when the master of the house withdrew to his parlour rather than join the communal meals in the hall. This situation was paralleled in farmhouses in which the farmer and his family retreated to a separate table near the fire, whilst the farm servants enjoyed the cold comfort of sitting at a long table some distance away in the same room (Fig. 240). William Cobbett bemoaned the decline in the 'home counties' of the tradition for the farm servants to

290 Early eighteenth-century overmantel painting in the panelled housekeepers room (possibly designed by James Smith *c.* 1645–1731) at Traquair House, Peebles, Scotland. This overmantel simultaneously incorportates the notion of a curtained bookcase and a curtained picture. Vernacular work will be found in lesser locations in important country houses.

live-in as part of the family (see pp. 8–9) but further afield this practice persisted. As late as the closing decades of Queen Victoria's reign some farmers were 'little lords on their small domains'.[69]

Despite these underlying trends towards social separation, segregation even, house-painters who evolved into artisan artists of the vernacular tradition found employment in gentry houses well into the eighteenth century. Such artists would have painted a bough pot on a chimney board or a 'landskip' on an overmantel panel (Fig. 55). In contexts such as these paintings could sustain damage by being kicked, or through the rising heat and fumes from the fire; but then these were regarded as 'furnishing pictures' not deployed in locations reserved for real works of art (Figs. 290, 291).

Because the 'work of art' is not our concern the normal art-historical approach is refreshingly irrelevant. Despite their ostensibly utilitarian imperatives the ver-

291　Overmantel from the Samuel McClellan House, South Woodstock, Connecticut. This work, by the American artist Winthrop Chandler, was painted in *c.* 1770 for his guardian, Samuel McClellan. Despite the time-lag, comparison with Fig. 290 demonstrates how close the vernacular traditions of Colonial America could be to those of the mother country. Webb Gallery of American Art, Shelburne Museum, Vermont.

nacular arts obeyed their own internal logic in which aesthetic values were arrived at, as much as sought. Some examples may serve to demonstrate the point. A skirting board can, as we have seen, be viewed as part of the repertoire of classically inspired design – but it is in origin, and generally speaking in practice, a functional detail. Like its painted equivalent (see p. 57), or the delft tiles shown in the same position in paintings by the Dutch masters of the seventeenth century, the skirting simply served to protect plaster walls from the injury they would otherwise sustain from mops and brooms. For good reason this 'base-board' was known in America as the 'wash-board'.[70] A painted skirting served much the same purpose in camouflaging minor damage or dirt. Similarly chair rails, as their name implies, protected walls from injury by furniture. These were the sort of features that were predicated on the practicalities of use, but there were other disciplines inspired by the logic of construction. For example, the bevel which defines the 'field' in a 'fielded panel' (Fig. 291) is a practical detail made visible – it helps to ensure that the wood has liberty to shrink within the grooves cut in the surrounding stiles and rails. There were similarly non-aesthetic reasons for the application of paints, distempers and limewash. They could serve as fire retardents on thatch, as a disinfectant, or as a means of consolidating a mud floor. Paint could be used by joiners as an informal glue or as a means of retaining the flexibility of putty. However prosaic these explanations may be, satisfying visual effects were achieved almost as a by-product.

The hands-on understanding which craftsmen possessed in a pre-industrial situation stands in marked contrast to the inevitable separation that resulted when machines intervened between the material being worked on and the 'operative'. This problem pre-dated full-scale mechanisation and may have begun with the advent of manufactures. In 1787 the house-painter-turned-artist William Williams expressed strong opposition to the by-laws which had been introduced in various towns and cities to limit the way in which trade signs were shown. These regulations had the effect of discouraging the use of signs the making of which had, according to Williams, been 'the nursery and reward of painters'. Such a training had enabled painters to asses 'the qualities and hues of the different pigments in their dry state, that [it was possible to] judge the goodness or deficiency of them when ground in oil'. By the second quarter of the eighteenth century a whole generation of London painters had become accustomed to purchasing ready-made paint (see below) and, so Williams believed, were unable to judge the quality of these materials.[71] This was a situation that occurred with numerous other crafts in which a particular material was separated from its origins, as for example with the use of Baltic timber by joiners and carpenters in Britain. This dislocation between origins, use and final destination may have assisted industrialisation, but it was to be one of the features which would damage the sort of integrity upon which the crafts were based.

The internal evidence provided by a hand-crafted object makes it susceptible to analysis. In the materials selected, in the traces left by the hand tools used to work those materials, one may learn much of the sequence of making and the logic of construction. As for the circumstances in which a craftsman worked, we are dependent upon the written record or pictorial representation. Trade-cards often combine these two forms of evidence.

From such sources we know that the sort of stock held by many eighteenth-century 'oil and colourmen' was more akin to a delicatessen than a builders' merchant or an emporium selling artists' materials. These shops stocked items like smoked hams, anchovies and olive oil, together with turpentine and pigments. From such documents we know that in London the Emerton dynasty of colourmen (active *c.* 1710–53) produced paint on a large scale using horse mills and that they sold their paints together with instructions. Consequently gentlemen could employ their household 'Servants, without the Assistance or Directions of a Painter' to decorate their houses.[72] This early form of 'DIY' was evidently designed to by-pass specialist tradesmen. As we have seen (p. 97, Fig. 149) it is from similar printed ephemera that we know that hat shops sold floor mats and oil cloths and that a carpenter would also serve as an undertaker (funeral director) or that a house-painter would, in addition, accept commissions to paint 'likenesses' of cattle, ships and even people.

As noted elsewhere the earliest features in a house will often be found under later panelling (Fig. 292) or in the farthest recesses of a dwelling high in the attic (e.g. Fig. 113). In places such as this one may even uncover a craftsman's message to posterity or his name and the date (Fig. 172). Obviously the degree of change and modernisation sustained by any dwelling is closely related to its age, older houses being likely to have experienced the most radical alterations. Also the principal rooms of a house, the more public spaces, would have always expressed the most up-to-date characteristics from the time they were built onwards. For these reasons 'front of

(facing page)

292   Chimney wall in the first floor front room of No. 2 High street, Abingdon, Oxfordshire (ex Berkshire). The archaeology of the small domestic interior is well exemplified here. Within this timber-frame building of the late sixteenth or early seventeenth century, an eighteenth-century interior was installed – as indicated by the 'shadow' of a large chimney piece (up to which the wall has been plastered and now leaving the bricks of the flue exposed). The walls were covered at this time with blue sugar paper, an unusual treatment. Subsequent changes are recorded in the chalked message:

> This room was batten'd
> & cover'd in October 1828
> by Mr Rowles
> & Mr Bayley

The battens would originally have been covered with hessian, which in turn would have been hung with wallpaper. The white marble chimney piece was also installed at this time although the grate is three or four decades later.

house' rooms would have been most subject to regular redecoration and modernisation. It will have been noted that the most elaborate mural schemes cited here have been found in upper rooms and bedrooms. This could imply that modernisation has swept away evidence of earlier decoration – or the explanation could be more subtle. In general, reception rooms were more likely to be graced by case furniture or even framed pictures. As these would have intruded over a pictorial mural scheme the latter were probably more often commissioned for bedchambers in upper rooms.

In considering the interiors of an historic house we are always in danger of making various assumptions that are not supported by the available evidence – not least with regard to the underlying architecture of a room, its fixtures and fittings and the movable furnishings and plenishings it would have contained at a given point in time. We may too easily assume that a stone wall is original when it may well have replaced one of timber frame. This can often be established during conservation work when 'chamfer-stops' to joists or a summer beam will be found deep within the masonry. We may also too easily presume that a window was always glazed or that they and floorboards or door locks were always regarded as fixtures – they were not.

Above all, the carpets, curtains and wallpaper which today provide vehicles for colour and pattern in the home were largely absent from the pre-industrial vernacular interior. Most people did without such comforts and embellishments or made do with painted carpets (floor cloths or painted boards) and stencilled walls (in place of patterned wallpaper). In the absence of curtains, shutters probably occupied a more important place in the scheme of things than they do today.

In most respects vernacular interiors were thought about in terms of their appearance during hours of daylight; artificial light was simply too expensive or too inadequate for them to have been considered in any other way. This was yet another reason why curtains were not much used in more modest interiors: they were expensive and unnecessary.[73] The bulk of the population rose at dawn and went to bed at sundown, with some exceptions such as the Yorkshire knitting parties which took place in the semidarkness of firelight (and, for economy and sociability, in one house). In contrast William Cowper (1731–1800) describes an upper middle-class home in his lines on a cosy winter's evening:

> Now stir the fire, and close the shutters fast,
> Let fall the curtain, wheel the sofa round.[74]

In the highly stratified societies of the past, hierarchies were manifest not only between houses but between rooms of differing importance within one dwelling – as

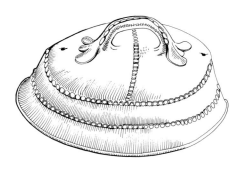

293   Curfew, late thirteenth century, 18 ins (45.5 cm) in diameter. The earthenware *couvre-feu*, or fire cover, was probably used at many social levels to both dampen down and retain a wood fire overnight. Being circular on plan this was designed for a central hearth. Later apsidal curfews for wall hearths were generally made in *repoussé* brass. Salisbury and South Wiltshire Museum.

with the species and quality of wood used for floorboards in each room (see pp. 92–3). Everything within the house reflected the status of its occupants, from the presence or absence of textiles to the type of candle that was burnt for artificial light. This order of precedence was similarly reflected in both the media and the pigments used in paints and distempers. The cheapest was whitewash although colour-wash distempers might be deployed in more significant rooms. As for oil paint, this was, for many, an impossible luxury. The connotations are clear in the phrase once commonly used in Charleston, South Carolina: 'Too poor to paint, too proud to whitewash'.[75] These were matters that were unconsciously understood by our forebears, but which now become apparent only through interpretation.

Appendix I

A Description of the Floor Cloth Manufactory of Hare's of Bristol from the 1816 Diary of Rolinda Sharples (1794–1838)[1]

The manufactory of oil cloth is also very well worth seeing. We went first into the weaving room. The length through which the shuttle passes is so great, as to require two men, one at each end. We next passed through a lofty building in which hung immense pieces of primed cloth, (from their light and even appearance they must have been streched on rollers). At the end we ascended a tremendous flight of narrow circular steps: on reaching the top saw a man and boy employed in stamping patterns. A stamp, made of pear wood, is pressed on a stone, on which was evenly laid the colour, it is then pressed, and hammered on the oil cloth, which had been previously prepared with a trowel. When it is finished breadth ways with one colour, it is stamped with another, between the pattern of the former, until completed. When a portion is finished it is let down and the operation recommenced on another.

On descending the stairs and crossing the court we entered the place where colours were ground. Immense wheels are kept in motion by a steam engine.

As a professional easel painter Miss Sharples would have had some understanding of the materials used in these manufacturing methods.

Appendix II

A True and perfect Inventory of all and singular the Goods Chattels and Credditts of Thomas Bayly[1] late of Marlborough in the County of Wilts mercer whereof he dyed possessed taken and appraised by us whose names are hereunto Subscribed the third day of February in the year of our Lord 1690/1[2]

In the Wash kitchen

	li	s	d
Item 1 pair old rackes and Dogs 4 little)			
Quivers one rownd 2 long ones)	01	15	00

In the Seller

4 Barrills 2 dozen « bottles)			
1 old powdring tubb and a vaute)	00	18	00

In the Kitchen

2 folding tables	00	10	00
3 side boards	00	03	00
1 Ring 7s 6 old leather Chaires 9s	00	16	00
2 shelves 3s 1 skreene 5s	00	08	00
1 Jack 10s 1 grate fire shovell and			
tounges all 15s	00	15	00
2 spitts 1 pott Hangles	00	03	00
pair Andirons	00	02	00
1 old Clock	00	10	00
Wood in the backside	02	00	00
1 Folding Table	00	10	00
1 pallatt Bed and old Bedsteed	01	00	00
6 Keane Chaires	00	18	00

In the Shopp

21 yards of wainskot	02	02	00
Drawers		16	00
3 Chaires		3	00

15 old Boxes		2	06
3 Curtaines and rods		10	00
1 Table Board 3 pickters other lumber		10	00
4 shop Chests 4 window grates	02	05	00
Brasse	03	11	06
Pewter	03	16	00
warming pan and tining ware		08	00
1 Fustian Bed Curtins 1 Dammas)			
Table Cloth 4 Diaper table Clothes)			
napkins and other linen in all)	10	10	00
and 1 Trunke)			

In the Garrit over the Kitchen Chamber

1 Bedsteed matt and Cord Curtains)			
2 old Feather Beds 2 rugs and Counterpan)			
2 Bolsters 4 pillowes Cradle Rugg)	06	00	00
Cradle 6 old Blankets 1 stand)			
1 old saddle and pillion 1 old Chest)			
2 Chaires 1 stoole 2 old window)			
Curtins in all			

In the Passage

1 small trookle Bedsted Cord and mat)			
1 Curtaine 1 old Flock Bolster 1 old)	00	08	00
Tubb and lumber			

In the Garrett over the Hall Chamber

Item 1 old bed 3 blankets 1 old rug)			
1 bedsted Curtains and vallians)			
1 Bolster 1 small pillow 1 canvas)	02	05	00
sheet 1 Bolster Case 2 side Boards)			
1 old Trunke 2 old Chaires and)			
2 old Stooles 2 old Boxes in all)			

	43	15	6

In the Closet in the Hall Chamber

Item 1 presse with wareing Apparell   05 00 00

In the Dineing Roome

Item 12 turkeywoorke Chaires   )
1 looking glasse pair Andirons   )
Firepan and tounges pair Billowes   )   04 00 00
2 pickters 1 table in all   )

In the Kitchin Chamber

1 Feather Bed 1 Flock bed   )
2 Bolsters one Feathers   )
Bedsteed Curtains and vallins   )
6 old Chaires 2 Chest Drawers   )
1 little Table 2 Cubbord Clothes   )
1 glasse Cubbord Fire pan and   )   8 05 00
Tounges paire Andions and Dogs   )
1 Lawnskip 2 looking glasses   )
2 Comb Boxes 3 window curtains   )
1 rug Blanket and Counterpan in all   )

In the Clossett

19 Bottles 2 Drawers 4   )
Boxes and some english books   )   15 00

In the Buttery

Item Jack 1 Childs Chaire   )
1 old portmantle pair tables   )   15 00

In the Little Room

6 Leather Chaires   )
1 table 2 window Curtain and rod   )   01 04 00
In Plate   )   41 06 09
1 pot and Lymback   01 00 00
Samuel Fowler   )   ——————
William Baylye   )   62 15 [ ]
) Appraisors   43 15 6
                    106[ ]
In Debts   232[ ]
In William Baylys hand   38[ ]
In Nathl Baylys hand   [   ]
Due for rent   15[ ]
            397-01=1
In bad debts   077-05-00
            474 06 2
his gold rings   002=05=00
            476=11=2

February 6th 1690/1 This inventory was Published
And Sworn to by Ann Bayly widow before me
                    Cornelius Yeate

Extracts from the Ledger of Michael Edkins of Bristol, Carriage, House, Sign and Ornamental Painter. A sample of entries relating to painting in domestic buildings.

1761
1st July   To Paint^g 2 Window
grates Green   £– 4 0

1762
9th April   Mr. Guillam, Bedminster
To Stopping with Puttey
and Painting a window
Shutter twice   – 0 8

To Painting a Chest   – 1 0

Mr. Austin, Bedminster
To Painting the
Window Shutter   – 0 6

1764
10th May   Mr. Wilson Snr.
To Painting 2 Garden Chairs
2 Lead Colour and
finish^g Green   – 5 0

Mr. Wilson Jnr.
To Paint^g 4 Windsor Chairs
3 times lead Colour and
finish^g Green   – 5 0

1765
July   Mr. James Coulsting
To Paint^g a press Bedstead
Red   – 2 6

13th Dec   Mr. Saunders
To painting Several Cannisters
Green etc. Smalting the
Sugar Loaves[1]   – 12 0

To painting the Inside of the
Window white and part of
the shop stone colour   – 4 0

1766
3rd June   To Painting Mr. Halls
Summer House Green
allow^g for one Coat myself viz.   – 6 0
The Half to paint 2 Windsor
Chairs Several Times lead
Colours and Finish Green   – 5 0
To D^o Garden Hutch   – 5 0

16th July   Mr. Williams, Redcliff
Street [merchant]
To paint^g a Cove 4 times
lead Colour   £– 4 0

1767
30th May   Mr. Robert Vigor [glass
manufacturer]
To Painting a parlour and
Painting Several times
Lead Colour and
finishing with best
Verdigrease in Varnish
47 yds – at 1s/0d   2 7 0

To Paint^g a folding Blind
[venetian blind?]
To D^o 16½y^d Stone Colour
in the Painting, Shelves
Wain-Scoat &c. at
0/3d yd   – 4 1½

To Paint^g 99½y^d Dead
  White – – – at os 6d yd   2   9   9

To Paint^g 14y^{ds} Stone Col^r
  In the Beaufet – at
  os/3d yd   –   3   6

To Paint^g a door and
  Wind^w Frames, Shutters
  Chocolate Col^r 6 yds at
  6s/3d   –   1   6
                                   5 10 10½

c. 1774
4th May   Mr. Smith, Nicholas Street
To paint^g a Cove several
  Times and finish^g it
  Pompad^r   –   5   0

1778
31 Jan^y   Mr. Crosse, Painter
To Work Done to 8 Chairs   – 10   6
To Verdigrease &c.   –   3   0

1781   To Paint^g a Transparency
  with figures of Rodney
  and Vaughn & writ^g   4   4   0

1786
8th April   Mr. Morgan, Confectioner
To Silk for Two
  Transparencys
To Paint^g 2 Transparencys
  with Pine Apples Writ^g
  &x. at 1/1,0 each   2   2   0

20th Dec   Mr. Chamberlain Cox, Baker
To Paint^g done at your House
  in Union Street pr
  Measurer's feet[2]   5 17   7½

1787   Doctor Duck
Varnishing the folding doors
  of the Parlour and Passage
  Doors   –   2   0

Appendix IV

House-Painting in Eighteenth-Century Scotland

Despite the 'Auld Alliance', and a tendency for the precocious use of French-inspired detailing in Scotland,
vernacular traditions persisted even for gentry houses.

Account Book of Sir John Foulis of Revelston 1671–1707[1]

29 July 1680	to Henry frazer for colouring a chimney and windows and below the hangings in a chamber in my lodging	£4. 15. 0
31 July 1680	to the painter againe till account for colouring ye gates	£2. 18. 0
20 May 1703	I have agreed w^t Laurie Hendersone for painting the roume of the hall whyt japand pannells, black borders, w^t pictures of flowers, men, etc., and gilded, the cornish marble, chimney marble and surbass marble, the picture frames japand, w^t flowers of all sorts, etc., for 10^{Lib} [pounds] Sterl [Sterling] and what I pleased to give more, he sought 11^{Lib}	

The Scottish Pound was, at this time, equal to 1s 8d English Sterling. The description given on 20 May 1703 may have resembled the painted panelling illustrated in Fig. 220. Unfortunately neither Henry Frazer nor Laurie Henderson appear in the *Register of Edinburgh Apprentices 1701–1755* or in the *Roll of Edinburgh Burgesses 1701–1760*.

The Norrie family of painters (both 'mechanic' and 'liberal') are listed in the *Register* as having apprentices bound to them as early as 1711 and as late as 1841. The following bill[2] was submitted by a member of this Edinburgh dynasty of painters in 1750:

To painting in his Lodging in the Abby a room in the first story and a closet measuring 107 yards @ 5^d a yard	£2. 4. 7d
To colouring on the outsides of seven doors 31 yards Chocolate colour in oil @ 6^d the yard	15s. 6d
To painting the corners of the old castle in imitation of stone	£2. 12. 0d
To part of a boat with different colours marking inside and doing the gun ports	10s. 0d
To 19 oars bright red thrice over and marking them @ 2s. each	£1. 18. 0d

Although this was a commission from Lord Glenorchy for work at Taymouth and for his apartments at Holyrood House ('the Abby') the diversity of work including both house and boat painting is comparable to the range of activities undertaken by Michael Edkins of Bristol (see Appendix III).

James Norrie and his sons (who trained as landscape painters in London under George Lambert 1700–65) could, at various times, claim the Scottish artists Alexander Runciman and Jacob More as former apprentices. Robert Norrie's trade-card[3] (designed by Runciman) lists him as 'Robert Norrie, Painter, at his Oil and Colour Warehouse, Edinburgh'.

HOUSE FINISHING IN EARLY EIGHTEENTH-CENTURY LONDON

Whilst resident in London in 1715 Lady Grisell Baillie (1692–1733) supervised the work done on a 'new house' – possibly one that had been acquired as 'a shell'.[4]

| 21 June | For screwing all the wainscote of new house @ 20^d a day without meat [meals]. | £0. 17. 0 |
| | For white washing the House 1s a foot [?] | £0. 15. 0 |

24 June	For repairing the Rooff of the new house	£0. 2. 6
30 July	For painting the house by Meas. [measure] @ 3^d a yeard	£5. 7. 6
	For glazing the windows £5 cleaning them all 10s	£1. 15. 0

It will be noted that where dates are given in these accounts, the summer months were favoured for house-painting.

Appendix V

Inventory: Swaledale Cottages

From the Poor Law Papers relating to Arkengarthdale, North Yorkshire. These papers are undated but are from the first decade or two of the nineteenth century, when even the poor, in this valley, lived in quite well-equipped houses – although some, like Anne Croft, may have been 'encouraged', by their children, to enter a workhouse. Transcripts of these are held by BEAMISH: The North of England Open Air Museum. There are a total of twenty-seven inventories in this series of which the following five are typical examples.

GEORGE STUBBS

a Clock
a Dresser and rales
a Corner cupboard
a Tea Table
a Kitchen table
Nineteen Dublers[1] and plates
a Wood bowl
a Cream pot
Three chairs
a Knife box
a Tea Kettle

Four stools
a Stand
Ten petty pans[2]
a Tin candle box
a Reckin
a Fire shovel
a Tin cover
a Bed and bedstead
Two Blankets
Two Bolsters
a Bed Quilt

MARGARET HUTCHINSON   *Rent 32/6 one room*

Invt. the Dwelling House

Two tables
a stand
a dresser and rales
Two chairs
an Iron pan
a tin can
Twelve plates and dishes
a Tiffany[3]
a hair temse[4]
a drippin pan
a cloathes brush

a hearth brush
a tin Funnell
a tin boiler
a butter boat
a fender
a tin grater
a chaff bed
Two blankets
Four pillows
Two bed quilts
a Frying pan
a spinning wheel

ROBERT STONES

In the Dwelling House

a Kitchen table
Four chairs
a box
a Dresser and rales
a Frying pan
a girdle
Three stools
a corner cupboard
a Fleak
a spinning wheel
a tine sile [?]
a Lanthorn
a Delf rack
Twenty one plates and dishes
Two beds
two bedsteads
Three blankets
Two quilts
a rug
Two tubs
a Sile[5]

a pair of wool cards
a tea kettle
three Iron pans
a pair of tongs
a Coulrake
a smoothing Iron
    and heaters
an Iron reckin

In the Stable

a cart saddle
Two pair of cart
    trappin
a pair of cart wheels
a Horse and cart
a braffam collar and
    hames
a wrinker collar
an Iron backband
a washing tub
a heifer in calf
Six hay rakes
a hay spade

THOMAS ROBINSON

In the Dwelling House

In the Kitchen

a Clock and case
an oval table
a square one
a delf rack
Thirteen plates and dishes
a corner cupboard
a tea table
Seven chairs
a round stand
a tin toaster
Thirty three pettie and
   other small tins
a funnel
a drippin tin
a tin cover
Two waiters
Cream pot and sugar tongs
other Two milk pots
a cloaths brush
Two pictures
a hair temse
a milk sile
a seeing glass
a pair of bellows
a Fleak
Two small racks

Two fenders
a fork
a pair of scissors
a hand brush
Two pair of tongs
an Iron pan
an end oven
a tea caddie
a tea kettle
Three tea pots
a glass and two cups
a tin Sheel [?]
a Box of tups [?]
a rope twiner
a saw
a chaff bed
a bedstead
Two blankets
a rugg
a pillow
a Bedstead
a feather bed
Two blankets
a rugg and a bolster

ANN CROFT   *Her sons furniture in the same house not mark'd*

In the Dwelling House

In the Kitchen

a Clock
a Dresser and rales
a Churn
an oval table
a square one
Two chairs
a tea kettle
a smoothing Iron and heater
a dog Iron sweeble[6] Clog
   and a brass plate mark'd
   John Hutton Esq.
   Marske Hall
a brass candlestick
an Iron candlestick
an Iron hand Speet[7]
Two long reckins[8]
an Iron range
Two little forks
a shovel coulrake and tongs
a Waiter
a tin candle box
an Iron
a Kettle pot
a seeing glass
a Hair sieve
a wood ladel
a brass pan
Two spoons
a pair of plated shoe buckles
a tin toaster
Four petty pans
a large washing pot
Two feather beds
One bedstead

Six feather bolsters
Two blankets
Three bed quilts
a frying pan
a Bakestone[9]
a Basket
a pair of wool cards
a Chest of drawers
Four pot milk bowls
a pair of butter scales
Three wood bowls
a cream pot
a milk pot
Two butter boards
a tin can
a Rolling pin
a paste bowl
a butter bowl
Twelve plates and
   dishes
Two tumbler glasses
a tea caddie
Four tea pots
another tea pot
a pint Two cream jugs

In the Stable

A cow and a bedstead and wool bed
Ann Croft told her son to go and sell her cow which he sold for £7. 7s. and paid [blank] at Reeth for some Fog[10] out of that and bought another cow at Richmond with the remainder of the money this is Ann Crofts own story and the house is here only her son paid some money for her.

Appendix VI

Witchcraft Detected & Prevented[1]

'The greater part of this highly curious little volume is selected from the ancient and scarce works of the principal writers on these subjects, particularly from Scott's Discovery of Witchcraft, The Book which supplied Shakespeare [sic] with his Witch and Wizard Lore.'[2]

A safe way to secure a House.

If you suspect your house will be robbed, and would secure it from thieves, as no doubt but you are desirous, consider the night what planet reigns, and is lord of the ascendant; and these are the characters, the Sun ☉ on Sunday, the Moon ☽ on Monday, Mars ♂ on Tuesday, Mercury ☿ on Wednesday, Jupiter ♃ on Thursday, Venus ♀ on Friday, Saturn ♄ on Saturday. Now consider on what night you do this, as to these planets and write on fair parchment these characters, ♌ ♈ ♑, and, supposing it to be on a Sunday, add the planetary character ☉ with this number, 1, 3, 5, 1–4, 1–7, and at that night, lay this under the earth, or covered with a tile in the middle of the house, as near as may be, sprinkle it over with the juice of nightshade, and so go to sleep as soon as you have thrice repeated them over, and if the thieves have power to enter the house, they shall have no power to get out again, or to carry any thing away till the sun rises; and if you be watchful, then you may easily apprehend them before they are able to depart.

And thus you may do any day in the week, adding the character of the planet that rules that day as I have set it down, to what is beside set down in order.

Appendix VII

Firewood for the Hearth

Beech-wood fires are bright and clear
If the logs are kept a year.
Oaken logs burn steadily
If the wood is old and dry.
Chestnut's only good, they say,
If the log is laid away.
But ash new or ash old
Is fit for a Queen with a crown of gold.

Birch and fir-logs burn too fast –
Blaze up bright but do not last.
Make a fire of elder-tree,
Death within your house you'll see.
It is by the Irish said
Hawthorn bakes the sweetest bread.
But ash green or ash brown
Is fit for a Queen with a golden crown.

Elm-wood burns like churchyard mould –
E'en the very flames are cold.
Poplar gives a bitter smoke
Fills your eyes and makes you choke.
Apple-wood will scent your room
With an incense-like perfume.
But ash wet or ash dry
For a Queen to warm her slipper by.

ANON
*(probably nineteenth century
but reflecting age-old understanding)*

Appendix VIII

Ambrose Heal Collection of Trade Cards: Floor Cloth Manufacturers

The following is a list of those manufacturers and retailers in London whose labels list floor cloths for sale.
It is drawn from the Heal Collection in the British Museum and from Ambrose Heal's
The London Furniture Makers.[1]

Mid-18th century	Barnes and Sons, Basinghall Street and City Road, Moorfields
Mid-18th century	Biggerstaff's and Walsh's, Islington
1818	H. Buckley, 161 Strand and 'Manufactory' near Westminster Bridge
c. 1810	Bulmer, 284 Strand
Mid-19th century	Carter and Company, 2 Cheapside near Paternoster Row
1790–1803	Thomas Cloake, Lower Moorfields, near Old Bethleham
1760–2	James Cox, near St Martins Lee Grand in Newgate Street
1768	Gerard Crawley, The Coffee Mill & Nimble Ninepence adjoining St Michael's Church in Cornhill
c. 1769	Crompton and Spinnages, Cockspur Street, Charing Cross
Early 19th century	Downing and Company, Knightsbridge and King's Road
1777–84	Gatfield and Co., St Margaret's Hill, Southwark
c. 1810	Hare and Co., 37 Newington Causeway
c. 1810	John Samuel Hayward, 37 Newington Causeway, Southwark and 12 Leadenhall Street
c. 1800	Matthew Heath, 18 Seething Lane, Tower Street
Mid-18th century	Thomas Iliffe, opposite the Hospital Gate, Newgate Street
Early 19th century	Morley's Original Floor-Cloth Manufactories, Knightsbridge and King's Road
Mid-18th century	B. Philpott, Wardrobe Court, Great Carter Lane, near St Paul's
Mid-18th century	James Platt, Newgate Street (succeeded by James Cox)
c. 1760	Pope and McLellan's
Late 18th century	Joshua Russell, 10 Blackman Street, Southwark

c. 1751	John Shepherd, opposite St Clements Church, Strand	Mid-18th century	Thomas Tillinghurst, Swithin's Lane, near Cannon Street
1844	Smith and Barber, opposite the Horse Barracks, Knightsbridge	Early 19th century	Thomas Weaver, 118 Long Acre (removed from Holborn)
Early 19th century	William South	Mid-18th century	Joseph Weston, Old Bethlehem, Bishopsgate
Early 19th century	Southgate and Mitchell, London Road, St George's Fields; Warehouse No. 44, Newgate Street	1763	Alexander Wetherstone, Portugal Street, Lincoln's Inn Fields
c. 1760	John Speer, Lion & Lamb, West side of Fleet Market	Mid-18th century	John White, Shoe Lane, Fleet Street (an address strongly associated with the production of trade signs – another activity with which painters were linked
c. 1750	Francis Thompson, The Three Chairs, St John's Lane, near Hick's Hall		

Glossary

ARCH A method of spanning the space between two points by means of a curve or curves. In the true arch this curve is composed of a series of individual stones known as *voussoirs*. Where an arch is cut from a monolithic block it is not a true arch and is structurally the same as a **lintel**. The single-centred arch is a characteristic of the Romanesque tradition. Medieval architecture used, and indeed in some respects was based upon the use of, the two and later four-centred arch.

ARCHITRAVE The lowest member of an **entablature**. The word is also applied to a door, window or fireplace surround.

ARK A chest with a barrel, curved or faceted top made by arkwrights.

ARRIS The sharp edge where two planes meet.

ASTRAGAL Narrow semicircular moulding. On a large scale this moulding is known as a 'torus'. The glazing bars of windows or bookcases are often astragals in section.

ASTYLAR A façade or similar elevation (e.g. panelling in a room) which uses the proportion rather than the detailing (columns, etc.) of the Classical Orders.

AUMBRY The early name for a built-in cupboard with a door. The early cupboard (cup-board) was simply an open shelf.

BALUSTER A species of small column (or pier). Usually found in groups as in the balusters which support the handrail of a staircase – hence 'balustrade'.

BATTEN DOOR See **ledge door**.

BAY One or several uniform divisions of a building often defined by structural features such as columns or piers. In timber-frame buildings the bay is often about 16 ft (4.9 m) but a half-bay may be as much as 9 ft (2.7 m).

BEAD A narrow moulding of convex form.

BED The natural way that stone lies in the quarry is referred to as 'the bed'. So that stone may 'weather' well it is generally laid 'on bed' by the mason.

BEVEL See **chamfer**.

BOB-TAIL The dovetailed extension sometimes found at the back of the seat of a Windsor chair to hold two additional sticks to provide extra support to the back.

BODGER A name given to the turners who used pole lathes in the Buckinghamshire beech woods where the legs of Windsor chairs were turned.

BOLECTION MOULDING A projecting moulding of ogee section often used to surround panels and to connect a higher plane to a lower one.

BOSS A feature used in both stone and wood to mask the intersections of ribs in vaulting or ceilings. The term is also used more generally to describe a decorative protuberance.

BRESSUMMER or **BREAST SUMMER** A horizontal structural beam built into the face of a wall to support a considerable load above a void as over a shop window. See also **summer beam**.

BUFFET A sideboard or a three-legged 'turned' or 'thrown' stool (also tuffet). A three-legged 'thrown' chair was known as a 'buffet chair'.

BURGAGE PLOT A tenure of land in a town held by a burgess, a citizen with full municipal rights.

BUTTERY A service room used for the storage of drink. Often paired with a **pantry**.

CAMES Slender rods of lead, milled in a 'plumber's vice' to impress grooves along their sides, designed to take glass in a 'leaded' window.

CARCASE The body of a piece of 'case' furniture.

CHAIR RAIL See **dado**.

CHAMFER The narrow surface or bevel produced by planing or tooling-off the **arris** on timber or masonry – also known as a **bevel** in larger-scale work.

CHIMNEY BOARD or **FIRE BOARD** A board designed to fit into a fireplace opening to seal it in summer. They were usually decorated.

CILL or **SILL** The lowest horizontal timber into which the studs of a timber-frame building are morticed. Also the horizontal member, of wood or stone, at the base of a window (window cill) or door (door cill).

CLOAM OVEN A type of bread oven made of earthenware (from the seventeenth to the early twentieth century) in Devon and Somerset.

COB A mixture of marl or chalk, gravel, dung and straw used for building walls. Known as 'wichert' in Buckinghamshire.

COLLAR A horizontal beam which 'ties' and sustains a pair of principal rafters approximately half way up their length.

CONSOLE A bracket – a console table is one in which the top is supported on a bracket, or brackets.

CORBEL A projecting stone, or timber, used as a support for a structural member or sculptural feature.

COURT-CUPBOARD At first a two-tiered buffet or side table which was later enclosed by doors but retaining vestigal traces of the original form. When fully enclosed, known as a 'press cupboard'.

COVE A wide concave moulding.

CRUCK Timbers used in pairs to provide the principal members of roof and wall and known as 'full crucks'. Such timbers were often arched and employed the natural curves of chosen trees. In early examples the whole diameter of the log was used. Eric Mercer has identified and defined 'base', 'jointed', 'middle', 'raised' and 'upper' crucks.

CUPBOARD-BED A bed enclosed by cupboard doors.

CURB ROOF See **gambrel roof**.

DADO The die-stone or pedestal to a column, in a room the area beneath and including the 'chair rail'. The chair rail is, in effect, the cornice to the pedestal or plinth.

DAIS The raised platform for the 'high table' in a medieval hall. Such a feature was once found in quite small houses.

DAUB Plaster (or to plaster) with cob or clay as in 'wattle and daub'.

DISTEMPER Whitewash or colour wash mixed with water and bound with **size**.

DOG-LEGGED STAIR A stair rising in two or more straight flights united by a landing and either without a 'well' or with a very narrow one.

DORMER WINDOW A window which rises vertically through a roof and provided with its own pitched roof (once also known as 'lucans' as they are still so termed in East Anglia).

DRAGON BEAM The diagonal beam supporting the joists in a building having a jetty on two adjacent sides. Also the diagonal rafter in a hipped roof.

ENTABLATURE The whole of the parts (in effect, the beam) of an order above a column. These parts comprise the **architrave**, the frieze and the cornice.

ENTASIS The diminution of the diameter (or width) of a column (or pilaster) in its top two thirds or so.

FEATHER EDGE A tapering of the edge of a board – a feature which is not appropriate to stone.

FIELDED PANEL A panel with a raised central area or 'field' – an effect produced by bevelling the surrounding edges of the panel.

FIGURE The decorative grain in wood.

FLAG STONE A paving stone.

FLOOR CLOTH or **OIL CLOTH** A canvas floor covering prepared with oil paint, plain or decorated. They were common before the introduction of linoleum in 1860. The use of oil cloth on kitchen tables persisted until it was displaced by plastics in the twentieth century.

FROG (in bricks) An indentation on the larger face or faces above and/or below a brick.

GABLET A small gable in a hipped roof devised (when open) to permit smoke to escape from the central hearth in the hall.

GALLET A chip of stone as produced when 'pitching' – see **pitched stone**.

GAMBREL ROOF or **CURB ROOF** A roof which is pitched in two sections, that is to say a roof with two angles of slope on each side of the ridge.

GESSO A composition composed of whiting (chalk) and size, used as a preparation on wood for paint and water gilding.

GIBB DOOR or **JIBB DOOR** A door which is fitted flush with the wall and without an **architrave** and decorated so as to be all but invisible. The word 'jibb' or 'gibb' occurs in a number of contexts as in a 'jibb bracket' (one that swings), the 'jib' of a crane or the 'jib sail' of a boat. From the Danish *gibbe*.

GREEN TIMBER Unseasoned timber – see also **seasoning**.

GRIP FLOOR A 'plaster' floor made of a mixture of lime and ash.

GUDGEON A 'hook' on which a strap hinge turns (also known as a **pintle**).

GUILLOCHE A band of decoration (Classical in origin) consisting of a series of interlacing circles.

HALL The principal and sometimes only room in a house of medieval type or, at a later date, an entrance lobby.

HALLIER A thatcher, or tiler.

HARR A primitive type of hinge where one side of a door projects at top and bottom providing a pair of 'horns' on which the door (or gate) swings.

HECK   A short internal wall separating a fireplace from an entrance lobby and often supporting a **mantel-tree** and fire hood.

HOOKED RUG   Made of rags or coarse wool pulled through a coarse canvas backing. In Northumberland and Durham they are known as 'hookies and proddies', in Cumbria as 'stobbie rugs' and in Scotland as 'clootie rugs'.

INTERSTICES   The narrow spaces, quirks, grooves or veins such as are found in carved work.

JAMB   An upright member flanking a door, window or fireplace.

JERKIN-HEAD   An end wall which is half gabled beneath a roof which is half hipped – a type common to thatch but also used with stone-tiled roofs. Despite the use of this feature in Britain the term is almost obsolete here although in current usage in America.

JETTY   In a timber-frame house the floor joists which project through the façade to support the external (and sometimes the internal) wall above.

JIBB DOOR   See **gibb door**.

JOGGLE   A **tenon** which is not part of either of the two members it unites – used in both wood and stone.

JOINER   A craftsman whose skills are employed at the bench and generally in a workshop, in contrast to the carpenter who works on buildings *in situ*.

KIDDERMINSTER CARPET   A decorative carpet without a pile, popular in the first half of the nineteenth century. In effect the different colours in these carpets are in separate although interlocking layers of fabric. With 'Scotch ingrain' carpets the colours do not form separate layers.

KING POST   The centre truss post that supports the tie beam and the **rafters** of the roof. When used in pairs they are known as 'queen posts' – crown posts are similar.

KNEE   A piece of timber forming a near right angle by natural growth and deriving strength from that fact.

LEDGE DOOR or **BATTEN DOOR**   A door in which vertical boards are united by horizontal 'ledges' or 'battens'.

LINTEL or **LINTOL**   A horizontal member bridging a void as over a doorway or window.

LIST CARPET   A coarse carpet without a pile made of strips of rag woven into conventional warp threads. Typical examples are striped in different colours. In textiles a 'list' is an alternative word for the selvage of woven fabric. In an architectural sense a 'list' is a synonym for a 'fillet' or an 'annulet'.

LONG-HOUSE   A building combining a home for man and his animals, the 'house-part' often being separated from the byre by a cross passage. The byre is generally one step lower than the 'house-part'.

MANTEL-TREE   The **bressummer** over a fireplace opening.

MASON'S MITRE   The form made when two mouldings, cut out of the solid, meet at an angle – a feature found in wood as in stone.

MEDULLARY RAY   The 'flash' that occurs in some woods such as oak.

MEGILP   A thickening medium used by painters for marbling and graining.

MENDLESHAM CHAIR   A chair the design of which incorporated turned balls. Most examples were made in fruitwood and date from the first quarter of the nineteenth century. Named after Mendlesham in Suffolk where the chairmakers (Daniel and Richard Day) were located.

MITRE   A joint or junction of two similar members each cut to the same angle which for a right angle would be 45 degrees.

MORTICE   A sinking in wood (or sometimes stone) designed to receive a tenon (or **joggle**).

MULLER   A stone used for grinding pigment on a ledger.

MULLION   The vertical division of a window composed of two or more 'lights'.

MUNTIN   An upright timber intermediate between other uprights as in the central upright in a framed door or the middle uprights in a plank and muntin screen. A word possibly related to **mullion**.

NAKED FLOORING   The framework of a floor (joists, etc.) before it is 'clothed' with floorboards.

NEWEL   The vertical post or posts in a stair which bear one end of the stairs or one end of the string and handrail.

NOGGING   Bricks laid in a non-structural way (e.g. herring bone) to emphasise their non-structural use.

OIL CLOTH   See **floor cloth**.

ORDERS   The Orders in Classical architecture are the elements identifiable as Doric, Ionic, Corinthian Composite, etc., each of which obeys fixed proportions (e.g. the ratio of column height to diameter) and certain decorative features and detailing.

OUTSHUT or **OUTSHOT**   An extension or lean-to formed along the side of a house and roofed over by extending one slop of the main roof down to the pole-plate of the extension.

PAMMENTS   A name given in East Anglia to earthenware floor tiles.

PANTRY   A service room for the storage of bread, etc.; often paired, across the cross passage, with the **buttery**.

PARGET   A coarse plaster.

PARLOUR   A private room (originally for conversation, etc.) into which members of the family or favoured guests could retreat. These rooms were generally without a fireplace until the seventeenth century.

PATERAE A small rondel or rosette popular as a result of the Classical Revival – originally referred to the round flat dish used to receive a sacrificial libation.

PEDIMENT In Classical architecture the low-pitched triangular gable – also used externally and internally as a decorative device (e.g. over doors and on furniture and mirror frames).

PENNANT A hard blue grit stone used for flooring or paving in and around Bristol and in South Wales.

PESS A drum-like hassock of rushes.

PIANO NOBILE An Italian term referring to the principal or first floor of a Palladian house. The high noble floor above the base (basement) or ground floor, also known as the *bel étage*.

PIER A post, rectangular in cross-section, or the column of brick or stonework between two windows – hence the terms 'pier table' or 'pier glass' for the furniture that occupied this position in an interior.

PINTLE See **Gudgeon**.

PITCH-BOARD A board made to resemble a large set-square and used to establish the pitch or angle of a flight of stairs or steps.

PITCHED STONE By the use of a pitching hammer and pitcher a mason 'roughed out' his work by the removal of large **gallets**. These gallets could be used for paving. The pitching hammer is of steel rather than iron and is long and narrow, two features that produce a harsher knock. The pitcher is not sharpened (to cut) but is near square ended in cross-section, to enable it to split the stone.

PLANK AND STUD or **PLANK AND MUNTIN** A type of early panelling often found used in screens and composed of a series of vertical **muntins** alternating with planks.

POLE-PLATE Now more generally known, if with less precision, as the wall-plate. Pole, in the sense of 'head', is the top 'plate' or beam on a wall.

QUARREL A lozenge or rectangular-shaped piece of glass in a leaded window.

RAFTERS In a roof the timbers which run from ridge to **pole-plate**.

RAIL Horizontal timber in framed buildings and horizontal **scantlings** in panelling or panelled furniture.

RAMPED STAIR The upward curve of a handrail to its **newel** post usually accompanied by the upward curve of the corresponding panelling.

REBATE (Pronounced 'rabbit' and spelt thus in early references.) An angle cut into the length of a piece of wood so as to receive a panel or similar element in a construction.

REREDOS In the context of the vernacular interior a slab of stone, or small wall, forming the back to a central open hearth. In an ecclesiastical context the reredos is the wall or screen at the back of an altar.

RETURN The continuation of a moulding round a corner on plan or elevation.

RISERS The vertical faces of stairs or steps.

RIVEN Split timber (as when using a riving iron, froe, or chit). In many respects a method which is favoured over sawing as it avoids cutting through the fibres of timber – e.g. riven shingles tend to last longer for this reason.

RUB JOINT Two accurately planed surfaces treated with glue and rubbed together to form a suction joint.

SAPWOOD The external layers (beneath the bark) of the trunk or branches of a tree – the layers which carry the sap. Sapwood is paler in colour than the bulk of the wood and, in most species, is soft and subject to woodworm.

SARKING BOARDS In roofs the insulation in the form of boards laid over rafters and under the roof covering. Characteristic of North America and Scotland and sometimes found in the north of England.

SCANTLINGS Timber (or stone) components which are consistent in their cross-sectional dimensions.

SCARF The joint (of which there are many variations) by means of which timber may be joined end to end.

SCRIBED To use a sharp implement to scratch a line – hence a 'scribed skirting'.

SCUMBLING The achievement of broken colour effects by removing or texturing a wet coat of paint to expose part of the coat beneath it.

SEASONING (OF TIMBER) The 'drying' of timber so as to remove the sap gradually and thereby limit warping and splitting. Methods used include 'air drying', 'water seasoning' and 'kiln drying'.

SECTION The profile through a building or across a moulding.

SEISE A type of settle common in Scotland.

SETTLE-BED A type of settle found in Ireland and in northeast North America and Canada. The seat folds forward to form an open box in which to make a bed.

SHIELING Summer dwelling.

SHINGLE A wooden tile used as a roof covering.

SHIPPON A byre or cow house.

SILL See **cill**.

SIZE A thinned glue derived from animal sources including white of egg, milk, bones, rabbit skin or fish.

SMOKE HOOD The precursor of the chimney, being a funnel (often of wattle and daub and even paper!) corbelled out over the fire. Early references to chimneys often allude to 'funnels'.

SNAPPING A LINE The use of a line, covered with chalk or charcoal, etc., held taught and then 'snapped', to produce a straight line, on the surface to be worked on.

Spear Reeds used by plasterers in place of laths.

Spere or **Spur** A short fixed internal screen often running at right angles to an outside wall. Various dialect and regional terms are also used for this feature.

Spline A thin narrow strip of wood which serves the same function between boards as the tongue in tongue-and-groove boards. Unlike the tongue a spline (like the **joggle**) is not part of either of the boards it unites (Fig. 74).

Sprigs Short (chip-like) square-sectioned headless nails used to hold glass in place in preparation for puttying.

Stained hangings Wall hangings which are stained, or sometimes painted, onto coarse canvas so as to resemble woven tapestry.

Stamm The base of the tree which widens near the 'bowl' to offer support to the living plant. As timber this, when inverted, could offer a natural 'jowl' or integral corbel of structural value or, when paired, could create a natural two-centred arch doorway (Fig. 188).

Stile An upright member in framed panelling or, with larger **scantlings**, vertical posts which are known as **studs**.

Stop As in 'chamfer-stop', the feature which terminates the **chamfer**.

String A raking beam or board into which the **treads** and **risers** of a staircase are 'housed'. Such members take three forms, the 'close string', 'open string' and the central 'bearing string'.

String course A decorative, usually projecting, thin course of brick or stone. Usually only found in interiors of 'first-rate' houses where it is often executed in plaster. Common on external elevations.

Studs Vertical timbers in a timber-framed wall – lighter-weight studs are known as **stiles**.

Summer beam The principal beam which supports the joists. The word, although archaic in Britain (where the cumbersome term 'bridging beam' is now used), is current in America. Also once known as a 'dormant tree'. See **bressummer** (**breast summer**).

Tenon A horn or protrusion in wood designed to fit into a **mortice**; see also **joggle**.

Torching-up A lining of coarse mortar or **parget** applied to the underside of a stone, slate or tiled roof for purposes of weatherproofing.

Transom or **Transome** A horizontal member as in the 'transom' (or transoms) of a mullioned window. This feature occurs between the **lintel** and the **cill** dividing the window horizontally into two or more zones. The window transom is rare in small domestic buildings. Also the horizontal member between a *lunette* (or fan light) and a door – sometimes known as a transom light.

Tread The **scantling** which forms the horizontal flat board in a staircase – or similar surface in stone steps.

Trennell or **Tree nail** An alternative word for a dowel.

Tridarn A Welsh term for a three-tiered **court-cupboard**.

Trimmers Subsidiary joists, etc., used in framing-up round a well in a 'naked floor' (see **naked flooring**), to make way for a chimney or staircase.

Trunk A chest 'dug out' of a log. Later used to describe a travelling trunk or chest.

Truss In carpentry, the collection of structural timbers that form a triangle and employed in series as the principal supports for a roof. These 'trusses' were usually 'offered-up' as entities and once in place they were united by purlins, etc.

Tuffet See **buffet**.

Vernacular Native language or idiom. A word that has become much associated with building as in vernacular architecture. (From the Latin *verna*, a home-born slave.)

Wainscot A term used for panelling or panelled furniture and originally referring specifically to oak.

Wall-plate See **pole-plate**.

Wattle Woven timber often made of oak rods with split ash or hazel strips or twigs woven into them.

Wichert See **cob**.

Winders Steps or stairs which, on plan, radiate wedge-shaped from a **newel**.

Withe The dividing masonry or brickwork separating two or more flues within one chimney.

Notes

Foreword

1   In the United States interior decoration was a popular concern throughout much of the twentieth century, and so it remains. This may have begun with the Centennial Exhibition of the Declaration of Independence (1776–1876) in Philadelphia, was encouraged by Edith Wharton and Ogden Codman in their book *The Decoration of Houses* (Charles Scribner's Sons, New York, 1897) and was carried forward in the next century by Elsie de Wolfe of New York, perhaps the first interior decorator in the modern sense of the word.

In Britain the situation was more confused with Victorian eclecticism, the Aesthetic Style and the Arts and Crafts Movement. This is not to say that America was not subject to these British fashions – it was. However the British also had to accommodate the souvenirs of Empire which added still further layers to this cultural melting-pot.

2   There are numerous individual studies of aspects of the vernacular interior (e.g. furniture and timber-frame construction) but few, if any, encompass and capture the more fugitive qualities of the vernacular interior as an entity.

3   Richard Gough, *History of Myddle* ed. by David Hey, Penguin Books, Harmondsworth, 1981, pp. 22, 244. Gough's book was written between 1700 and 1702. In it he also makes reference to 'wild Humphrey' Kinaston who, having abandoned his castle at Myddle, 'sheltered himself in a Cave' (p. 56). The memoire also describes timber-framed houses rebuilt in stone (p. 111), converting old houses into byres (p. 57), demolishing a barn and setting it up 'for a dwelling house' (p. 151), and building a 'faire house', a 'handsome pile' which was 'whoaly built in sixteen weeks' (p. 160).

4   C. Carson, N. F. Barka, W. M. Kelso, G. W. Stone and D. Upton, 'Impermanent architecture in the Southern Colonies', *Winterthur Portfolio*, Wilmington, Delaware, Vol. 16, Nos. 2, 3, 1981, pp. 135–96.

5   For example Bob Machin, 'The lost cottages of England: an essay on impermanent building in post-medieval England', Vernacular Architecture Group, 1997 Winter Meeting at which this printed paper was circulated.

6   Christopher Dyer, 'History and vernacular architecture', *Vernacular Architecture*, Vol. 28, 1997, pp. 1–7.

7   J. Ayres, *Building the Georgian City*, Yale University Press, New Haven and London, 1998, p. 5 and fig. 6. It could be argued that, for a privileged few, the suburb first appeared in the orbit of London as a result of the development of the leaf spring for carriages (*c.* 1670). It was, however, the advent of the railway which was to cause the widespread development of suburbia, a trend that was reinforced by the internal combustion engine in the twentieth century.

8   John Wood, *An Essay Towards a Description of Bath*, Vol. I first published 1742, Vols. II and III first published 1743. It is in these earlier editions of the *Essay* that Wood provided, at the end of the last volume, 'A Table of Distances Between the Principal Parts of the City of Bath' as this related to the fares charged by sedan chair men. Within the City walls they charged a flat fee but Wood was of the opinion that this discriminated against his extra-mural developments.

9   Ibid., p. 91.

10 Neil Burton, ed., *Georgian Vernacular*, London, 1996. For the persistence of the timber-frame tradition see, in this same publication, David Martin, 'The decline of traditional methods of timber framing in the south-east of England', pp. 27–33. For bond timbers see Dan Cruickshank and Neil Burton, *Life in the Georgian City*, London, 1990, p. 109. Also Ayres, *Building the Georgian City*, 1998, pp. 39, 85, 112, 116, 134.

11 There are many examples of such tradesmen-architects who are known to have possessed a wider knowledge, among them the Smiths of Warwick and the Bastards of Blandford – and of course John Wood the elder of Bath.

12 Neil McKendrick, John Brewer and J. H. Plumb, *The Birth of a Consumer Society: The Commercialization of Eighteenth-Century England*, London, 1983.

13 Isaac Ware, *The Complete Body of Architecture*, T. Osborne and J. Shipton, London, 1756, p. 291.

14 J. T. Smith, *Nollekens and His Times* (1828), Turnstile Press, London, 1949, p. 130. This statement occurs in relationship to Charles Townley's very grand house at No. 7 Park Street, now Queen Anne's Gate, Westminster.

For social history and its relevance to domestic life see for example Peter Burke, *Popular Culture in Early Modern Europe* (1978), Scolar Press, Aldershot, 1994; and Peter Borsay, *The English Urban Renaissance*, Clarendon Press, Oxford, (1989) 1991.

For Colonial American domestic life see Richard L. Bushman, *The Refinement of America: Persons, Houses, Cities*,

Vintage Books, Random House, New York, 1993. For early post-Colonial domestic life see Jane C. Nylander, *Our Own Snug Fireside: Images of the New England Home 1760–1860*, Yale University Press, New Haven and London, 1994.

15 George Eliot, *Middlemarch* (1871–2), Book I, Chapter 3. Charles L. Eastlake (1835–1906) not to be confused with Charles L. Eastlake (1793–1865). The younger man's *Hints . . .* (Longmans, Green and Co., London, 1868) was criticised for its 'medieval predilections' but it was equally concerned with post-medieval vernacular traditions, e.g. fig. v, which illustrates a 'Farm house kitchen, Chambercombe, Devon'.

16 Authorities on vernacular furniture in the British Isles include B. D. Cotton (English chairs and Manx furniture), A. Davies (Wales), the late Christopher Gilbert (England), Claudia Kinmouth (Ireland) and R. Ross Noble (Scotland) – among others.

17 In particular Lorna Weatherill, *Consumer Behaviour and Material Culture in Britain 1660–1760*, Routledge, London and New York, (1988) 1996. For probate inventories see, for example, F. G. Emmison, *Elizabethan Life: Home, Work and Land*, Essex County Council, Chelmsford, 1976; and John S. Moore, *The Goods and Chattels of our Forefathers: Frampton Cotterell and District Probate Inventories 1539–1804*, Phillimore, Chichester, 1976.

18 Most important of these were the late Nina and Bertram Little (see the numerous publications by Nina Fletcher Little).

Introduction

1   William Howitt, *The Rural Life of England* (1838), Longman, London, 1844, p. 403.

2   E.g. Skellig Michael (*c.* AD 700), Co. Kerry and the cleits of St Kilda (resembling igloos – but built of stone and used to store the meat of sea birds).

3   Timber-frame buildings were generally prepared in the carpenter's yard with their components numbered for assembly on site.

4   Letter from *The Times* to the author dated 7 June 1978. See Astragal, *Architects' Journal*, London, 28 June 1978, p. 1237, which quotes this letter.

5   D. Parsons, ed., *Stone: Quarrying and Building in England AD 43–1525*, Phillimore Press, Chichester, 1990, Chapter 9.

6   Now in the collections of the Museum of London. This was by no means an isolated example. See J. M. Swann, 'Shoes concealed in buildings', Northampton Museum and Art Gallery *Journal*, No. 6. In Ireland it was customary to bury a horse's skull under the floor of a house as a builder's sacrifice.

7   For builders' offerings see Timothy Easton, 'Spiritual middens', in Paul Oliver, ed., *The Encyclopedia of Vernacular Architecture of the World*, Cambridge University Press, Cambridge, 1997; also the same author's 'Ritual marks on historic timbers', *Weald and Downland Museum 'Newsletter'*, Sussex, Spring 1999, pp. 22–8; and Ralph Merrifield, *The Archaeology of Ritual and Magic*, Batsford, London, 1987. For a very brief summary of the rise of the architectural profession see J. Ayres, *Building the Georgian City*, Yale University Press, New Haven and London, 1998, Chapter 1.

Chapter 1: The Vernacular Interior

1   Anon., *Builder's Dictionary*, A. Bettesworth and C. Hitch, London, 1734. No author given but attributed by contemporaries to James Ralph.

2   Richard Neve, *The City and Country Purchaser*, London, 1726, p. 22.

3   Including inventories.

4   Ian Bradley, 'The question mark over the future of the middle classes', *The Times*, 7 January 1975.

5   Isaac Ware, *The Complete Body of Architecture*, T. Osborne and J. Shipton, London, 1756, p. 693.

6   H. Muthesius, *Das englische Haus*, Berlin, 1904–5 (*The English House*, Crosby Lockwood Staples, London, 1979).

7   In Britain the 'gambrel' is today sometimes used to describe a hipped roof with a pair of 'gablets'.

8   William Cobbett, *Rural Rides 1821–32* (1885), Webb & Bower, Exeter, 1984, pp. 114–17.

9   Lorna Weatherill, *Consumer Behaviour and Material Culture in Britain 1660–1760*, Routledge, London and New York, (1988) 1996, Chapter 4.

10 Christopher Morris, ed., *The Journeys of Celia Fiennes*, Cresset Press, London, 1947, p. 136.

11 Ibid., p. 204.

12 William Harrison, *Description of England* (1577) ed. by F. J. Furnival, Vol. II, London, 1877, p. 239.

13 Richard Carew, *The Survey of Cornwall* (1602), B. Law, London, 1769, pp. 64, 66–7.

14 John Wood, *A Description of Bath* (1749), W. Bathoe, London, 1765, pp. 3–5. Significantly, Wood returned to his native Bath in 1727.

15 J. T. Smith, *Nollekens and His Times* (1829), Vol. II, London, 1919, p. 102.

16 M. W. Barley, *The English Farmhouse and Cottage*, Routledge and Kegan Paul, London, 1961, ill. 22b.

17 J. Ayres, *Building the Georgian City*, Yale University Press, New Haven and London, 1998, p. 71, figs. 97–8.

18 J. C. Loudon, *An Encyclopaedia of Cottage, Farm, and Villa Architecture*, Longman, London, (1833) 1836, from the first sentence of the Introduction. William Atkinson's *Views of Picturesque Cottages*, T. Gardiner, London, 1805, in part 'intended as hints for the improvement of village scenery.'

19 See Doré's views of the capital in Gustave Doré and Blanchard Jerrold, *London a Pilgrimage*, Grant and Co., London, 1872.

20 Mona Duggan, *Ormskirk: The Making of a Modern Town*, Sutton Publishing, Stroud, 1998, pp. 55–6.

21 For example Prince Albert's designs for model houses which were erected beside the 1851 Exhibition in the grounds of 'Hyde Park Barracks' (see C. H. Gibbs-Smith, *The Great Exhibition of 1851*, HMSO, London, 1950, p. 139).

Chapter 2: Heat and Light

1   Eric Mercer, *English Vernacular Houses*, HMSO, London, 1975, p. 23.

2   The British Record Society (website: http://britishrecordsociety.org.uk) is currently publishing a county by county series of texts on the *Hearth Taxes* 1660s to 1670s.

3   M. W. Barley, *The English Farmhouse and Cottage*, Routledge and Kegan Paul, London, 1961, p. 13. The whole question of detached kitchens is a matter of debate. See *Vernacular Architecture*, Vol. 32, 2001, articles by J. T. Smith, pp. 16–19 and David and Barbara Martin, pp. 20–33.

4   Hugh D. Roberts, *Downhearth to Bar Grate*, Hugh D. Roberts, Bath, 1981.

5   Alison Kelly, *English Fireplaces*, Country Life, London, 1968, p. 11.

6   Stuart Piggott, *Ancient Europe from the Beginnings of Agriculture to Classical Antiquity*, Edinburgh University Press, Edinburgh, (1965) 1973, p. 247.

7   F. G. Emmison, *Elizabethan Life*, Essex County Council, Chelmsford, 1976, p. 25.

8   John Wood, *A Description of Bath* (1749), W. Bathoe, London, 1765, p. 416, quoting Aubrey.

9   Photograph of the Mitford dogwheel, Beamish Open Air Museum, neg. 9840 – another example may be seen in the kitchen at No. 1 Royal Crescent, a house museum administered by the Bath Preservation Trust.

10 The references to spit dogs come from Wood's *Description* (1765, pp. 416–17) and J. Seymour Lindsay, *Iron and Brass Implements . . .* (1927), Tiranti, London, 1964, p. 22, quoting Dr Caius.

11 Lindsay, *Iron and Brass Implements*, 1964, fig. 81, p. 17.

12 Christopher Morris, ed., *The Journeys of Celia Fiennes*, Cresset Press, London, 1947, p. 11. Celia Fiennes writing *c.* 1685.

13 British Library, Department of Manuscripts, Add X 15537, Folio 170.

14 Barley, *The English Farmhouse and Cottage*, 1961, p. 94.

15 Morris, ed., *The Journeys of Celia Fiennes*, 1947, p. 161.

16 Ibid., p. 262, and Oliver Rackham, *Trees and Woodland in the British Landscape* (1976), Phoenix Press, London, 2001, p. 85.

17 Iorwerth C. Peate, *Tradition and Folk Life, a Welsh View*, Faber and Faber, London, 1972, p. 42.

18 Alexander Fenton, *Scottish Country Life*, John Donald, Edinburgh, 1976, p. 193.

19 Ibid., p. 198.

20 William Howitt, *The Rural Life of England* (1838), Longman, London, 1844, p. 238.

21 Emmison, *Elizabethan Life*, 1976, p. 25.

22 Jane C. Nylander, *Our Own Snug Fireside*, Yale University Press, New Haven and London, 1994, p. 186.

23 Now in the Frilandsmuseet, Copenhagen.

24 I. F. Grant, *Highland Folk Ways*, Routledge and Kegan Paul, London, 1961, fig. 35c, p. 164.

25 For the 'Little Ice Age' see Rackham, *Trees and Woodland in the British Landscape*, 2001, p. 189, and Brian Fagan, *The Little Ice Age . . . 1300–1850*, Basic Books/Perseus Group, New York, 2000.

26 R. T. Mason, *Framed Buildings of the Weald* (1964), Coach Publishing House, Horsham, 1969, pp. 76–7. See also Mercer, *English Vernacular Houses*, 1975, p. 62.

27 Royal Commission on Historical Monuments, *Westmorland*, London, 1936, Preface, p. lxi.

28 For many years evidence for this in the north of England remained to be discovered (see Mercer, *English Vernacular Houses*, 1975, p. 21) but a smoke-blackened crown post has now been recorded at Baxby Hall, Husthwaite, North Yorkshire (Barbara Hutton, 'North Yorkshire vernacular houses', *Current Archaeology*, No. 74, Vol. 7, No. 3, November 1980.

29 Grant, *Highland Folk Ways*, 1961, p. 163.

30 William Harrison, *Description of England* (1577) ed. by F. J. Furnival, Vol. II, London, 1877, pp. 239, 240.

31 W. G. Hoskins, 'The rebuilding of rural England 1570–1640', *History Today*, 1955, pp. 104–11, republished as Chapter 7 in *Provincial England*, Macmillan, London, 1963. Whilst this thesis has been revised to take in local variation, its basic tenets have been largely maintained with huge regional variations in terms of date.

32 Mason, *Framed Buildings*, 1969, p. 44. Mason argues that W. G. Hoskins's thesis for the 'Great Rebuilding' should be termed the 'Second Rebuilding', the first and more radical being in the fifteenth century.

33 Ibid., p. 77.

34 David and Barbara Martin, 'Detached Kitchens or Adjoining Houses – A Response', *Vernacular Architecture*, Vol. 32, 2001, p. 22.

35 An example may be seen in the hill farmhouse from Coscib, near Cushendall, now in the Ulster Folk Museum.

36 Timothy Easton, 'The painting of historic brick', *Weald and Downland Museum 'Newsletter'*, Sussex, Spring 2001, pp. 26–8. See also Maurice Barley, *Houses and History*, Faber and Faber, London, 1986, p. 179.

37 J. Ayres, 'Ancient High House and Northeycote Farm', *Architects Journal*, Vol. 86, No. 47, 25 November 1987, pp. 50–5, fig. 60. In this house the chimney, where it emerged from the roof, was given more ribs on the more visible side by the road – a mark of prestige.

38 Quoted by Nicholas Cooper, *Houses of the Gentry 1480–1680*, Yale University Press, New Haven and London, 1999, p. 45.

39 Frederick Edwards, *Our Domestic Fire-places*, London, 1870, pp. 15, 219. These were also known as a valance or, in France, as a *tour de cheminée* – see Peter Thornton, *Authentic Décor*, Weidenfeld and Nicolson, London, 1984, p. 27.

40 Timothy Easton, 'Ritual marks on historic timbers', *Weald and Downland Museum 'Newsletter'*, Sussex, Spring 1999, pp. 22–8, citing Ralph Merrifield, *The Archaeology of Ritual and Magic*, Batsford, London, 1987.

41 Richard Harris, '. . . Marks to be seen on buildings in the Museum', *Weald and Downland Museum 'Newsletter'*, Sussex, Spring 1999, pp. 29–30.

42 An example of this use of brick nogging has been recorded at Bury Lodge, Enfield of *c.* 1600 – photo held by National Monuments Record, London.

43 Mason, *Framed Buildings*, 1969, p. 55.

44 A feature now destroyed.

45 Batty Langley, *The London Prices of Bricklayer's Materials and Works*, London, 1748, p. 46.

46 J. Ayres, *Building the Georgian City*, Yale University Press, New Haven and London, 1998, pp. 198–9.

47 Ibid., pp. 198–9, fig. 296.

48 Nina Fletcher Little, *American Decorative Wall Painting 1700–1850* (1952), Dutton, New York, 1972, pp. 72, 76.

49 R. T. Gunther, ed., *The Architecture of Sir Roger Pratt*, Oxford University Press, Oxford, 1928, p. 192, quoted by Peter Thornton, *Seventeenth-Century Interior Decoration in England, France and Holland*, Yale University Press, New Haven and London, 1978, p. 344, endnote 27.

50 An example of this black-over-white technique was recorded at Middle Maur Sowton, a farmhouse dating back at least to 1671 (now destroyed) – Michael Laithwaite in *Transactions of the Devon Archaeological Society*, Vol. 10, No. 3, 1971, pp. 77–83.

51 Nathaniel Lloyd, *A History of the English House*, Architectural Press, London, (1931) 1975, p. 275, figs. 306–7 (early sixteenth century) and Ayres, *Building the Georgian City*, 1998, p. 198, fig. 295 (dated 1719). The method was also used in Renaissance Italy – see *Vasari on Technique* ed. by G. Baldwin Brown, Dent, London, 1907, p. 19 and Chapter 12, p. 243, fig. xi.

52 Thornton, *Seventeenth Century Interior Decoration*, 1978, p. 68, quoting Pepys's *Diary*, 19 January 1666.

53 Barley, *The English Farmhouse and Cottage*, 1961, p. 168.

54 Peate, *Tradition and Folk Life*, 1972, p. 41.

55 C. Malcolm Watkins, 'North Devon pottery and its export to North America in the 17th century', US *National Museum Bulletin*, No. 225, Smithsonian Institution, Washington, DC, 1960.

56 Peter Brears, *The Old Devon Farmhouse*, Devon Books, Tiverton, 1998, p. 31.

57 Bertram Frank, 'Salt boxes of the North Yorkshire Moors', *The Dalesman*, December 1970.

58 Emyr Estyn Evans, *Irish Folk Ways*, Routledge and Kegan Paul, London, 1957, p. 65.

59 Linda Hall, 'Yeoman or gentleman? Problems in defining social status in 17th and 18th-century Gloucestershire', *Vernacular Architecture*, Vol. 22, 1991, p. 8.

60 Isaac Ware, *The Complete Body of Architecture*, T. Osborne and J. Shipton, London, 1756, p. 554.

61 Gwenno Caffell, 'The carved slates of Dyffryn Ogwen', *Current Archaeology*, No. 74, Vol. 2, No. 3, November 1980.

62 Peate, *Tradition and Folk Life*, 1972, p. 39; Lindsay, *Iron and Brass Implements*, 1964, p. 16.

63 Brears, *The Old Devon Farmhouse*, 1998, p. 60, Cat. 139–45 illustrated p. 113. See also Lindsay, *Iron and Brass Implements*, 1964, p. 55, figs. 329, 332–4.

64 Mona Duggan, *Ormskirk: The Making of a Modern Town*, Sutton Publishing, Stroud, 1998, p. 57.

65 E.g. Mezzotint by J. Boydell after Zoffany, *Mr. Foote in the Character of Major Sturgeon*, 1765.

66 Quoted by Nina Fletcher Little, *Country Arts in Early American Homes*, Dutton, New York, 1975, p. 112.

67 The National Portrait Gallery, London.

68 Ambrose Heal Collection of Trade Labels, British Museum, Department of Paintings and Drawings.

69 Ambrose Heal Collection, British Museum. Quoted by Ambrose Heal in his *The London Furniture Makers*, Batsford, London, 1953, p. 143. A newly discovered chimney board is illustrated as item 65 in the catalogue of the Exhibition *The Fashionable Fireplace* by Christopher Gilbert and Anthony Wells-Cole, Leeds City Art Gallery, 1985.

70 Larwood and Hotten, *History of Signboards*, London, 1866, p. 521, quoting 'a monthly sheet entitled *The London Register* for April [1762?] . . . under the title of "Particular Account of the Great Exhibition in Bow Street . . ."'

71 This incident may have derived from an actual event said to have taken place in the court of King François I of France (see Thornton, *Seventeenth Century Interior Decoration*, 1978, pp. 386–7, endnote 85).

72 Illustrated by Thornton, *Seventeenth Century Interior Decoration*, 1978. See also his footnote that refers to a similar one in a private collection in London in 1950.

73 Little, *Country Arts in Early American Homes*, 1975, p. 13.

74 Very few trade-labels in the Heal Collection mention fire boards.

75 Some of the American examples illustrated by Nina Fletcher Little have painted flowers arranged in a vase strikingly similar to plate 14 in John Stalker and George Parker's *A Treatise of Japaning and Varnishing* (1688), Tiranti, London, 1971.

76 Morris, ed., *The Journeys of Celia Fiennes*, Macdonald, London, 1982, Introduction, p. 30.

77 Ibid., pp. 176–7.

78 Edwards, *Our Domestic Fire-places*, 1870, p. 25.

79 L. A. Shuffrey, *The English Fireplace*, Batsford, London, 1912, p. 175 and Appendix.

80 Nicolas Gauger, *Mechanique du Feu* (The Mechanism of Fire), translated by J. T. Desaguliers, London, 1716, pp. xi, xv.

81 Ibid., Vol. II, Part I, p. 48.

82 Ibid., Vol. II, Part III, p. 64.

83 B. Anthony Bax, *The English Parsonage*, John Murray, London, 1964, p. 124.

84 Sixteenth-century faience stove tiles of central European type have been excavated in the City of London (collection: Museum of London) but if Continental ceramic stoves were used in early modern Britain this was probably a cosmopolitan sophistication confined to the capital.

85 Even in New England there were occasional exceptions to this generalisation. See Josephine H. Peirce, *Fire on the Hearth*, Pond-Ekberg, Springfield, MA, 1951, p. 33.

86 Ibid., p. 39.

87 Shuffrey, *The English Fireplace*, 1912, p. 224.

88 Christopher Morris, ed., *Selections from William Cobbett's Rural Rides 1821–32*, Webb & Bower, Waltham Abbey, (1984) 1992, p. 131, see also pp. 122–3.

89 Raymond Lister, *Decorative Cast Ironwork in Great Britain*, Bell and Sons, London, 1960, p. 106. See also *Who's Who in American History*, Marquis, Chicago, 1963.

90 J. C. Loudon, *An Encyclopaedia of Cottage, Farm, and Villa Architecture*, Longman, London, (1833) 1836, p. 656.

91 Michael Owen, *Antique Cast Iron*, Blandford Press, Poole, Dorset, 1977, p. 74.

92 Lister, *Decorative Cast Ironwork*, 1960, pp. 108–9.

93 Maria Hartley and Joan Ingilby, *Life and Tradition in the Yorkshire Dales*, Dent, London, 1968, pp. 3, 4.

94 Howitt, *The Rural Life of England*, 1844, p. 238.

95 Lindsay, *Iron and Brass Implements*, 1964, pp. 41, 46, 50.

96 Quoted by E. H. Pinto, *Treen and Other Wooden Bygones*, Bell and Sons, London, 1969, p. 114.

97 Christopher Hawkins, 'Lights for mediaeval worshippers', *Country Life*, December 1974.

98 Evans, *Irish Folk Ways*, 1957, fig. 27.

99 Examples in the Welsh Folk Museum at St Fagans.

100 Grant, *Highland Folk Ways*, 1961, p. 184. Also Lindsay, *Iron and Brass Implements*, 1964, p. 46.

101 Old village woman recorded by Gertrude Jekyll: Gertrude Jekyll and Sidney R. Jones, *Old English Household Life*, Batsford, London, (1925), 1975, p. 19.

102 Therle Hughes, *Cottage Antiques*, Lutterworth Press, London, 1967, p. 163.

103 Gilbert White, *Natural History of Selborne*, letter of 1 November 1775 – also quoted in full by Lindsay, *Iron and Brass Implements*, 1964, pp. 41–3.

104 Peter Borsay, *The English Urban Renaissance*, Clarendon Press, Oxford, (1989) 1991, p. 156.

105 Peter Brears, *Book of English Country Pottery*, David and Charles, Newton Abbot, 1974 illustrates (p. 17) a slip decorated wall sconce from Halifax by Samuel Catherall dated 1869.

106 Evans, *Irish Folk Ways*, 1957, p. 89.

107 Pinto, *Treen and Other Wooden Bygones*, 1969, p. 118.

108 Sir Hugh Platt, *The Jewel House of Arts and Nature*, London, 1594, pp. 31–2.

109 See Platt and the engraving by Robert William Buss (1804–75) showing a wood engraver working in his studio at night – Victoria and Albert Museum, E3100-1931.

110 P. V. Glob, *De Nosten Ukendte*, Dansk Kulturhistorisk Museumsforenig, 1971, p. 61.

Chapter 3: Walls

1 Iorwerth C. Peate, *The Welsh House*, Hugh Evans and Sons, Liverpool, 1946, p. 91, quoting respectively *The Royal Commission on Land in Wales, Minutes of Evidence*, and the *Report of the Commissioners on Education* (1847).

2 Ibid., p. 91.

3 C. F. Innocent, *The Development of English Building Construction* (1916), David and Charles, Newton Abbot, 1971, p. 129.

4 Ibid., p. 125.

5 Ibid., p. 132.

6 S. O. Addy, *The Evolution of the English House* (1898), George Allen and Unwin, London, 1933, pp. 48, 49, 128.

7 Known in Lincolnshire and in the south of England as 'stud and mud', or 'daub and stower' in the north, or 'raddle and daub' in Cheshire and Lancashire. Innocent, *The Development of English Building Construction*, 1971, p. 133.

8 W. G. Hoskins, 'The rebuilding of rural England 1570–1640',

History Today, 1955, pp. 104–11. The 'Great Rebuilding' is now seen to have occurred at different times in different regions.

9   This remarkable survival is described in many books, among them Nathaniel Lloyd's *A History of the English House*, Architectural Press, London, (1931) 1975, pp. 6, 7, and more recently by Jane Grenville, *Medieval Housing*, Leicester University Press, London and Washington, (1997) 1999, p. 33 with illustration of related examples. List of 'Dendrochronology results for buildings dated before 1300', *Vernacular Architecture*, Vol. 30, 1999, p. 51.

10 V. F. Penn, 'Wall-painting in a house in High Street Walsall, Staffordshire', *South Staffordshire Archaeological and Historical Society Transactions 1974–75*, Vol. VI, pp. 62–4. The house (of the early sixteenth century) was recorded informally as it was being demolished in 1969. The seventeenth-century (?) painted decoration was arranged vertically between closely spaced studs and took the form of a series of repeat scrolls with leaves and fruit based on the strawberry – similar to Fig. 228 here.

11 For example a late sixteenth-century scheme painted in the interior of an attic room in the George and Dragon Inn, Beaumaris, North Wales. An external example of the sixteenth century at Shell Manor, Himbleton, Worcestershire is illustrated by Abbott Lowell Cummings, *The Framed Houses of Massachusetts Bay 1625–1725*, Harvard University Press, Cambridge, MA. and London, 1979, fig. 135.

  A further example of paint used to represent internal structural features has been recorded in the 'supra-vernacular' Burn Hall, Thornton-le-Fylde (near Fleetwood) – see M. F. McClintock and R. C. Watson, 'Domestic wall painting in the North West', *Vernacular Architecture*, Vol. 14, 1938, p. 56.

12 Joseph Gwilt, *An Encyclopaedia of Architecture* (1842), Longmans, Green and Co., London, 1876, p. 564.

13 Margaret Wood, *The English Mediaeval House*, Phoenix House, London, 1965, Chapter 9, 'Development of the screen: internal partitions'. See also Emyr Estyn Evans, *Irish Folk Ways*, Routledge and Kegan Paul, London, 1957, p. 64, which mentions the 'sconce' of Cumberland and the 'jamb wall' or 'hollan wall' of Ulster and southern Scotland.

14 Innocent, *The Development of English Building Construction*, 1971, pp. 139–40, fig. 30.

15 'No. 10 High Street', Royal Commission on Historical Monuments, *Stamford*, 1977.

16 Wood, *The English Mediaeval House*, 1965, p. 146.

17 M. W. Barley, *The English Farmhouse and Cottage*, Routledge and Kegan Paul, London, 1961, p. 122.

18 L. F. Salzman, *Building in England down to 1540*, Clarendon Press, Oxford, 1952, p. 258, quoting John Ripley who provided such panelling for Westminster Palace in 1532 for the sum of 21d.

19 William Harrison, *Description of England* (1577) ed. by F. J. Furnival, Vol. II, London, 1877, p. 235.

20 F. G. Emmison, *Elizabethan Life*, Essex County Council, Chelmsford, 1976, p. 22.

21 R. T. Mason, *Framed Buildings of the Weald* (1964), Coach Publishing House, Horsham, 1969, p. 83.

22 Eric Mercer, *English Vernacular Houses*, HMSO, London, 1975, pp. 14–15.

23 Peter Beacham, ed., *Devon Building*, Devon Books, Exeter, 1990, p. 39 fig. 2.7, and a house at Spaxton, near Bridgewater, Somerset, inspected by the author.

24 Emmison, *Elizabethan Life*, 1976, p. 9.

25 Nathaniel Lloyd, *A History of the English House*, Architectural Press, London, (1931) 1975, p. 78.

26 John Fowler and John Cornforth illustrate one of the rooms at Clandon stripped of its hangings to reveal similar wood lining – *English Decoration in the 18th Century*, Barrie and Jenkins, London, (1974) 1978, p. 123, fig. 108.

27 Christopher Morris, ed., *The Journeys of Celia Fiennes*, Cresset Press, London, 1947, p. 66. The entry, in the journal for 1697, concerns the panelling of Hinchinbrooke Hall, Huntingdonshire.

28 Isaac Ware, *The Complete Body of Architecture*, T. Osborne and J. Shipton, London, 1756, p. 469.

29 Salzman, *Building in England*, 1952, p. 346. Such fish skin was bought in 1355 for 9d for use at Westminster.

30 John Stalker and George Parker, *A Treatise of Japaning and Varnishing* (1688), Tiranti, London, 1971, p. 2.

31 Joseph Moxon, *Mechanick Exercises: or, the Doctrine of Handy-Works* (1677), Dan. Midwinter and Tho. Leigh, London, 1703, pp. 108–9.

32 Ibid., pp. 108–9.

33 Ibid., p. 113.

34 Batty Langley, *The Builder's Jewel* R. Ware, London, (1741) 1754, pp. 4, 5. See also plate 76, 'To proportion cornices to Rooms of any height', plate 77, 'Mouldings for Pannels', plate 78, 'Mouldings for tabernacle Frames', plate 79, 'A Cove ¼ of the entire Height', which also shows the chimney-breast end of a room with tabernacle frame.

35 Peter Nicholson, *New Practical Builder*, London, 1823–5, p. 230.

36 William Salmon, *Polygraphice: Or the Arts of Drawing, Engraving, Etching, Limning, Painting, Varnishing, Japanning and Gilding &c* (1672), London, 1701, Vol. II, Chapter 17.

37 Mary Ellen Best's 1840 watercolour of the eighteenth-century (?) Steward's Room at Whitby Abbey House shows a delft tile 'skirting' possibly influenced by Dutch custom – Holland being a short distance from Whitby across the North Sea. See Caroline Davidson, *The World of Mary Ellen Best*, Chatto and Windus, London, 1985, fig. 71, pp. 70–1.

38 John Harvey, *Mediaeval Craftsmen*, Batsford, London, 1975, p. 155, and J. Ayres, *Building the Georgian City*, Yale University Press, New Haven and London, 1998, pp. 131, 139.

39 Cited by Ayres, *Building the Georgian City*, 1998, p. 202.

40 J. C. Loudon, *An Encyclopaedia of Cottage, Farm, and Villa Architecture*, Longmans London, (1833) 1836, p. 1274.

41 Innocent, *The Development of English Building Construction*, 1971, p. 138, quoting Professor Thorold Rogers, and Ayres, *Building the Georgian City*, 1998, pp. 201, 202.

42 Barley, *The English Farmhouse and Cottage*, 1961, p. 237.

43 This recipe is very similar to one given by Sir Hugh Platt, *The Jewel House of Arts and Nature*, London, 1594, p. 76.

44 Harvey, *Mediaeval Craftsmen*, 1975, p. 146.

45 Salzman, *Building in England*, 1952, p. 155; for types of parget, see Ayres, *Building the Georgian City*, 1998, p. 199.

46 Wilfred Kemp, *The Practical Plasterer*, Crosby Lockwood and Son, London, (1893) 1926, p. 145. See also Ayres, *Building the Georgian City*, 1998, pp. 196, 197.

47 Kemp, *The Practical Plasterer*, 1926, pp. 67, 70.

48 Harvey, *Mediaeval Craftsmen*, 1975, plate 45.

49 Loudon, *Encyclopaedia*, 1836, p. 274.

50 B. Anthony Bax, *The English Parsonage*, John Murray, London, 1964, p. 124.

51 Ayres, *Building the Georgian City*, 1998, fig. 302, p. 203.

Chapter 4: Doors and Doorways

1   The gates (now in the British Museum) for the palace of Shalmaneser III (858–824 BC) at Balawat in modern Iraq are harre-hung. Doors of this type remained in use in nineteenth-century Egypt (Letters page, *County Life*, 28 January 1965).

2   A. T. Lucas, 'Wattle and straw mat doors in Ireland', *Arctica, Studia Ethnographica Upsaliensia*, XI, pp. 16–35, fig. 7.

3   S. O. Addy, *The Evolution of the English House* (1898), George Allen and Unwin, London, 1933, p. 64.

4   I. F. Grant, *Highland Folk Ways*, Routledge and Kegan Paul, London, 1961, p. 165.

5   Iorwerth C. Peate, *The Welsh House*, Hugh Evans and Sons, Liverpool, 1946, p. 123.

6   J. Evans, *Letters . . . in North Wales in 1798*, C. and R. Baldwin, London, 1804, p. 161.

7   Translated from the Irish by Lucas, 'Wattle and Straw Mat Doors in Ireland', p. 24.

8   Although for small cupboard doors one slab of wood was sufficiently substantial for these projecting horns to create harre hinges, this was not possible on an architectural scale. The direct successor to the harre hinge is the pin hinge but these are most suitable for lightweight cupboard doors in furniture, etc.

9   R. T. Mason, *Framed Buildings of the Weald* (1964), Coach Publishing House, Horsham, 1969, pp. 73–6.

10 An example may be seen in the front door of the Coscib Farmhouse at the Ulster Folk Museum. Between 1700 and 1840 Ireland as a whole saw a fourfold increase in population hence the deforestation – Oliver Rackham, *Trees and Woodland in the British Landscape* (1976), Phoenix Press, London, 2001, p. 90.

11 A double door of this type is illustrated in the *Journal of the Cork Historical and Archaeological Society*, Vol. 76, 1971. A. T. Lucas, 'A straw roof lining at Stradbally, Co. Waterford'. A vertically dividing half-door of the early seventeenth century remains in place in the seventeenth-century core of Beech House, Upper Swainswick, Bath, and in the Almshouses at Chipping Camden, Gloucestershire, (*Country Life*, 15 August 1963, letters page) which are hinged centrally, each half leading to a different lodging.

12 Joseph Moxon, *Mechanick Exercises: or, the Doctrine of Handy-Works* (1677), Dan. Midwinter & Tho. Leigh, London, 1703, pp. 18–22.

13 Grant, *Highland Folk Ways*, 1961, pp. 165–6.

14 Moxon, *Mechanick Exercises*, London, edition printed for J. Moxon 1677–83, p. 160.

15 This architectural detail is now in the National Museum of Antiquities, Edinburgh. The Steyning Manor Farm example is similarly wood-lined.

16 Bernard Hughes, 'English domestic locks', *The Connoisseur Year Book*, London, 1957, pp. 100–8.

17 Moxon, *Mechanick Exercises*, 1703, pp. 18–22.

18 Hughes, 'English domestic locks', 1957, pp. 100–8.

19 Alexander Fenton, *Scottish Country Life*, John Donald, Edinburgh, 1976, p. 188, quoting the *Memoir of George Hope* by his daughter, 1881, p. 231.

20 '*The First Book of Architecture by Andrea Palladio* (1570) translated out of the Italian w^th: diverse other designs necessary to the art of well building by Godfrey Richards', first published in London in 1663, p. 145.

21 Richards's edition (1667) of Palladio's *First Book of Architecture*, p. 145, also Richard Neve, *The City and Country Purchaser*, London, 1726, pp. 127–8.

22 Isaac Ware, *The Complete Body of Architecture*, T. Osborne and J. Shipton, London, 1756, pp. 439, 458. In large houses a door could more easily be of a 1 : 2 proportion without being impossibly low. Even so, status could still be implied by door width (and corresponding height) as in the late sixteenth-century great hall of Shaw House, Newbury, where the door leading from the dais to the private apartments is some 4 ins wider (and some 8 ins higher) than the two doors at the lower end of the hall which lead to the service wing.

23 J. C. Loudon, *An Encyclopaedia of Cottage, Farm, and Villa Architecture*, Longman, London, (1833) 1836, pp. 39, 49.

Chapter 5: Windows

1   Henry Laver, 'Ancient types of huts at Athelney', *Somerset Archaeological and Natural History Society*, Vol. 55, 1909, pp. 175–80.

2   The informant was speaking in Irish. A. T. Lucas, 'Wattle and straw mat doors in Ireland, *Arctica, Studia, Ethnographica Upsaliensia*, XI, p. 16.

3   Richard Carew, *The Survey of Cornwall*, London, 1602, also 1769 edition. See also S. O. Addy, *The Evolution of the English House* (1898), George Allen and Unwin, London, 1933, pp. 146, 147, 151.

4   L. F. Salzman, *Building in England down to 1540*, Clarendon Press, Oxford, 1952, p. 93.

5   Ibid., p. 94. Today masons use the word 'mould' in reference to their zinc templates – although in the past wood and sheet iron was used for this purpose.

6   Ibid., p. 174.

7   Lucas, 'Wattle and straw mat doors in Ireland', p. 22. In England workshops are known to have gone without glass in their windows until the 1880s – see J. Ayres, *Building the Georgian City*, Yale University Press, New Haven and London, 1998, p. 189.

8   Ayres, *Building the Georgian City*, 1998, p. 191.

9   Salzman, *Building in England*, 1952, p. 256.

10 H. Chandlee Forman, *Old Buildings, Gardens and Furniture in Tidewater, Maryland*, Cambridge, MD, 1967, p. 21.

11 B. Anthony Bax, *The English Parsonage*, John Murray, London, 1964, p. 153.

12 William Harrison, *Description of England* (1577) ed. by F. J. Furnival, Vol. II, London, 1877, p. 236.

13 For lattice doors to cheeserooms, see Pamela M. Slocombe, *Wiltshire Farmhouses and Cottages 1500–1850*, Wiltshire Buildings Record, Devizes, 1988, p. 32, figs. 42, 43; Iorwerth C. Peate, *The Welsh House*, Hugh Evans and Sons, Liverpool, 1946, p. 185.

14 J. Evans, *Letters . . . in North Wales in 1798*, C. and R. Baldwin, London, 1804, p. 160.

15 Salzman, *Building in England*, 1952, p. 173.

16 Quoted in ibid., p. 173.

17 Thomas More, *Utopia*, (1516) translated by Paul Turner, Penguin Books, London, 1965, Book II, p. 72.

18 Sir Hugh Platt, *The Jewel House of Art and Nature*, London, 1594, pp. 76–7.

19 Lucas, 'Wattle and straw mat doors in Ireland', p. 17.

20 S. O. Addy, *The Evolution of the English House* (1898), George Allen and Unwin, London, 1933, p. 64. These mud houses also had doors of 'harden'.

21 Peate, *The Welsh House*, 1946, p. 186.

22 Salzman, *Building in England*, 1952, p. 185.

23 Quoted by Addy, *The Evolution of the English House*, 1933, p. 132.

24 *Encyclopaedia Britannica*, 11th edition, 1910–11, see 'pane'.

25 Department of Manuscripts, No. 37.339.

26 Platt, *The Jewel House of Art and Nature*, 1594, pp. 38–9 which concerns tracing drawings through glass.

27 Mark Girouard, *Robert Smythson and the Elizabethan Country House*, Yale University Press, New Haven and London, 1983, pp. 195–6, fig. 123. The timber frontage of Sir Paul Pindar's House (*c.* 1600) from London, which has abrupt bay windows of this kind, is preserved in the Victoria and Albert Museum.

28 The earliest documented specialist plane-maker identified so far is Thomas Granford (active 1687–1713) at the sign of the Three Planes, Queen Street, London. W. L. Goodman, revised by Jane

and Mark Rees, *British Planemakers from 1700*, 3rd edition, Roy Arnold, Needham Market, 1993.

29 J. H. Peel, *An Englishman's Home*, Cassell, London, 1972, p. 151. See also Ayres, *Building the Georgian City*, 1998, Appendix I.

30 *Captain Hall in America* by 'an American' (the author is revealed, on p. 5, to have been a woman). Carey and Lea, Philadelphia, 1830, p. 13. The subject of the book was Captain Basil Hall, R.N. Andrew Derrick, '1670 Sash Window Revealed in Newmarket', Suffolk Historic Buildings group, *Newsletter No. 9*, Spring 1997, pp. 9–11.

31 John Woodforde, *Georgian Houses for All*, Routledge and Kegan Paul, London, p. 113.

32 Christopher Morris, ed., *The Journeys of Celia Fiennes*, Cresset Press, London, 1947, p. 339.

33 Harold Hughes and Herbert L. North, *The Old Cottages of Snowdonia* (1908), Snowdonia National Park Society, Capel Curig, Gwynedd, Wales, 1979, p. 61.

34 See particularly Hentie Louw, 'The origin of the sash window', *Architectural History*, No. 26, 1983, pp. 49–72.

35 For the sash shutters in the White Hart see F. W. B. Charles, *Conservation of Timber Buildings*, Hutchinson, London, 1986, p. 224. Horman quoted by C. F. Innocent, *The Development of English Building Construction* (1916), David and Charles, Newton Abbot, 1971, p. 261.

36 Blair Gift, Metropolitan Museum of Art, New York, 45–114.

37 M. W. Barley, *The English Farmhouse and Cottage*, Routledge and Kegan Paul, London, 1961, pp. 263–4.

38 Information from Nick Tyson of the Regency Town House, Hove, 2001.

39 Ayres, *Building the Georgian City*, 1998, p. 145.

40 Morris, ed., *The Journeys of Celia Fiennes*, 1947, p. 74.

41 *Chamber's Encyclopaedia*, 1862, see 'glass'.

42 J. C. Loudon, *An Encyclopaedia of Cottage, Farm, and Villa Architecture*, Longman, London, (1833) 1836, p. 154.

43 Hentie Louw, 'The rise of the metal window . . . c. 1750–1783', *Construction History*, Vol. 3, 1987.

44 Barley, *The English Farmhouse and Cottage*, 1961, pp. 267–8.

45 Bax, *The English Parsonage*, 1964, p. 143.

46 Ibid., p. 143.

47 Lorna Weatherill, *Consumer Behaviour and Material Culture in Britain 1660–1760*, Routledge, London and New York, (1988) 1996, p. 8.

48 Ivan and Elizabeth Hall, *Georgian Hull*, Hull Civic Society, Hull, 1978/9, p. 109, and Ayres, *Building the Georgian City*, 1998, p. 227.

49 *A Catalogue of the House and Gardens at Chelsea, and all thereunto belonging, of the Most Noble Robert Earl of Orford*, 1747, p. 9. The effects remaining in Sir Robert Walpole's Chelsea house were sold by Mr Cock on 13 April 1747.

50 Marcus Wiffen, *The Eighteenth Century Houses of Williamsburg*, revised edition, Colonial Williamsburg Foundation, 1984, p. 20. It is perhaps possible that the use of fly screens was a Colonial innovation and that Robert Walpole, the 1st Earl of Orford (1676–1745), had been introduced to them by his near neighbour in Chelsea, Sir Hans Sloane (1660–1753), who had spent some years in Jamaica.

51 Sir Ambrose Heal, *The London Furniture Makers*, Batsford, London, 1953, p. 15.

52 Illustrated in Charles Saumarez Smith, *Eighteenth Century Decoration . . .* , Weidenfeld and Nicolson, London, 1993, pp. 208–9, fig. 202.

53 Loudon, *Encyclopaedia*, 1836, p. 342.

54 The 1853 watercolour drawings of Renishaw Hall, Derbyshire, by Mrs Campbell Swinton show venetian blinds in use in the Oak Parlour and transparent blinds painted in imitation of stained glass. Both watercolours are reproduced in John

Cornforth, *English Interiors 1790–1848*, Barrie and Jenkins, London, 1978, plates 71, 73.

55 Nathaniel Whittock, *The Decorative Painters' and Glaziers' Guide*, London, 1827, p. 188. Another source of information is the unpublished thesis by William J. Jedlick, 'Landscape window shades of the nineteenth century in New York State and New England', New York State Historical Society, Cooperstown. The Abby Aldrich Rockefeller Folk Art Collection at Williamsburg, Virginia, holds a photocopy of this thesis. See also Elaine Eff, 'The painted window screens of Baltimore, Maryland', *The Clarion*, Museum of American Folk Art, New York, Spring 1976, pp. 5–12. This article discusses a late manifestation of these externally painted screens introduced to Baltimore in 1913 by a Czechoslovak immigrant named William Oktavec.

56 Loudon, *Encyclopaedia*, 1836, p. 34.

57 Ibid., p. 341.

Chapter 6: Floors

1 L. F. Salzman, *Building in England down to 1540*, Clarendon Press, Oxford, 1952, p. 146.

2 Henry Best, *Rural Economy in Yorkshire 1641*, Surtees Society, Durham, 1857, p. 107, 'For Makinge and Mendinge of Earthen Floores'.

3 J. Binns, *The Miseries and Beauties of Ireland*, Longman, London, 1837, pp. 1, 112.

4 Henry Aldrich (1647–1710), *Elementa Architecturæ*, 1789 – only Book I and part of Book II were published, in an edition of about ten copies.

5 *Building News*, 3 September 1869, quoted by C. F. Innocent, *The Development of English Building Construction* (1916), David and Charles, Newton Abbot, 1971, p. 100.

6 Iorwerth C. Peate, *The Welsh House*, Hugh Evans and Sons, Liverpool, 1946, p. 173.

7 *Chamber's Encyclopaedia*, 1862, see 'carpets'. In eighteenth-century Stockholm this continued as a Christmas tradition. See Peter Thornton, *Authentic Décor*, Weidenfeld and Nicolson, London, 1984, p. 181, which reproduces a drawing of 1798 that illustrates such a custom.

8 Sir Hugh Platt, *The Jewel House of Art and Nature*, London, 1594, p. 76.

9 Peate, *The Welsh House*, 1946, p. 172.

10 Harold Hughes and Herbert L. North, *The Old Cottages of Snowdonia* (1908), Snowdonia National Park, Denbigh, 1979, pp. 65–6.

11 Translation quoted by B. Anthony Bax, *The English Parsonage*, John Murray, London, 1964, p. 47. For the Latin original with the revolting details in full, see Nathaniel Lloyd, *A History of the English House*, Architectural Press, London, (1931) 1975, p. 80.

12 T. Hudson Turner, *Some Account of Domestic Architecture*, 2nd edition, London, 1877, p. 93.

13 Innocent, *The Development of English Building Construction*, 1971, p. 158.

14 Isaac Ware, *The Complete Body of Architecture*, T. Osborne and J. Shipton, London, 1756, p. 123.

15 Innocent, *The Development of English Building Construction*, 1971, p. 161, quoting T. W. Troup writing mainly about Norfolk. See also B. Lawrence Hurst, 'Concrete and the structural use of cements in England before 1890', *Proc. Inst. Civ. Engrs. Structs. & Bldgs*, No. 116, August/November 1996, pp. 285–6, which discusses lime-ash floors.

16 Ware, *The Complete Body of Architecture*, 1756, p. 123.

17 I am indebted to Mr James Chapman of Norwich City Architects' Department for this information.

18   Christopher Morris, ed., *The Journeys of Celia Fiennes*, Casset Press, London, 1947, p. 153.

19   Ibid., p. 268.

20   Further information on English limestones which are capable of being polished so as to appear like 'marble' may be found in 'The use of Purbeck marble in mediaeval England', an unpublished thesis by James Ayres for the Institute of Education, London University, 1961.

21   Morris, ed., *The Journeys of Celia Fiennes*, 1947, p. 12, written *c.* 1685.

22   See J. Ayres, *Building the Georgian City*, Yale University Press, New Haven and London, 1998, p. 97.

23   Peate, *The Welsh House*, 1946, p. 174.

24   Joseph Wright, *The English Dialect Dictionary*, Vol. IV, 1903, p. 527, see 'pitch'.

25   Peate, *The Welsh House*, 1946, p. 174.

26   In some houses slates were cut to fit neatly under the feet of long-case clocks to prevent dust gathering underneath. Sometimes these pieces of slate were carved to resemble a pile of books. Information in a letter to the author from Mrs Gwenno Caffell, 16 January 1981.

27   The term 'Flanders brick' may be a folk memory distorting the historical use in Britain of imported flooring tiles. Henry Yevele is known to have used at Westminster Palace '8000 tiles of Flanders for paving floors'. See Salzman, *Building in England down to 1540*, 1952, p. 145. Examples of 'Bath brick' may be seen in Bridgewater Museum.

28   Quoted by Dorothy Hartley, *Made in England*, Eyre Methuen, London, (1939) 1977, p. 136.

29   See *Scottish Home and Country*, the magazine of the Scottish Women's Rural Institutes, Vol. 11, No. 3, March 1935.

30   Marie Hartley and Joan Ingilby, *Life and Tradition in the Yorkshire Dales*, Dent, London, 1968, p. 4.

31   Peate, *The Welsh House*, 1946, p. 172.

32   S. O. Addy, *The Evolution of the English House* (1898), George Allen and Unwin, London, 1933, pp. 134–5.

33   S. R. Jones, *The Village Homes of England*, Studio, London, 1912, p. 114.

34   Hartley, *Made in England*, 1977, pp. 136–8, and Jane C. Nylander, *Our Own Snug Fireside*, Yale University Press, New Haven and London, 1994, p. 119.

35   Addy, *The Evolution of the English House*, 1933, p. 135.

36   I am indebted to the late Mrs George Morris of Washington, DC, for showing me these examples. The two English floors have been illustrated by John Fowler and John Cornforth, *English Decoration in the 18th Century*, Barrie and Jenkins, London, 1974. The Crowcombe Court floor also occurs in Christopher Hussey's *English Country Houses, Early Georgian 1715–1760*, Country Life, London, 1955.

37   John Cornforth, *English Interiors 1790–1848: The Quest for Comfort* Barrie and Jenkins, London, 1978, fig. 110, p. 93.

38   William Wordsworth, *Personal Talk*, London, 1888, quoted by Lloyd, *History of the English House*, 1975.

39   Very good American examples are illustrated by Nina Fletcher Little, *American Decorative Wall Painting 1700–1850*, E. P. Dutton, New York, 1952, plate xi and fig. 160. A reproduction of a floor of this kind may be seen in the textile room at the American Museum in Britain.

40   J. C. Loudon, *An Encyclopaedia of Cottage, Farm, and Villa Architecture* (1833), London, 1842, p. 344.

41   Ian Gow, 'A stencilled room and a painted floor: the archaeology of Edinburgh's New Town', Architectural Heritage Society of Scotland *Bulletin*, No. 8, September 1981.

42   Addy, *The Evolution of the English House*, 1898, p. 26.

43   Turner, *Some Account of Domestic Architecture*, 1877, p. 92.

44   Richard Carew, *The Survey of Cornwall* (1602), London, 1769, pp. 66–7.

45   William Aiton, of Strathaven, *General View of the Agriculture of Ayr*, Glasgow, 1811, pp. 114–15.

46   M. E. Wood, *The English Medieval House*, Dent, London, 1965, p. 67, regarding *sol*: floor.

47   Quoted by F. G. Emmison, *Elizabethan Life*, Essex County Council, Chelmsford, 1976, p. 9, regarding Gilbert Isaac's will.

48   Joseph Moxon, *Mechanick Exercises* (1677), Dan. Midwinter & Tho. Leigh, London, 1703, pp. 149–53.

49   Information kindly supplied by Mr James Chapman of Norwich City Architects' Department.

50   Moxon, *Mechanick Exercises*, 1703, p. 150.

51   Morris, ed., *The Journeys of Celia Fiennes*, 1947, p. 345.

52   Innocent, *The Development of English Building Construction*, 1971, p. 163, fig. 52.

53   Best, *Rural Economy in Yorkshire 1641*, 1857, p. 125.

54   *Chamber's Encyclopaedia*, 1862, see 'floors'.

55   Bax, *The English Parsonage*, 1964, p. 122.

56   Rodris Roth, *Floor Coverings in 18th Century America*, Smithsonian Press, Washington, DC, 1967, p. 19, quotes Mrs John Adams writing from Paris in 1784, 'then a man-servant with foot brushes drives round your room dancing here and there like a Merry Andrew. This is calculated to take from your foot every atom of dirt, and leave the room in a few moments as he found it.'

57   Caroline Halsted, *Investigations or Travels in the Boudoir*, London, 1837, p. 17.

58   The long table in the Chelsea Arts Club, Church Street, London, has for years been scrubbed with beer and sand to produce such an effect. For the use of these methods in England, see Fowler and Cornforth, *English Decoration in the 18th Century*, 1978, p. 210, which cites Hannah Glass (1760), Samuel and Sarah Adams' *The Complete Servant* (1825, p. 280), *The Housekeeping Book of Susannah Whatman* of the 1770s (ed. by Thomas Balston, 1956), Mrs Boscawen's *Admiral's Widow* (1787, plate 23) and M. Gorsley's *A Tour of London*, Vol. I (1772, p. 73).

59   See S. W. Wolsey and R. W. P. Luff, *Furniture in England, The Age of the Joiner*, Arthur Barker, London, 1968, p. 50, fig. 1.

60   Turner, *Some Account of Domestic Architecture*, 1877, p. 98.

61   Ibid.

62   Carew, *The Survey of Cornwall*, 1769, pp. 18–19. Information on marram-grass mats from the leaflet issued in 1982 by the Bodeilio Weaving Centre in Anglesey.

63   Christopher Gilbert, James Lomax and Anthony Wells-Cole, *Country House Floors, 1660–1850*, Exhibition Catalogue, Temple Newsom, Leeds, 1987, p. 101, ref. item TN EA 36/56(24).

64   Roth, *Floor Coverings in 18th Century America*, 1967.

65   R. T. H. Halsey and Charles O. Cornelius, *A Handbook of the American Wing*, Metropolitan Museum of Art, New York, 1924.

66   Quoted by Roth, *Floor Coverings in 18th Century America*, 1967, p. 17.

67   I am indebted to Sir Robert Spencer Nairn of Nairn Floors International Ltd. and to Miss Andrea Kerr of Kirkcaldy Museum and Art Gallery for this information.

68   I am indebted to Mr Anthony Davis and Mr Ronald Clarke of Coventry City Art Gallery and Museum for this information.

69   John Smith, *The Art of Painting in Oyl* (1676), London, 1705, p. 77.

70   Butcher's edition of *The Art of Painting in Oyl*, London, 1821, p. 22.

71   R. Barnes, 'Papers on Floor-Cloth Manufacture 1857–61', manuscript in National Art Library, London (MS. L 1911–1939 II R.C.H. 1 B), p. 15. Joseph Barnes's successor John Barnes operated from the City Road, Moorfields, London from 1774 to

1779 and as John Barnes & Son from 1780 to 1785. See Bodleian Library Exhibition Catalogue, *A Nation of Shopkeepers*, Oxford, Autumn 2001, Cat. 7, p. 7.

72 Photograph in the Feilden Collection within the Ambrose Heal Collection at the British Museum, 30.2.

73 Letter from Charles Carroll of Annapolis, MD, 24 February 1767, to William Anderson, a London merchant, quoted by Roth, *Floor Coverings in 18th Century America*, 1967, p. 12.

74 Ambrose Heal Collection, British Museum, 91.24.

75 Roth, *Floor Coverings in 18th Century America*, 1967, p. 12.

76 Loudon, *Encyclopaedia*, 1842, p. 346.

77 Charles L. Eastlake, *Hints on Household Taste* (1868), 3rd edition (revised), London, 1872, pp. 51–2.

78 Ambrose Heal Collection, British Museum, 30.24, the trade-card of Southgate and Mitchell.

79 Virginia Surtees, *Charlotte Canning*, John Murray, London, 1975.

80 Ambrose Heal Collection, British Museum, 30.30. 'Leghorn' was a widely used English name for Livorno, Italy.

81 Also in the Heal Collection.

82 Heal Collection, 30.11, 30.12.

83 Illustrated in the *Art-Journal Catalogue*, 1862, p. 42.

84 Ambrose Heal Collection, British Museum, 72.103.

85 Heal Collection 30.4. In 1804 Mr Booth purchased at the same address, 19 New Spring Gardens, floor cloth from Downing & Co, Receipt, Ambrose Heal Collection, British Museum, 30.9.

86 Wayne and Ruger of Charlestown advertised in 1768 that they sold 'Floor Cloths, painted as neat as any from London'. Roth, *Floor Coverings in 18th Century America*, 1967, pp. 12–13.

87 Ambrose Heal Collection, British Museum, 30.4.

88 Little, *American Decorative Wall Painting*, 1972, p. 76.

89 *Chamber's Encyclopaedia*, London, 1862, see 'floors'.

90 Ibid.

91 *Encyclopaedia Britannica*, 11th edition, 1910–11, see 'floorcloth'.

92 Fowler and Cornforth, *English Decoration in the 18th Century*, 1974, p. 216.

93 These *Travels* were published in London in 1794 and are quoted by Roth, *Floor Coverings in 18th Century America*, 1967, p. 29. See also Nylander, *Our Own Snug Fireside*, 1994, p. 122.

94 Halsted, *Investigations*, 1837, pp. 18–19.

95 *Chamber's Encyclopaedia*, London, 1862, see 'list' and 'fillet'.

96 *Country House Floors* Exhibition Catalogue, Temple Newsom House, Leeds, 1987, p. 95.

97 See Bax, *The English Parsonage*, 1964, p. 155, quoting Julius Hare's *The Story of My Life*, Vol. I, p. 137.

98 Halsted, *Investigations*, 1837, p. 9.

99 Ibid., pp. 10–11, 12.

100 Barnstaple Museum, north Devon has a very fine and rare Axminster table carpet of this period.

101 Loudon, *Encyclopaedia*, 1842, p. 344.

102 Lady Llanover, ed., *The Autobiography and Correspondence of Mary Granville, Mrs. Delany*, Vol. III, London, 1861, p. 176.

103 Loudon, *Encyclopaedia*, 1842, p. 345.

104 Ibid, p. 345

105 Halsted, *Investigations*, 1837, p. 16.

106 M. E. B, *Hookies and Proddies*, information sheet published by Abbot Hall Art Gallery and Museum, Kendal, *c*. 1980.

107 Ibid.

108 Flora Thompson, *Lark Rise in Candleford* (1939), Penguin, London, 1973, p. 19.

Chapter 7: Ceilings

1 F. G. Emmison, *Elizabethan Life*, Essex County Council, Chelmsford, 1976, pp. 9, 13.

2 Desmond McCourt and E. Estyn Evans, 'A late 17th-century farmhouse at Shantallow near Londonderry', *Ulster Folklife*, Vol. 14, 1968, pp. 14–23.

3 M. W. Barley, *The English Farmhouse and Cottage*, Routledge and Kegan Paul, London, 1961, Chapter 5, 'The highland zone'.

4 A. T. Lucas, 'Straw roof lining at Stradbally, Co. Waterford', *Journal of the Cork Historical and Archaeological Society*, Vol. 76, 1971, pp. 81–3. For an illustration of such a 'base coat' of straw, see J. Cox and John R. L. Thorpe, *Devon Thatch*, Devon Books, Tiverton, 2001, p. 51.

5 Lucas, 'Straw roof lining . . .', 1971, p. 83.

6 Ibid, p. 83.

7 Peter Nicholson, Edward Lomax and Thomas Gunyon, *Encyclopaedia of Architecture . . . Nicholson's Dictionary . . .* 2 vols, Peter Jackson, London, 1852. Summer beams were also known as 'somers', 'girders' and 'dormants'. See also C. F. Innocent, *The Development of English Building Construction* (1916), David and Charles, Newton Abbot, 1971, p. 164. Despite the survival of the term 'breast-summer' or 'bressummer', the member which supports the joists is now often known in Britain as a 'bridging beam' (Richard Harris, *Timber-Framed Buildings*, Shire Publications, Aylesbury, 1978, p. 26) or as a 'girder' (James Stevens Curl, *Encyclopaedia of Architectural Terms*, Donhead, Shaftesbury, 1992).

8 Innocent, *The Development of English Building Construction*, 1971, p. 163, fig. 52.

9 Information from Mr James Chapman, Norwich City Architects' Department.

10 Illustrated by Victor Chinnery, *Oak Furniture . . .*, Antique Collectors Club, Woodbridge, 1979, p. 36, fig. 1:9; Timothy Easton, 'Ritual marks on historic timber', *Weald and Downland Museum 'Newsletter'*, Spring 1999, pp. 22–8.

11 Innocent, *The Development of English Building Construction*, 1971, p. 160.

12 Ibid., p. 161, quoting F. W. Troup.

13 Information from Mr James Chapman, Norwich City Architects' Department.

14 The reeds no doubt came from the nearby marshes known as the Somerset Levels.

15 Royal Commission on Historical Monuments, *Stamford*, HMSO, London, 1977, p. lxix. For further discussion of these plaster floor/ceilings, see B. L. Hurst, 'Concrete and the structural use of cements in England before 1890', *Proceedings of the Institution of Civil Engineers*, No. 116, August/November 1996, p. 285.

16 William Harrison, *Description of England* (1577) ed. by F. J. Furnival, Vol. II, London, 1877, Chapter 12, p. 235.

17 Information from Mr James Chapman, Norwich City Architects' Department.

18 Herbert Cescinsky and Ernest Gribble, *Early English Furniture and Woodwork*, George Routledge, London, 1922, Vol. I, p. 202, fig. 205.

19 Joseph Gwilt, *Encyclopaedia of Architecture*, revised by Wyatt Papworth, London, 1876, p. 601.

20 This very remarkable house was described by Nikolaus Pevsner, *North Somerset and Bristol*, Penguin Books, 1958, p. 199, before its outrageous destruction.

21 E. Guy Dawber and W. Galsworthy Davie, *Cottages and Farmhouses in the Cotswolds*, Batsford, London, 1905, p. 15.

22 Innocent, *The Development of English Building Construction*, 1971, p. 167.

23 Sir Balthazar Gerbier, *Counsel and Advice to all Builders*, London, 1663, p. 81.

24 John and Jane Penoyre, *Decorative Plasterwork in the Houses of Somerset 1500–1700*, West Country Books, Tiverton, 1994.

25 I am indebted to the Hon. Desmond Guinness for drawing my attention to this example of Irish plasterwork.

26 J. T. Smith, *Nollekens and His Times* (1829), Vol. II, London, 1919, p. 102.

27 Ibid., p. 174.

28 J. C. Loudon, *Encyclopaedia of Cottage, Farm, and Villa Architecture*, Longman, London, (1833) 1836, p. 273, para. 566.

29 Ibid., p. 273, para. 568.

30 Gwilt, *Encyclopaedia*, 1876, p. 679, para. 2251.

31 I am indebted to my father, Arthur J. J. Ayres (1902–1985) for this information.

Chapter 8: Stairs

1 M. W. Barley, *The English Farmhouse and Cottage*, Routledge and Kegan Paul, London, 1961, p. 63.

2 Ibid., p. 63.

3 Margaret Wood's thesis for the 'first-floor hall' (*The English Mediaeval House*, Phoenix House, London, 1965) was first seriously contested by John Blair (G. Meirion-Jones and M. Jones, eds., *Manorial Domestic Buildings in England and Northern France*, Society of Antiquaries, London, 1993) and is well summarised by Edward Impey, 'The Manor House: Boothby Pagnell, Lincolnshire', *Country Life*, 29 July 1999.

4 The peel towers of the far north of England derive their name from the 'pele' or 'pale', as in the paling which originally surrounded these towers (S. O. E. D.). The type may date back to the late twelfth century (Pendragon Castle, Cumbria), are more typical of the fourteenth century, but are most numerous in their vernacular form from the early seventeenth century down to about 1700 – of this last phase about 180 survive. See Barley, *The English Farmhouse and Cottage*, 1961, pp. 8–9 and the same author's *Houses and History*, Faber and Faber, London, 1986, p. 250.

5 Barley, *The English Farmhouse and Cottage*, 1961, p. 170.

6 Samuel Johnson, *A Journey to the Western Islands of Scotland* (1775), 1886, p. 28.

7 S. O. Addy, *The Evolution of the English House* (1898), George Allen and Unwin, London, 1933, p. 63. This good example of a 'chaamer' from Staveley, Yorkshire, is illustrated and described by S. R. Jones in *The Village Homes of England*, London, 1912, p. 118.

8 For East Anglian examples see Barley, *The English Farmhouse and Cottage*, 1961, p. 68.

9 Joseph Gwilt, *Encyclopaedia of Architecture*, revised by Wyatt Papworth, London, 1876, p. 647, 'solid steps were housed into the carriage.'

10 Addy, *The Evolution of the English House*, p. 77.

11 J. C. Loudon, *Encyclopaedia of Cottage, Farm, and Villa Architecture*, Longman, London, (1833) 1836, p. 79, fig. 37. A slight variation on this system is illustrated by Alexander Fenton and Bruce Walker, *The Rural Architecture of Scotland*, John Donald, Edinburgh, 1981, p. 159, fig. 145, North Lodge, Rossie Priory, Abernyte, Perthshire. The London-based architectural practice of Donald Insall and Partners has used this type of stair in restored historic buildings such as the Benjamin Franklin House, Craven Street, London – with the evident approval of the authorities.

12 Barley, *The English Farmhouse and Cottage*, 1961, p. 11.

13 Ibid., p. 158.

14 Ibid., p. 73.

15 Nicholas Cooper (*Houses of the Gentry 1480–1680*, Yale University Press, New Haven and London, 1999, p. 313) has argued that Palladian influence in Britain may be present as early as the late sixteenth century in houses such as Hardwick Hall – or could this be the persistence of the first-floor hall discussed above?

16 C. F. Innocent, *The Development of English Building Construction* (1916), David and Charles, Newton Abbot, 1971, pp. 168–70.

17 Barley, *The English Farmhouse and Cottage*, 1961, p. 73.

18 Ibid., p. 84.

19 Nathaniel Lloyd, *A History of the English House*, Architectural Press, London, (1931) 1975, fig. 819.

20 Barley, *The English Farmhouse and Cottage*, 1961, p. 114. Other examples include the stair in the service wing of Shaw House (*c.* 1585), Newbury, Berkshire and another in Queen Hoo Hall (1580s) – for the latter see John Cornforth, *Country Life*, 15 March 1962, p. 596, fig. 8.

21 Barley, *The English Farmhouse and Cottage*, 1961, p. 138.

22 I am indebted to Arthur Ayres (1902–85) for this information.

23 For Boston Manor see the article by Arthur Oswald in the magazine *Country Life*, 18 March 1965, and for the Colchester example see the National Monuments Record photograph BB 51/2357. A painted staircase of this kind of *c.* 1630 is at Sutton House, east London (*Country Life*, 3 November 1999). In 2001 similar painted work was discovered on the walls, where a seventeenth-century staircase had once been located in Ightham Mote, Kent.

24 The late Charles Montgomery noted the way in which wood-turners might throw a mahogany column for a tea table or a master pattern for casting the columns of a pair of brass andirons. Charles Montgomery and Patricia E. Kane, eds., *American Art: 1750–1810 Towards Independence*, New York Graphic Society, Boston, 1976, p. 53.

25 Barley, *The English Farmhouse and Cottage*, 1961, pp. 219–20.

26 Gwilt, *Encyclopaedia*, 1876, p. 648.

27 Ibid., p. 569.

28 Batty Langley, *The Builder's Jewel*, R. Ware, London, 1754, p. 38. It should be noted that a staircase demands more headroom when descending than when ascending. Loudon, *Encyclopaedia*, 1836, p. 1141. Gwilt, *Encyclopaedia*, 1876, fig. 785.

29 Loudon, *Encyclopaedia*, 1836, p. 1141.

30 Gwilt, *Encyclopaedia*, 1876, fig. 785.

31 Ibid., fig. 787.

Chapter 9: Paint and Painting

1 E.g. Ian C. Bristow, *Interior House-Painting, Colour and Technology 1615–1840*, Yale University Press, New Haven and London, 1996. For the reasons outlined the work of the 'upholder' is excluded from this book – see Geoffrey Beard, *Upholsterers and Interior Furnishing in England 1530–1840*, Yale University Press, New Haven and London, 1997.

2 Robert Dossie, *The Handmaid to the Arts*, Vol. I, London, 1758, p. 2.

3 For a discussion of this and other matters see J. Ayres, *Building the Georgian City*, Yale University Press, New Haven and London, 1998, Chapters 8, 9, and J. Ayres, *The Artist's Craft*, Phaidon, Oxford, 1985, pp. 86–133.

4 Russet was a very bright red pigment which rapidly faded to brown. It was made from brazil wood. The Summers trade-lable is illustrated on the letters page in the magazine *Country Life*, 17 March 1960.

5 Marjorie Reeves, *Sheep Bell and Ploughshare*, Moonraker Press, Bradford on Avon, Wiltshire, 1978, p. 106. A. S. Davidson, *Marine Art and Liverpool*, Waine Research Pub., Wolverhampton, 1986, pp. 85–6.

6 John Abbot, quoted by Ayres, *Building the Georgian City*, 1998, p. 199. John Martin manuscript, 1699–1701, p. 6, Sir John Soane's Museum, London.

7   A mussel shell in use as a container for paint is shown in *St Luke Painting the Virgin and Child*, school of Quinten Massys (1465–1530), National Gallery, London.

8   Collapsible metal tubes for oil paint were invented in 1841 by John G. Rand, an American portrait-painter working in London (see Ayres, *The Artist's Craft*, 1985, p. 115). Bladder colours were messy – in 1739–40 Jeffery Whitaker, a member of a Wiltshire farming family of Bratton, 'rode over to Bradford [on Avon] ¾ after 4 for paint, it got out of the bladder and painted my cloathes.' Reeves, *Sheep Bell and Ploughshare*, 1978, pp. 20–1.

9   R. Campbell, *The London Tradesman*, London, 1747, pp. 103–4.

10   Edkins manuscript, Bristol Central Library, Reference Division, B20196 Strong Room.

11   Meggitt's trade-label illustrated in Ayres, *Building the Georgian City*, 1998, figs. 317–18. Having served as printer to the University of Oxford, Whittock moved to London in 1828. See Bodleian Library Exhibition Catalogue, *A Nation of Shopkeepers*, Autumn 2001, Cat. 332, p. 141.

12   John Abbott manuscript and sketch book, Devon Record Office, Exeter (404 M/B1 B2). Copies in the Royal Albert Memorial Museum, Exeter and in the National Art Library (V&A), London.

13   For dyes, see Bristow, *Interior House-Painting*, 1996, Chapter 7.

14   Joan Lane, *Apprenticeship in England 1600–1914*, University College London Press, London, 1996.

15   For distempered mud floors, see Harold Hughes and Herbert L. North, *The Old Cottages of Snowdonia* (1908), Snowdonia National Park Society, Capel Curig, Gwynedd, Wales, 1979, p. 65. Whitewashing thatch – see C. F. Innocent, *The Development of English Building Construction* (1916), David and Charles, Newton Abbot, 1971, p. 212, and for limewash as a disinfectant, see Ayres, *Building the Georgian City*, 1998, p. 209.

16   Joseph Gwilt, *Encyclopaedia of Architecture*, revised by Wyatt Papworth, Vol. I , London, 1876, p. 693.

17   I have used the edition of 1701 but the British Library contains, in addition to this and the first edition, other copies dated 1673, 1675, 1681 and 1685.

18   Robert Dossie, *The Handmaid to the Arts* (1758), London, 1764, Preface, p. xx.

19   I have excluded books translated into English such as G. P. Lomazzo (1584) 1598, and accounts in larger compendiums of information. The treatise *On The Various Arts* by Theophilus (thought to have been written in the eleventh century) omits certain important chapters, some think because of pressure from the guilds (see John Harvey, *Medieval Craftsmen*, Batsford, London, 1975, pp. 50, 54), whilst Cennino Cennini's *The Craftsman's Handbook* (1437) is too much a product of the Renaissance to be considered characteristic of later vernacular traditions.

20   John Smith, *The Art of Painting in Oyl* (1676), London, 1705, p. 1.

21   Ibid., p. 1.

22   Dossie, *The Handmaid to the Arts*, 1764, Section III. 'Levigation': to grind to a powder, especially with a liquid.

23   L. F. Salzman, *Building in England down to 1540*, Clarendon Press, Oxford, 1952, pp. 157, 158. On p. 171 Salzman cites Horace Walpole's *Anecdotes of Painting in England* (1762) with its reference to the use of oil paint in England as early as 1239.

24   Innocent, *The Development of English Building Construction*, 1971, p. 1.

25   Wilfred Kemp, *The Practical Plasterer*, Crosby Lockwood and Son, London, (1893) 1926, Chapter 17.

26   Salzman, *Building in England*, 1952, pp. 159, 170.

27   The ochre was quarried and ground in a windmill near Wheatley, Oxon. Yellow ochre was also found in Cumberland and Anglesea, Ayres, *The Artist's Craft*, 1985, p. 127, fig. 180.

28   See Ayres, *The Artist's Craft*, 1985, pp. 98–102. Harvey, *Mediaeval Craftsmen*, 1975, p. 54. Dossie (*The Handmaid to the Arts*, 1764) gives instructions on the preparation of 'Nut oil . . . [which] is oil of walnuts'.

29   William Salmon, *Polygraphice: Or, The Arts of Drawing, Engraving . . . &c* (1672), Vol. II, London, 1701, Chapter 2, Recipes viii–xvi.

30   Edward Edwards, *Anecdotes of the Painters*, Leigh and Sotheby, London, 1808, p. 15. Müntz worked for Horace Walpole at Strawberry Hill. Dossie in *The Handmaid to the Arts* mentions that 'Mr Müntz has published a treatise on the subject of painting methods', Preface to 1764 edition, p. xi. The book Edwards refers to is J. H. Müntz, *Encaustic: or Count Caylus's Method of Painting in the Manner of the Ancients*, London, 1760. For a fuller account of Müntz's book on *Encaustic* see Ayres, *The Artist's Craft*, 1985, p. 95.

31   Gesso is made of a mixture of whitening and size similar to whitewash except that the proportion of size is greater, though weaker solutions are usually used for the final coats.

32   Harvey, *Mediaeval Craftsmen*, 1975, p. 164.

33   Related to casein paint was glue made from cheese. 'Mr Roubiliac, when he had to mend a broken antique [marble], would mix grated Gloucester cheese with his plaster, adding the grounds of porter and the yoke of an egg; which mixture, when dry forms a hard cement.' J. T. Smith, *Nollekens and His Times* (1829), Vol. II, London, 1919, p. 4.

34   Butcher's edition of Smith, *The Art of Painting in Oyl*, London, 1821, pp. 31–2. Innocent, *The Development of English Building Construction*, 1971, p. 59.

35   Innocent, *The Development of English Building Construction*, 1971, p. 159.

36   Lansdowne manuscript, British Library, quoted by W. A. D. Englefield, *History of the Painter-Stainers Company of London*, Chapman & Dodd, London, 1923, p. 13.

37   The Stainers are first recorded as a City Company in 1268, the Painters in 1283. See Nicholas Mander, 'Painted cloths: history, craftsmen and techniques', *Textile History*, Vol. 28, No. 2, 1997, pp. 131, 133.

38   Ibid.; E. Matley Moore, 'The painted cloths of Owlpen Manor', *Gloucestershire Country Life*, 25 August 1944; 'Painted cloths', *Transactions of the Worcester Archaeological Society*, 3rd series, Vol. 8, 1982.

39   Anthony Wells-Cole, *Art and Decoration in Elizabethan and Jacobean England*, Yale University Press, New Haven and London, 1997, pp. 275–89.

40   Mander, 'Painted cloths', 1997, p. 120; F. G. Emmison, *Elizabethan Life*, Essex County Council, Chelmsford, 1976, p. 78.

41   For illustrations of Dalecarlia hangings see the article by Per Bjurstrom, 'The gospel according to Dalcarlia', *F.M.R.*, English edition, Peterborough, November/December 1988. For these hangings shown in context see Charles Holme, *Peasant Art in Sweden, Lapland and Iceland*, The Studio, London, Paris, New York, 1910, plate 5.

42   Wells-Cole, *Art and Decoration*, 1997, pp. 275–6.

43   Tessa Watt, *Cheap Print and Popular Piety 1550–1640*, Cambridge University Press, Cambridge, (1991) 1996, p. 193.

44   William Harrison, *Description of England* (1577) ed. by F. J. Furnival, Vol. I, London, 1877, p. 235.

45   M. A. Havinden, ed., *Household and Farm Inventories in Oxfordshire 1550–90*, HMC, London, 1965, p. 113.

46   Mander, 'Painted cloths', 1997, p. 120.

47   Watt, *Cheap Print*, 1996, pp. 203, 209, 212, 219.

48 P. A. Kennedy, ed., *Nottinghamshire Household Inventories*, Thornton Society Record Series, Vol. 22, Nottingham, 1963.

49 I, Richard III, cap. 12, quoted by Mander, 'Painted cloths', 1997, p. 131 – he is quoting The Act of Parliament.

50 Mander, 'Painted cloth', 1997, p. 132.

51 Now in Colchester Museum – in fragmentary condition.

52 Mander, 'Painted cloths', 1997, p. 121, quoting from John Aubrey, *Brief Lives* ed. by O. Lawson Dick, 1960, p. 118.

53 Watt, *Cheap Print*, 1996, see especially Chapter 5, 'Stories for walls'.

54 Ibid., p. 192.

55 Ibid., pp. 191, 194.

56 *Henry IV*, Part II, II, i, 143–7 (1590–1?). So popular was the story of *The Prodigal Son* that a butcher in St Helen's, Worcestershire, is known to have owned such a stained hanging. Watt, *Cheap Print*, 1996, p. 204.

57 *Merry Wives of Windsor*, IV, v, 6–8 (1597?). This reference is either to a wall painting or a stained hanging.

58 *Love's Labours Lost*, V, ii, 574–8.

59 Duncan Thomson, *Painting in Scotland 1570–1650*, Trustees of the National Galleries of Scotland, Edinburgh, 1975, p. 38.

60 *Henry IV*, Part II, II, i, 143–7.

61 Christopher Hussey, 'Owlpen Manor, Gloucestershire', *Country Life*, Vol. 110, 9 November 1951, and *Shorter O.E.D.*, 'Hards or Hurds: the coarser parts of flax or hemp: tow'.

62 Watt, *Cheap Print*, 1996, p. 199, citing articles by Elsie Matley Moore, the chief authority on stained hangings before Nicholas Mander.

63 Reprinted in full by Dover, New York (2 vols.) as Sir Charles Lock Eastlake, *Methods and Materials of Painting of the Great Schools and Masters*, Vol. I, 1960, pp. 95–7 for the transcript with the original Latin text as a footnote. Charles L. Eastlake (1793–1865) the author of *Materials . . .* should not be confused with Charles L. Eastlake (1835–1906) whose *Hints on Household Taste* (1868) is cited on pp. xi, 97 . In addition to the Abbott manuscript (see note 12 above) a third account of the methods used may be found in Jim Murrell, 'John Guillim's book: a heraldic painter's Vade Mecum', *Walpole Society*, Vol. 57, 1993/4. I am indebted to Ann Ballantyne for drawing my attention to this.

64 Emmison, *Elizabethan Life*, 1976, p. 78.

65 John Abbott manuscript of 1662–3 (see note 12 above).

66 Watt, *Cheap Print*, 1996, p. 198. Mrs Phelps was the principal of Troy Female Seminary in New York. A 'theorem painting' was a picture stencilled on velvet.

67 One of these rather grand essays in the technique, painted in *c.* 1660 by Jan and Daniel Smit of Amsterdam, once hung in Hornsberg Manor, Kalmar County, Sweden – I am grateful to Prof. Lena Johannesson of the University of Linköping, Sweden for this information – the hanging depicts the story of Alexander the Great. In Britain it is recorded that, at an earlier date, stained hangings of this quality were designed by Holbein and (a very young) Thomas More – see Mander, 'Painted cloths', 1997, pp. 126–35.

68 Of these the late sixteenth-century hangings in the Golden Cross, Oxford, are important, as are the examples not seen by the author, at Yarde Farm, Kingsbridge, Devon.

69 For example the stained hangings at Anne of Cleves Museum, Sussex; Gainsborough Old Hall, Lincolnshire; Luton Museum, Bedfordshire; and Ipswich Museum, Suffolk.

70 A hanging of the Owlpen/Munslow school was on the London art market (Rutland Gallery) in the late twentieth century and is at present on loan to the Victoria and Albert Museum, London.

71 Hussey, 'Owlpen Manor', 9 November 1951. Earlier *Country Life* articles on 'Owlpen and its hangings' include Elsie Matley Moore (25 August 1944) and Mrs Trent-Stoughton (6 October 1906).

72 Mander, 'Painted cloths', 1997, p. 132.

73 See Peter Thornton, *Seventeenth Century Interior Decoration . . .*, Yale University Press, New Haven and London, 1978, pp. 141–2, figs. 113–14.

74 An engraving of this event together with an extensive description of this 'Machinery' is in the British Library, Map Room, K top XXVI 7. p. 1.

75 Trade-label for Michael Kirby of Clerkenwell, London, whose label of *c.* 1740–50 cites 'Sarsenet' for this purpose (Vol. I Trade Cards 27.100(1) p. 198 in the Metropolitan Museum, New York) and Nathaniel Whittock, *The Decorative Painters' and Glaziers' Guide* also favoured this material. For the use of silk for this purpose see Appendix III, for 8 April 1786. The full title of Gillray's engraving is *Exhibition of a Democratic Transparency, – with its Effect upon Patriotic Feelings* (1799) illustrated in the Exhibition Catalogue *James Gillray: The Art of Caricature*, by Richard Godfrey with Mark Hallett, Tate Britain, London, 2001, Cat. No. 67, p. 104.

76 Jerry Sampson, *Wells Cathedral: West Front*, Sutton Publishing, Stroud, Gloucestershire, 1998, Chapter 3.

77 Jonathan Alexander and Paul Binski, eds., *Age of Chivalry*, Royal Academy of Arts Catalogue published in association with Weidenfeld and Nicolson, London, 1987, p. 249, Cat. No. 137.

78 Sir Henry Wotton, *Elements of Architecture*, London, 1624, p. 96.

79 Watt, *Cheap Print*, 1996, p. 199 quoting a complaint of 1601 recorded by Sir William and Heywood Townsend, *Megalopsychy* (1682), cited by Croft-Murray, *Decorative Painting in England, 1537–1837*, Vol. I , 1962, p. 30. The references to 'posts' could refer to the multicoloured bollards used in sixteenth-century gardens. See Roy Strong, *The Artist and the Garden*, Yale University Press, New Haven and London, 2000, p. 18, fig. 5.

80 J. C. Loudon, *Encyclopaedia of Cottage, Farm, and Villa Architecture*, Longman, London, (1833) 1836, p. 274.

81 I am indebted to Mr James Chapman of Norwich City Architects' Department for this information.

82 Christopher Morris, ed., *The Journeys of Celia Fiennes*, Cresset Press, London, 1947, p. 149.

83 Lane, *Apprenticeship in England*, 1996, pp. 6, 101.

84 Salzman, *Building in England*, 1952, p. 159.

85 Nina Fletcher Little, *American Decorative Wall Painting 1700–1850*, E. P. Dutton, New York, 1952, p. 3.

86 J. H. Bettey, *The Suppression of the Monasteries in the West Country*, Alan Sutton, Gloucester, 1989, pp. 104–5.

87 Eric Mercer, *English Vernacular Houses*, HMSO, London, 1975, p. 96, fig. 67.

88 I am indebted to Mr David Whitcombe, the farmer whose house it is, for permitting me both to see and photograph his house on numerous visits. Despite the incongruity of the pebble dashing which shrouds the house, it is a remarkable example of a 'long-house' with a cross passage (one door to which is now blocked). One end, the floor of which is about 18 ins (45.7 cm) lower than the 'hall', was always known by Mr Whitcombe's father as 'the bottom end'. It probably once housed cattle.

89 See, for example, the decoration from the Red House, Sproughton, Suffolk, now exhibited in the Christchurch Mansion, Ipswich – see Arthur Oswald, *Country Life*, 26 August 1954, p. 647, fig. 11.

90 John Cornforth, 'Queen Hoo Hall, Hertfordshire' *Country Life*, 15 March 1962, p. 598, figs. 11, 12.

91 Illustrated by Nathaniel Lloyd, *A History of the English House*, Architectural Press, London, (1931) 1975, p. 403, fig. 695. A scheme, very similar to the Oxford example, has also been

recorded in the Old Blue Boar Inn, St John's Street, Winchester (Winchester Museum).

92 Englefield, *The History of the Painter-Stainers Company*, 2nd edition, London 1936, p. 68.

93 Watt, *Cheap Print*, 1996, p. 218.

94 Ibid, p. 193.

95 William Shakespeare, *The Rape of Lucrece* (1594), lines 244–5 – see Watt, *Cheap Print*, 1996, p. 219.

96 M. R. Apted, *The Painted Ceilings of Scotland 1550–1650*, HMSO, Edinburgh, 1966.

97 Anders Bugge, *Norwegian Stave Churches*, translated by Ragnar Christopherson, Dreyers Forlag, Oslo, 1953, illustrates examples in churches from the first half of the seventeenth century, plates 28, 91, 109. For domestic examples dating down to the eighteenth century (some of which imitate plaster ceilings) see Jocasta Innes, *Scandinavian Painted Décor*, Cassell, London, 1990, and Maita di Niscemi *et al.*, *Manor Houses and Castles of Sweden*, Antique Collector's Guide, Woodbridge, Suffolk, 1998.

98 Duncan Thomson, *Painting in Scotland 1570–1650*, Trustees of the National Galleries of Scotland, 1975, p. 12.

99 Ibid., pp. 11–13, 38–9.

100 For example in the chapel of Gray's Almshouses (1635), Taunton, Somerset.

101 Trevor Fawcett, *The Rise of English Provincial Art . . . 1800–1830*, Clarendon Press, Oxford, 1974, p. 17.

102 J. L. Nevinson, 'The embroidery patterns of Thomas Trevelyan', *Walpole Society*, Vol. 41, 1968. I am grateful to Margaret Swain for lending me her copy of this article.

103 E. A. Entwisle, *The Book of Wallpaper* (1954), Kingsmead Reprints, Bath, 1970, pp. 24–7.

104 In 1698 Celia Fiennes noted that the brick pillars to Patshull Park, near Shrewsbury were surmounted by 'stone heads on which stood a Turkey Cock on each, cut in stone and painted proper', in the heraldic meaning of the word. Morris, ed., *The Journeys of Celia Fiennes*, 1947 p. 229.

105 I am greatly indebted to Michael Gray of the Merchant's House Trust, Marlborough, for all his knowledge, advice and help.

106 Michael Gray, *The Merchant's House, Marlborough*, Official Guide, n.d., *c*. 2000

107 A similar version in which the 'echo' is sounded in timber is at Hatfield House, Hertfordshire, *c.* 1610.

108 Arthur Oswald, 'Boston Manor House, Middlesex', *Country Life*, 18 March 1965.

109 Anthony Woodward, 'Sutton House, London, E9', *Country Life*, 3 November 1994.

110 Colchester example, see NMR Photograph BB51/2357.

111 Peter de Hooch's painting of the interior of *Amsterdam Town Hall* is in the Thyssen-Bornemisza Collection. Striped wall hangings of this kind may have been of worsted – see Peter Thornton, *Authentic Décor*, Weidenfeld and Nicolson, London, 1984, pp. 86–7. Other sources of inspiration could be striped wool 'dornix' (Thornton, *Seventeenth Century Interior Decoration*, 1978, plate viii) or the wall hangings of paned-together fabric in the Queen's Closet at Ham House (1670s) which Timothy Easton has suggested may have been the type of scheme which inspired emulation in paint in vernacular interiors in Suffolk.

112 Daniel Defoe, *A Tour Through the Whole Island of Great Britain* (1724), Yale University Press, New Haven and London, 1991, p. 78.

113 Morris, ed., *The Journeys of Celia Fiennes 1685–1712*, Macdonald/Webb & Bower, London and Sydney, 1982, pp. 236–7. The 'good pictures' may be the paintings of Durdans now at Berkeley Castle, Gloucestershire – see John Harris, *The Artist and the Country House*, Sotheby Parke Bernet, London and New York, 1979, p. 61, plate 54.

114 The 'killing' of knots to prevent the resin in them erupting was also known as 'knotting'.

115 Bristow, *Interior House Painting*, 1996, p. 107 – and information from the late Arthur J. J. Ayres (1902–1985).

116 Other examples are recorded in a house of 1696 formally at Botolph Lane, London – watercolour drawing by E. W. Tristram reproduced by Ralph Dutton, *The English Interior 1500–1900*, Batsford, London, 1978, plate 56. An American example as late as 1784–7, attributed to the English painter John Hazlitt (brother of the essayist William H.), is illustrated by Little, *American Decorative Wall Painting*, 1972, fig. 36.

117 Margaret Jourdain, *English Interior Decoration 1500–1830*, Batsford, London, 1950, fig. 56. Lloyd, *A History of the English House*, 1975, p. 407.

118 No less than thirteen of these works by Canaletto, now at Windsor Castle, were described as 'Door Pieces' by Joseph Smith in his catalogue of pictures acquired by George III, quoted by Jourdain, *English Interior Decoration*, 1950, pp. 33–4.

119 This could be James or Jacques Regnier or, by 1762, Miss Celeste Regnier – she was the fourth wife of the Huguenot sculptor, Louis Francois Roubiliac – see Tessa Murdoch, ed., *The Quiet Conquest – The Huguenots 1685–1985*, Exhibition Catalogue, Museum of London, 1985, item 242, Heal Collection, British Museum, Department of Prints and Drawings. Another Regnier card is in the Metropolitan Museum, New York, Trade Cards, Vol. III, p. 90.

120 Ivan and Elizabeth Hall, *Georgian Hull*, William Session/Hull Civic Society, York and Hull, 1978/9, p. 58.

121 James Ayres, *Two Hundred Years of English Naïve Art 1700–1900*, Exhibition Catalogue, Art Services International, Alexandria, VA, 1996, pp. 13–14. Also illustrated by Ayres, *Building the Georgian City*, 1998, fig. 286.

122 Peter Lord, *Artisan Painters/Arlunwyn Gwlad*, Exhibition Catalogue, National Library of Wales, Aberystwyth, 1993, p. 16.

123 Panel now in the Museum of Welsh Life, St Fagans, Cardiff, illustrated by Iorwerth C. Peate, *Tradition and Folk Life, A Welsh View*, Faber and Faber, 1972, fig. 3.

124 Horace Walpole, *Anecdotes of Painting in England* (1762–71), 'Collected by the late George Virtue', Vol. 4, 1787, p. 59.

125 Walpole, *Anecdotes*, Vol 4, 1787, pp. 19–20. George I came to the throne in 1714.

126 For later examples see Little, *American Decorative Wall Painting*, 1952, Part 1, Chapter 3.

127 John Stalker and George Parker, *Treatise of Japaning and Varnishing*, Oxford, 1688, p. 79.

128 Loudon, *Encyclopaedia*, 1836, p. 277.

129 Morris, ed., *The Journeys of Celia Fiennes*, 1947, p. 85.

130 Stalker and Parker, *Treatise of Japaning and Varnishing*, 1688, p. 82.

131 Salmon, *Polygraphice*, 1701, Chapter 15, items III, IV, V.

132 Reproduced in James Ayres, *The Shell Book of the Home in Britain* (Faber and Faber, London, 1981 – the first-version of the present book) as figs. 152 and 153.

133 Little, *American Decorative Wall Painting*, 1952, plate 1.

134 Smith, *The Art of Painting in Oyl*, 1705, p. 73.

135 Dossie, *The Handmaid to the Arts*, 1758, Part I, Chapter 2.

136 A. E. Richardson and H. Donaldson Eberlein have noted in *The Smaller English House of the Later Renaissance*, London, 1925, p. 31, that the new style did not find favour with all; Sir Willian Chambers for one 'professed contempt for the macaronic attitude of the Brothers Adam'.

137 Some authorities have argued that this was not simulated until about 1817 at which date George Morant of New Bond Street, London, sent J. B. Papworth a sample. See Jourdain, *English Interior Decoration*, 1950, pp. 68, 76.

138 Taken from the index in Whittock's *Guide*.

139   Whittock, *Guide*, 1827, pp. 104, 115.
140   Reconstructed examples can be seen in the Ulster Folk and Transport Museum, Cultura Manor, Holywood, Northern Ireland.
141   S. O. Addy, *The Evolution of the English House* (1898), George Allen and Unwin, London, 1933, p. 133.
142   Abbott Lowell Cummings, *The Framed Houses of Massachusetts Bay 1625–1725*, Harvard University Press, Cambridge, MA and London, 1979, p. 196, figs. 265, 266. Other examples have been rather poorly reconstructed in a series of rooms in the Peter Wentz Farmstead of 1758 in Montgomery County, PA.
143   Addy, *The Evolution of the English House*, 1933, pp. 133–4.
144   Little, *American Decorative Wall Painting*, (1952) 1972.
145   Susan Denyer, *Traditional Buildings and Life in the Lake District*, Victor Gollanz/National Trust, London, 1991, p. 60.
146   I am indebted to Ian Gow for this information. In Edinburgh decorative painting was dominated by the Norrie family from the mid-eighteenth to the mid-nineteenth centuries. Later the painter and decorator David Ramsay Hay (1798–1866) was to become 'Scotland's first Interior Decorator' – see Ian Gow, *The Scottish Interior*, Edinburgh University Press, Edinburgh, 1992, frontispiece.
147   For details of the designers responsible for Grosvenor Place, see Walter Ison, *The Georgian Buildings of Bath* (1948), Kingsmead Reprints, Bath, 1969 – although Shew is not listed by either Ison or by Howard Colvin, *A Biographical Dictionary of British Architects 1600–1840* (1955), Yale University Press, New Haven and London, 1995.
148   E. A. Entwisle, *The Book of Wallpaper* (1954), Kingsmead Reprints, Bath, 1970, p. 107. Jean Lipman, *Rufus Porter Rediscovered* (1968), Clarkson N. Potter Inc., New York, 1980 – see Chapter 'The Young Jack-of-all-Trades'.
149   Loudon, *Encyclopaedia* (1833), Vol. I, reprint of 1846 edition, Donhead Publishing, Shaftesbury, 2000, pp. 274, 276, fig. 514.
150   St James's Square, Bath was built *c.* 1790–3 to designs by the Bath glazier and architect John Palmer (1738–1817) – so this scheme presumably dates from a later redecoration of the house, although no earlier scheme was found. The Spitalfields example was illustrated by Dan Cruickshank, 'Painting the town', *Country Life*, 19 April 1990, p. 160.
151   Peter Lord, *Artisan Painters/Arlnwyn Gwlad*, 1993, p. 13. See also p. 17 in the same publication for a panelled room painted, in the early nineteenth century, with a tropical paradise by Robert Hughes.
152   Francis W. Reader, 'Mural decoration', *Archaeological Journal*, Vol. 95, London, 1938, Part I, in which Reader describes a group of murals as 'mostly of an uncultured nature'.
153   Salzman, *Building in England*, 1952, p. 159.
154   Ibid., p. 167.
155   Addy, *The Evolution of the English House*, 1933, p. 134.
156   Found in Christ's College, Cambridge, see Entwisle, *The Book of Wallpaper*, 1970, plates 1, 2.
157   Dossie, *The Handmaid to the Arts* (1758), Vol. II, 1764, Part VI, Appendix.
158   Probably the seventeenth-century term for Florentine stitch used to produce the then fashionable and well-known zig-zag pattern.
159   Trade-card for Edward Batling, Ambrose Heal Collection, British Museum.
160   Entwisle, *The Book of Wallpaper*, 1970, p. 57.
161   Dossie, *The Handmaid to the Arts*, Vol. II, 1764, Part VI, Appendix.
162   Loudon, *Encyclopaedia*, 1842, pp. 277–8.
163   A. S. Jennings and G. C. Rothery, *The Modern Painter and Decorator*, Vol. II, Caxton Publishing Co., London, 1920, p. 85. Willesden paper like Willesden canvas (green tarpaulin) was probably treated with enprammonium hydroxide to inhibit rot.

164   Reader, 'Mural decoration', 1938. See also James Ayres, *British Folk Art*, Barrie and Jenkins, London, 1977, pp. 107–10.
165   As is confirmed by the provenanced examples in The Building of Bath Museum.
166   Entwisle, *The Book of Wallpaper*, 1970, pp. 57–60. In *The House Decorator and Painters' Guide*, London, 1840, the virtues of stencilling are discussed. This book gives advice on the decoration of very grand interiors. On the title page the authors, H. W. and A. Arrowsmith, declare themselves to be 'Decorators to her Majesty'.
167   Jennings and Rothery, *The Modern Painter and Decorator*, Vol. II, 1920, p. 69.
168   Christopher Thomson, *Autobiography of an Artisan*, London, 1847, p. 271.
169   Stalker and Parker, *Treatise*, 1688, pp. 79, 80.
170   Daniel Defoe, *The Complete English Tradesman*, London, 1727, p. 258. See also Ayres, *Building the Georgian City*, 1998, pp. 36–7.
171   R. Campbell, *The London Tradesman*, London, 1747, p. 104.
172   Ian Bristow (*Interior House-Painting*, 1996) does not cite the Aromatic Paint Company but makes reference (p. 117) to aromatic paint in T. H. Vanherman, *The Painter's Cabinet and Colourman's Repository* (1828), pp. 18–19, 30–3.
173   Edwards, *Anecdotes of the Painters*, London, 1808, pp. 31, 44.
174   It should be added that in a number of restorations X-ray cameras are used to establish whether or not nails are old and woodwork original. This was done when investigating the staircase of the Paca House in Annapolis, MD. See the magazine *Antiques*, New York, January 1977, p. 163.
175   Morgan Phillips and Christopher Whitney, 'The restoration of original paints at the Otis House', *Old-Time New England*, Bulletin of the Society for the Preservation of New England Antiquities, Vol. 62, No. 1, Summer 1971, serial 225 – to name but one of many of the earlier studies of this kind.

Chapter 10: Furniture

1   Robert Roberts, *The Classic Slum: Salford Life in the First Quarter of the Century*, Manchester University Press, Manchester, 1971, p. 17.
2   Lorna Weatherill, *Consumer Behaviour and Material Culture in Britain 1660–1760*, Routledge, London, (1988) 1996, p. xvi.
3   Richard Bushman, *The Refinement of America* (1992), Vintage Books/Random House, New York, 1993.
4   Weatherill, *Consumer Behaviour*, 1996, p. 196.
5   Oliver Goldsmith, quoted by Geoffrey Wills, *English Furniture 1550–1760*, Guinness Superlatives, London, 1971, p. 17.
6   J. C. Loudon, *Encyclopaedia of Cottage, Farm, and Villa Architecture*, Longman, London, (1833) 1836, p. 633.
7   For a more complete understanding of this complex subject (or rather series of subjects) reference should be made to Christopher Gilbert, *English Vernacular Furniture 1760–1900*, Yale University Press, New Haven and London, 1991; Claudia Kinmonth, *Irish Country Furniture 1700–1950*, Yale University Press, New Haven and London, 1993; B. D. Cotton, *The English Regional Chair*, Antique Collectors Club, Woodbridge, Suffolk, 1990 and the same author's *Traditional Manx Furniture*, Manx National Heritage, Douglas, Isle of Man, 1993.
8   Skara Brae was continuously inhabited for about six hundred years from *c.* 3100–2500 BC. David Clarke and Patrick Maguire, *Official Guide to Skara Brae*, Historic Scotland, Edinburgh, (1989) 1995, p. 18.
9   In a house from Mule, Bordo, Faeroe Islands, now in the Frilandsmuseet, Copenhagen.

10 Emyr Estyn Evans, *Irish Folk Ways*, Routledge and Kegan Paul, London, 1957, p. 93.

11 Usually from the same tree, as the grain will confirm.

12 *Stollen* means a supportive post or foot. See Gislind M. Ritz, *The Art of Painted Furniture*, Van Nostrand Reinhold Company, 1970, English language edition, New York, 1971, p. 9 and figs. 157–60.

13 An example of this can be seen at the American Embassy, Grosvenor Square, London, where the mitre at the base of the stone revetment rising from the pavement is deteriorating rapidly.

14 Joseph Moxon, *Mechanick Exercises* (1677), Dan. Midwinter & Tho. Leigh, London, 1703, p. 89.

15 S. W. Wolsey and R. W. P. Luff, *Furniture in England: The Age of the Joiner*, Praeger, New York, 1969, p. 44.

16 F. G. Emmison, *Elizabethan Life*, Essex County Council, Chelmsford, 1976, p. 16.

17 S. O. Addy, *The Evolution of the English House* (1898), George Allen and Unwin, London, 1933, pp. 76–9.

18 Sir John Summerson in his revised edition of Addy, ibid., p. 79.

19 Mark Girouard, *Life in the English Country House*, Yale University Press, New Haven and London, (1978) 1979, p. 104. The decline in the use, if not the importance, of the great hall occurred even earlier with the rich merchants of London and Bristol – by the late fifteenth century. See Roger H. Leech, 'The symbolic hall . . .', *Vernacular Architecture*, Vol. 31, 2000.

20 Note by Summerson in Addy, *The Evolution of the English House*, 1933, p. 79.

21 Weatherill, *Consumer Behaviour*, 1996, pp. 86–7, 187, 206.

22 J. T. Smith, *Nollekens and His Times* (1828), Vol. II, Turnstile Press, London, 1949, p. 228.

23 Quoted by Geoffrey Wills, *English Furniture 1760–1900*, London, 1971, p. 113.

24 Evans, *Irish Folk Ways*, 1957, p. 88.

25 Peter Brears, *Traditional Food in Yorkshire*, Donald, Edinburgh, 1987, pp. 28, 241, fig. 44.

26 Moxon, *Mechanick Exercises*, 1703, p. 122.

27 This traditional term occurs in Robert Manwaring's *Cabinet and Chair Maker's Real Friend and Companion*, London, 1765.

28 Thomas H. Ormsbee, *The Windsor Chair*, Deerfield Books, New York, 1962, p. 16. This book is primarily concerned with American Windsors.

29 J. Ayres, *Building the Georgian City*, Yale University Press, New Haven and London, 1998, pp. 52, 57, 61.

30 Jane Toller, *Country Furniture*, David and Charles, Newton Abbot, 1973, pp. 38–9.

31 Information appended to the label in the British Museum by Mrs Bernard Croft-Murray together with a photograph of a William Webb chair. Therle Hughes in *Cottage Antiques*, Lutterworth Press, London, 1967, p. 23, quotes 'Stubbs' Manufactory' which offered 'all sorts of Yew Tree, Gothic and Windsor Chairs, Alcoves and rural Seats, Garden Machines, Dyed Chairs &c.' on a trade-card of 1790–1803. See also Gilbert, *English Vernacular Furniture* 1991, p. 116.

32 Gilbert, *English Vernacular Furniture*, 1991, p. 109.

33 The metamorphosis of the English Windsor into the American version may be attributed entirely to the use of different materials. In America the 'sticks' of the back were often made from hickory which permitted more elongated lines than was possible with English ash. Furthermore, in America the seats were traditionally of pine or some other such softwood. The elm seats in England were strong enough if only 1½ins (3.8 cm) thick, but pine had to be at least 2 ins (5 cm) thick, and the point at which the legs entered the seat had to be kept well to the centre if splitting was to be avoided. To reduce their apparent thickness the seats of American examples were elaborately dished and chamfered. All these features resulted in the more elongated forms and exaggerated angles of the American Windsor. Occasionally such characteristics will be found in English Windsor chairs such as the mid-eighteenth-century example once owned by Oliver Goldsmith and now in the Victoria and Albert Museum (538–1872).

34 Helen Comstock, ed., *Concise Encyclopaedia of American Antiques*, Vol. I, Hawthorn Books, New York, 1958, Chapter on 'Windsor chairs' by Marvin D. Schwartz, pp. 59–61.

35 'Correspondence', *Country Life*, 8 April 1976. An article by J. Geraint Jenkins, 'A Chiltern chair bodger', occurs in the same journal for 29 September 1955 giving details of manufacture. See also Gilbert, *English Vernacular Furniture*, 1991, p. 117, fig. 185.

36 Toller, *Country Furniture*, 1973, p. 43.

37 Gilbert, *English Vernacular Furniture*, 1991, pp. 106, 108, 111, 112, 114.

38 J. C. Loudon, *Encyclopaedia of Cottage, Farm, and Villa Architecture* (1833), Vol. I, reprint of 1846 edition, Donhead, Shaftesbury, Dorset, 2000, p. 319.

39 Ibid., Vol. I, p. 319.

40 J. Gloag, *Mr. Loudon's England*, Oriel Press, Newcastle upon Tyne, 1970. Jill Lever, *Architect's Designs for Furniture*, RIBA, Trefoil Books, London, 1982, pp. 19, 20. Wills, *English Furniture 1760–1900*, 1971, p. 199 for ref. to William Dalziel and Edward Buckton Lamb.

41 Ormsbee, *The Windsor Chair*, p. 191.

42 Thomas Sheraton, *The Cabinet Dictionary*, London, 1803, p. 145.

43 Gilbert, *English Vernacular Furniture*, 1991, fig. 197, chair inscribed: 'William John/Carpenter/fecit October 21 1778'.

44 Toller, *Country Furniture*, 1973, p. 43 and Gilbert, *English Vernacular Furniture*, 1991, p. 188.

45 Cotton, *The English Regional Chair*, 1990, and Michael Owen Jones, *The Hand Made Object and its Maker*, University of California Press, Berkeley, CA and London, 1975.

46 Gilbert, *English Vernacular Furniture*, 1991, p. 101.

47 Cotton, *The English Regional Chair*, 1990; Cotton, *Traditional Manx Furniture*, 1993; Kinmouth, *Irish Country Furniture*, 1993.

48 Gilbert, *English Vernacular Furniture*, 1991, pp. 103, 105, 107.

49 Peter C. D. Brears, *The English Country Pottery*, David and Charles, Newton Abbot, 1971, p. 13.

50 Wills, *English Furniture 1550–1760*, 1971, p. 7. As we have seen, wheelwrights too were makers of Windsor chairs.

51 Iona and Peter Opie, *Oxford Dictionary of Nursery Rhymes*, Clarendon Press, Oxford, 1951.

52 Randle Holme, *The Academy of Armory*, written 1648–9, published in Chester, 1688, Vol. III, Chapter 14, fig. 73.

53 Chairs of turners' work, known to the author in Scandinavia (where birch was the wood most favoured), have four legs and are rectangular on plan. An example may be seen in Urnes Church, Norway. The Low Countries are a more likely source of the type, as both chairs and stools of triangular plan are illustrated in the paintings by artists such as Jan Steen.

54 R. W. Symonds, 'The craft of the English turner', *Apollo*, London, May 1939, p. 223. See also accession card for a seventeenth-century turned chair in the Victoria and Albert Museum (W.24-1913).

55 Penelope Eames, *Furniture in England, France and the Netherlands from the Twelfth to the Fifteenth Century*, Furniture History Society, London, 1977, pp. 192–4, plates. 54, 55a, 55b.

56 Gilbert, *English Vernacular Furniture* 1991, pp. 105, 107, 110; Herbert Cesinsky and Ernest R. Gribble, *Early English Furniture and Woodwork*, Vol. II, Routledge, London, 1922, p. 184; S. W. Wolsey and R. W. P. Luff, *Furniture in England: The Age of the Joiner*, Arthur Baker, London, 1968, pp. 65–78, fig. 88; Benno M. Forman, *American Seating Furniture 1630–1730*, Winterthur,

W. W. Norton, New York and London, 1988, 'Seating made by turners', pp. 65–131.

57   In the collection of the Victoria and Albert Museum (P.51-1962).

58   Toller, *Country Furniture*, 1973, pp. 45–6.

59   An example can be seen in the Dutch House at Newcastle, Delaware.

60   Oliver Rackham, *Trees and Woodland in the British Landscape* (1976), Phoenix Press, London, 1990, p. 90.

61   Kinmonth, *Irish Country Furniture*, 1993, pp. 10–13.

62   Evans, *Irish Folk Ways*, 1957, p. 85.

63   A chair of this 'hedge carpenter' type but with a thick seat is illustrated by Michael S. Bird, *Canadian Country Furniture 1675–1950*, Stoddart, Boston Mills Press, Erin, Ontario, 1994, fig. 77.

64   Kinmonth, *Irish Country Furniture*, 1993, pp. 21–7, 134.

65   Ibid., pp. 15, 34, 35.

66   Evans, *Irish Folk Ways*, 1957, pp. 85, 93, quoting W(illiam) M(offat), *The Western Isle*, 1724, Canto 2.

67   Loudon, *Encyclopaedia*, 1836, p. 317.

68   Ibid, p. 317. The word 'jib' may be a verb meaning 'to swing' as in the jib of a crane. Peter Nicholson refers to a 'jibb' or 'jib door' which he defines as one 'which is flush with the surface of the wall, being generally papered over, the same as the room, the design being to conceal the door as much as possible, in order to preserve the symmetry . . . of the room'; Nicholson, *New Practical Builder*, London, 1823–5, p. 183, plate L.

69   An example may be seen in the American Museum in Britain at Bath. See also the magazine *Antiques*, New York, March 1968. See Russell Hawes Kettle, *The Pine Furniture of Early New England*, Dover, New York, 1929, ill. 69, and Ralph and Terry Kovel, *American Country Furniture 1780–1875*, Crown, New York, 1965, p. 13. Michael S. Bird, *Canadian Country Furniture 1675–1950*, Stoddart/Boston Mills Press, Toronto, 1994, illustrates a number of 'sleep benches' or 'bench-beds', figs. 29, 480–5, 578–82.

70   *Antiques*, New York, March 1968, p. 345. I have found no examples of these settles in Scotland.

71   Kinmonth, *Irish Country Furniture*, 1993, pp. 82–90.

72   For Guernsey, see Gilbert, *English Vernacular Furniture*, 1991, pp. 133, 134, figs. 218, 219, and for Jersey, George S. Knocker, 'The Jersey kitchen, La Tchuisinne Jerriaise', *Société Jersiaise Bulletin*, 1932, p. 27.

73   William Harrison, *Description of England* (1577) ed. by F. J. Furnival, Vol. II, London, 1877, p. 240.

74   Wills, *English Furniture 1550–1860*, 1971, p. 32, quoting Evelyn's *Sylva* (1664).

75   L. F. Grant, *Highland Folk Ways* (1961), Routledge and Kegan Paul, London, 1975, p. 169.

76   H. J. Hansen, ed., *European Folk Art*, Thames and Hudson, London, 1968, pp. 26–7.

77   Peter Thornton, *Authentic Décor*, Weidenfeld and Nicolson, London, 1984, pp. 46–7.

78   Jean Cuisenier, *French Folk Art*, Kodansha International Ltd, Tokyo, New York and San Francisco, 1977, figs. 82–4.

79   Loudon, *Encyclopaedia*, 1836, plate 1291.

80   Excavations on Fyfield Down in Wiltshire revealed a long-house with a bed outshot associated with twelfth-century pottery. Eric Mercer, *English Vernacular Houses*, HMSO, London, 1975, p. 35.

81   Desmond McCourt and Emyr Estyn Evans, 'A late 17th century farmhouse at Shantallow near Londonderry', *Ulster Folklife*, Vol. 14, 1968, pp. 14–23. 'Though the outshot (on the ground floor) projects only 3 ft [91.4 cm] externally it has been given an internal depth of 3 ft 6 in [106.7 cm] by reducing the

width of the outside wall to 18 in [45.7 cm] as compared with the thickness of 2 ft [61 cm] in the rest of the house.'

82   Kinmonth, *Irish Country Furniture*, 1993, pp. 153–5.

83   For the high status 'cloth of estate' see Peter Thornton, *Seventeenth Century Interior Decoration in England, France and Holland*, Yale University Press, New Haven and London, 1978, pp. 57–9, 149–54. Such cloths were also employed in yeoman houses.

84   Marie Hartley and Joan Ingilby, *Life and Tradition in the Yorkshire Dales*, Dent, London, 1968, p. 6.

85   James Orchard Halliwell, *Dictionary of Archaic Words* (1850), Bracken Books, London, 1989, p. 111 quoting *Tusser's Five Hundred Points*, Vol. II, 1573, p. 5.

86   A number of highly sophisticated medieval food cupboards survive with pierced tracery panels. See, for example, Cescinsky and Gribble, *Early English Furniture and Woodwork*, Vol. II, 1922, p. 35, fig. 36.

87   Quoted by Wolsey and Luff, *Furniture in England*, 1968, p. 35.

88   Ibid., pp. 36–7.

89   Gilbert, *English Vernacular Furniture*, 1991, p. 45.

90   Weatherill, *Consumer Behaviour*, 1996, pp. 39–46.

91   Ibid., p. 52.

92   Ibid., p. 194, citing H. J. Perkin, 'The social causes of the British Industrial Revolution', *Transactions of the Royal Historical Society*, 1968, pp. 123–43, reference to the *British Magazine* of 1763.

93   A very late manifestation that did not occur until families lived on board the boats, after the decline of the canals (due to the advent of the railways); see A. J. Lewery, *Narrow Boat Painting*, David and Charles, Newton Abbot, 1974.

94   Eric Mercer, *Furniture 700–1700*, Weidenfeld and Nicolson, London, 1969, pp. 30, 43. A number fairly complete examples of painted medieval furniture survive. John Harvey, *Mediaeval Craftsmen*, Batsford, London, 1975, p. 155, cites documentary evidence (of 1483) for early joiners having painting equipment in their workshops. Apparently these craftsmen also made saddle-bows which, like the furniture, would be painted.

95   Joan Liversidge, *Furniture in Roman Britain*, Tiranti, London, 1955, p. 16.

96   Grant, *Highland Folk Ways*, 1975, p. 207.

97   Loudon, *Encyclopaedia*, 1836, p. 347.

98   Evans, *Irish Folk Ways*, p. 93.

99   Iowerth C. Peate, *Tradition and Folk Life*, Faber and Faber, London, 1972, p. 51.

100 Halliwell, *Dictionary*, 1989, p. 618.

101 *Oxford English Dictionary*.

102 For 'limning', see William Salmon, *Polygraphice: Or, The Arts of Drawing . . . &c* (1672), London, 1701, 'an art whereby in water colours we strive to resemble Nature . . .' For statistics on ownership of pictures, see Weatherill, *Consumer Behaviour*, 1996, p. 168, table 8: 1.

103 Sir Balthazar Gerbier, *Counsel and Advice to All Builders . . .*, London, 1663, pp. 84, 85.

104 For a rather grand version of one of these frames of *c*. 1620, as described by Gerbier, see J. Ayres, *The Artist's Craft*, Phaidon, Oxford, 1985, p. 124, fig. 175.

105 See the introduction by Benno M. Forman (p. xxiv) in Charles Montgomery's edition of Joseph Moxon's *Mechanick Exercises* (1677), Praeger, New York, 1970.

106 Moxon, *Mechanick Exercises*, 1703, pp. 106–8.

107 John Stalker and George Parker, *A Treatise of Japaning and Varnishing*, Oxford, 1688, p. 70.

108 *The Practical Carver and Gilder's Guide*, printed by Simpkin Marshall and Co. for Brodie and Middleton, *c*. 1880, pp. 145–6.

109 Drawing of Samuel Pepys's library at York Buildings, London, *c*. 1693, reproduced (oddly) by Cornforth, *English Interiors 1790–1848*, Barrie & Jenkins, London, 1978, p. 88.

110 Prince Hoare, *Epochs of the Arts*, London, 1813, pp. 87–8.

111 Christopher Morris, ed., *The Journeys of Celia Fiennes*, Cresset Press, London, 1947, p. 85, written in 1697.

112 Jane C. Nylander, *Our Own Snug Fireside: Images of the New England Home 1760–1860*, Yale University Press, New Haven and London, 1993, p. 40, fig. 37.

113 Quoted by Richard L. Bushman, *The Refinement of America . . .* , Vintage Books, Random House Inc., New York, 1995, p. 206.

114 Not all mirrors used plate glass but all glass was subject to tax (by weight) and large mirrors required heavy plate glass. For production methods for glass see Ayres, *Building the Georgian City*, 1998, pp. 189–94.

115 John Michael Montias, *Artists and Artisans in Delft: A Socio-Economic Study of the Seventeenth Century*, Princeton University Press, Princeton, NJ, 1982, Chapter 8, 'Art collections in seventeenth century Delft'.

116 Weatherill, *Consumer Behaviour*, 1996, p. 179.

117 Giovanni Paolo Lomazzo, *Tracte Containing the Artes of Curious Paintinge, Carvinge and Buildinge*, translated by Richard Haydocke, Oxford, 1598, Chapter 3.

118 Late eighteenth, early nineteenth-century trade-label, Ambrose Heal Collection 90.15, British Museum, Department of Prints and Drawings. The label concludes 'NB Ships' Liknesses taken'.

119 Richard Jefferies, *Hodge and His Masters* (1880), Alan Sutton, Stroud, 1992, p. 94. Demelza Spargo, ed., *This Land is Our Land: Aspects of Agriculture in English Art*, Royal Agriculture Society and The Mall Galleries, London (exhibited 5–29 January 1989). Christiana Payne, *Toil and Plenty: Images of the Agricultural Landscapes 1780–1890*, Yale Center for British Art, Yale University Press, New Haven and London, 1993–4 (Exhibition New Haven and Nottingham). Elizabeth Moncrieff with Stephen and Iona Joseph, *Farm Animal Portraits*, Antique Collectors' Club, Woodbridge, Suffolk, 1996.

120 Edmund Bartell, *Hints for Picturesque Improvements in Ornamental Cottages*, London, 1804, pp. 50–1.

121 Loudon, *Encyclopaedia*, (1836) 1842, p. 165.

122 *The Practical Carver and Gilder's Guide*, c. 1880, p. 168.

123 Peter Thornton, *Seventeenth Century Interior Decoration*, Yale University Press, New Haven and London, 1978, pp. 252–3, figs. 240, 241.

124 *The Practical Carver and Gilder's Guide*, c. 1880, p. 167.

125 Ibid, p. 165.

126 M. K. Ashby, *Joseph Ashby of Tysoe* (1961), Merlin Press, London, 1974, p. 172.

127 George S. and Helen McKearin, *American Glass*, Crown Publishers, New York, (1941) 1963, p. 179.

128 Brears, *The English Country Pottery*, 1971.

129 Edward H. Pinto, *Treen and Other Wooden Bygones*, G. Bell and Sons, London, 1969.

130 For an account of the last sheaf of corn see Peate, *Tradition and Folk Life*, 1972, p. 119, and Jo Cox and John R. L. Thorp, *Devon Thatch*, Devon Books, Tiverton, 2001, p. 79. For an illustration of the corn dolly made from the final wheatsheaf of the harvest hanging from the ceiling in the main room of a farmhouse in Yockleton, Shropshire see Peate, *Tradition and Folk Life*, 1972, fig. 50.

Conclusion: The Vernacular Interior in Context

1 A number of papers have been published on this question in *Vernacular Architecture* including John Blair, 'Posts or crucks? Building on the north/eastern cruck boundary', Vol. 15, 1984, p. 39; N. W. Alcock and John Blair, 'Crucks: new documentary evidence', Vol. 17, 1986, p. 36; Sylvia Colman, 'Base-cruck usages in Suffolk', Vol. 21, 1990, p. 10; Eric Mercer, 'Cruck distribution: a social explanation', Vol. 27, 1996, p. 1.

2 R. T. Mason, *Framed Buildings of the Weald*, Coach Publishing House, Horsham, 1964, Chapter 3, 'Distinctive House Types', The Wealden House, pp. 37–41, which cites 'isolated examples as far away as Exeter and York'. Jane Grenville, *Medieval Housing*, Leicester University Press, London and Washington, DC, (1997) 1999, pp. 189–90.

3 W. G. Hoskins, 'The rebuilding of rural England 1570–1640', *Past and Present*, Vol. 4, 1953, pp. 44–59; R. Machin, 'The Great Rebuilding: a reassessment', *Past and Present*, Vol. 73, 1973, pp. 33–56. This rebuilding is now seen to have begun as early as the fifteenth century in counties like Somerset and as late as the early eighteenth century in remote parts of the north of England. It is arguable that, in distant parts of the British Isles, this 'rebuilding' did not take place until the twentieth century. See also Colin Platt, *The Great Rebuildings . . .* , University College London Press, London, 1994.

4 Lorna Weatherill, *Consumer Behaviour and Material Culture in Britain 1660–1760*, Routledge, London and New York, (1988) 1996, p. 43. For an American study of this kind, see Richard L. Bushman, *The Refinement of America: Persons, Houses, Cities*, Vintage Books, Random House, New York, 1903. At an altogether different social level Mark Girouard's *Life in the English Country House*, Yale University Press, New Haven and London, 1978, has as its subtitle *A Social and Architectural History*.

5 The distinction between 'front of house' (prestige) and 'back stage' (simplicity) is reflected in the mid-sixteenth-century door-head illustrated as Figs. 105, 106.

6 Catherine Hall, 'The early formation of Victorian domestic ideology', in S. Burman, ed., *Fit Work for Women*, Croom Helm, London, 1979, pp. 15–32. Hall demonstrates that the origins of this outlook may be dated back to the 1780s and the Evangelicals of the Clapham Sect with women like Hannah More arguing the case for a more conservative and domestic role for women in contrast to Mary Wollstonecraft's *Vindication of the Rights of Women* (1792). In the eighteenth century women were excluded from direct engagement in the building trades (see Joan Lane, *Apprenticeship in England 1600–1914*, London University Press, London, 1995, p. 39). Treve Rosoman (1992) has pointed out that the trade-labels of Abraham Price (c. 1715), James Wheeley (c. 1754) and Richard Masefield (c. 1760s) illustrating wallpaper-shop interiors, all show that women predominate as customers. Women, though, were excluded from participating in the overall design of a house and its interiors, although there were always exceptions like Bess of Hardwick. See J. Ayres, *Building the Georgian City*, Yale University Press, New Haven and London, 1998, p. 27, quoting James Peacock's *Nutshells* (1785) which implies an entirely masculine discussion of domestic architecture.

7 Matthew Johnson, *Housing Culture . . .* , Smithsonian Institution Press, Washington, DC, 1993, p. 120.

8 Lane, *Apprenticeship in England*, 1996, p. 78, quoting George Herbert, a shoemaker. The freedom and 'life' found in the late Stuart woodcarving of the school of Gibbons owes much to its speed of execution.

9 Isaac Ware, *The Complete Body of Architecture*, London, 1756, p. 291. See also Dan Cruickshank and Neil Burton, *Life in the Georgian City*, Viking, London, 1990, ill. on p. 107.

10 I coined this phrase for the exhibition *Rooms Concise: Glimpses of the Small Domestic Interior* shown for the launch of the first edition of this book at the RIBA Heinz Gallery, London, 1981.

11 This was a widely used phrase in pre-industrial English-speaking communities. See for example Abbott Lowell Cummings, *The Framed Houses of Massachusetts Bay 1625–1725*, Harvard

University Press, Cambridge, MA. and London, 1979, p. 40 quoting the Boston Selectmen of 1660.

12 Walter Cahn, *Masterpieces: Chapters in the History of an Idea*, Princeton University Press, Princeton, NJ, 1979, and also Lane, *Apprenticeship in England*, 1996, p. 75.

13 See F. Rainsford-Hannay, *Dry Stone Walling*, Faber and Faber, London, 1957. For farmers and thatching the following example is instructive: in 1735 George Domett, a farmer at Hawkchurch on the Devon/Dorset border, conveyed his property to one of his sons including crops, livestock and farm implements; the latter comprised 'some old reed and sparrs' for thatching. See Jo Cox and John R. L. Thorp, *Devon Thatch*, Devon Books, Tiverton, 2001, p. 73. Thatching was by no means confined to country districts but reference in eighteenth-century trade directories for large cities list halliers (e.g. *Sketchley's Bristol Directory* for 1775) could equally well signify tilers. For halliers or helliers see Edwin Welch, *Plymouth Building Accounts of the sixteenth and seventeenth centuries*, Devon and Cornwall Record Society, New Series, Vol. 12, 1967, Torquay – numerous references and Glossary.

14 See Lane, *Apprenticeship in England*, 1996, pp. 39, 45; Donna J. Rilling, *Making Houses: Crafting Capitalism*, University of Pennsylvania Press, Philadelphia, 2001, pp. 13–15, 53–4; and Ayres, *Building the Georgian City*, 1998, pp. 7, 90, 93, 102, 109, 212, figs. 44, 162, 163, 204, 315.

    The practice of women taking over their late husband's businesses and similar traditions seems to have also been characteristic of trades other than those connected to building. See Philippa Glanville and Jennifer Faulds Goldsborough, *Women Silversmiths 1685–1845*, Thames and Hudson, London, 1990 (published in association with the National Association of Women in the Arts, Washington, DC).

15 Lane, *Apprenticeship in England*, 1996, pp. 2–3, 6–7, and Marcus Whiffen, *The 18th Century Houses of Virginia*, revised edition, Colonial Williamsburg Foundation, 1984, p. 26; also W. J. Rorabaugh, *The Craft Apprentice from Franklin to the Machine Age in America*, Oxford University Press, New York and Oxford, 1986.

16 E. Anthony Wrigley, 'Urban growth and agricultural change: England and the Continent in the early modern period', in Peter Borsay, ed., *The Eighteenth Century Town 1688–1820*, Longman, London and New York, 1990, pp. 39–82.

17 Alan Everitt, 'Country, county and town: patterns of regional evolution in England', in ibid., pp. 97, 104–6.

18 Jennifer Lang, *Pride Without Prejudice: The Story of London's Guilds and Livery Companies*, Perpetua Press, London, 1975, p. 11. Lang lists seventy-seven guilds with charters dating between 1393 and 1709, of which about half are for trades which, historically, involved such judgment.

19 For example R. S. Neal (*Bath, a Social History 1680–1850*, Routledge, London and Boston, 1981, p. 68) has found that in Bath the City companies paraded their privileges through the streets of the spa for the last time in 1765 and that by 1776 their powers were all but extinguished.

20 Lane, *Apprenticeship in England*, 1996, pp. 3–4, 18–19, 38, 81–9, 217, 226.

21 Everitt, 'Country, county and town', 1990, p. 106.

22 Malcolm Airs, *The Tudor and Jacobean Country House: A Building History*, Sutton Publishing in association with the National Trust, Stroud, (1995) 1998, Chapter 17, 'Home life'. Airs follows Girouard in arguing that some craftsmen-architects like John Smythson (d. 1634) lived on the scale of lesser gentry.

23 Oliver Rackham, *Trees and Woodland in the British Landscape* (1976), Phoenix Press, London, 2001, pp. 83, 189. Between *c.* 1540 and 1553 the price of 'underwood' (firewood) rose by 75 percent because of the cold winters. See also Brian Fagan, *The*

24 *Little Ice Age* (2000), Basic Books/Perseus Group, New York, 2002.

    Trinity College, Cambridge, retains the iron fire basket purchased in 1702–3 for £12 for use on the central hearth of its open hall, where it remained in use until 1866. See Margaret Wood, *The English Medieval House*, Phoenix House, London, 1965, p. 259.

25 For a localised study of this transition, see Pat Ryan, 'The building of rural Ingatestone, Essex, 1556–1601 – "Great Rebuilding" or "Housing Revolution"', *Vernacular Architecture*, Vol. 31, 2000, pp. 11–25.

26 For a discussion of the lingering status of the hall at a time of its declining use, see Roger H. Leech, 'The symbolic hall: historical context and merchant culture in the early modern city', *Vernacular Architecture*, Vol. 31, 2000, pp. 1–10. For the Wealden hall, see Johnson, *Housing Culture*, 1993, pp. 58, 82.

27 For an example of a chimney piece in an open hall in Somerset see the mid to late fifteenth-century Priest's House at Muchelney, Somerset, although the chimney may be an early sixteenth-century insertion the status of the house and its proximity to Muchelney Abbey may justify an earlier dating for this flue.

28 Anthony Garvan, *Architecture and Town Planning in Colonial Connecticut*, Yale University Press, New Haven, 1951, in which the Ulster 'Plantations' are discussed on pp. 20, 30–1, 114, 116, 140–1.

29 Unlike J. Frederick Kelly (in *The Early Domestic Architecture of Connecticut*, Yale University Press, New Haven, 1924), this is meant in a general sense, rather than as a particular series of plans showing the growth and evolution of a specific house type.

30 Jamestown, Virginia, founded 1607, Plymouth Plantation, Massachusetts, founded 1620. Robert P. Multhauf, 'America's Wooden Age', in Charles E. Peterson, ed., *Building Early America*, Astragal Press, Mendham, NY, 1976, pp. 23–34.

31 Fulke Clifton's list published in London in 1630 of *The Provisions Needfull of Such as Intend to Plant Themselves in New England* – a copy of this list is in Lincoln Cathedral Library. In addition to tools it includes nails, locks and hinges for doors.

32 Cummings, *The Framed Houses of Massachusetts Bay*, 1979, p. 40.

33 Charles Montgomery, *A History of American Pewter*, Winterthur, Praeger, New York, 1973, Chapter 2, 'The American pewterer and his craft', pp. 20–41. This chapter demonstrates the decline in the control of craft organisation.

34 Cummings, *The Framed Houses of Massachusetts Bay*, 1979, p. 42.

35 Charles Dickens, *American Notes*, 1842, Chapter 16, which quotes from this letter.

36 Jean Lipman, *Rufus Porter Rediscovered: Artist, Inventor, Journalist, 1792–1884* (1968), Clarkson N. Potter, New York, 1980. As a house-painter Porter produced remarkable scenic murals which are illustrated in Lipman.

37 Rorabaugh, *The Craft Apprentice*, 1986, p. 60.

38 J. F. C. Harrison, *The Common People* (1984), Fontana Press/ Collins, Glasgow, 1989, Part III, 'The Working Class (1780–1880)', Chapter 10, 'In the workshop of the world.' See also E. P. Thompson, *The Making of the English Working Class*, Gollancz, London, (1963) 1991.

39 Nicholas Barbon, *An Apology for the Builder*, London, 1685, pp. 2–4, 16–17.

40 John and Jane Penoyre, 'The Somerset dendrochronology project: phase 3', *Vernacular Architecture*, Vol. 30, 1999, pp. 54–7. Grenville, *Medieval Housing*, 1999, includes numerous refs, but see pp. 161–2 and plan of burgage plots at Kingsbridge, Devon on p. 163.

41 For early examples of speculative building, see John Summerson, *Georgian London* (1945), Barrie and Jenkins, London, 1988, p. 16. See also Elizabeth McKellar, *The Birth of*

Modern London . . . 1660–1720, Manchester University Press, Manchester and New York, 1999; T. R. Liszka and L. E. M. Walker, eds., *The North Sea World in the Middle Ages*, Portland, OR, 2001; and J. Roding and L. H. van Voss, eds., *The North Sea and Culture (1550–1800) . . .* , Hilversum, 1996.

42 Tessa Watt, *Cheap Print and Popular Piety 1550–1640*, Cambridge University Press, Cambridge, (1991) 1996, p. 193.

43 Christopher Morris, ed., *The Journeys of Celia Fiennes 1685–c. 1712*, Macdonald/Webb & Bower, London and Sydney, 1982, for Nottingham see pp. 86–7, for Liverpool see pp. 160–1.

44 William Leybourne's revised edition (1680) of Stephen Primatt's *The City and Country Purchaser and Builder* (1667), and Joseph Moxon's *Mechanick Exercises or Doctrine of Handy Works*, published in instalments from 1678 and as a complete book in 1684 and again in 1703.

45 For a brief account of Mandey's library see Ayres, *Building the Georgian City*, 1998, p. 13 and endnotes 25–26 on p. 250.

46 R. Campbell, *The London Tradesman*, London, 1747, pp. 158, 159.

47 For example these regulations insisted that the pendent signs, which were so common before the days of street numbering, were, following the Great Fire of 1666, to be carved in stone in relief and built flush into the brick frontages of houses – as was done at first. In this position signs were far less visible and by the mid-eighteenth century almost all premises in the City of London were identified by sign boards hung from sign irons projecting out over the street. See J. Ayres, 'Signs', in Edwin Mullins, ed., *The Arts of Britain*, Phaidon, Oxford, 1983, pp. 64–5.

48 McKellar, *The Birth of Modern London*, 1999, p. 71.

49 For example, the woodcarver Grinling Gibbons (1648–1721) was a Draper by patrimony being admitted to the Company in 1672.

50 Barbon, *Apology for the Builder*, 1685, p. 2.

51 The Act for rebuilding Warwick followed closely on the London Act with whole paragraphs repeated – see Peter Borsay, *The English Urban Renaissance: Culture and Society in the Provincial Town 1660–1710*, Clarendon Press, Oxford, (1989) 1991, p. 90.

52 Frederick D. Nichols 'Restoring Jefferson's University', in Peterson, ed., *Building Early America*, 1976, pp. 319–39.

53 The fire at Warwick (1694) was preceded by a similar disaster at Northampton (1675). In 1736 the *Northampton Mercury* was able to refer to the 'friendly emulation' evident in the way in which the two towns were rebuilt. See Borsay, *The English Urban Renaissance*, 1991, pp. 18–19.

54 If the example illustrated is thought to be an exception, see Geoffrey Wills, *English Looking Glasses . . . 1670–1820*, Country Life, London, 1965, fig. 41, p. 81, showing a similar but more elaborate mirror of this kind of *c*. 1735.

55 Weatherill, *Consumer Behaviour*, 1996, p. 47.

56 John A. Biggs, 'The Bastards of Blandford', unpublished thesis, Architectural Association, London, 1987/9, pp. 34 and 52, quoting letter of 6 July 1752 from John Bastard to Sir Peter Thompson MP – by the mid-eighteenth century the Bastards were able to refer to a new type of roof in a pattern book 'lately published by Mr. Halfpenny' (*Twelve Beautiful Designs for Farmhouses*, 1750). See also Joseph Rykwert, 'On oral transmission of architectural theory', A. A. Files, No. 6, May 1984, cited by McKellar, *The Birth of Modern London*, 1999.

57 Summerson, *Georgian London*, 1988, Chapter 3, 'Foundation stones of wealth', regarding the financing of urban housing schemes.

58 Roger W. Moss, 'The origins of the Carpenters' Company of Philadelphia', in Peterson, ed., *Building Early America*, 1976, p. 38. For Eyre see Rilling, *Making Houses*, 2001, p. 88

59 Christopher Dyer, 'History and vernacular architecture', *Vernacular Architecture*, Vol. 28, 1997, p. 1 – with reference to the study of the wider history and its relationship to traditional buildings.

60 Christopher Hill, *The World Turned Upside Down* (1972), Penguin Books, London, 1982, p. 203. Hill argues that migrating craftsmen may have been amongst the chief supporters of the Ranters.

61 Neal, *Bath*, 1981, p. 99 with reference to John Locke's *Two Treatises of Government*, 1690. See Borsay, *The English Urban Renaissance*, 1991, and, for the 'long eighteenth century', Borsay, ed., *The Eighteenth Century Town*, 1990.

62 Peter Burke, *Popular Culture in Early Modern Europe*, Scolar Press, Aldershot, 1994, pp. 28, 270–86.

63 An example of the use of external plasterwork can be seen on the cornice of the rear elevation of Calke Abby, Derbyshire. From the 1760s plasterers were employed to apply stucco to external elevations, and in earlier centuries such tradesmen were probably responsible for the application of 'rough cast'.

64 Ayres, *Building the Georgian City*, 1998, is organised by trades.

65 Lane, *Apprenticeship in England*, 1996, p. 33.

66 Walter Rose in *The Village Carpenter*, Cambridge University Press, Cambridge, (1937) 1946, is conscious of the distinction between carpentry and joinery, but his account of his family business in the nineteenth century implies that the one firm, and possibly the same individuals, would undertake both types of work in the village and a five-mile radius round it. Hentie J. Louw, 'Demarcation disputes between English carpenters and joiners from the 16th century to the 18th century', *Construction History*, Vol. 5, London, 1989, pp. 3–20.

67 Charles E. Peterson, ed., *The Carpenters Company of the City and County of Philadelphia: 1786 Rule Book*, reprint, Astragal Press, Mendham, NY, 1992.

68 Peter Burke, *Popular Culture*, 1994, pp. 23–9, 270–81.

69 S. O. Addy, *The Evolution of the English House* (1898), George Allen and Unwin, London, 1933, pp. 76, 79. For farmers 'on their small domains' see Rose, *The Village Carpenter*, 1946, p. 38.

70 Rilling, *Making Houses*, 2001, p. 176.

71 William Williams, *An Essay on the Mechanic of Oil Colours, considered under these heads: Oils, Varnishes and Pigments*, Bath, 1787, pp. 10–11, 35–6. See also J. Ayres, *The Artist's Craft*, Phaidon, Oxford, 1985, pp. 17–18, 86.

72 For a summary of the diversification of the stock held by eighteenth-century 'oil and colourmen' see Campbell, *The London Tradesman*, 1747, pp. 105, 106, and Ayres, *The Artists's Craft*, 1985, p. 130. See also the Ambrose Heal Collection of Trade-Labels in the British Museum, Department of Prints and Drawings, London.

73 Curtains often denoted social class, between 1675 and 1725 a Yeoman farmer was more likely to own a clock and some books than to have curtains at his windows. See Weatherill, *Consumer Behaviour*, 1996, pp. 172, 177, table 8:1.

74 John Corry, *The Life of William Cowper*, London, 1803, p. 52.

75 Information from a lecture on Charleston, SC. given by Carter Hudgins at a conference on 'The Interpretation of Georgian Towns' held at the Paul Mellon Centre for British Art, London, on 18 July 2001.

Appendix I

1 A transcript of this diary is in Bristol City Museum and Art Gallery.

Appendix II

1 As a textile merchant Bayly's household boasted more window and bed curtains than was probably typical at this time.

2 See pp. 144, 122, 147, 148, 149 and Figs. 172, 183, 210, 211, 212 for this house in Marlborough.

Appendix III

1   Smalt was ground glass, blue in colour, which was sprinkled over gold size to which it adhered. The sugar loaves, probably a carved wood sign, were evidently represented wrapped in blue 'sugar paper' – see Fig. 292.
2   Price arrived at by an independent measurer after the work had been carried out.

Appendix IV

1   Ed. by A. W. Cornelius Hallen, Edinburgh University Press for the Scottish Record Society, Edinburgh, 1894.
2   Scottish Record Office GD112/21/78.
3   The card is reproduced in *The Discovery of Scotland*, National Gallery of Scotland Exhibition Catalogue (section on 'Decorative Painting'), Edinburgh, 1978.
4   See Robert Scott Moncrieff, ed., *Household Book of Lady Grisell Baillie 1692–1733*, T. A. Constable for the Scottish Record Society, Edinburgh, 1911. I am indebted to Pricilla Minay of Edinburgh for supplying me with these notes in 1982.

Appendix V

1   'dubler': a large earthenware platter or dish; originally a wood trencher.

2   'petty pan': a white iron mould for pastry.
3   'tiffany': a fine gauze, usually used as a flour sieve (for bolting) – finer than a *temse*.
4   'temse': a sieve
5   'sile': a milk strainer.
6   'sweeble': a swivel.
7   'speet' (or 'spiet' or 'spit')
8   'reckins': hooks for pots
9   'bakestone': a circular iron plate for baking cakes, etc., sometimes with an iron bow top; originally a flat stone.
10   'Fog': a second crop of grass.

Note: I am indebted to John Gall for this information.

Appendix VI

1   I am indebted to John Gall for drawing my attention to this publication.
2   By a member of the School of Black Art, Italy, published by P. Buchan, Peterhead, Scotland, 1823, pp. 48–9

Appendix VIII

1   See also the Ambrose Heal, *The London Furniture Makers*, Batsford, London, 1953, p. 143. I am indebted to Mrs Bernard Croft Murray's notes on the Heal collection in the British Museum, Department of Prints and Drawings.

Bibliographical Note

Interest in the Decorative Arts began with the sort of connoisseurship that was, quite literally, at home in the English country house, the Scottish castle and the establishments of the Ascendancy in Ireland. Whilst not offering this explanation one economic historian has recently observed that 'discussions of domestic interiors tend to concentrate on the élite'. Lorna Wetherill discusses this point in her book *Consumer Behaviour and Material Culture in Britain 1660–1760* (Cambridge, (1988) 1996, p. 32). In these circumstances some publications in this field contain relevant material but in general this is insufficient to justify a Bibliography for a book on vernacular interiors. Consequently such references are to be found here in the Endnotes. An exception to this generally rather meagre body of published work is N. W. Alcock's *People at Home: Living in a Warwickshire Village 1500–1800* (Phillimore, Chichester, 1993). This invaluable book ties-in surviving buildings with their inventories in the village and parish of Stoneleigh.

Index

The following index excludes endnotes and glossary. Illustrations appear as Fig. numbers in bold type at the end of the entry.

Photographic Credits